D0382315

enVisionMATH
Common Core

Authors

Randall I. Charles
Professor Emeritus
Department of Mathematics
San Jose State University
San Jose, California

Janet H. Caldwell
Professor of Mathematics
Rowan University
Glassboro, New Jersey

Mary Cavanagh
Executive Director of Center for Practice,
Research, and Innovation in Mathematics
Education (PRIME)
Arizona State University
Mesa, Arizona

Juanita Copley
Professor Emerita, College of Education
University of Houston
Houston, Texas

Warren Crown
Professor Emeritus of Mathematics Education
Graduate School of Education
Rutgers University
New Brunswick, New Jersey

Francis (Skip) Fennell
L. Stanley Bowlsbey Professor of Education and
Graduate and Professional Studies
McDaniel College
Westminster, Maryland

Stuart J. Murphy
Visual Learning Specialist
Boston, Massachusetts

Kay B. Sammons
Coordinator of Elementary Mathematics
Howard County Public Schools
Ellicott City, Maryland

Jane F. Schielack
Professor of Mathematics
Associate Dean for Assessment and
Pre K-12 Education, College of Science
Texas A&M University
College Station, Texas

William Tate
Edward Mallinckrodt Distinguished University
Professor in Arts & Sciences
Washington University
St. Louis, Missouri

Mathematicians

David M. Bressoud
DeWitt Wallace Professor of Mathematics
Macalester College
St. Paul, Minnesota

Roger Howe
Professor of Mathematics
Yale University
New Haven, Connecticut

Gary Lippman
Professor of Mathematics and Computer Science
California State University East Bay
Hayward, California

PEARSON

Glenview, Illinois • Boston, Massachusetts • Chandler, Arizona • Upper Saddle River, New Jersey

Consulting Author

Grant Wiggins
Researcher and Educational Consultant
Hopewell, New Jersey

ELL Consultant

Jim Cummins
Professor
The University of Toronto
Toronto, Canada

Common Core State Standards Reviewers

Elizabeth Baker
Mathematics Coordinator
Gilbert Public Schools
Gilbert, Arizona

Amy Barber
K-12 Math Coach
Peninsula School District ESC
Gig Harbor, Washington

Laura Cua
Teacher
Columbus City Schools
Columbus, Ohio

Wafa Deeb-Westervelt
Assistant Superintendent for
Curriculum, Instruction, and
Professional Development
Freeport Public Schools
Freeport, New York

Lynn Gullette
Title 1 Math Intervention
Mobile County Public Schools
Gilliard Elementary
Mobile, Alabama

Director of Mathematics
Birmingham City Schools
Birmingham, Alabama

Kelly O'Rourke
Elementary School Assistant Principal
Clark County School District
Las Vegas, Nevada

Piper L. Riddle
Evidence-Based Learning Specialist
Canyons School District
Sandy, Utah

Debra L. Vitale
Math Coach
Bristol Public Schools
Bristol, Connecticut

Diane T. Wehby
Math Support Teacher
Birmingham City Schools
Birmingham, Alabama

Scott Foresman·Addison Wesley
enVisionMATH® Common Core

Copyright © 2012 by Pearson Education, Inc., or its affiliates. All Rights Reserved. Printed in the United States of America. This publication is protected by copyright, and permission should be obtained from the publisher prior to any prohibited reproduction, storage in a retrieval system, or transmission in any form or by any means, electronic, mechanical, photocopying, recording, or likewise. For information regarding permissions, write to Rights Management & Contracts, Pearson Education, Inc., One Lake Street, Upper Saddle River, New Jersey 07458.

Pearson, Scott Foresman, Pearson Scott Foresman, and enVisionMATH are trademarks, in the U.S. and/or in other countries, of Pearson Education Inc., or its affiliates.

Common Core State Standards: © Copyright 2010. National Governors Association Center for Best Practices and Council of Chief State School Officers. All rights reserved.

UNDERSTANDING BY DESIGN® and UbD™ are trademarks of the Association for Supervision and Curriculum Development (ASCD), and are used under license.

ISBN-13: 978-0-328-67262-2
ISBN-10: 0-328-67262-9

7 8 9 10 V063 15 14 13

Grade 4 Topic Titles

Common Core

Standards for Mathematical Content

Domain: Operations and Algebraic Thinking
Topics: 1 and 2

Domain: Number and Operations in Base Ten
Topics: 3, 4, 5, 6, 7, 8, 9, and 10

Domain: Number and Operations—Fractions
Topics: 11, 12, and 13

Domain: Measurement and Data
Topics: 14 and 15

Domain: Geometry
Topic: 16

Standards for Mathematical Practice

- ✔ Make sense of problems and persevere in solving them.
- ✔ Reason abstractly and quantitatively.
- ✔ Construct viable arguments and critique the reasoning of others.
- ✔ Model with mathematics.
- ✔ Use appropriate tools strategically.
- ✔ Attend to precision.
- ✔ Look for and make use of structure.
- ✔ Look for and express regularity in repeated reasoning.

Domain: Operations and Algebraic Thinking

Topic **1** **Multiplication and Division: Meanings and Facts**

Topic **2** **Generate and Analyze Patterns**

Domain: Number and Operations in Base Ten

Topic **3** **Place Value**

Topic **4** **Addition and Subtraction of Whole Numbers**

Topic **5** **Number Sense: Multiplying by 1-Digit Numbers**

Topic **6** **Developing Fluency: Multiplying by 1-Digit Numbers**

Topic **7** **Number Sense: Multiplying by 2-Digit Numbers**

Topic **8** **Developing Fluency: Multiplying by 2-Digit Numbers**

Topic **9** **Number Sense: Dividing by 1-Digit Divisors**

Topic **10** **Developing Fluency: Dividing by 1-Digit Divisors**

Domain: Number and Operations—Fractions

Topic **11** **Fraction Equivalence and Ordering**

Topic **12** **Adding and Subtracting Fractions and Mixed Numbers with Like Denominators**

Topic **13** **Extending Fraction Concepts**

Domain: Measurement and Data

Topic **14** **Measurement Units and Conversions**

Topic **15** **Solving Measurement Problems**

Domain: Geometry

Topic **16** **Lines, Angles, and Shapes**

Grade 4 Contents

Common Core

Standards for Mathematical Practice

- ✔ Make sense of problems and persevere in solving them.
- ✔ Reason abstractly and quantitatively.
- ✔ Construct viable arguments and critique the reasoning of others.
- ✔ Model with mathematics.
- ✔ Use appropriate tools strategically.
- ✔ Attend to precision.
- ✔ Look for and make use of structure.
- ✔ Look for and express regularity in repeated reasoning.

Grade 4 Domain Colors

● **Domain: Operations and Algebraic Thinking**
Topics: 1 and 2

● **Domain: Number and Operations in Base Ten**
Topics: 3, 4, 5, 6, 7, 8, 9, and 10

● **Domain: Number and Operations—Fractions**
Topics: 11, 12, and 13

● **Domain: Measurement and Data**
Topics: 14 and 15

● **Domain: Geometry**
Topic: 16

Standards for Mathematical Content

Domain
Operations and Algebraic Thinking

Clusters
- Use the four operations with whole numbers to solve problems.
- Gain familiarity with factors and multiples.
- Generate and analyze patterns.

Standards
4.OA.1, 4.OA.2, 4.OA.3, 4.OA.4, 4.OA.5

Topic 1 — Multiplication and Division: Meanings and Facts

Topic 2 · Generate and Analyze Patterns

Standards for Mathematical Content

Domain
Operations and Algebraic Thinking

Cluster
• Generate and analyze patterns.

Standard
4.OA.5

Topic 3 · Place Value

Standards for Mathematical Content

Domain
Number and Operations in Base Ten

Cluster
• Generalize place value understanding for multi-digit whole numbers.

Standards
4.NBT.1, 4.NBT.2, 4.NBT.3

Standards for Mathematical Content

Domain
Number and Operations in Base Ten

Clusters
• Generalize place value understanding for multi-digit whole numbers.
• Use place value understanding and properties of operations to perform multi-digit arithmetic.

Standards
4.NBT.3, 4.NBT.4, 4.OA.3

Standards for Mathematical Content

Domain
Number and Operations in Base Ten

Clusters
• Use place value understanding and properties of operations to perform multi-digit arithmetic.
• Use the four operations with whole numbers to solve problems.

Standards
4.NBT.3, 4.NBT.5, 4.OA.3

Standards for Mathematical Content

Domain
Number and Operations in Base Ten

Clusters
• Use place value understanding and properties of operations to perform multi-digit arithmetic.
• Use the four operations with whole numbers to solve problems.

Standards
4.NBT.1, 4.NBT.5, 4.NBT.6, 4.OA.3

Standards for Mathematical Content

Domain
Number and Operations—Fractions

Clusters
• Extend understanding of fraction equivalence and ordering.
• Gain familiarity with factors and multiples.

Standards
4.NF.1, 4.NF.2, 4.OA.4, 4.OA.5

Topic 13   **Extending Fraction Concepts** *(continued)*

Topic 14   **Measurement Units and Conversions**

Standards for Mathematical Content

Domain
Measurement and Data

Cluster
• Solve problems involving measurement and conversion of measurements from a larger unit to a smaller unit.

Standards
4.MD.1, 4.MD.2

Topic 15 — Solving Measurement Problems

Standards for Mathematical Content

Domain
Measurement and Data

Clusters
• Solve problems involving measurement and conversion of measurements from a larger unit to a smaller unit.
• Represent and interpret data.

Standards
4.MD.2, 4.MD.3, 4.MD.4

Topic 16 — Lines, Angles, and Shapes

Standards for Mathematical Content

Domain
Geometry

Clusters
• Draw and identify lines and angles, and classify shapes by properties of their lines and angles.
• Geometric measurement: understand concepts of angle and measure angles.

Standards
4.G.1, 4.G.2, 4.G.3, 4.MD.5, 4.MD.5.a, 4.MD.5.b, 4.MD.6, 4.MD.7, 4.OA.5

Problem-Solving Handbook

Scott Foresman·Addison Wesley

enVisionMATH®
Common Core

Problem-Solving Handbook

Use this Problem-Solving Handbook throughout the year to help you solve problems.

Pictures help me understand!

Explaining helps me understand!

Everybody can be a good problem solver!

There's almost always more than one way to solve a problem!

Don't give up!

Problem-Solving Process

Read and Understand

© Answer these questions to make sense of problems.

❷ What am I trying to find?
- Tell what the question is asking.

❷ What do I know?
- Tell the problem in my own words.
- Identify key facts and details.

Plan and Solve

© Choose an appropriate tool.

❷ What strategy or strategies should I try?

❷ Can I show the problem?
- Try drawing a picture.
- Try making a list, table, or graph.
- Try acting it out or using objects.

❷ How will I solve the problem?

❷ What is the answer?
- Tell the answer in a complete sentence.

Strategies
- Show What You Know
- Draw a Picture
- Make an Organized List
- Make a Table
- Make a Graph
- Act It Out/ Use Objects
- Look for a Pattern
- Try, Check, Revise
- Write an Equation
- Use Reasoning
- Work Backward
- Solve a Simpler Problem

Look Back and Check

© Give precise answers.

❷ Did I check my work?
- Compare my work to the information in the problem.
- Be sure all calculations are correct.

❷ Is my answer reasonable?
- Estimate to see if my answer makes sense.
- Make sure the question was answered.

Using Bar Diagrams

© Bar diagrams are tools that will help you understand and solve word problems. Bar diagrams show how the quantities in a problem are related.

Problem 1

Carrie helps at the family flower store in the summer. She keeps a record of how many flower bouquets she sells. How many bouquets did she sell on Monday and Wednesday?

Carrie's Sales

Days	Bouquets Sold
Monday	19
Tuesday	22
Wednesday	24
Thursday	33
Friday	41

Bar Diagram

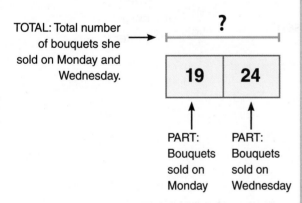

TOTAL: Total number of bouquets she sold on Monday and Wednesday. → **?**

| 19 | 24 |

PART: Bouquets sold on Monday   PART: Bouquets sold on Wednesday

19 + 24 = ▪

 Think I can add to find the total.

Problem 2

Kim is saving to buy a sweatshirt from the college her brother attends. She has $18. How much more money does she need to buy the sweatshirt?

$32

Bar Diagram

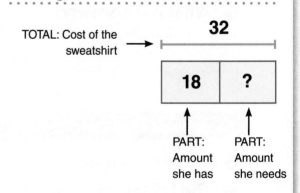

TOTAL: Cost of the sweatshirt → **32**

| 18 | ? |

PART: Amount she has   PART: Amount she needs

32 − 18 = ▪

 Think I can subtract to find the missing part.

Pictures help me understand!

Don't trust key words!

Problem 3

Tickets to a movie on Saturday cost only $5 each no matter what age you are. What is the cost of tickets for a family of four?

Bar Diagram

TOTAL: Total cost of the tickets →

?

| 5 | 5 | 5 | 5 |

↑ PART:
Cost of
each ticket

4 × 5 = ▪

Think I can multiply because the parts are equal.

Problem 4

Thirty students traveled in 3 vans to the zoo. The same number were in each van. How many students were in each van?

Bar Diagram

TOTAL: Total number of students →

30

| ? | ? | ? |

↑ PART:
Number in
each van

30 ÷ 3 = ▪

Think I can divide to find how many are in each part.

Problem-Solving Strategies

© These are tools for understanding and solving problems.

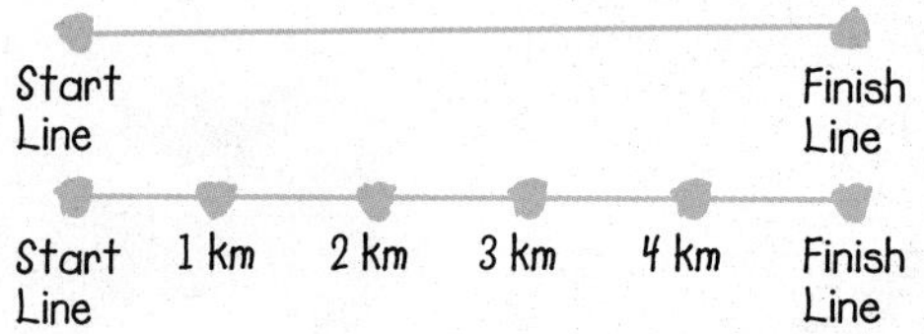

Strategy	Example	When I Use It
Draw a Picture	The race was 5 kilometers. Markers were at the starting line and the finish line. Markers showed each kilometer of the race. Find the number of markers used.	Try drawing a picture when it helps you visualize the problem or when the relationships such as joining or separating are involved.
Make a Table	Phil and Marcy spent all day Saturday at the fair. Phil rode 3 rides each half hour and Marcy rode 2 rides each half hour. How many rides had Marcy ridden when Phil rode 24 rides?	Try making a table when: • there are 2 or more quantities, • amounts change using a pattern.
Look for a Pattern	The house numbers on Forest Road change in a planned way. Describe the pattern. Tell what the next two house numbers should be.	Look for a pattern when something repeats in a predictable way.

Draw a Picture example:

Start Line — Finish Line

Start Line · 1 km · 2 km · 3 km · 4 km · Finish Line

Make a Table example:

Rides for Phil	3	6	9	12	15	18	21	24
Rides for Marcy	2	4	6	8	10	12	14	16

Look for a Pattern example:

3   6   10   15   ?   ?

Everybody can be a good problem solver!

MATHEMATICAL PRACTICES

Strategy	Example	When I Use It
Make an Organized List	How many ways can you make change for a quarter using dimes and nickels?	Make an organized list when asked to find combinations of two or more items.

1 quarter =

1 dime + 1 dime + 1 nickel
1 dime + 1 nickel + 1 nickel + 1 nickel
1 nickel + 1 nickel + 1 nickel + 1 nickel + 1 nickel

Strategy	Example	When I Use It
Try, Check, Revise	Suzanne spent $27, not including tax, on dog supplies. She bought two of one item and one of another item. What did she buy? $8 + $8 + $15 = $31 $7 + $7 + $12 = $26 $6 + $6 + $15 = $27	Use Try, Check, Revise when quantities are being combined to find a total, but you don't know which quantities.

Dog Supplies Sale!
Leash $8
Collar $6
Bowls $7
Medium Beds $15
Toys $12

Strategy	Example	When I Use It
Write an Equation	Maria's new CD player can hold 6 discs at a time. If she has 204 CDs, how many times can the player be filled without repeating a CD? Find $204 \div 6 = n$.	Write an equation when the story describes a situation that uses an operation or operations.

Even More Strategies

© These are more tools for understanding and solving problems.

Strategy	Example	When I Use It
Act It Out	How many ways can 3 students shake each other's hand?	Think about acting out a problem when the numbers are small and there is action in the problem you can do.
Use Reasoning	Beth collected some shells, rocks, and beach glass. **Beth's Collection** 2 rocks 3 times as many shells as rocks 12 objects in all How many of each object are in the collection?	Use reasoning when you can use known information to find unknown information.
Work Backward	Tracy has band practice at 10:15 A.M. It takes her 20 minutes to get from home to practice and 5 minutes to warm up. What time should she leave home to get to practice on time? Time Tracy leaves home **?** ← 20 minutes ← Time warm up starts ← 5 minutes ← Time practice starts **10:15**	Try working backward when: • you know the end result of a series of steps, • you want to know what happened at the beginning.

MATHEMATICAL PRACTICES

Strategy	Example	When I Use It
Solve a Simpler Problem	Each side of each triangle in the figure at the left is one centimeter. If there are 12 triangles in a row, what is the perimeter of the figure? I can look at 1 triangle, then 2 triangles, then 3 triangles. perimeter = 3 cm perimeter = 4 cm perimeter = 5 cm	Try solving a simpler problem when you can create a simpler case that is easier to solve.
Make a Graph	Mary was in a jump rope contest. How did her number of jumps change over the five days of the contest? **Mary's Contest Results**	Make a graph when: • data for an event are given, • the question can be answered by reading the graph.

Writing to Explain

Ⓒ Good written explanations communicate your reasoning to others. Here is a good math explanation.

Explaining helps me understand!

Writing to Explain What happens to the area of the rectangle if the lengths of its sides are doubled?

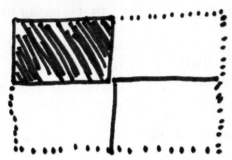

■ = $\frac{1}{4}$ of the whole rectangle

The area of the new rectangle is 4 times the area of the original rectangle.

Tips for Writing Good Math Explanations ...

A good explanation should be:
- correct
- simple
- complete
- easy to understand

Math explanations can use:
- words
- pictures
- numbers
- symbols

Problem-Solving Recording Sheet

Ⓒ This helps you organize your work and make sense of problems.

Name _Benton_

Teaching Tool
1

Problem-Solving Recording Sheet

Problem:

Suppose your teacher told you to open your math book
to the facing pages whose page numbers add to 85.
To which two pages would you open your book?

Find?

Two facing page
numbers

Know?

Two pages.
Facing each other.
Sum is 85.

Strategies?
Show the Problem
☑ Draw a Picture
☐ Make an Organized List
☐ Make a Table
☐ Make a Graph
☐ Act It Out/Use Objects

☐ Look for a Pattern
☑ Try, Check, Revise
☑ Write an Equation
☐ Use Reasoning
☐ Work Backwards
☐ Solve a Simpler Problem

Show the Problem?

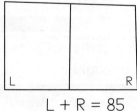

L + R = 85
L is 1 less than R

Solution?

I'll try some numbers in the middle.
40 + 41 = 81, too low
How about 46 and 47?
46 + 47 = 93, too high
Ok, now try 42 and 43.
42 + 43 = 85.

Answer?

The page numbers are 42
and 43.

Check? Reasonable?

I added correctly.
42 + 43 is about 40 + 40 = 80
80 is close to 85.
42 and 43 is reasonable.

TT 1

Copyright © Pearson Education, Inc., or its affiliates. All Rights Reserved. 4

Getting to Know Your Math Book

Before you start working on lessons, look through your textbook. Here are some questions to help you learn more about your book—and about the math you will learn this year.

How many of the topics in your book are about fractions?

Which of the problem-solving strategies on pages xviii–xix would you use when numbers are repeating in a predictable way?

What shape is used in exercise 7 on page 40?

What game board is featured on page 17 for exercises 44–47?

Look at the picture on page 186. What kind of problems do you think you will be doing in this topic?

What tool will you use in Lesson 16–5 on page 431?

What is the last page number in your book?

What is the first word in the glossary under M?

Topic 1

Multiplication and Division: Meanings and Facts

▼ Goldfish have been kept as pets for more than 1,000 years. How many goldfish can you keep in a 10-gallon tank? You will find out in Lesson 1-6.

Topic Essential Questions

- How can patterns and properties be used to find some multiplication facts?
- How can unknown multiplication facts be found by breaking them apart into known facts?
- How can unknown division facts be found by thinking about a related multiplication fact?

Vocabulary

Choose the best term from the box.

- breaking apart
- factor
- product
- multiples

1. In the number sentence $8 \times 3 = 24$, 8 is a _?_.

2. In the number sentence $2 \times 6 = 12$, 12 is the _?_.

3. $191 + 67 = (191 + 9) + 58$ is an example of using the _?_ strategy.

4. To find _?_ of the number 3, multiply numbers by 3.

Patterns

Find the term that comes next in the pattern.

5. 2, 4, 6, 8, ▨

6. 20, 25, 30, 35, ▨

7. 6, 9, 12, 15, ▨

8. 8, 16, 24, 32, ▨

9. 7, 14, 21, 28, ▨

10. 11, 22, 33, 44, ▨

Arrays

Copy each array and circle equal groups of 3.

11. ▨ ▨ ▨ ▨
    ▨ ▨ ▨ ▨
    ▨ ▨ ▨

12. ▨ ▨ ▨
    ▨ ▨ ▨

© 13. **Writing to Explain** Henry is thinking of a whole number. He multiplies the number by 5, but the result is less than 5. What number is Henry thinking about? Explain.

Interactive Learning

Topic 1

Pose the problem. Start each lesson by working together to solve problems. It will help you make sense of math.

Lesson 1-1

© **Use Tools** Solve. Use place-value blocks or draw a picture to help.

Marcy built a wall 6 blocks wide and 4 blocks high. How many blocks did she use?

Lesson 1-2

© **Look for Patterns** Use a hundred chart to solve this problem.

How many fingers are there on four hands? Five hands? Six hands? Describe patterns you see.

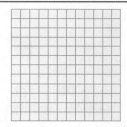

Lesson 1-3

© **Generalize** Solve any way you choose.

Find two ways to arrange 10 desks in equal rows. Then write number sentences for each arrangement and describe how these number sentences are similar.

Lesson 1-4

© **Use Structure** Use grid paper to complete this task.

Draw two 4 × 6 arrays on grid paper. Write a multiplication sentence for the first array. Divide the second array into two smaller arrays. Make each represent a multiplication fact that you already know. Write the multiplication sentence for each of these smaller arrays. How do the totals for the two 4 × 6 arrays compare? How do you know?

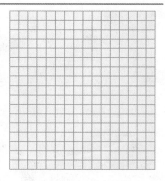

Lesson 1-5

© **Look for Patterns** Copy and complete the table.

Five people go to the movies. The total cost including transportation for 1, 2, 3, and 4 people is shown in the table. If the pattern continues, how much will it cost for 5 people? Describe patterns you found.

No. of People	1	2	3	4	5
Cost	$16	$22	$28	$34	?

Lesson 1-6

Use Tools Solve. Use counters to help.

Sophia has 8 sticker sheets and she wants to give 2 sheets to each of her friends. How many friends will receive sticker sheets?

Lesson 1-7

Use Tools Solve. Use counters to help.

How can you use counters to make an array to show 2 × 6? How many different multiplication and division sentences can you write that are represented by the array?

Lesson 1-8

Model Solve any way you choose.

Four friends want to share 4 books. How many books would each friend get? What number sentence could you use to represent this? Could four friends share 0 books? Explain.

4 books			
?	?	?	?

Lesson 1-9

Use Structure Explain how multiplication or division can be used to solve this problem.

Carly reads a book with 32 chapters. She has 8 days to read it. She wants to read the same number of chapters each day. How many chapters should she read each day?

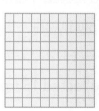

Lesson 1-10

Model Solve. Tell how you found the solution.

Sarah has two pets. Her cat, Max, weighs 8 pounds. Her dog, Pete, weighs 6 times as much. How much does Pete weigh?

© **Common Core**

4.OA.1 Interpret a multiplication equation as a comparison, e.g., interpret 35 = 5 × 7 as a statement that 35 is 5 times as many as 7 and 7 times as many as 5. Represent verbal statements of multiplicative comparisons as multiplication equations. Also **4.OA.2**

Meanings of Multiplication

How can multiplication be used when equal groups are combined?

How many ducks are there in 4 rows of 3? To find the total, multiply the number of equal groups by the number in each group. Objects arranged in equal rows form an <u>array</u>.

4 rows of 3

Another Example ## How can multiplication be used when you only know the number in one group?

You have learned addition facts. Now you will use them to help you learn to multiply.

Rudi and Eva collect plastic frogs. Rudi collected 5 frogs. Eva collected 3 times as many frogs. How many frogs did Eva collect?

A 3 frogs

B 5 frogs

C 10 frogs

D 15 frogs

Rudi's frogs

Eva's frogs
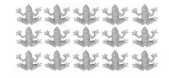

Eva collected 3 times as many frogs as Rudi.

Multiply by 3:

$3 \times 5 = 15$

Eva collected 15 frogs. The correct choice is **D**.

Explain It

1. Jon and Bill collect sports cards. Jon collected 6 sports cards. Bill collected 4 times as many sports cards. Write a multiplication sentence that shows how many sports cards Bill collected.

2. Sara and Molly each have a set of crayons. Molly has 8 crayons in her set. Sara has 24 crayons in her set. Sara says she has 3 more crayons than Molly. Is she correct? Explain.

There are 4 rows. Each row has 3 rubber ducks.

Repeated Addition: $\underbrace{3 + 3 + 3 + 3}_{\text{adding 4 rows of 3}} = 12$

Multiplication: $4 \times 3 = 12$

factors   product

12 is 4 times as many as 3.

The product is the answer to a multiplication problem. Factors are the numbers multiplied together to find the product.

The same rubber ducks can be arranged in another way.

Each group has 4 rubber ducks.

Repeated Addition: $4 + 4 + 4 = 12$

Multiplication: $3 \times 4 = 12$

12 is 3 times as many as 4.
There are 12 rubber ducks in all.

Guided Practice*

MATHEMATICAL PRACTICES

Do you know HOW?

In **1** and **2**, write an addition sentence and a multiplication sentence for each picture below.

1.

2.

Do you UNDERSTAND?

3. Model Beth saw 2 groups of 4 moths. Draw a picture to show 2 groups of 4. Then draw an array to show 2×4.

4. How could you use repeated addition to find the total number of objects in 3 groups of 2?

5. Martha has 5 rubber ducks. Jim has twice as many rubber ducks. How many rubber ducks does Jim have?

Independent Practice

Leveled Practice In **6** through **8**, write an addition sentence and a multiplication sentence for each picture.

6.

7.

8.

In **9** through **11**, write a multiplication sentence for each addition sentence.

9. $3 + 3 + 3 + 3 = 12$

10. $5 + 5 + 5 + 5 + 5 = 25$

11. $8 + 8 + 8 = 24$

Animated Glossary
www.pearsonsuccessnet.com

For another example, see Set A on page 32.

12. Which number is thirty-three thousand, three in standard form?

    A   333,003

    B   303,003

    C   303,033

    D   33,003

13. Betsy's school needs $2,000 to send the band to the state finals. So far, they have raised $465 in a fundraiser. How much more money do they need?

14. Jacob, Hannah, and their grandmother visited the petting zoo. One scoop of animal food cost two dollars. How much did their grandmother pay to buy a scoop for each child?

© 15. Writing to Explain Without multiplying, how do you know that a 4×4 array will have more items than a 3×3 array?

16. Taylor helped his father with the grocery shopping. He bought three bags of cheese sticks. Each bag contained 8 cheese sticks. How many cheese sticks were there in all?

    A   3 cheese sticks

    B   16 cheese sticks

    C   24 cheese sticks

    D   30 cheese sticks

17. Sam is setting the table for a family dinner. He needs to put two forks at each place setting. Ten people will come for dinner. Write a multiplication sentence to show how many forks Sam needs.

© 18. Think About the Structure Harry arranged the marbles in the pattern shown to the right. Which number sentence best represents Harry's arrangement of marbles?

    A   3 groups of 9 marbles   **C**   2 groups of 13 marbles

    B   4 groups of 5 marbles   **D**   4 groups of 7 marbles

19. Lisa has 2 rings. Tina has 4 times as many rings. How many rings does Tina have?

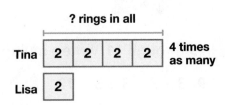

Mixed Problem Solving

National Animals	Facts
Australia: Kangaroo	Kangaroos move at a rate of about 18 feet per second for several hours.
Canada: Beaver	Adult male and female beavers can weigh over 55 pounds.
India: Bengal Tiger	A typical male Bengal Tiger's body length measures 72 inches not including the length of its tail or 120 inches including its tail.
Thailand: Thai Elephant	On May 19, 1998, it was approved that March 13 would be marked as Thai Elephants Day.
United States: Bald Eagle	The Bald Eagle has been a symbol for the United States since June 20, 1782.
Botswana: Zebra	The life expectancy of a zebra can be 40 years.

1. How far can a kangaroo travel in 5 seconds?

? Distance a kangaroo can jump in 5 seconds

18	18	18	18	18

↑
Feet jumped per second

2. How long can the tail of a male Bengal Tiger be?

120 inches

72 inches	?

3. About how many beavers weigh the same as a 165 pound adult?

4. In what year will the 25th anniversary of Thai Elephants Day occur?

5. The Continental Congress adopted the Great Seal of the United States in 1782. The American Revolution started 7 years earlier. In what year did the American Revolution begin?

6. The largest of all zebras is the Grevy's zebra. A male Grevy's zebra, on average, weighs 431 kilograms. The average female Grevy's zebra weighs 386 kilograms. How much more does a male Grevy's zebra weigh than a female Grevy's zebra?

7. A Bald Eagle can lay 1 to 3 eggs a year. What is the largest number of eggs a Bald Eagle can lay in 8 years?

8. A female Bengal Tiger can measure about 60 inches in length, not including her tail. About how many inches longer is the male Bengal Tiger than the female Bengal Tiger?

Lesson
1-2

Common
Core

4.OA.5 Generate a number
or shape pattern that
follows a given rule. Identify
apparent features of the
pattern that were not
explicit in the rule itself.

Patterns for Facts

What are the patterns for multiples of 2, 5, and 9?

A **multiple** is the product of a number and any whole number.

○ multiples of 2

▢ multiples of 5

△ multiples of 9

41	42	43	44	45	46	47	48	49	50
51	52	53	54	55	56	57	58	59	60
61	62	63	64	65	66	67	68	69	70
71	72	73	74	75	76	77	78	79	80

Guided Practice*

MATHEMATICAL PRACTICES

Do you know HOW?

In **1** through **4**, skip count to find the number that comes next.

1. 5, 10, 15, ▨   **2.** 40, 42, 44, ▨

3. 60, 65, 70, ▨   **4.** 45, 54, 63, ▨

In **5** through **8**, find the product.

5. 9×3 **6.** 2×9

7. 5×8 **8.** 9×6

Do you UNDERSTAND?

© **9. Generalize** In the chart above, what pattern do you see for the numbers that have both red circles and green squares?

10. How do you know that 73 is not a multiple of 2? Explain using the pattern for multiples of 2.

11. Felix is sorting socks. He has 11 pairs of socks. How many socks does he have in all?

Independent Practice

In **12** through **15**, skip count to find the number that comes next.

12. 18, 27, 36, ▨   **13.** 72, 74, 76, ▨   **14.** 2, 4, 6, ▨   **15.** 88, 90, 92, ▨

In **16** through **30**, find each product.

16. 6×2 **17.** 5×3 **18.** 2×5 **19.** 8×5 **20.** 9×4

21. 2×7 **22.** 5×9 **23.** 3×9 **24.** 9×6 **25.** 8×2

26. 2×3 **27.** 7×9 **28.** 5×6 **29.** 7×6 **30.** 5×5

Animated Glossary
www.pearsonsuccessnet.com

*For another example, see Set B on page 32.

To find multiples of 2, skip count by 2s.

(42), (44), (46), (48),
(50), (52), (54), (56)...

All multiples of 2 are even numbers.

To find multiples of 5, skip count by 5s.

| 45 | 50 | 55 | 60 |
| 65 | 70 | 75 | 80 | ...

All multiples of 5 have a 0 or 5 in the ones place.

To find multiples of 9, skip count by 9s.

45 , 54 , 63 , 72 ...

The digits of multiples of 9 add to 9 or a multiple of 9.

For 99, for example, $9 + 9 = 18$, and 18 is a multiple of 9.

Problem Solving

© MATHEMATICAL PRACTICES

31. How many legs are there on

  a 9 flies with 6 legs each?

  b 5 spiders with 8 legs each?

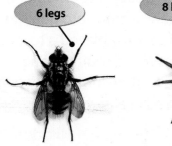
6 legs

8 legs

32. In wheelchair basketball, players use sports chairs that have 2 large wheels and 3 small wheels. If there are 5 players, how many

  a large wheels do the sports chairs have?

  b small wheels do the sports chairs have?

  c wheels do the sports chairs have in all?

33. Jody is working on her model train. She adds 9 pieces of track. Each piece of track is attached with 5 screws. How many screws does she need in all?

  A 15 screws   **C** 54 screws

  B 45 screws   **D** 90 screws

© **34. Model** Each pentagon shown below has 5 sides. How many sides are there in all? Skip count by 5s to find the answer. Then, write the multiplication sentence.

© **35. Reason** Use the digits 2, 5, and 9 to make as many 3-digit numbers as you can. Put the numbers in order from least to greatest.

36. Which expression has a product of 40?

  A 2×10 **C** 8×5

  B 5×6 **D** 9×8

Lesson
1-3

ⓒ
Common
Core

4.OA.1 Interpret a
multiplication equation
as a comparison, e.g.,
interpret 35 = 5 × 7 as a
statement that 35 is 5 times
as many as 7 and 7 times
as many as 5. Represent
verbal statements of
multiplicative comparisons
as multiplication equations.

Multiplication Properties

How can properties help you multiply?

Multiplication properties can help you
remember basic facts.

3 groups of 2 (6 in all)

Commutative Property of Multiplication
Two numbers can be multiplied in any
order and the product will be the same.

2 groups of 3 (6 in all)

$$3 \times 2 = 2 \times 3$$

Guided Practice*

Do you know HOW?

In **1** through **4**, find the product.

1. 0×5 **2.** 1×6

3. 1×0 **4.** 1×9

In **5** and **6**, copy and complete.

5. $4 \times 7 = 7 \times \blacksquare$

6. $6 \times 10 = \blacksquare \times 6$

Do you UNDERSTAND?

7. When you multiply any number by
one, what is the product?

ⓒ **8.** **Model** In a soccer tournament,
Matt's team scored zero goals in
each game. They played a total of
6 games. Write a multiplication
sentence to show how many goals
they scored in all.

Independent Practice

In **9** through **18**, find the product.

9. 1×5 **10.** 5×0 **11.** 3×9 **12.** 0×8 **13.** 0×3

14. 4×0 **15.** 9×4 **16.** 6×7 **17.** 5×6 **18.** 1×1

In **19** through **26**, find the missing number.

19. $4 \times 5 = \blacksquare \times 4$ **20.** $9 \times 12 = 12 \times \blacksquare$ **21.** $5 \times 0 = \blacksquare \times 5$ **22.** $9 \times 8 = \blacksquare \times 9$

23. $8 \times 11 = \blacksquare \times 8$ **24.** $1 \times 9 = \blacksquare \times 1$ **25.** $6 \times 4 = \blacksquare \times 6$ **26.** $7 \times 5 = \blacksquare \times 7$

Animated Glossary
www.pearsonsuccessnet.com

*For another example, see Set B on page 32.

Zero Property of Multiplication
The product of any number and zero is zero.

2 groups of 0

$2 \times 0 = 0$

Identity Property of Multiplication
The product of any number and one is that number.

1 group of 7

$1 \times 7 = 7$

Problem Solving

MATHEMATICAL
PRACTICES

For **27** and **28**, use the table at the right.

27. Reason Annie has 6 packages of tennis balls. How many packages of yellow ping-pong balls would Annie need to have so that she has an equal number of ping-pong balls and tennis balls?

28. If Annie and her three friends each bought 1 package of baseballs, how many baseballs do they have in all?

Type of Ball	Number in each Package
Baseball	1
Tennis Balls	3
Ping-Pong Balls	6

29. Writing to Explain How do you know that $23 \times 15 = 15 \times 23$ without finding the products?

30. The Appalachian Trail is 2,174 miles long. If Andy hiked the entire trail one time, how many miles did he hike?

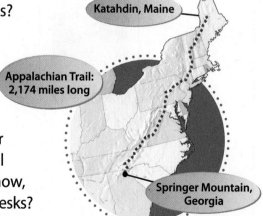

Katahdin, Maine

Appalachian Trail: 2,174 miles long

Springer Mountain, Georgia

31. Persevere Mrs. Grayson has 27 students in her class. She wants to rearrange the desks in equal groups. If the desks are in 9 groups of 3 desks now, what is another way that she could arrange the desks?

Tip *Use a multiplication property.*

A 3 groups of 9 desks   **C** 5 groups of 6 desks

B 2 groups of 13 desks   **D** 4 groups of 7 desks

© Common Core

4.OA.4 Find all factor pairs for a whole number in the range 1–100. Recognize that a whole number is a multiple of each of its factors. Determine whether a given whole number in the range 1–100 is a multiple of a given one-digit number. Determine whether a given whole number in the range 1–100 is prime or composite.

3, 4, 6, 7, and 8 as Factors

How can you break apart facts?

Each skateboard has 4 wheels.

Darnel is replacing the wheels on 8 skateboards. Each skateboard has 4 wheels. How many wheels does he need in all?

Use the Distributive Property to break apart a problem into two simpler problems.

Another Example **Are there different ways to break apart a fact?**

Darnel's boss asks him to replace the wheels on 7 inline racing skates. Each skate has 5 wheels. How many wheels does he need?

Find 7×5.

You can break apart the first factor or the second factor.

One Way

The second factor, 5, can be broken into $3 + 2$.

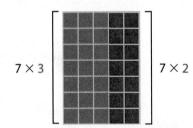

7×3 7×2

$7 \times 5 = (7 \times 3) + (7 \times 2)$

$21 + 14 = 35$

Another Way

The first factor, 7, can be broken into $5 + 2$.

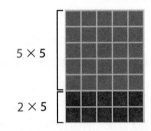

5×5

2×5

$7 \times 5 = (5 \times 5) + (2 \times 5)$

$25 + 10 = 35$

Darnel needs 35 wheels.

Explain It

1. In the example above, explain how the products 21 and 14 were found.

2. What is another way to break apart the fact 7×5?

Find 8 × 4.

Break apart 8 into 3 + 5.

$8 × 4 = (3 × 4) + (5 × 4)$

$12 + 20 = 32$

So, $4 × 8 = 32$

Find 8 × 4.

Break apart 8 into 2 + 6.

$8 × 4 = (2 × 4) + (6 × 4)$

$8 + 24 = 32$

Darnel needs 32 wheels in all.

Guided Practice*

MATHEMATICAL PRACTICES

Do you know HOW?

In **1** through **3**, use breaking apart to find each product.

1. $6 × 8 = (6 × 4) + (6 × \boxed{})$

$\boxed{} + \boxed{} = \boxed{}$

2. $7 × 3 = (7 × 1) + (\boxed{} × 2)$

$\boxed{} + \boxed{} = \boxed{}$

3. $9 × 5 = (9 × 1) + (9 × \boxed{})$

$\boxed{} + \boxed{} = \boxed{}$

Do you UNDERSTAND?

4. Use Structure In Exercise 2, what is another way to break apart the 7 in 7 × 3?

5. On Friday, Darnel received a box of skateboard wheels from the factory. The box contained 12 sets of 4 wheels. How many wheels were there in all?

 Break apart 12 into 10 + 2.

Independent Practice

Leveled Practice In **6** through **24**, use breaking apart to find each product.

6. $5 × 10 = (5 × 5) + (5 × \boxed{})$

7. $1 × 3 = (1 × \boxed{}) + (1 × 2)$

8. $7 × 11 = (7 × 1) + (7 × \boxed{})$

9. $4 × \boxed{} = (4 × 3) + (4 × 9)$

10. $9 × 9$

11. $6 × 7$

12. $3 × 5$

13. $7 × 6$

14. $4 × 7$

15. $4 × 9$

16. $9 × 7$

17. $6 × 3$

18. $7 × 8$

19. $8 × 8$

20. $6 × 4$

21. $6 × 9$

22. $9 × 3$

23. $8 × 6$

24. $7 × 12$

Animated Glossary
www.pearsonsuccessnet.com

DIGITAL

In **25** through **28**, copy and complete by filling in with 6, 7, or 8.

25. $(8 \times 2) + (8 \times 4) = 8 \times$ ▢

26. $(7 \times 3) + (7 \times 5) = 7 \times$ ▢

27. $(6 \times 3) + (6 \times 4) = 6 \times$ ▢

28. $(9 \times 5) + (9 \times 3) = 9 \times$ ▢

In **29** through **34**, compare using $<$, $>$, or $=$ to fill in each ◯.

29. 8×4 ◯ 6×4

30. 3×7 ◯ 4×7

31. 3×6 ◯ 9×2

32. 11×5 ◯ 12×4

33. 2×12 ◯ 4×6

34. 9×9 ◯ 8×10

Problem Solving

MATHEMATICAL
PRACTICES

© **35. Reason** How many eggs are in

a 2 dozen? **b** 6 dozen? **c** 10 dozen?

 Remember 1 dozen = 12.

For **36** and **37**, use the table at the right.

36. In the Aztec calendar, each year has a number from 1 to 13. It also has one of 4 signs, as shown in the table. It takes 4×13 years to go through one complete cycle of the years. How many years is this?

 Break apart 13 into 10 + 3.

Aztec Year Names (first 16 years)			
2-House	3-Rabbit	4-Reed	5-Flint
6-House	7-Rabbit	8-Reed	9-Flint
10-House	11-Rabbit	12-Reed	13-Flint
1-House	2-Rabbit	3-Reed	4-Flint

© **37. Generalize** The year 2006 is 7-Rabbit in the Aztec calendar. In what year will 11-Rabbit occur?

© **38. Persevere** Jamal, Vera, and Tanya took a vacation. They traveled the distances shown in the table at the right. Who walked the farthest?

A Jamal

C Vera

B Tanya

D They all walked the same distance.

Hiker	Distance walked
Jamal	9 miles each day for 8 days
Vera	8 miles per day for 4 days and 4 miles a day for 8 days.
Tanya	7 miles each day for 5 days then 5 miles a day for 7 days.

39. Tickets for a car festival cost $24 each. How can you use what you know about multiples of 12 to find the cost of three tickets?

40. Critique Reasoning Jillian says that the product of 11 × 12 is 1,212. Is this reasonable? Why or why not?

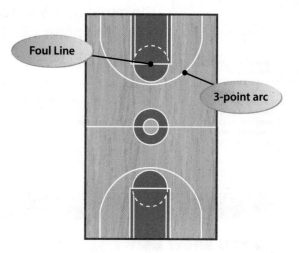

Use the diagram and table at the right to answer **41** through **43**.

41. Damian makes five shots from beyond the arc. How many points are scored?

42. Writing to Explain Vicki scores six baskets inside the arc and six free throws. Li scores six baskets from beyond the arc. Without multiplying, explain why each girl scores the same total.

43. Reason In his last basketball game, Andrew scored 15 points. Which of the following is **NOT** a way he could have scored his points?

   A Five 3-point shots

   B Three 3-point shots in the first half and two 3-point shots in the second half

   C Three 2-point shots

   D Five 2-point shots and five foul shots

Type of Shot	Points
Foul shot	1
Basket made inside arc	2
Basket made beyond arc	3

For **44** through **47**, use the diagram at the right.

Write a multiplication sentence to find the total number of

44. white pieces.

45. squares with pieces.

46. white squares.

47. Model Write an addition sentence and a multiplication sentence to find the number of squares on a chessboard.

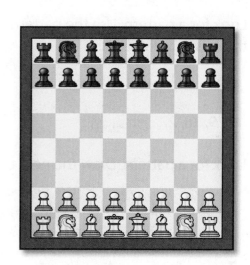

Lesson
1-5

Common Core

4.OA.3 Solve multistep word problems posed with whole numbers and having whole-number answers using the four operations, including problems in which remainders must be interpreted. Represent these problems using equations with a letter standing for the unknown quantity. Assess the reasonableness of answers using mental computation and estimation strategies including rounding. Also **4.OA.5**

Problem Solving

Look for a Pattern

Ella is learning how to play a waltz on the piano. Her teacher gives her a beginner's exercise for her left hand.

The music shows 4 measures. If this pattern continues, how many notes will she play in 8 measures?

3, 6, 9, 12, ▮, ▮, ▮, ▮

Guided Practice*

MATHEMATICAL PRACTICES

Do you know HOW?

Solve. Find a pattern.

© 1. **Generalize** Julia is printing files. The first file is 2 pages, the second file is 4 pages, the third file is 6 pages, and the fourth file is 8 pages. If this pattern continues, how many pages will be in the eighth file?

Do you UNDERSTAND?

© 2. **Use Structure** What multiplication facts can you use to help find the answer to Problem 1? Why?

© 3. **Write a Problem** Write a problem that uses a pattern for multiples of 5. Then answer your question.

Independent Practice

MATHEMATICAL PRACTICES

Look for a pattern. Use the pattern to find the missing numbers.

4. 5, 10, 15, 20, ▮, ▮, ▮, ▮

5. 9, 18, 27, ▮, ▮, ▮, ▮

Look for a pattern, Draw the next two shapes.

6.

7.

Applying Math Practices

- What am I asked to find?
- What else can I try?
- How are quantities related?
- How can I explain my work?
- How can I use math to model the problem?
- Can I use tools to help?
- Is my work precise?
- Why does this work?
- How can I generalize?

For another example, see Set D on page 32.

What do I know? The pattern for the first 4 measures is: **3, 6, 9, and 12.**

What am I asked to find? The number of notes she will play in 8 measures

Find a pattern. Skip count by 3s.

3, 6, 9, 12,...

What are the next four numbers?

3, 6, 9, 12, 15, 18, 21, 24

Ella plays 24 notes in 8 measures.

Is the answer reasonable?

There are 12 notes in 4 measures.

The number of notes in 8 measures is double the number in 4 measures.

The answer is reasonable.

Look for a pattern. Copy and complete each number sentence.

8. 30 + 5 = 35
300 + 5 = 305
3,000 + 5 = ▢
30,000 + 5 = ▢

9. 50 + 5 = 55
505 + 50 = 555
5,005 + 550 = ▢
50,505 + 5,050 = ▢

10. 60 + 8 = 68
600 + 80 = 680
6,000 + 800 = ▢
60,000 + 8,000 = ▢

11. Kaylee delivers invitations to everyone on her floor of her apartment building. There are 10 apartments on her floor. The numbers of the first four apartments are 2, 4, 6, and 8. If the pattern continues, what are the rest of the apartment numbers?

ⓒ **12. Generalize** Look for a pattern in the table below to find the missing numbers.

300	320	340	▢	380
400	▢	440	460	▢
500	520	▢	560	580

13. Kerry has a newspaper route. The first four houses she delivers to are numbered 322, 326, 330, and 334. If this pattern continues, what will the next four numbers be?

14. Marvin is looking for a radio station on the AM dial. He tries these three stations: 1040, 1080, and 1120. If this pattern continues, what will be the next three numbers?

ⓒ **15. Model** Jonas saves coins in his piggy bank. He drops in these groups of coins: 1 penny, 2 nickels, 3 dimes, 4 quarters, 5 pennies, 6 nickels, 7 dimes, and 8 quarters. If this pattern continues, what are the next four groups of coins?

ⓒ **16. Model** Suppose there are 18 bowls arranged in this pattern: big bowl, little bowl, big bowl, little bowl, and so on. Is the last bowl a big bowl or a little bowl? Explain.

Lesson
1-6

© Common Core

4.OA.2 Multiply or divide to solve word problems involving multiplicative comparison, e.g., by using drawings and equations with a symbol for the unknown number to represent the problem, distinguishing multiplicative comparison from additive comparison.

Meanings of Division

When do you divide?

A museum wants to display a collection of 24 gems on four shelves, placing the same number of gems on each shelf. How many gems will be on each shelf?

Choose an Operation Think about sharing. Divide to find the number in each group.

24 gems on 4 shelves

Another Example **How can you divide to find the number of groups?**

You have learned subtraction facts. Now you will use them to help you divide.

Terri has 24 gems. She wants to display them on shelves. She decides to display 4 gems on each shelf. How many shelves does she need?

Choose an Operation Think about repeated subtraction. Divide to find the number of groups.

What You Show

To find the number of shelves, put 4 gems in each group. How many groups are there?

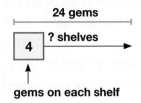

Terri needs 6 shelves.

What You Write

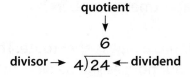

Explain It

1. How can repeated subtraction be used to find the number of shelves needed to hold 24 gems if each shelf holds 6 gems?

2. Explain what the quotient represents in each of the examples above.

What You Show

Think of sharing the gems equally among the 4 shelves. How many gems are on each shelf?

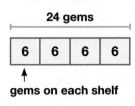

24 gems

| 6 | 6 | 6 | 6 |

↑ gems on each shelf

What You Write

divisor
↓
$24 \div 4 = 6$
↑   ↑
dividend   quotient

Each shelf should have 6 gems.

Guided Practice*

MATHEMATICAL PRACTICES

Do you know HOW?

In **1** and **2**, draw pictures to help you divide.

1. You put 18 people into 3 rows. How many people are in each row?

2. Rocco is putting 14 drawings into 2 art binders. How many drawings are in each binder?

Do you UNDERSTAND?

© **3. Use Structure** Explain how you could use repeated addition to check the answer to the example above.

4. Sixteen players came to soccer practice. They formed four teams with the same number of players per team. How many players were on each team?

Independent Practice

Leveled Practice In **5** through **7**, copy and complete the diagrams to help you divide.

5. Kevin is arranging 12 chairs in 3 equal groups. How many chairs are in each group?

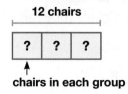

12 chairs

| ? | ? | ? |

↑ chairs in each group

6. Meg has 36 beads. Each bracelet has 9 beads. How many bracelets does she have?

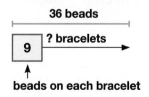

36 beads

| 9 | ? bracelets →

↑ beads on each bracelet

7. A farmer has 15 fruit trees. He plants 3 trees in each row. How many rows are there?

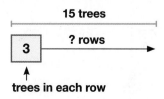

15 trees

| 3 | ? rows →

↑ trees in each row

*For another example, see Set E on page 33.

In **8** through **11**, draw pictures to solve each problem.

8. Jeff puts 25 quarters into 5 equal groups. How many quarters are in each group?

9. Sally has 12 flower bulbs and divides them into 4 equal groups. How many flower bulbs are in each group?

10. Jena is making apple pies. She has 33 apples. She's putting 11 in each pie. How many pies will Jena make?

11. There are 30 stuffed bears in a gift shop arranged in 5 equal rows. How many bears are in each row?

Problem Solving

MATHEMATICAL PRACTICES

In **12** through **15**, use the table at the right.

12. How many students will be in each row for Mrs. Raymond's class photo?

ⓒ **13. Reason** How many more students will be in each row for Mr. Peterson's class than for Mr. Chen's class?

14. In which class will there be 7 students in each row?

ⓒ **15. Reason** If 3 students were absent from Miss Clifford's class on picture day, how many fewer students would be in each row?

Class Picture Day	
Each class must be arranged into three equal rows.	
Name of Teacher	**Number of Students**
Mrs. Raymond	24
Mr. Chen	18
Miss Clifford	21
Mr. Peterson	27

Data

16. A fish store tells you that you need 2 gallons of water for each goldfish. How many goldfish can you keep in a 10-gallon tank?

ⓒ **17. Persevere** Ray collects toy cars. He stores them in special boxes that fit 6 cars each. He had a total of 48 cars. Today he got 12 more cars. How many boxes will Ray need to store all of his cars now?

A 2 boxes

B 6 boxes

C 8 boxes

D 10 boxes

ⓒ **18. Think About the Structure** The drama club collects 242 bottles and 320 cans in a fundraiser. Each is worth a nickel. However, the recycling machine rejects 48 cans. Which expression shows how many nickels they raised?

A $(242 + 320) - 48$

B $242 + 320 + 48$

C $(320 - 242) + 48$

D $(320 - 242) - 48$

Algebra Connections

Properties and Number Sentences

Remember multiplication properties can be used to help you solve multiplication problems:

- Commutative Property
  $3 \times 2 = 2 \times 3$
- Associative Property
  $(5 \times 2) \times 4 = 5 \times (2 \times 4)$
- Identity Property
  $9 \times 1 = 9$
- Zero Property
  $8 \times 0 = 0$

Example: $8 \times 5 = \boxed{} \times 8$

Think *The Commutative Property of Multiplication means you can multiply numbers in any order.*

Since $8 \times 5 = 5 \times 8$, the value of $\boxed{}$ must be 5.

Copy and complete. Check your answers.

1. $39 \times \boxed{} = 39$

2. $\boxed{} \times 12 = 12$

3. $(8 \times 5) \times 2 = \boxed{} \times (5 \times 2)$

4. $20 \times 4 = 4 \times \boxed{}$

5. $6 \times \boxed{} = 5 \times 6$

6. $15 \times 3 = \boxed{} \times 15$

7. $\boxed{} \times 8 = 8 \times 9$

8. $1 \times \boxed{} = 24$

9. $\boxed{} \times 25 = 0$

10. $0 = \boxed{} \times 9$

11. $16 \times \boxed{} = 16$

12. $\boxed{} \times 5 = 6 \times (4 \times 5)$

13. $12 \times 0 = \boxed{}$

14. $7 \times \boxed{} = 0$

15. $7 \times (1 \times \boxed{}) = (7 \times 1) \times 3$

· ·

For **16** through **18**, use the information in the table to find the answer.

16. Write two number sentences to represent the number of seats in 6 rows.

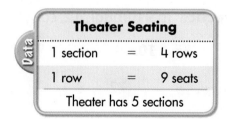

Theater Seating		
1 section	=	4 rows
1 row	=	9 seats
Theater has 5 sections		

17. No one is sitting in the last row of the theater that is otherwise filled. How many seats are being used?

18. How many rows of seats does the theater have?

Lesson
1-7

©
**Common
Core**

4.OA.1 Interpret a
multiplication equation
as a comparison, e.g.,
interpret 35 = 5 × 7 as a
statement that 35 is 5 times
as many as 7 and 7 times
as many as 5. Represent
verbal statements of
multiplicative comparisons
as multiplication equations.

Relating Multiplication and Division

<u>Operations that undo each other</u>
are inverse operations. Multiplying by
3 and dividing by 3 are inverse operations.

Each trading card sheet has 3 rows
with 2 pockets in each row. How many
pockets are on each sheet?

**3 rows
of 2**

Guided Practice*

© **MATHEMATICAL PRACTICES**

Do you know HOW?

In **1** and **2**, copy and complete each
fact family.

1. 8 × ▢ = 32   **2.** 6 × 9 = ▢

   32 ÷ ▢ = 4   54 ÷ ▢ = 9

   32 ÷ ▢ = ▢   54 ÷ 9 = ▢

   ▢ × ▢ = 32   9 × ▢ = ▢

In **3** and **4**, write the fact family for each
set of numbers.

3. 3, 6, 18   **4.** 5, 7, 35

Do you UNDERSTAND?

5. Why are there four number
sentences in the example above?

6. Is 2 × 6 = 12 part of the fact family
from the example above?

7. Why is 3 + 3 = 6 **NOT** in the fact
family of 2, 3, and 6?

© **8. Reason** If you know 7 × 9 = 63,
what division facts do you know?

Independent Practice

Leveled Practice In **9** through **12**, copy and complete each fact family.

9. 5 × ▢ = 35   **10.** 9 × ▢ = 72   **11.** 3 × ▢ = 18   **12.** 2 × ▢ = 24

   35 ÷ 7 = ▢   72 ÷ 8 = ▢   18 ÷ 6 = ▢   24 ÷ 12 = ▢

   ▢ × ▢ = 35   ▢ × ▢ = 72   ▢ × ▢ = 18   ▢ × ▢ = 24

   35 ÷ ▢ = ▢   72 ÷ ▢ = ▢   18 ÷ ▢ = ▢   24 ÷ ▢ = ▢

**Animated Glossary
www.pearsonsuccessnet.com**

A fact family shows all the related multiplication and division facts for a set of numbers. You can use fact families to help you remember division facts.

This is the fact family for 2, 3, and 6:

$2 \times 3 = 6$	$6 \div 2 = 3$
$3 \times 2 = 6$	$6 \div 3 = 2$

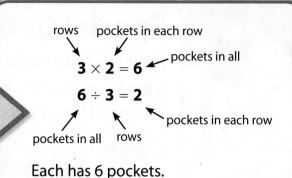

rows   pockets in each row

$3 \times 2 = 6$ ← pockets in all

$6 \div 3 = 2$

pockets in all   rows   pockets in each row

Each has 6 pockets.

In **13** through **20**, write a fact family for each set of numbers.

13. 7, 8, 56   **14.** 2, 8, 16   **15.** 6, 7, 42   **16.** 6, 6, 36

17. 3, 8, 24   **18.** 7, 10, 70   **19.** 6, 5, 30   **20.** 5, 8, 40

Problem Solving

Ⓒ MATHEMATICAL PRACTICES

Ⓒ **21. Persevere** How many years did it take to release all 50 quarters? Write a division fact you can use to find this quotient.

State Quarters

First quarters released	1999
Number of new quarters each year	5

22. In the fact family for the numbers 5, 6, 30, which term does **NOT** describe 5 or 6?

  A factor   **C** product

  B divisor   **D** quotient

23. Josh practiced his drums two hours before dinner and three hours after dinner. How many hours did he practice in all?

  A 3 hours   **C** 5 hours

  B 4 hours   **D** 6 hours

Ⓒ **24. Model** Write the fact family that has 9 as a factor and 45 as a product.

Ⓒ **25. Reason** Why does the fact family for 64 and 8 have only two number sentences?

Lesson
1-8

©
Common
Core

4.OA.2 Multiply or divide
to solve word problems
involving multiplicative
comparison, e.g., by using
drawings and equations
with a symbol for the
unknown number to
represent the problem,
distinguishing multiplicative
comparison from additive
comparison. Also 4.OA.3

Special Quotients

How can you divide with 1 and 0?

A sandwich is cut into 8 pieces. How many people can have 1 piece each? Find $8 \div 1$.

1 group of 8

8 people can have 1 piece of sandwich

Dividing by 1

Think What number times 1 equals 8?

$1 \times 8 = 8$

So, $8 \div 1 = 8$.

Rule: Any number divided by 1 is itself.

Guided Practice*

© MATHEMATICAL
PRACTICES

Do you know HOW?

In **1** through **8**, use multiplication facts to help you divide.

1. $9 \div 9$ **2.** $5 \div 1$

3. $0 \div 4$ **4.** $7 \div 1$

5. $3\overline{)0}$ **6.** $1\overline{)1}$

7. $1\overline{)2}$ **8.** $6\overline{)6}$

Do you UNDERSTAND?

9. What multiplication sentence can help you find $0 \div 8$?

10. What multiplication sentence can help you find $8 \div 8$?

© **11. Writing to Explain** If none of the sandwich is left, how many pieces can 4 people have?

Independent Practice

Use multiplication facts to help you divide.

12. $1\overline{)3}$ **13.** $8\overline{)0}$ **14.** $2\overline{)0}$ **15.** $4\overline{)4}$

Copy and complete by writing $>$, $<$, or $=$ for each $\bigcirc$.

16. $7 \div 7 \bigcirc 2 \div 2$ **17.** $0 \div 5 \bigcirc 3 \div 1$ **18.** $4 \div 1 \bigcirc 4 \div 4$

19. $6 \div 6 \bigcirc 0 \div 4$ **20.** $9 \div 1 \bigcirc 4 \div 1$ **21.** $3 \div 3 \bigcirc 6 \div 1$

22. $0 \div 3 \bigcirc 0 \div 8$ **23.** $0 \div 5 \bigcirc 5 \div 5$ **24.** $8 \div 1 \bigcirc 6 \div 1$

25. $0 \div 9 \bigcirc 0 \div 7$ **26.** $0 \div 1 \bigcirc 1 \div 1$ **27.** $7 \div 1 \bigcirc 0 \div 6$

For another example, see Set F on page 33.

1 as a Quotient

To find $8 \div 8$, think 8 times what number equals 8?

$$8 \times 1 = 8$$

So, $8 \div 8 = 1$.

Rule: Any number (except 0) divided by itself is 1.

Dividing 0 by a Number

To find $0 \div 8$, think 8 times what number equals 0?

$$8 \times 0 = 0$$

So, $0 \div 8 = 0$.

Rule: 0 divided by any number (except 0) is 0.

Dividing by 0

To find $8 \div 0$, think 0 times what number equals 8?

There is no such number.

Rule: You cannot divide by 0.

Problem Solving

MATHEMATICAL
PRACTICES

28. Three friends decided to buy tickets to a play. Anne spent $25, Saul spent $32, and Ryan spent $28. Write these numbers from least to greatest.

29. Tony's family is driving 70 miles to a fair. They have already traveled 30 miles. They are traveling at a speed of 40 miles per hour. How many hours will it take them to complete the trip?

30. On a trip to the beach, the Torrez family brings 5 beach balls for their 5 children.

   a If the beach balls are divided evenly, how many beach balls will each child get?

   b If the children give the 5 balls to 1 parent, how many balls will the parent have?

© **31. Persevere** If $\square \div \triangle = 0$, what do you know about $\square$?

   A $\square$ cannot equal 0.

   B $\square$ must equal 0.

   C $\square$ must equal 1.

   D $\square$ must equal $\triangle$.

© **32. Write a Problem** Write a word problem in which 5 is divided by 5 and another problem in which 5 is divided by 1.

33. In one season, a baseball team will practice 3 times a week. If there are 24 practices, how many weeks will the team practice in the season?

24 practices

3   ? weeks

Practices in one week

© **34. Model** Write a fact family for 3, 3, and 9.

Lesson
1-9

© Common Core

4.OA.2 Multiply or divide to solve word problems involving multiplicative comparison, e.g., by using drawings and equations with a symbol for the unknown number to represent the problem, distinguishing multiplicative comparison from additive comparison. Also **4.OA.3**

Using Multiplication Facts to Find Division Facts

How does multiplication help you divide?

Matt wants to buy 28 super bouncy balls to give as prizes. How many packs does Matt need to buy?

Choose an Operation Divide to find the number of equal groups.

7 balls in each pack

Guided Practice*

 MATHEMATICAL PRACTICES

Do you know HOW?

In **1** through **6**, use multiplication facts to help you divide.

1. 27 ÷ 9   **2.** 40 ÷ 5

3. 24 ÷ 4   **4.** 66 ÷ 6

5. 9)63   **6.** 9)81

Do you UNDERSTAND?

7. What multiplication fact could you use to help you find 72 ÷ 9?

© **8. Model** Matt has 40 super bouncy balls to put in 10 bags. He puts the same number in each bag. What multiplication fact can you use to find the number of balls in each bag?

Independent Practice

Leveled Practice In **9** through **27**, use multiplication facts to help you find the quotient.

9. ▢ × 3 = 27   27 ÷ 3 = ▢   **10.** ▢ × 8 = 40   40 ÷ 8 = ▢

11. ▢ × 6 = 42   42 ÷ 6 = ▢   **12.** ▢ × 7 = 63   63 ÷ 7 = ▢

13. 7)49   **14.** 3)27   **15.** 6)48   **16.** 7)21   **17.** 4)16

18. 9)36   **19.** 5)15   **20.** 2)10   **21.** 6)36   **22.** 2)14

23. 3)24   **24.** 4)32   **25.** 2)18   **26.** 7)35   **27.** 7)56

How many groups of 7 are in 28?

Change this to a multiplication sentence:

What number times 7 equals 28?

☐ × 7 = 28   4 × 7 = 28

There are two ways to write division facts.

28 ÷ 7 = 4

or

$$4 \over 7\overline{)28}$$

Matt needs to buy 4 packs of bouncy balls.

Problem Solving

MATHEMATICAL PRACTICES

For **28** and **29**, use the table at the right.

© **28. Construct Arguments** On a field trip to the aquarium, Shana spends $24 in the gift shop. Which item can Shana buy the most of? Explain.

29. How many mini-flags can Shana buy if she uses all of her money?

Price List	
Postcard packs	$3
Mini-flags	$6
Sea lion toy	$8

For **30**, use the diagram at the right.

© **30. Model** People started riding carousels in the United States in 1835. The carousel drawing at the right has a total of 36 horses with an equal number of horses on each circle. Write a division fact you can use to find the number of horses on the outer circle.

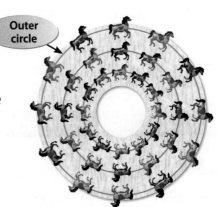

Outer circle

31. Carson plays a card word game. She gives the same number of cards to each of 4 players. If there are 20 cards in all, how many cards does each player get?

© **32. Persevere** The total lunch bill for six people is $52. They add an $8 tip and split the bill evenly. How much is each person's equal share of the total bill?

A $6   C $10

B $8   D $12

Lesson
1-10

Common
Core

4.OA.2 Multiply or divide
to solve word problems
involving multiplicative
comparison, e.g., by using
drawings and equations
with a symbol for the
unknown number to
represent the problem,
distinguishing multiplicative
comparison from additive
comparison. Also 4.OA.3

Problem Solving

Draw a Picture and Write an Equation

A stegosaurus was 5 times as long as a velociraptor.
If a velociraptor was 6 feet long, how long
was a stegosaurus?

Stegosaurus:
? feet long

Velociraptor:
6 feet long

Guided Practice*

 MATHEMATICAL PRACTICES

Do you know HOW?

Solve. Write an equation to help you.

1. Manuel has a collection of coins, all
   of which are nickels and quarters.
   He has 8 nickels and three times as
   many quarters.

   a How many quarters does he have?

   b How many coins does Manuel
   have in all?

Do you UNDERSTAND?

© 2. **Use Tools** How did the picture in the
   example above help you to write an
   equation?

3. A ceratosaurus was 5 times the
   length of a microvenator. A
   microvenator was 4 feet long.
   Use this information to write a
   problem you can solve by writing
   an equation. Then solve.

Independent Practice

 MATHEMATICAL PRACTICES

4. 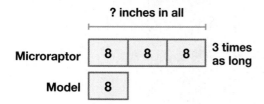 **Science** For the science fair, Joe made
   a model of a microraptor, one of the smallest
   dinosaurs ever discovered. He made his model
   8 inches long. The actual dinosaur was 3 times
   the length of Joe's model. How long was
   the microraptor?

? inches in all

| Microraptor | 8 | 8 | 8 | 3 times as long |
| Model | 8 | | | |

Applying Math Practices

- What am I asked to find?
- What else can I try?
- How are quantities related?
- How can I explain my work?
- How can I use math to model the problem?
- Can I use tools to help?
- Is my work precise?
- Why does this work?
- How can I generalize?

What do I know? A velociraptor was 6 feet long. A stegosaurus was 5 times as long as a velociraptor.

What am I asked to find? The length of a stegosaurus

Draw a picture.

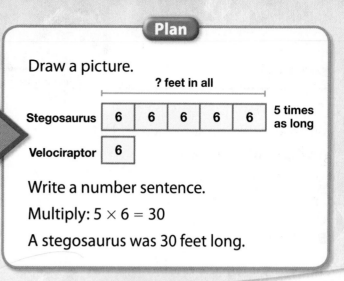

Write a number sentence.

Multiply: $5 \times 6 = 30$

A stegosaurus was 30 feet long.

---

5. Reason Carmen's recipe calls for three times as many carrots as peas. If Carmen uses 2 cups of peas, how many cups of carrots, c, will she use?

c cups of carrots in all

| Carrots | 2 | 2 | 2 | 3 times as many |
| Peas | 2 | | | |

6. Rae's recipe calls for twice as many tomatoes as peppers. She uses 2 cups of peppers. How many cups of tomatoes, x, will she use in all?

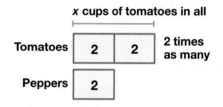

7. Persevere Marley, Jon, and Bart swim a relay race. Jon swims two more laps than Marley. Bart swims twice as many laps as Marley. If Marley swims 3 laps, how many laps do they swim all together? Explain.

8. Be Precise Jack's dog has a rectangular pen. The length is two feet longer than the width. The width is 6 feet. Write an equation to find the perimeter. What is the perimeter of the pen?

9. Matilda is 9 years old. Her mother is 4 times as old as she is. Use the model below to find the age of Matilda's mother, y.

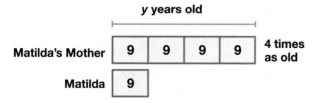

10. Think About the Structure Four relay team members run an equal part of an 8-mile race. Which equation could you use to find n, the number of miles each relay team member runs?

A $4 + n = 8$

B $4 \times n = 8$

C $4 + 4 + 4 + 4 = n$

D $2 \times 2 = n$

Set A, pages 6–8

Write an addition sentence and a multiplication sentence.

$5 + 5 + 5 = 15$

$3 \times 5 = 15$

Remember multiplying is the same as adding the same number over and over.

Set B, pages 10–11 and 12–13

When you multiply any number by 0, the product is 0.
$9 \times 0 = 0$

When you multiply a number by 2, the product is always even.
$2 \times 8 = 16$

Remember you can change the order of factors when you multiply.

1. 10×0 **2.** 9×2

3. 12×3 **4.** 5×7

Set C, pages 14–17

Use the Distributive Property to break apart a problem into two simpler problems.

Find 4×6.

Break apart 6 into $3 + 3$.

$(4 \times 3) + (4 \times 3)$

$12 \quad + \quad 12 \quad = \quad 24$

So, $4 \times 6 = 24$.

Remember there is more than one way to break apart a fact.

Use breaking apart to find each product.

1. 4×3 **2.** 6×5

3. 9×9 **4.** 8×3

Set D, pages 18–19

Look for a pattern. Tell the missing numbers.

1, 5, 9, 13, ▢ **,** ▢

Find the pattern.

$1 + 4 = 5$

$5 + 4 = 9$

$9 + 4 = 13$

Finish the pattern.

$13 + 4 = 17$

$17 + 4 = 21$

The missing numbers are 17 and 21.

Remember that in some patterns you do not add the same number each time.

1. 2, 10, 18, 26, ▢ , ▢ , ▢

2. 1, 2, 4, 7, 11, 16, 22, ▢ , ▢ , ▢

3. 3, 6, 9, 12, ▢ , ▢ , ▢

4. 5, 11, 17, 23, ▢ , ▢ , ▢

Katherine is making 6 lunches. She has 30 carrot sticks. How many carrot sticks go in each lunch?

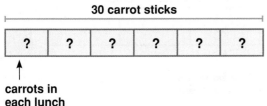

30 carrot sticks

There are 5 carrot sticks in each lunch.

Remember a fact family shows all of the related facts for a set of numbers.

Copy and complete each fact family.

1. $5 \times \boxed{} = 40$

$\boxed{} \div 5 = 8$

$8 \times 5 = \boxed{}$

$\boxed{} \div 8 = \boxed{}$

2. $7 \times 9 = \boxed{}$

$\boxed{} \div 7 = 9$

$9 \times \boxed{} = 63$

$63 \div \boxed{} = 7$

Find $36 \div 4$.

What number times 4 equals 36?

$\boxed{} \times 4 = 36$

$9 \times 4 = 36$

So, $36 \div 4 = 9$.

Remember zero divided by any number is zero.

1. $4\overline{)4}$ **2.** $2\overline{)18}$

3. $7\overline{)28}$ **4.** $2\overline{)0}$

5. $8\overline{)56}$ **6.** $8\overline{)48}$

Marisol has 8 pennies in her collection. She has four times as many quarters as pennies. How many coins are in Marisol's collection?

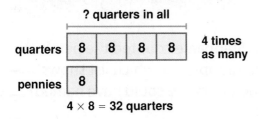

? quarters in all

quarters | 8 | 8 | 8 | 8 | 4 times as many

pennies | 8

$4 \times 8 = 32$ quarters

Add 8 pennies to find how many coins are in Marisol's collection.

$32 + 8 = 40$ coins in all

Remember you can draw a picture to help you write an equation.

Draw a picture and write an equation to solve.

1. The length of Mel's basement is 9 times the length of a broom. The length of a broom is 3 feet. What is the length of the basement?

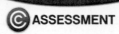
Multiple Choice

1. Which has the same value as 3×5? (1-1)

A $5 + 3$

B $5 + 5 + 5$

C $5 + 5 + 5 + 3$

D $3 + 3 + 3 + 3$

2. Grant made 4 California state flags for the school play. Each flag had 1 bear. How many bears did Grant need? (1-3)

A 0

B 1

C 4

D 5

3. Which is a way to find 7×8? (1-4)

A $32 + 32$

B $35 + 14$

C $35 + 8$

D $35 + 21$

4. Alfonzo applies numbers on the back of football jerseys. Below are the first five numbers he applied. If the pattern continues, what are the next three numbers he will apply? (1-5)

9, 18, 27, 36, 45, ▨, ▨, ▨

A 54, 63, 72

B 54, 63, 71

C 63, 64, 72

D 63, 72, 81

5. Three friends have 27 water balloons to share equally. How many water balloons will each friend get? (1-6)

27 water balloons

| ? | ? | ? |

↑
Water balloons
each friend gets

A 9

B 8

C 7

D 6

6. What is $35 \div 7$? (1-9)

A 7

B 6

C 5

D 4

7. Each flower has 5 petals.

If Stephanie counted the petals in groups of 5, which list shows numbers she could have named? (1-2)

A 15, 20, 25, 30

B 15, 20, 34, 40

C 12, 15, 18, 30

D 10, 12, 14, 16

8. What is the quotient of $0 \div 8$? (1-8)

9. Diego wanted to paint his fence. It takes him 7 minutes to paint one section of a fence. How many minutes would it take him to paint 6 sections? (1-2)

10. Sue collected 5 rocks. Angie collected 4 times as many rocks as Sue. What number sentence can be used to find the number of rocks Angie collected? (1-10)

? rocks in all

Angie	5	5	5	5	4 times as many
Sue	5				

11. What number makes the number sentence true? (1-3)

$7 \times 5 = \blacksquare \times 7$

12. What multiplication expression can be broken apart into $(3 \times 10) + (3 \times 10)$ using the distributive property? (1-4)

13. What number makes both number sentences true? (1-7)

$4 \times \blacksquare = 32$
$32 \div 4 = \blacksquare$

14. What multiplication sentences are in the same fact family as $63 \div 9 = \blacksquare$? (1-9)

15. The length of the kitchen counter at Sal's house is 9 times the length of a book. The length of the book is 8 inches. What is the length of the kitchen counter? Draw a picture and write an equation to solve. (1-10)

16. Gene is counting his pennies. Below are the first six numbers that he says aloud while he is counting. If the pattern continues, what are the next three numbers that Gene will say? (1-5)

6, 12, 18, 24, 30, 36,

17. Write a multiplication sentence for $4 + 4 + 4 + 4 + 4 + 4 = 24$. (1-1)

18. What multiplication fact can help you find $7 \div 7$? (1-8)

19. Matthew has 12 baseball cards. He wants to put the same number on each of 4 pages. How many cards should be on each page? Draw a picture to help divide. (1-6)

20. Jen has a collection of 45 corn husk dolls that she wants to arrange in equal groups. Write a fact family that shows how Jen could arrange her corn husk dolls. (1-7)

Mr. Harrison's class has been learning about earth science. Mr. Harrison and several students brought their rock collections to school. Mr. Harrison brought in a catalog that sells the two different rock display containers shown below.

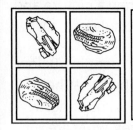

Display Box

Holds 4 rocks

$3

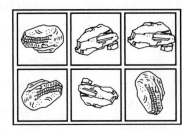

Display Box

Holds 6 rocks

$5

1. Maggie wants to buy several display boxes that hold 6 rocks each. She has $20 to spend. How many display boxes can she buy? Write a division fact that shows how you found your answer.

2. Travis has filled 3 of the containers that hold 4 rocks. How many rocks does Travis have? Write a multiplication fact to show your answer.

3. Lynette has 24 rocks in her collection. How many 6-rock containers does she need to display all her rocks? How many 4-rock containers does she need? Which option is less expensive?

4. Write and answer the hidden question or questions. Then, solve the problem.

   Angela has 18 rocks. She bought 2 containers that hold 6 rocks each. How many more 6-rock containers does she need to buy? How much money will she spend on containers in all?

5. Ramirez went rock hunting every 7 days. He collected 3 rocks each time he went. Copy, extend, and complete the table below to find out how many days it took for Ramirez to collect 24 rocks.

Days	7	14			
Rocks	3				

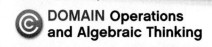

Topic
2

Generate and Analyze Patterns

▼ How many years will it take an animal symbol to repeat in the Chinese calendar? You will find out in Lesson 2-2.

Topic Essential Questions
• How can patterns be used to describe how two quantities are related?
• How can a relationship between two quantities be shown using a table?

Review What You Know!

Vocabulary

Choose the best term from the box.

- compare
- multiply
- divide
- regroup

1. To put together equal groups to find the total number, you __?__.

2. To decide if 4 has more ones or fewer ones than 8, __?__ the numbers.

3. To separate into equal groups, you __?__.

Number Patterns

Write the missing number in each pattern.

4. 3, 6, 9, 12, ☐, 18   **5.** 4, 8, 12, ☐, 20, 24

6. 8, 7, 6, ☐, 4, 3   **7.** 30, 25, 20, 15, ☐, 5

Multiplication Facts

Find each product.

8. 4×3 **9.** 3×5 **10.** 7×2

11. 5×6 **12.** 2×4 **13.** 3×7

Division Facts

Find each quotient.

14. $20 \div 4$ **15.** $10 \div 5$ **16.** $18 \div 6$

17. $28 \div 4$ **18.** $24 \div 6$ **19.** $56 \div 8$

© **20. Writing to Explain** Janelle bought 4 cans of tennis balls. There are 3 balls in each can. How many tennis balls did she buy? Explain how you solved the problem.

Topic 2

Interactive Learning

Pose the problem. Start each lesson by working together to solve problems. It will help you make sense of math.

Applying Math Practices

- What am I asked to find?
- What else can I try?
- How are quantities related?
- How can I explain my work?
- How can I use math to model the problem?
- Can I use tools to help?
- Is my work precise?
- Why does this work?
- How can I generalize?

Lesson 2-1

Ⓒ **Look for Patterns** Look for patterns in the arrangement of blocks at the right.

What will be the 10th shape in the pattern? Tell how you decided.

1 2 3 4 5 6

Lesson 2-2

Ⓒ **Look for Patterns** Look for patterns in the number sequences at the right.

What is a rule for finding each of the next three numbers in each sequence? Tell how you decided.

18, 21, 24, 27, ⬜, ⬜, ⬜

17, 19, 21, 23, ⬜, ⬜, ⬜

40, 36, 32, 28, ⬜, ⬜, ⬜

Lesson 2-3

Ⓒ **Use Tools** Copy and complete the table at the right to solve this problem.

There are 3 juice boxes in 1 pack, 6 in 2 packs, and 9 in 3 packs. How many juice boxes are there in 4 packs? In 5 packs? Look for patterns to complete the table. Describe the patterns you found.

Number of Packs	Number of Juice Boxes
1	3
2	6
3	9
4	⬜
5	⬜
6	⬜
10	⬜
100	⬜

Lesson 2-4

© **Reason** Look for patterns in the tables on your recording sheet.

For each table, use the patterns you find to give a rule in words that tells how to find the value of one quantity when you know the value of the other quantity.

Price of Item	Total Cost of Item and Shipping
$19	$25
▢	$36
$18	▢
$23	▢

In	2	9	▢	8
Out	6	▢	15	▢

Nelson's Age	4	10	8	▢	▢
Pam's Age	2	8	6	▢	▢

Lesson 2-5

© **Reason** Use cubes to build the towers shown at the right.

Look for patterns in the number of cubes and the arrangement of cubes in each tower. Using your patterns, what will the next two towers look like? Tell how you decided.

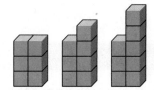

Lesson 2-6

© **Reason** Solve any way you choose. You may use two-color counters.

Nolan has collected 14 baseball cards, including cards from the Rangers, the Astros, and the Titans. He has 3 Astros cards. He has 5 fewer Titans cards than Rangers cards. How many of each kind of card are in Nolan's collection?

Lesson
2-1

© Common Core

4.OA.5 Generate a number or shape pattern that follows a given rule. Identify apparent features of the pattern that were not explicit in the rule itself.

Repeating Patterns

How can you continue a repeating pattern?

Rashad is making patterns with shapes. What three shapes should come next in this pattern?

A repeating pattern is <u>made up of shapes or numbers that form a part that repeats.</u>

Guided Practice*

© **MATHEMATICAL PRACTICES**

Do you know HOW?

1. Draw the next three shapes to continue the pattern.

2. Write the next three numbers to continue the pattern.
9, 2, 7, 6, 9, 2, 7, 6, 9

Do you UNDERSTAND?

© **3. Communicate** In the example above, describe the pattern using words.

4. What is the 10th shape in the pattern below? How do you know?

Independent Practice

In **5–8**, draw the next three shapes to continue the pattern.

5.

6. ↑↓←⇒↑↓←⇒↑

7.

8.

In **9–10**, write the next three numbers to continue the pattern.

9. 1, 1, 2, 1, 1, 2, 1, 1, 2

10. 5, 7, 4, 8, 5, 7, 4, 8, 5, 7, 4

11. Make a pattern using the digits 2, 8, 9.

12. Make a pattern using the digits 0, 3, 4.

Animated Glossary
www.pearsonsuccessnet.com

Step 1

Find the part that repeats.

These 4 shapes make up the part that repeats.

Step 2

Continue the pattern.

Problem Solving

MATHEMATICAL PRACTICES

13. Hilda is making a pattern with the shapes below. If she continues the pattern, what will the 11th shape in the pattern be? Draw a picture to show the shape.

14. Marcus is using shapes to make a pattern. He has twice as many circles as squares. Make a pattern that will use all the shapes.

15. Look for Patterns Louisa put beads on a string to make a bracelet. She used a blue bead, then three green beads, then a blue bead, then three green beads, and so on, until she used 18 green beads. How many beads did she use in all?

16. Estimation A box of toy blocks has 108 blocks. Jiang used 72 of the blocks to make a building. About how many blocks are left in the box? Explain how you estimated.

17. The table shows the number of students in each grade at a school.

Which grade has more than 145 but fewer than 149 students?

A First   **C** Second

B Third   **D** Fourth

Grade	Number of Students
First	142
Second	158
Third	146
Fourth	139

18. Writing to Explain Balloons are sold in bags of 30. There are 5 giant balloons in each bag. How many giant balloons will you get if you buy 120 balloons? Explain.

Lesson
2-2

Common Core

4.OA.5 Generate a number or shape pattern that follows a given rule. Identify apparent features of the pattern that were not explicit in the rule itself.

Number Sequences

What is the pattern?

The house numbers on a street are in a pattern. If the pattern continues, what are the next three numbers?

Guided Practice*

Do you know HOW?

In **1** and **2**, find a rule for the pattern. Use your rule to continue each pattern.

1.

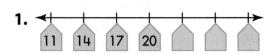

2. 48, 42, 36, 30, 24, ▢, ▢, ▢

Do you UNDERSTAND?

3. In the example above, suppose 16 is the 1st number in the pattern. What is the 10th number?

4. Rudy is using "add 2" as his rule to make a pattern. He started with 4 and wrote the numbers below for his pattern. Which number does not belong in this pattern? Explain.

4, 6, 8, 9, 10, 12

Independent Practice

© **Use Structure** In **5–13**, find a rule for the pattern. Use your rule to continue each pattern.

5. 21, 18, 15, ▢, ▢

6. 4, 11, 18, ▢, ▢

7. 5, 10, 15, ▢, ▢

8. 5, 7, 9, ▢, ▢, 15

9. 250, 300, 350, ▢, ▢

10. 92, 80, 68, ▢, ▢

11. 790, 780, 770, ▢, ▢

12. 16, 27, 38, ▢, ▢

13. 96, 101, 106, ▢, 116, ▢

In **14–16**, use the rule to create a pattern.

14. Rule: Add 4
43, ▢, ▢, ▢, ▢

15. Rule: Subtract 15
120, ▢, ▢, ▢, ▢

16. Rule: Subtract 9
99, ▢, ▢, ▢, ▢

*For another example, see Set B on page 58.

Find a rule for the pattern.

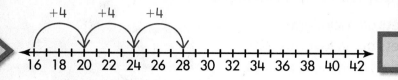

+4   +4   +4

16 18 20 22 24 26 28 30 32 34 36 38 40 42

Each number is 4 more than the number before it.

Use your rule to continue the pattern.

Rule: Add 4.

$$28 + 4 = 32$$
$$32 + 4 = 36$$
$$36 + 4 = 40$$

The next numbers in the pattern are 32, 36, and 40.

Problem Solving

MATHEMATICAL PRACTICES

17. Orlando delivers mail. He sees that one mailbox does not have a number. If the numbers are in a pattern, what is the missing number?

27 29 ☐ 33 35 37 39

18. In the Chinese calendar, each year has an animal as a symbol. There are 12 animals. It was the year of the snake in 2001 and will be again in 2013. The year 2005 was the year of the rooster. The next year of the rooster will be 2017. Make a number sequence that shows the pattern for the next five years of the rooster.

19. Suppose you were born in the year of the snake. How old will you be the next time the year of the snake is celebrated?

The pattern of animals repeats every 12 years.

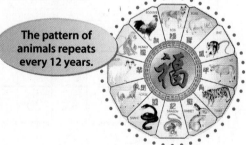

20. Persevere The numbers below are in a pattern.

24, 27, 30, 33

Which number would be part of the pattern?

A 34   **C** 39

B 38   **D** 44

21. Generalize Mia counted the pencils in groups of 6.

Which list shows numbers Mia named?

A 24, 36, 48, 52   **C** 6, 12, 24, 32

B 6, 24, 48, 56   **D** 12, 18, 24, 30

Common Core

4.OA.5 Generate a number or shape pattern that follows a given rule. Identify apparent features of the pattern that were not explicit in the rule itself.

Extending Tables

What pairs of numbers fit a pattern?

There are 3 leaflets on 1 cloverleaf.
There are 9 leaflets on 3 cloverleaves.
There are 12 leaflets on 4 cloverleaves.
How many leaflets are there on
2 cloverleaves? on 5 cloverleaves?

A cloverleaf has 3 leaflets.

Guided Practice*

 MATHEMATICAL PRACTICES

Do you know HOW?

In **1** and **2**, copy and complete each table.

1.

Number of Boxes	Total Number of Hats
2	6
5	15
7	21
■	27

2.

Number of Cars	2	3	5	9
Total Number of Wheels	8	12	20	■

Do you UNDERSTAND?

3. In the example above, 4 and 12 are a pair of numbers that fit the pattern. Does the pair 6 and 16 fit the pattern? Explain.

④ 4. Reasonableness A rule for this table is "add 5 to my age."

My Age	Joe's Age
5	10
8	13
9	15

Which number does not belong?

Independent Practice

In **5–7**, copy and complete each table.

5.

Number of Spiders	Number of Legs
1	8
2	■
3	24
4	32
■	56

6.

Regular Price	Sale Price
$29	$22
$25	$18
■	$16
$22	■
$19	$12

7.

Weight of Book in Ounces	9	11	12	16
Total Weight of Carton in Ounces	18	20	21	■

8. For each table in 5–7, write another pair of numbers that could be in the table.

*For another example, see Set C on page 58.

Draw pictures to show what you know.

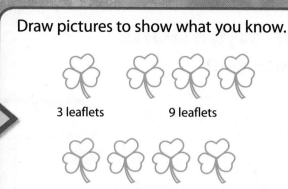

3 leaflets   9 leaflets

12 leaflets

Fill in a table by using a rule.

Rule: Multiply by 3

Number of Cloverleaves	Number of Leaflets
1	3
2	6
3	9
4	12
5	15

Problem Solving

MATHEMATICAL
PRACTICES

For **9** and **10**, the table at the right shows the number of batteries needed for different numbers of one kind of flashlight.

9. How many batteries do 8 flashlights need? 10 flashlights?

© **10. Writing to Explain** How many more batteries do 6 flashlights need than 4 flashlights? Explain how you found your answer.

Batteries for Flashlights	
Number of Flashlights	Number of Batteries
1	3
4	12
7	21

© **11. Persevere** What is the greatest number you can make using each of the digits 1, 7, 0, and 6 once?

12. A penguin can swim 11 miles per hour. At this speed, how far can it swim in 3 hours? Use a table to help.

13. Alan has 35 fewer coins than Suzy has. Which of these shows the number of coins that Alan and Suzy could have?

　A Alan 65, Suzy 105　　**C** Alan 105, Suzy 65

　B Alan 105, Suzy 70　　**D** Alan 70, Suzy 105

14. If the pattern at the right continues, how long will each side of the next square be?

　A 8 feet　　　**C** 10 feet

　B 9 feet　　　**D** 11 feet

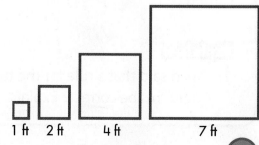

1 ft   2 ft   4 ft   7 ft

Common
Core

4.OA.5 Generate a number or shape pattern that follows a given rule. Identify apparent features of the pattern that were not explicit in the rule itself.

Writing Rules for Situations

What is a math rule for the situation?

Alex and his older brother Andy have the same birthday. If you know Alex's age, how can you find Andy's age? Look for a pattern in the table and find a rule.

Alex's age	2	4	6	7	9
Andy's age	8	10	12	13	15

Another Example **What other rules are there for pairs of numbers?**

Nell saves some of the money she earns. The table shows how much she earned and how much she saved for five days. What is a rule for the table? What are the missing numbers?

Earned	65¢	45¢	50¢	30¢	
Saved	50¢	30¢		15¢	25¢

Step 1

Find a rule for the table.

Look for a pattern.

Earned	65¢	45¢	50¢	30¢	
Saved	50¢	30¢		15¢	25¢

Each time, the amount saved is 15¢ less than the amount earned.

Rule: Subtract 15¢ from the amount earned.

Step 2

Check that your rule works for all pairs.

65¢ − 15¢ = 50¢
45¢ − 15¢ = 30¢
30¢ − 15¢ = 15¢   Your rule works for each pair.

What amount is 15¢ less than 50¢?
50¢ − 15¢ = 35¢

25¢ is 15¢ less than what amount?
25¢ = ▨ − 15¢   15¢ + 25¢ = 40¢

The missing amounts are 35¢ saved and 40¢ earned.

Explain It

1. David said that a rule for the table above is "Add 15¢." Could this be correct? Explain.

Find a rule for the table.

Compare each pair of numbers. Look for a pattern.

Alex's age	2	4	6	7	9
Andy's age	8	10	12	13	15

In each pair, Andy's age is 6 more than Alex's age. You say a rule for the table is "add 6."

Check that your rule works for all pairs.

Rule: Add 6.

$2 + 6 = 8$
$4 + 6 = 10$
$6 + 6 = 12$
$7 + 6 = 13$
$9 + 6 = 15$

Your rule works for each pair.

Guided Practice*

Do you know HOW?

In **1** and **2**, use the table below.

Hours Worked	4	8	7	2	6
Amount Earned	$24	$48		$12	

1. Write a rule for the table.

2. What are the missing numbers?

Do you UNDERSTAND?

3. In the example above, what does the rule "add 6" mean in the problem?

4. Marty uses the rule "subtract 9" for his table. If the first number in Marty's table is 11, what is the second number in that pair?

Independent Practice

MATHEMATICAL PRACTICES

© **Use Tools** In **5–9**, find a rule for the table. Use your rule to complete the table.

5.

Earned	$15	$12	$17	$9	$11
Spent	$7		$9		$3

6.

Earned	$14	$18	$12	$16	$8
Saved	$7	$9			$4

7.

Price	$36	$28	$33	$40	$25
Discount	$24	$16		$28	

8.

Number of Chairs	Number of Legs
3	12
2	8
5	20
7	
	36

9.

Number of Teams	Number of Players
4	20
3	15
5	
6	30
8	

For **10** and **11**, use the table at the right.

10. The table shows the ages of a velvet mesquite tree and a saguaro cactus plant at a garden. When the velvet mesquite tree was 48 years old, how old was the saguaro cactus?

© **11. Reasonableness** Phil says the saguaro cactus is about 100 years older than the velvet mesquite tree. Is his estimate reasonable? Explain.

12. Use the table below. How many eggs can 4 ostrich hens lay in one year? 5 ostrich hens?

Plant's Age in Years	
Velvet Mesquite Tree	**Saguaro Cactus**
1 year	36
15	50
67	102
48	▩

An ostrich hen can lay 50 eggs in a year. A male ostrich helps care for the eggs.

Number of Ostrich Hens	1	2	3	4	5
Number of Eggs	50	100	150	▩	▩

© **Use Structure** For **13** and **14**, the table shows the number of baskets that Betty needs for different numbers of apples. She needs to put an equal number of apples into each basket.

Betty's Apple Baskets					
Number of Apples	28	56	7	21	14
Number of Baskets	4	▩	1	3	2

13. How many baskets does Betty need for 56 apples?

A 8 **B** 7 **C** 6 **D** 5

14. What is a rule for the table?

A Subtract 24. **C** Divide by 7.

B Subtract 6. **D** Add 12.

15. An art museum has 47 paintings in one room and 24 paintings in another room. Which is the best estimate of the total number of paintings in these two rooms?

A 50 **C** 80

B 70 **D** 100

16. Esther is 8 years older than Manuel. Which of these shows the ages that Esther and Manuel could be?

A Esther 15, Manuel 23

B Esther 16, Manuel 15

C Esther 15, Manuel 7

D Esther 7, Manuel 15

Mixed Problem Solving

In the 1800s and 1900s, several inventions helped to change life around the world. The time line shows the dates of some of these inventions and discoveries.

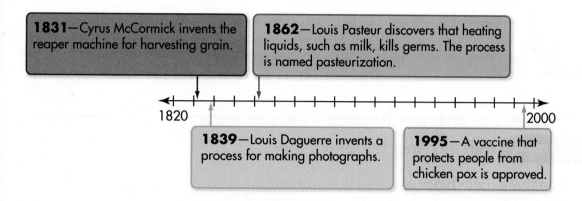

1831—Cyrus McCormick invents the reaper machine for harvesting grain.

1862—Louis Pasteur discovers that heating liquids, such as milk, kills germs. The process is named pasteurization.

1820

2000

1839—Louis Daguerre invents a process for making photographs.

1995—A vaccine that protects people from chicken pox is approved.

1. Which invention was made about 10 years before a process for making photographs was invented?

2. How many years after the discovery of pasteurization was the chicken pox vaccine approved?

3. Which invention or discovery was made before 1900 but after 1850?

4. How many years have passed since the year that a chicken pox vaccine was approved?

For **5** and **6**, use the table below.

Year	Invention
1804	Steam Locomotive
1885	Gasoline-powered Automobile
1934	Diesel Train in U.S.

Data

5. How many years passed between the first steam locomotive and U.S. diesel train?

6. How many years ago was the gasoline-powered automobile invented?

© **7. Model** Solve the problem. Use the strategy Make a Table.

The reaper machine could cut wheat and move it to the side for harvesting. One reaper machine could do the work of 5 people. How many reapers could do the work of 20 people?

Lesson
2-5

Common
Core

4.OA.5 Generate a number or shape pattern that follows a given rule. Identify apparent features of the pattern that were not explicit in the rule itself.

Geometric Patterns

grid paper

cubes

How can you describe block towers?

Talisa made three block towers. She recorded her pattern. If she continued the pattern, how many blocks would be in a 10-story tower? a 100-story tower?

Stories: 1   2   3

Blocks: 4   8   12

Another Example **Making Another Block Tower**

Luis made three more block towers. He recorded his pattern. If he continued the pattern, how many blocks would a 5-story tower have?

Number of Stories	1	2	3
Number of Blocks	1	3	6

Build the next two towers.

Number of Stories	1	2	3	4	5
Number of Blocks	1	3	6	▨	▨

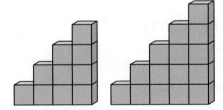

A 4-story tower has 10 blocks, and a 5-story tower has 15 blocks.

Explain It

1. How many blocks would Luis need for a 6-story tower? Explain.

2. How many stories is a tower made of 36 blocks?

Build the next two towers.

Number of Stories	1	2	3	4	5
Number of Blocks	4	8	12		

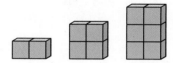

| 1 story 4 blocks | 2 stories 8 blocks | 3 stories 12 blocks | 4 stories 16 blocks | 5 stories 20 blocks |

A rule for the pattern in the table is "multiply by 4."

$$5 \times 4 = 20$$
$$10 \times 4 = 40$$
$$100 \times 4 = 400$$

A 10-story tower would have 40 blocks.

A 100-story tower would have 400 blocks.

Guided Practice*

MATHEMATICAL PRACTICES

Do you know HOW?

In **1** and **2**, draw the next two towers in the pattern. You may use grid paper to help. Find the missing numbers in each table.

1.

Number of Stories	1	2	3	4	5
Number of Blocks	2	4	6		

2.

Number of Stories	1	2	3	4	5	
Number of Blocks	2	3	4	5		7

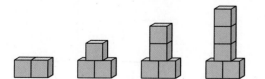

Do you UNDERSTAND?

3. In the example above, why does multiplication work to get from the first number to the second number in a number pair?

4. In Exercise 1, how many blocks would a 10-story tower have?

5. Lionel made the three block towers below. If he continued the pattern, how many blocks would a 100-story tower have?

© **6. Writing to Explain** How many blocks would you need to make a 15-story tower in Exercise 2? Explain how you know.

eTools
www.pearsonsuccessnet.com

For another example, see Set D on page 59.

In **7–10**, use patterns to find the missing numbers in each table.
You may draw the next two figures on grid paper to help.

7.

Number of Stories	7	6	5	4	3
Number of Blocks	21	18	15		

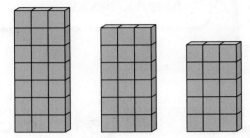

8.

Number of Stories	1	2	3	4	5
Number of Blocks	4	8	12		

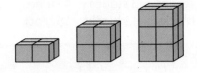

9.

Number of Rows	2	3	4	5	6
Number of Squares	3	5	7		

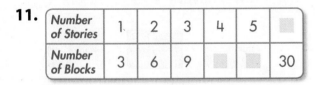

10.

Number of Rows	1	2	3	4	5
Number of Small Triangles	1	4	9		

In **11–13**, use the patterns in the block towers or
squares to copy and complete each table.

11.

Number of Stories	1	2	3	4	5	
Number of Blocks	3	6	9			30

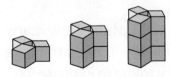

12.

Length of Each Side	1	2	4	6	9
Sum of All Sides	4	8	16		

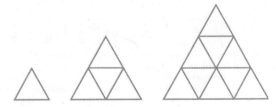

1 unit   2 units   4 units

13.

Number of Stories	1	2	3	4	5
Number of Blocks	2	6	12		

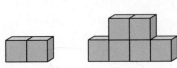

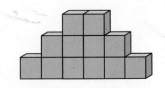

14. Jon used 15 blocks to make a tower. Next he used 12 blocks to make a tower, and then 9 blocks to make a tower. If he continued the pattern, what rule could he use for this table?

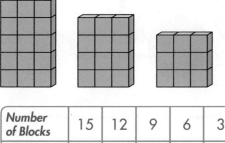

Number of Blocks	15	12	9	6	3
Number of Stories	5	4	3	2	1

15. Dean is making picture frames. He uses the same number of wood pieces in each frame. The table shows the number of wood pieces that he needs for different numbers of frames.

Number of Frames	6	7	8	9	10
Number of Wood Pieces	24	28		36	40

How many wood pieces does Dean need for 8 picture frames?

A 30 **C** 34

B 32 **D** 36

16. Stonehenge is an ancient monument in England made up of a pattern of rocks that looks like this:

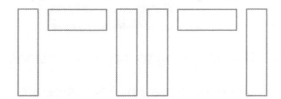

Draw the shape that comes next.

17. Maura made these three block towers. If she continued the pattern, how many blocks would a 10-story tower have? How many blocks would a 100-story tower have?

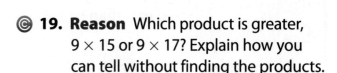

18. Persevere What two 1-digit factors could you multiply to get a product of 48?

19. Reason Which product is greater, 9 × 15 or 9 × 17? Explain how you can tell without finding the products.

20. Estimation Lily has 75¢. A stamp costs 39¢. Does she have enough money to buy 2 stamps? Explain.

21. Leon ran twice as many laps around the track as Sam. Sam ran 6 laps. How many laps did they run in all?

22. Construct Arguments Eduardo spent $3.78 on groceries. He paid with a $5 bill. How do you know that his change included at least two pennies?

Common Core

4.OA.5 Generate a number or shape pattern that follows a given rule. Identify apparent features of the pattern that were not explicit in the rule itself. Also **4.OA.3**

Problem Solving

Hands-On
counters

Act It Out and Use Reasoning

Juana collected old pennies, nickels, and dimes. Her collection has at least one of each kind of coin.

How many of each kind of coin does Juana have?

nickel

penny

dime

Juana's Collection
2 pennies
2 fewer nickels than dimes
10 coins in all

Another Example ## What are other kinds of relationships?

Ken's Collection of Dimes, Nickels, and Pennies
3 nickels
4 more dimes than nickels
15 coins in all

How many of each coin are in his collection?

Read and Understand

What do I know?
There are 15 coins in all, and 3 of the coins are nickels.

There are 4 more dimes than nickels.

Use objects to show what you know.

Plan and Solve

Use reasoning to make conclusions.

Since there are 3 nickels, there are 12 pennies and dimes together.

Try 3 nickels, 7 dimes, and 5 pennies. Since $3 + 7 + 5 = 15$, this is correct.

There are 5 pennies, 3 nickels, and 7 dimes in the collection.

Explain It

1. Which number of coins in Ken's collection is given to you? Which information do you need to find?

2. Explain how you know 7 is the number of dimes in the solution above.

DIGITAL
eTools
www.pearsonsuccessnet.com

What do I know? Juana has 10 coins in all, and 2 of the coins are pennies.

There are 2 fewer nickels than dimes.

Use objects to show what you know.

Use reasoning to make conclusions.

She has 2 pennies, so there are 8 nickels and dimes together.

Try 1 nickel and 7 dimes. $2 + 1 + 7 = 10$, but 1 nickel is not 2 fewer than 7.

Try 3 nickels and 5 dimes. Since $2 + 3 + 5 = 10$, this is correct.

There are 2 pennies, 3 nickels, and 5 dimes in Juana's collection.

Guided Practice*

MATHEMATICAL PRACTICES

Do you know HOW?

Find the number of each kind of stamp in the collection. Use counters.

1. Ricardo has 9 stamps in all. He has 2 nation stamps and 3 more inventor stamps than flower stamps.

   Nation Stamps = ▓
   Inventor Stamps = ▓
   Flower Stamps = ▓

Do you UNDERSTAND?

2. What did you do to find the number of inventor stamps in Ricardo's collection?

© 3. **Write a Problem** Write a problem about coin collections that you can solve by using reasoning.

Independent Practice

MATHEMATICAL PRACTICES

Solve. Use counters or draw pictures to help.

© 4. **Persevere** Find the number of each kind of object in Anya's collection.

Anya's Collection of Minerals, Gemstones and Rocks
6 minerals
3 fewer gemstones than rocks.
15 objects in all.

Minerals = ▓
Gemstones = ▓
Rocks = ▓

Applying Math Practices
- What am I asked to find?
- What else can I try?
- How are quantities related?
- How can I explain my work?
- How can I use math to model the problem?
- Can I use tools to help?
- Is my work precise?
- Why does this work?
- How can I generalize?

---

*For another example, see Set E on page 59.

5. There are 10 fish in all in Percy's fish tank. Four of the fish are angel fish. There are 4 more mollie fish than tetra fish. How many of each kind of fish are in the tank?

© **6. Reason** Norah's dog weighs 9 pounds more than her cat. Her dog weighs 6 pounds less than Jeff's dog. Norah's cat weighs 7 pounds. How much does Jeff's dog weigh?

The students in Mr. Cole's class voted on which kind of collection their class should start. The graph shows the results. Use the graph for **7–9**.

7. Which collection got five votes?

8. Which collection got the greatest number of votes?

9. How many more votes did the collection with the most of votes get than the collection with the fewest votes?

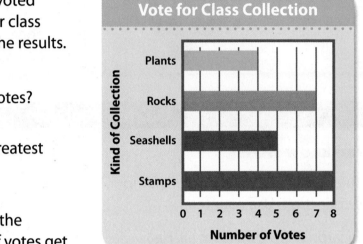

10. Isadora has 15 seashells in her collection. She has some oyster shells, some conch shells, and 6 clam shells. She has 2 fewer clam shells than oyster shells. How many conch shells does she have?

11. Lyn, Kurt, and Steve wrote a riddle about their ages. Lyn is 7 years older than Steve. Steve is 5 years old. The sum of their ages is 25 years. How old is Kurt?

© **12. Model** Sondra wants to buy 2 plates and 3 towels. What is the total cost of her items?

Item	Price
Flashlight	$9
Plate	$7
Towel	$4
Fishing net	$8
Umbrella	$3

Data

© **13. Think About the Structure** At the town pet show, Dina saw 48 pets. There were 6 birds and 7 cats. The remaining pets were dogs. Which number sentence shows one way to find the number of dogs, d, that were at the pet show?

A $6 + 7 + d = 48$

B $48 + 6 \div 7 = d$

C $48 - d \times 7 = 6$

D $6 \times 7 \times 48 = d$

Extending Tables

Use 🔧 tools
Spreadsheet/Data/Grapher eTool

Use a rule to complete the table.

Number of Lions	1	2	3	4	5
Number of Legs	4	8	▨	16	20

Step 1 ↗ Go to the Spreadsheet/Data/Grapher eTool. Use the arrow tool to select at least 2 rows and 6 columns. Set the number of decimal places at zero using the .00 pull-down menu. Enter *Lions, 1, 2, 3, 4, 5* in row 1. Enter *Legs* in column A of row 2.

Step 2 Try the rule "multiply by 4." Cell B2 is in column B, row 2. In cell B2, type = *4*B1*. This means "multiply 4 by the value in cell B1." The product will be shown in cell B2. In cell C2, type = *4*C1*. In cell D2, type = *4*D1* and so on for cells E2 and F2.

Step 3 Check that the numbers match those in the table above. This means the rule "multiply by 4" is correct. The missing number is 12.

F2	20					
	A	B	C	D	E	F
1	Lions	1.00	2.00	3.00	4.00	5.00
2	Legs	4.00	8.00	12.00	16.00	20.00

Practice

Copy each table, find a rule, and fill in the missing cell.

1.

Bud's Age	2	4	6	9
Spot's Age	7	9	▨	14

2.

Days	1	2	3	4
Toys Made	7	▨	21	28

Set A, pages 40–41

© **INTERVENTION**

Draw the next three shapes to continue the pattern.

Find the part that repeats.

Then continue the pattern.

Remember to first find the part of the pattern that repeats.

Draw the next three shapes or numbers to continue the pattern.

1.

2. 3, 5, 7, 9, 3, 5, 7, 9, 3, 5, 7

Set B, pages 42– 43

Find a rule to use to continue the pattern.

24,   21,   18,   15,   12,   ▨,   ▨,   ▨,
-3 -3 -3 -3 -3 -3 -3

Rule: Subtract 3
The next numbers in the pattern are 9, 6, and 3.

Remember to check that your rule works with all of the given numbers.

Write a rule and continue the pattern.

1. 5, 7, 9, ▨, ▨, ▨

2. 22, 18, 14, ▨, ▨, ▨

Set C, pages 44–45, 46–48

Look at the table below. How can you use the pattern to complete the table? What is the rule?

Regular price	Sale price
$43	$38
$45	$40
$46	$41
$47	▨

$43 - 5 = 38$

$45 - 5 = 40$

$46 - 5 = 41$

The sale price is $5 less than the regular price.

$47 - 5 = 42$

When the regular price is $47,
the sale price is $42. The rule is "subtract 5."

Remember to look for patterns and ask "What is a rule?"

Copy and complete each table and find a rule.

1.

Alice's age	Dina's age
3	12
5	14
8	17
12	▨

2.

Earned	Spent
$22	$5
$34	$17
▨	$21
$45	▨

3.

Trucks	1	2	3	4
Wheels	6	12	18	▨

4.

Earned	$12	$18	$24	$30
Saved	$4	$6	▨	$10

If Sam continues the pattern, how many blocks would a 5-story tower have? a 10-story tower?

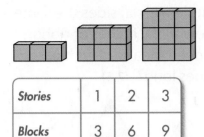

Stories	1	2	3
Blocks	3	6	9

A pattern in the table is multiply by 3. So, use 5 × 3 to find the number of blocks in a 5-story tower.
5 × 3 = 15
There are 15 blocks in a 5-story tower.

A 10-story tower would have 10 × 3 or 30 blocks.

Remember to use the number pairs in a table to find a rule or make predictions.

In **1** and **2**, write the missing numbers and a rule.

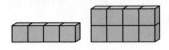

1.

Stories	1	2	3	4
Blocks	4	8		

2. Draw the next two figures in the pattern. Use grid paper.

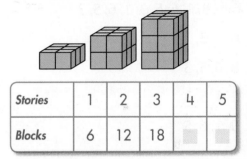

Stories	1	2	3	4	5
Blocks	6	12	18		

When you solve a problem by acting it out, follow these steps.

Choose objects to act out the problem.

Show what you know using the objects.

Use reasoning to make conclusions.

Find the answer.

Remember to decide what the objects represent before you begin.

Solve. Find the number of each kind of sticker in Ben's collection.

1. **Ben's Sticker Collection**
   - 3 kinds of stickers with 17 stickers in all
   - 6 star stickers
   - 3 fewer smiley face stickers than planet stickers

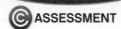
Multiple Choice

1. Football players came out of the tunnel in the pattern shown below.

What number belongs on the blank jersey? (2-2)

A 26

B 25

C 24

D 22

2. What are the next three numbers in this pattern? (2-1)

6, 5, 3, 1, 6, 5, 3, 1, 6, 5, 3

A 6, 3, 1

B 6, 5, 3

C 1, 5, 3

D 1, 6, 5

3. What rule can be used to find the number of legs on 7 grasshoppers? (2-4)

Number of Grasshoppers	3	5	7	9
Number of Legs	18	30		54

A Add 15.

B Divide by 5.

C Multiply by 5.

D Multiply by 6.

4. Kayla is cutting ribbon to go around cards. Each card is shaped like a triangle with all sides the same length. How many inches of ribbon does she need for a card with each side 7 inches long? (2-5)

2 inches   3 inches   4 inches

Side Length in Inches	2	3	4	7
Inches of Ribbon	6	9	12	

A 15

B 18

C 21

D 24

5. Coach Kim needs to form teams that all have the same number of players. The table shows the number of teams formed for different numbers of players.

Number of Players	24	32	40	72
Number of Teams	3	4		9

What rule can be used to find how many teams are formed if there are 40 players? (2-4)

A Divide by 8.

B Divide by 6.

C Multiply by 6.

D Subtract 21.

6. Hank had a party at the zoo. He used the table below to find the total price of admission for groups of different sizes.

Total Number of Children	Total Admission Price
3	$21
5	$35
7	■
9	$63

What is the total cost of admission for 7 children? (2-3)

7. Joe has 18 pets. His pets are birds, hamsters, and 10 fish. He has 2 fewer birds than hamsters. How many birds does he have? (2-6)

8. What is a rule for the pattern? (2-2)

29, 24, 19, 14, 9

9. Look at this pattern of numbers.
5, 7, 2, 8, 5, 7, 2, 8, 5, 7, 2, …

Write the next 3 numbers in the pattern. (2-1)

10. Lockers in a school are lined up in the pattern shown below. Write the number that belongs on the blank locker. (2-2)

11. Kelly is making mobiles cut from strips of wood that are shaped like pentagons. How many inches of wood does she need for a pentagon with sides that are each 5 inches long? (2-5)

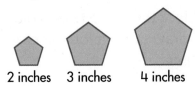

2 inches   3 inches   4 inches

Inches in One Side	2	3	4	5
Inches of Wood	10	15	20	■

12. There are 24 cars in the lot. Fourteen cars are silver the rest are blue or red. There are 6 more blue cars than red cars. How many cars are red? (2-6)

13. The table shows the number of boxes of juice in different numbers of cartons.

Total Number of Cartons	Total Number of Juice Boxes
3	9
5	15
7	■
8	24

How many juice boxes would you get in 7 cartons? Explain how you know. (2-3)

Make a pattern of block towers like the one shown.

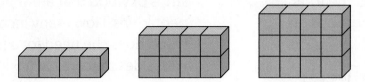

1. Your block tower will have 5 blocks in each story. On a separate sheet, draw the first four block towers in your pattern. Add one story each time.

2. Copy and complete the table for your pattern on a separate sheet.

Number of Stories	1	2	3	4	5
Number of Blocks	5				

3. How many blocks would you need for a 6-story tower in your pattern?

Make a pattern of house numbers beginning with 63.

4. Write the numbers of your pattern on a separate sheet.

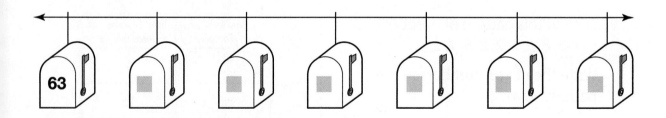

5. What is the rule for your number pattern?

6. Using your pattern, what house numbers will be on the 3 mailboxes to the left of the mailbox with house number 63?

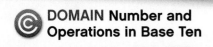
Topic
3

Place Value

▼ "Baby," the snake, weighs 403 pounds. Is it the heaviest snake that is living in captivity? You will find out in Lesson 3-4.

Review What You Know!

Vocabulary

Choose the best term from the box.

- odd
- even
- period
- number line

1. A group of three digits in a number separated by a comma is a ?.

2. A ? is a line that shows numbers in order using a scale.

3. The number 8 is an ? number.

4. The number 5 is an ? number.

Comparing Numbers

Compare each set of numbers using >, < or =.

5. 13 ◯ 10   6. 7 ◯ 7   7. 28 ◯ 29

8. 14 ◯ 5   9. 43 ◯ 34   10. 0 ◯ 1

11. 52 ◯ 52   12. 13 ◯ 65   13. 22 ◯ 33

Place Value

Tell if the underlined digit is in the ones, tens, or hundreds place.

14. 34<u>6</u>   15. <u>1</u>7   16. 9<u>2</u>1

17. <u>1</u>06   18. 3<u>3</u>   19. <u>4</u>7

20. <u>2</u>17   21. <u>3</u>20   22. 81<u>0</u>

23. 1,00<u>6</u>   24. <u>9</u>99   25. 1,4<u>0</u>5

© 26. **Writing to Explain** How does using commas to separate periods help you read large numbers?

Topic Essential Questions
- How are greater numbers read and written?
- How can whole numbers be compared and ordered?

Interactive Learning

Pose the problem. Start each lesson by working together to solve problems. It will help you make sense of math.

Applying Math Practices

- What am I asked to find?
- What else can I try?
- How are quantities related?
- How can I explain my work?
- How can I use math to model the problem?
- Can I use tools to help?
- Is my work precise?
- Why does this work?
- How can I generalize?

Lesson 3-1

© **Use Structure** Solve using place-value blocks.

An airplane flies at an altitude of 1,358 feet. How can you show this number using place-value blocks?

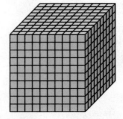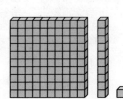

Lesson 3-2

© **Reasonableness** Solve using what you know about place value.

In the number 770, what is the relationship between the value of the first 7 and the value of the second 7? Explain.

© **Reason** Use place-value blocks and a place-value chart to complete this task.

I have a group of 1,345 ball-point pens and a group of 1,380 felt-tip pens. Which group has more? Tell how you decided.

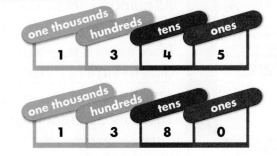

© **Reason** The depths of the Atlantic, Indian, and Pacific Oceans are shown on the recording sheet to the right. A robotic submarine can dive to a depth of 26,000 feet below sea level. Which ocean(s) can the submarine explore all the way to the bottom? Tell how you decided.

Comparing and Ordering Whole Numbers

1. Record the data your teacher gives you:
   robotic sub (maximum depth, 26,000 feet)
   depth of Atlantic Ocean (28,232 feet)
   depth of Pacific Ocean (35,840 feet)
   depth of Indian Ocean (23,376 feet)

© **Generalize** Solve. Look for patterns to help.

List 5 numbers that are between 300 and 400 but closer to 300 than 400. Then list 5 numbers between 300 and 400 that are closer to 400 than 300. Use a variety of digits. Write and explain how the digits in the numbers can be used to determine whether a number is closer to 300 or 400.

© **Use Tools** Solve using any method.

Daryl has some shirts and pants as shown to the right. What are all of the possible combinations of shirts and pants he can wear? How many different outfits can he make? How do you know you found them all?

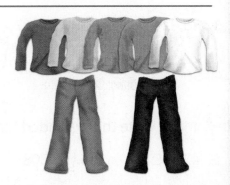

Lesson
3-1

Common
Core

4.NBT.2 Read and write multi-digit whole numbers using base-ten numerals, number names, and expanded form. Compare two multi-digit numbers based on meanings of the digits in each place, using >, =, and < symbols to record the results of comparisons. Also 4.NBT.1

Representing Numbers

Hands-On place-value blocks

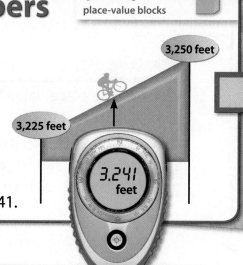

3,250 feet

3,225 feet

3,241 feet

How can you read and write 3- and 4-digit numbers?

All numbers are made from the digits 0, 1, 2, 3, 4, 5, 6, 7, 8, and 9.

Place value is the value of the place a digit has in a number.

Jill is 3,241 feet above sea level.

There are different ways to represent 3,241.

Another Example How can you show 3,241 on a place-value chart?

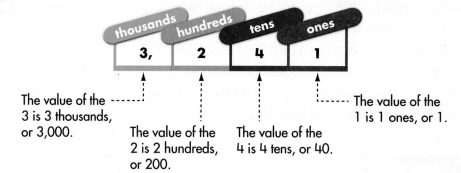

thousands	hundreds	tens	ones
3,	2	4	1

The value of the 3 is 3 thousands, or 3,000.

The value of the 2 is 2 hundreds, or 200.

The value of the 4 is 4 tens, or 40.

The value of the 1 is 1 ones, or 1.

Explain It

1. If you showed 3,421 in a place-value chart, how would it look different from the example above?

Guided Practice*

MATHEMATICAL PRACTICES

Do you know HOW?

In **1** through **4**, write the word form and tell the value of the red digit in each number.

1. 15,324
2. 135,467
3. 921,382
4. 275,206

In **5** and **6**, write the expanded form.

5. 42,158
6. 63,308

Do you UNDERSTAND?

7. If Jill climbed 100 feet more, how many feet above sea level would she be?

8. **Use Structure** What is the value of the 2 in 3,261? The 3? The 1?

9. Write one hundred one thousand, eleven in standard form.

Animated Glossary
www.pearsonsuccessnet.com

DIGITAL

You can represent numbers using place-value blocks.

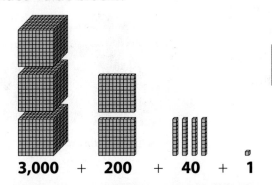

3,000 + 200 + 40 + 1

A number written in a way that shows only its digits is in **standard form**.

3,241

Write a comma between the thousands and the hundreds.

A number written as the sum of the values of its digits is in **expanded form**.

3,000 + 200 + 40 + 1

A number written in words is in **word form**.

three thousand, two hundred forty-one

Independent Practice

For **10** and **11,** write each number in standard form.

10.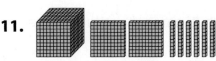

11.

For **12** and **13,** write each number in standard form and expanded form.

12. Eighty-three thousand, nine hundred two

13. Three hundred twenty-one thousand, two hundred nine

For **14–17,** write each number in word form.

14. 300,000 + 8,000 + 20 + 9

15. 123,414

16. 1,205

17. 9,876

Problem Solving

MATHEMATICAL PRACTICES

© **18. Be Precise** Which digit is in the same place in all three numbers below? Name the place-value position.

574,632   24,376   204,581

19. A city counted 403,867 votes in the last election. Write this number in word form.

20. A town library has 124,763 books and 3,142 DVDs. This year, they bought 1,000 books and 2,000 DVDs. How many books does the library have now?

  A 5,142 books   **C** 125,763 books

  B 23,142 books   **D** 134,763 books

© **21. Writing to Explain** Ben used place-value blocks to show the number 3,564. Then he added six more thousand cubes. What was the new number? Explain.

Common Core

4.NBT.1 Recognize that in a multi-digit whole number, a digit in one place represents ten times what it represents in the place to its right. Also **4.NBT.2**

Place Value Relationships

Hands-On
place-value blocks

How are the digits in a multi-digit number related to each other?

Kiana collected 110 bottle caps. What is the relationship between the values of the digit 1 in each place?

110 bottle caps

.Guided Practice*

MATHEMATICAL PRACTICES

Do you know HOW?

In **1** through **2**, name the values of the given digits.

1. the 7s in 7,700

2. the 4s in 442

In **3** through **4**, what is the relationship between the values of the given digits?

3. the 7s in 7,700

4. the 4s in 442

Do you UNDERSTAND?

5. Reason Is the value of the first 4 ten times as great as the value of the second 4 in 4,043? Explain why or why not.

6. Reason Is the value of the 2 in 230 ten times as great as the value of the 3 in the same number? Explain why or why not.

Independent Practice

MATHEMATICAL PRACTICES

Look for Patterns In **7–22,** name the values of the given digits in the numbers below.

7. the 4s in 6,448

8. the 3s in 433

9. the 6s in 6,674

10. the 1s in 5,711

11. the 5s in 4,559

12. the 2s in 722

13. the 9s in 4,998

14. the 4s in 844

15. the 8s in 8,800

16. the 7s in 2,773

17. the 2s in 225

18. the 1s in 1,138

19. the 5s in 5,590

20. the 6s in 2,366

21. the 8s in 688

22. the 9s in 9,993

DIGITAL
eTools
www.pearsonsuccessnet.com

The first 1 is in the hundreds place. Its value is 100.

The second 1 is in the tens place. Its value is 10.

How is 100 related to 10?

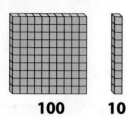

100   **10**

100 is ten times as much as 10. The first 1 is worth ten times as much as the second 1!

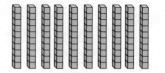

10 tens   **1 ten**

When two digits next to each other in a number are the same, the digit on the left is always ten times as great as the digit on the right.

Problem Solving

23. Reason What can you say about the 3s in the number 43,335?

24. Critique Reasoning Mia says that in the number 5,555, all the digits have the same value. Is she correct? Explain why or why not.

25. Writing to Explain Sal says he is thinking of a 3-digit number in which all of the digits are the same. He says that the value of the digit in the tens place is 80. How can you find the value of the digit on the left and the right of the tens place?

26. Which of the following names the value of the 4s in the number 4,449?

A   4,000, 400, 40   C   4,000, 40, 4

B   4,000, 400, 4   D   400, 40, 4

27. The number 6,644 contains two sets of digits in which one digit is ten times as great as the other. Find the values of the digits in each set.

28. In the number 6,339, which places contain digits where one digit is ten times as great as the other?

29. In the number 7,882, if you move from the 8 in the hundreds place to the 8 in the tens place, what happens to the value of the 8?

30. Look for Patterns In the number 222, what is the relationship between the 2s? Think about the value of each 2 to help you find your answer.

31. Critique Reasoning Vin says that in the number 4,346, one 4 is 10 times as great as the other 4. Is he correct? Explain why or why not.

32. Describe the relationship between the values of the two 7s in the number 737.

Lesson
3-3

©

Common Core

4.NBT.2 Read and write multi-digit whole numbers using base-ten numerals, number names, and expanded form. Compare two multi-digit numbers based on meanings of the digits in each place, using >, =, and < symbols to record the results of comparisons.

Comparing Numbers

How do you compare numbers?

When you compare two numbers you find out which number is greater and which number is less.

Which building is taller, the Taipei 101 Tower in Taiwan or the Willis Tower in Chicago?

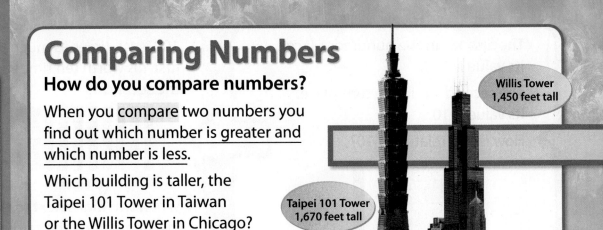

Willis Tower
1,450 feet tall

Taipei 101 Tower
1,670 feet tall

Another Example **How can you use place-value charts and number lines to compare numbers?**

Compare 13,456 and 13,482 using a place-value chart. Then show these two numbers on a number line.

On a place-value chart, line up the digits by place value. Compare the digits starting from the left.

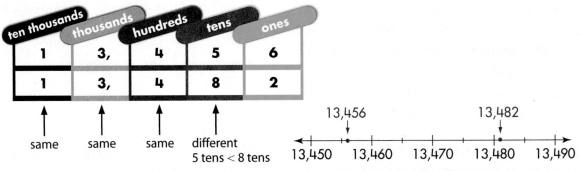

ten thousands	thousands	hundreds	tens	ones
1	3,	4	5	6
1	3,	4	8	2

same · same · same · different
5 tens < 8 tens

13,456 · 13,482

13,450 · 13,460 · 13,470 · 13,480 · 13,490

So 13,456 **is less than** 13,482.

On the number line, 13,456 is to the left of 13,482.

13,456 < 13,482

Explain It

1. In this example, why don't you need to compare the digits in the ones place?

2. Why can't you tell which number is greater by just comparing the first digit in each number?

Animated Glossary
www.pearsonsuccessnet.com

DIGITAL

You can use symbols.

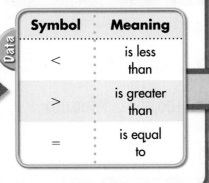

Symbol	Meaning
<	is less than
>	is greater than
=	is equal to

You can compare 1,670 and 1,450 using place-value blocks.

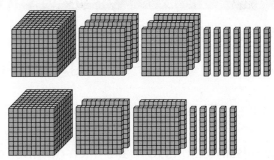

The place-value blocks show that 1,670 is greater than 1,450.

$$1,670 > 1,450$$

So, the Taipei 101 Tower is taller than the Willis Tower.

Guided Practice*

 MATHEMATICAL PRACTICES

Do you know HOW?

Compare the numbers. Use <, >, or =.

1.

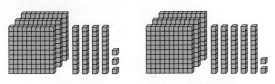

343 ◯ 352

2. 2,561 ◯ 2,261

3. 35,000 ◯ 35,100

4. 672,444 ◯ 672,444

Do you UNDERSTAND?

© **5. Critique Reasoning** Cara says that since 4 is greater than 1, the number 42,310 is greater than the number 142,310. Do you agree? Why or why not?

© **6. Writing to Explain** The height of the Willis Tower is 1,450 feet. The Petronas Towers in Malaysia are each 1,482 feet tall. Which is taller? Explain how you know.

7. Draw a number line to compare the numbers.

1,462 ◯ 1,521

Independent Practice

Compare the numbers. Use <, >, or =.

8.

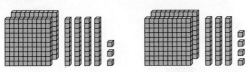

243 ◯ 234

9.

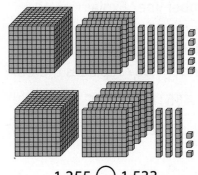

1,355 ◯ 1,533

Compare the numbers. Use <, >, or =.

10. 679 ◯ 4,679

11. 9,642 ◯ 9,642

12. 5,136 ◯ 5,631

13. 13,682 ◯ 13,782

14. 805,224 ◯ 800,554

15. 100,000 ◯ 100,001

Write the missing digits to make each number sentence true.

16. ▢24 > 896

17. 7,6▢7 < 7,617

18. 82,29▢ = 82,2▢0

19. ▢,000 < 1,542

20. 53,▢12 > 53,812

21. 912,185 > 912,▢85

Problem Solving

MATHEMATICAL PRACTICES

🌐 **Social Studies** For **22** and **23**, use the pictures at the right.

© **22. Persevere** Which building is taller, the Willis Tower or the Empire State Building? How do you know?

23. Which building is shorter, the Empire State Building or the John Hancock Center?

Empire State Building
1,250 feet tall

© **24. Reason** Mark is thinking of a 4-digit number. Janna is thinking of a 5-digit number. Whose number is greater? How do you know?

© **25. Communicate** Suppose you are comparing 1,272 and 1,269. Do you need to compare the ones digits? Which number would be farther to the right on the number line? Explain.

26. Which number sentence is true if the number 1,537 replaces the box?

A 1,456 > ▢

C 1,598 < ▢

B ▢ = 1,256

D ▢ > 1,357

Willis Tower
1,450 feet tall

John Hancock Center
1,127 feet tall

Algebra Connections

Greater, Less, or Equal

The two sides of a number sentence can be equal or unequal. A symbol $>$, $<$, or $=$ tells how the sides compare. Sometimes reasoning can help you tell if one side is greater.

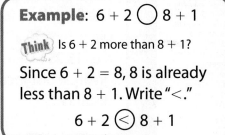

Example: $6 + 2 \bigcirc 8 + 1$

Think Is $6 + 2$ more than $8 + 1$?

Since $6 + 2 = 8$, 8 is already less than $8 + 1$. Write "$<$."

$6 + 2 \text{\small\textcircled{$<$}} 8 + 1$

Tip

$>$	$<$	$=$
is greater than	is less than	is equal to

Copy and complete. Replace the circle with $<$, $>$, or $=$. Check your answers.

1. $3 + 4 \bigcirc 2 + 7$

2. $9 + 1 \bigcirc 5 + 4$

3. $5 + 3 \bigcirc 6 + 3$

4. $2 + 9 \bigcirc 1 + 8$

5. $4 + 6 \bigcirc 4 + 7$

6. $8 + 6 \bigcirc 9 + 5$

7. $18 + 2 \bigcirc 16 + 4$

8. $15 + 5 \bigcirc 15 - 5$

9. $14 + 4 \bigcirc 12 + 4$

10. $20 - 3 \bigcirc 20 - 1$

11. $21 - 2 \bigcirc 19 - 2$

12. $27 + 3 \bigcirc 26 + 4$

· ·

For **13** and **14**, copy and complete each number sentence. Use it to help solve the problem.

13. Al and Jiro had some toy animals. Al had 8 lizards and 3 frogs. Jiro had 11 lizards and 2 frogs. Who had more toy animals?

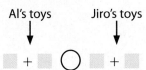

Al's toys   Jiro's toys

■ + ■ ◯ ■ + ■

14. The number below each block tells how many are in a set. Val used all of the small and large cylinders. Jen used all of the small and large cubes. Who used more blocks?

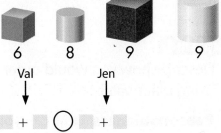

6   8   9   9

Val   Jen

■ + ■ ◯ ■ + ■

© **15. Write a Problem** Write a problem using this number sentence: $9 + 2 > 4 + 5$.

Lesson

3-4

Common
Core

4.NBT.2 Read and write multi-digit whole numbers using base-ten numerals, number names, and expanded form. Compare two multi-digit numbers based on meanings of the digits in each place, using >, =, and < symbols to record the results of comparisons.

Ordering Numbers

How do you compare more than two numbers?

Three planes fly to various points around the world. The first plane flies 18,188 kilometers. The second plane flies 20,275 kilometers. The third plane flies 15,251 kilometers. Which plane traveled the greatest distance? Which plane traveled the least distance?

Plane 1	18,188 km
Plane 2	20,275 km
Plane 3	15,251 km

Another Example **How do you order numbers?**

The areas of 3 land masses are shown in the table at the right. Which shows the areas in order from **least** to **greatest**?

A 950,000; 410,000; 690,000

B 410,000; 950,000; 690,000

C 690,000; 950,000; 410,000

D 410,000; 690,000; 950,000

Data

Land Mass	Areas (in square miles)
A	410,000
B	950,000
C	690,000

Step 1 Plot the numbers on a number line.

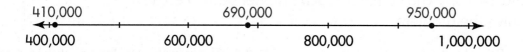

Step 2 Order the numbers. On a number line, numbers to the right are greater.

Reading from left to right: 410,000; 690,000; 950,000

The correct choice is **D**.

Explain It

1. Describe how you would order the land masses' areas using place value.

©2. **Reasonableness** How can you rule out choices A and C as the correct answer?

You can use a place-value chart to help you solve this problem.

ten thousands	thousands	hundreds	tens	ones
1	8,	1	8	8
2	0,	2	7	5
1	5,	2	5	1

2 > 1
So 20,275 is the greatest.

5 < 8
So 15,251 is the least.

You can use symbols to show how the numbers compare. The symbol > means greater than, and the symbol < means less than.

20,275 > 18,188
15,251 < 18,188

Plane 2 travels the greatest distance. Plane 3 travels the least distance.

Guided Practice*

Do you know HOW?

In **1** through **4**, copy and complete by writing > or < for each ◯.

1. 2,643 ◯ 2,801   **2.** 6,519 ◯ 6,582

3. 785 ◯ 731   **4.** 6,703 ◯ 6,699

In **5** and **6**, order the numbers from least to greatest.

5. 7,502   6,793   6,723

6. 80,371   15,048   80,137

Do you UNDERSTAND?

© **7. Writing to Explain** Why would you look at the hundreds place to order these numbers?

32,463   32,482   32,947

8. Compare the area of a country that is 435,789 square miles to the area of a country that is 435,699 square miles. Which is greater?

Independent Practice

In **9** through **20**, copy and complete by writing > or < for each ◯.

9. 221,495 ◯ 210,388   **10.** 52,744 ◯ 56,704

11. 138,752 ◯ 133,122   **12.** 4,937 ◯ 4,939

13. 22,873 ◯ 22,774   **14.** 912,706 ◯ 913,898

15. 412,632 ◯ 412,362   **16.** 999,999 ◯ 990,999

17. 506,521 ◯ 500,692   **18.** 397,239 ◯ 97,329

19. 62,219 ◯ 68,016   **20.** 859,316 ◯ 867,255

Leveled Practice In **21** through **24**, copy and complete the number lines. Then use the number lines to order the numbers from greatest to least.

21. 27,505   26,905   26,950

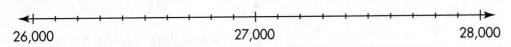

26,000   27,000   28,000

22. 422,100   422,700   422,000

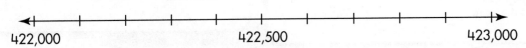

422,000   422,500   423,000

23. 7,502   7,622   7,523   7,852

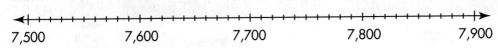

7,500   7,600   7,700   7,800   7,900

24. 3,030 3,033 3,003

3,000   3,050

In **25** through **32**, write the numbers in order from least to greatest.

25. 57,535 576,945 506,495

26. 18,764 18,761 13,490

27. 25,988 25,978 25,998

28. 87,837 37,838 878,393

29. 43,783 434,282 64,382

30. 723,433 72,324 72,432

31. 58,028 85,843 77,893

32. 849,551 940,039 485,903

Problem Solving

MATHEMATICAL PRACTICES

33. Critique Reasoning Aaron added 57 and 20 and said the answer is greater than 100. Is Aaron correct?

34. Model Write three numbers that are greater than 780,000 but less than 781,000.

35. Reason Could you use only the hundred thousands place to order 462,524, 463,524, and 562,391?

36. Describe how to order 7,463, 74,633, and 74,366 from least to greatest.

37. The heaviest snake living in captivity in the United States is a Burmese Python named "Baby." An average Anaconda snake weighs 330 pounds. Which snake weighs more?

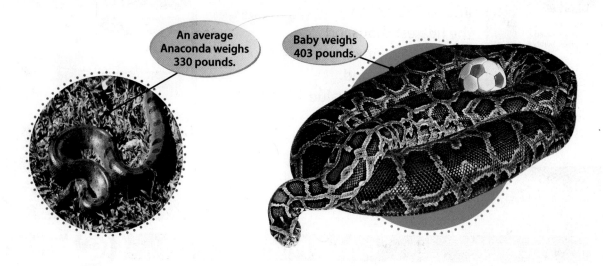

An average Anaconda weighs 330 pounds.

Baby weighs 403 pounds.

38. Which list of numbers is in order from least to greatest?

A	1,534	1,576	1,563
B	18,732	18,723	18,765
C	234,564	234,568	234,323
D	383,847	383,848	383,849

39. Which airplane is heavier?

Airplane	Weight (pounds)
A	602,999
B	610,345

40. The chart below shows the number of game cards owned by the top collectors in one school. Which student had the most cards?

A Shani **C** Ariel

B Lin **D** Jorge

Collector	Number of cards
Shani	3,424
Ariel	3,443
Lin	2,354
Jorge	2,932

41. A large city has a population of 420,000 people. This population is between which numbers?

A 400,000 and 440,000

B 300,000 and 340,000

C 410,000 and 419,000

D 430,000 and 500,000

Common
Core

4.NBT.3 Use place value
understanding to round
multi-digit whole numbers
to any place.

Rounding Whole Numbers

How can you round numbers?

Round 292,430 to
the nearest thousand
and to the nearest
hundred thousand.
You can use place value
to round numbers.

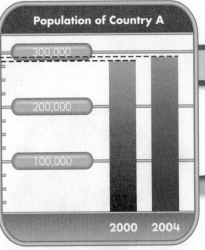

Population of Country A

292,430

281,421

300,000

200,000

100,000

2000   2004

Guided Practice*

MATHEMATICAL
PRACTICES

Do you know HOW?

In **1** through **6**, round each number
to the place of the underlined digit.

1. 128,955

2. 85,639

3. 9,924

4. 194,542

5. 160,656

6. 149,590

Do you UNDERSTAND?

7. Writing to Explain Explain how to
round a number when 7 is the digit
to the right of the rounding place.

8. A country's population was 421,906.
Round 421,906 to the nearest
hundred thousand.

Independent Practice

Leveled Practice In **9** through **28**, round each number to the place
of the underlined digit. You may use a number line to help you.

9. 493,295

░░,000

10. 39,230

░,000

11. 77,292

░,░0

12. 54,846

░0,000

13. 4,028

14. 668,365

15. 453,280

16. 17,909

17. 1,406

18. 55,560

19. 21,679

20. 417,547

21. 117,821

22. 75,254

23. 9,049

24. 666,821

25. 2,420

26. 900,985

27. 9,511

28. 73,065

For another example, see Set E on page 83.

Round 292,430 to the nearest thousand.

thousands place

292,430

If the digit to the right of the rounding place is 5 or more, add 1 to the rounding digit. If it is less than 5, leave the rounding digit alone.

292,000

Since 4 < 5, leave the rounding digit as is. Change the digits to the right of the rounding place to zeros.

So, 292,430 rounds to 292,000.

Round 292,430 to the nearest hundred thousand.

hundred thousands place

292,430

The digit to the right of the rounding place is 9.

300,000

Since the digit is 9, round by adding 1 to the digit in the hundred thousands place.

So, 292,430 rounds to 300,000.

Problem Solving

MATHEMATICAL
PRACTICES

For **29** and **30**, use the table at the right.

29. For each zoo in the chart, round the attendance to the nearest hundred thousand.

Ⓒ **30. Reason** Which zoo had the greatest number of visitors?

Zoo Attendance	
Zoo D	234,679
Zoo E	872,544
Zoo F	350,952

Ⓒ **31. Model** Write four numbers that round to 700 when rounded to the nearest hundred.

Ⓒ **32. Reason** Write a number that when rounded to the nearest thousand and hundred will have a result that is the same.

33. Jonas read that about 760,000 people will graduate from high school in the next four years. Jonas thinks this number is rounded to the nearest ten thousand. What would the number be if it was rounded to the nearest hundred thousand?

Ⓒ **34. Persevere** Liz had attended class every day since she started school as a kindergartner. She said she had been in school for about 1,000 days. What could the actual number of school days be if she rounded to the nearest ten?

35. When rounded to the nearest ten thousand, which number would be rounded to 120,000?

   A 123,900   **C** 128,770

   B 126,480   **D** 130,000

36. A fruit market sold 3,849 apples, 3,498 oranges, and 3,894 pears in one day. Write these numbers in order from greatest to least.

Common Core

4.NBT.1 Recognize that in a multi-digit whole number, a digit in one place represents ten times what it represents in the place to its right.

Problem Solving

Make an Organized List

Arthur is tiling a bathroom wall. He has 520 wall tiles. He wants to arrange them in patterns of hundreds and tens.

Using only hundreds and tens blocks, how many ways can he make 520?

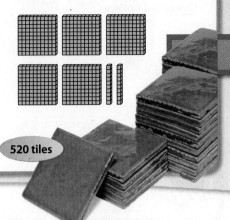

520 tiles

Guided Practice*

MATHEMATICAL PRACTICES

Do you know HOW?

Solve. Make an organized list to help you.

1. It costs Celia 50¢ admission to enter the aquarium. How many different ways can Celia pay the admission using only quarters, dimes, and nickels?

Do you UNDERSTAND?

2. What were the titles for the columns of your list in Problem 1?

© 3. **Write a Problem** Write a problem that you can solve using an organized list.

Independent Practice

MATHEMATICAL PRACTICES

Solve.

4. Using only hundreds blocks and tens blocks, list the ways to show 340.

5. Simon asked Margaret to guess a number. He gave these hints.
   - The number has 3 digits.
   - The digit in the 100s place is less than 2.
   - The digit in the 10s place is greater than 8.
   - The number is even.

   What are the possible numbers?

6. Make a list showing the ways you can make a dollar using only quarters, dimes, and nickels using no more than one nickel and no more than 9 dimes.

Applying Math Practices

- What am I asked to find?
- What else can I try?
- How are quantities related?
- How can I explain my work?
- How can I use math to model the problem?
- Can I use tools to help?
- Is my work precise?
- Why does this work?
- How can I generalize?

*For another example, see Set F on page 83.

What do I know? I can use only hundreds blocks and tens blocks.

What am I asked to find? All of the combinations that show a total of 520

Record the combinations using an organized list.

Hundreds	5	4	3	2	1	0
Tens	2	12	22	32	42	52

There are 6 ways to make 520.

The answer is reasonable because the combinations have 5 or fewer hundreds blocks.

7. Persevere Lou's sandwiches are made with either wheat or white bread and have only one type of cheese—Swiss, Cheddar, American, or Mozzarella. How many different kinds of sandwiches can Lou make?

8. A magazine has a total of 24 articles and ads. There are 9 ads. How many articles are there?

24 articles and ads

9	?

9. Model Janie is making a bracelet. She has 1 red bead, 1 blue bead, and 1 white bead. How many possible ways can Janie arrange the beads?

10. Reason What two numbers have a sum of 12 and a difference of 4?

11. Alan has a cat, a goldfish, and a dog. He feeds them in a different order each day. How many different ways can he feed his pets?

12. Heather is writing a 3-digit number. She uses the digits 1, 5, and 9. What are the possible numbers she can write?

13. At the driving range, James wants to buy 200 golf balls. The golf balls are sold in buckets of 100, 50, and 10 golf balls. How many different ways can James buy 200 golf balls?

14. Heather asks the cashier to break a $20 bill. She gets back only $5 and $10 bills. How many different ways can the cashier give Heather $20 back?

50 golf balls

100 golf balls

10 golf balls

Set A, pages 66–67

Write the number below in standard form, expanded form, and word form.

Standard form: 4,016

Expanded form: 4,000 + 10 + 6

Word form: four thousand, sixteen

Remember that the digit 0 is sometimes needed to hold a place in a number.

Write each number in standard form.

1. 1,000 + 5   **2.** 300 + 20 + 7

3. 7,000 + 800 + 60 + 4

4. 9,000 + 300 + 5

Write each number in expanded form and word form.

5. 8,214   **6.** 620

Set B, pages 68–69

Find the values of the digit 4 in the number 441.

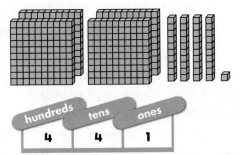

The first 4 is in the hundreds place. Its value is 400.
The second 4 is in the tens place. Its value is 40.

Remember that when two digits next to each other in a number are the same, the one on the left is always 10 times greater than the one on the right.

Name the values of the given digits.

1. the 8s in 188   **2.** the 7s in 774

3. the 1s in 6,811   **4.** the 3s in 2,339

5. the 4s in 4,457   **6.** the 9s in 9,924

Set C, pages 70–72

Compare 798,682 and 796,241.
Line up the digits by place value.
Compare the digits starting from the left.

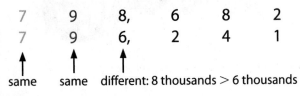

798,682 > 796,241

Remember, compare one place at a time.

Compare. Use <, >, or =.

1. 44,974 ◯ 91,719

2. 121,356 ◯ 21,356

3. 14,751 ◯ 14,851

4. 592,600 ◯ 592,600

Set D, pages 74–77

Order these numbers from least to greatest.

345,671   346,716   46,716

Since 46,716 is a 5-digit number, it's the least. Line up the other numbers by place value starting from the left. Find the first place where the digits are different.

345,671
346,716

5 thousands < 6 thousands

46,716   345,671   346,716

Remember, the number with the fewest digits is the least number.

Write the numbers in order from least to greatest.

1. 312,846   111,310   96,782

2. 79,230   7,923   79,233

Write the numbers in order from greatest to least.

3. 683,419   75,312   621,327

4. 23,912   23,812   24,812

Set E, pages 78–79

Round 764,802 to the nearest hundred thousand.

hundred thousands place

7̲64,802   The digit to the right of the rounding place is 6.

8̲00,000   Since 6 > 5, round by adding 1 to the digit in the hundred thousands place.

So, 764,802 rounds to 800,000.

Remember to look at the number to the right of the rounding place. Then change the digits to the right of the rounding place to zeros.

Round each number to the place of the underlined digit.

1. 166̲,742   **2.** 76̲,532

3. 5̲,861   **4.** 432̲,741

5. 1̲32,505   **6.** 2̲57,931

Set F, pages 80–81

Using only hundreds and tens blocks, how many ways can you make 440?

What do I know?   I can use only hundreds blocks and tens blocks

What am I being asked to find?   All of the combinations that make a total of 440

Record the combinations using an organized list.

Hundreds	4	3	2	1	0
Tens	4	14	24	34	44

Remember that the way you organize a list can help you find all the possibilities in a problem.

Solve. Make an organized list to help you.

1. Troy collects plastic banks. He has three different plastic banks: a pig, a cow, and a frog. How many ways can he arrange his banks on a shelf?

Multiple Choice

© ASSESSMENT

1. Which is greater than 49,324? (3-3)

   A 49,342

   B 49,322

   C 49,314

   D 39,424

2. A small country covers a total of 58,560 square miles. Which number is less than 58,560? (3-3)

   A 68,570

   B 58,650

   C 58,560

   D 58,500

3. On Thursday, 71,593 people attended a football game. On Sunday, 71,595 people attended, and on Monday, 71,586 people attended. Which lists these numbers in order from least to greatest? (3-4)

   A 71,586   71,593   71,595

   B 71,586   71,595   71,593

   C 71,593   71,595   71,586

   D 71,595   71,593   71,586

4. Carrie has 340 marbles to put in vases. She wants the vases to hold either 100 marbles or 10 marbles. Which is a way she can arrange the marbles? (3-6)

   A 34 hundreds

   B 3 hundreds 40 tens

   C 1 hundred 24 tens

   D 2 hundreds 24 tens

5. The table shows the areas of four states. Which of the four states has the least area? (3-4)

State	Area (sq. mi)
Montana	147,042
Oklahoma	68,898
Oregon	98,381
Wyoming	97,814

   A Montana

   B Oklahoma

   C Oregon

   D Wyoming

6. The place-value blocks show the number of students at a school. How many students are there? (3-1)

   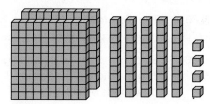

   A 145

   B 154

   C 245

   D 254

7. Which number will have the same result, when rounded to the nearest ten or hundred? (3-5)

   A 97

   B 118 and 5

   C 179

   D 5,091

8. What is the standard form of 80,000 + 5,000 + 700 + 8? (3-1)

9. Betsy is making a flag. She can choose three colors from red, white, blue, and yellow. How many choices does Betsy have? (3-6)

10. What is 259,809 rounded to the nearest ten thousand? (3-5)

11. The U. S. Constitution contains 4,543 words, including the signatures. What is 4,543 rounded to the nearest hundred? (3-5)

$$\xleftarrow{\hspace{0.3em}}\underset{4,500}{\;}\;+\;+\;+\;\underset{4,543}{\bullet}\;+\;+\;+\;+\;\underset{4,600}{\;}\xrightarrow{\hspace{0.3em}}$$

12. In the number 7,725, which places contain digits where one digit is ten times as great as the other? (3-2)

13. Write the number shown by the place-value blocks in word form. (3-1)

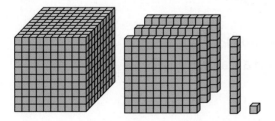

14. The number 57,733 contains two sets of digits in which one digit is ten times as great as the other. What are the values of the digits in each set? (3-2)

15. The table shows the seating capacities of three sports stadiums. How would you write the seating capacities in order from least to greatest? (3-4)

Stadium	Seating Capacity
Baseball	41,610
Football	61,500
Soccer	60,950

16. Tammy wants to get change for 30¢. The only coins she can get are quarters, nickels, and dimes. How many different ways can she get 30¢ using only these coins? (3-6)

17. What are the values of the 5s in the number 54,753? (3-2)

18. Jeff is thinking of a 5-digit number. Rick is thinking of a 6-digit number. Whose number is greater? How do you know? (3-3)

19. The sale prices for three homes are $212,599, $209,699, and $220,499. Write the home prices in order from greatest to least. (3-4)

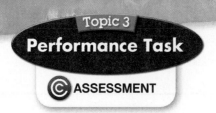
The table shows the land area for ten countries.

Country	Land area (km²)
New Zealand	268,680
Panama	78,200
Egypt	995,450
Turkey	780,580
Japan	377,835
Mozambique	784,090
Norway	307,442
France	547,030
Costa Rica	51,129
Chile	756,950

1. Write the land area of Turkey in word form.

2. Write the land area of Costa Rica in expanded form.

3. If you added the land area of Mozambique and Norway, would the sum be greater than or less than the land area of Egypt? Explain your reasoning.

4. List the countries with the three largest land areas from greatest to least.

5. List the countries with the three smallest land areas from least to greatest.

6. Which countries have a land area in which the value of one digit is ten times as great as the value of another digit?

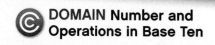

Topic 4

Addition and Subtraction of Whole Numbers

▼ The lunar rover set the surface speed record on the moon. Find out the rover's estimated speed in Lesson 4-3.

Review What You Know!

Vocabulary

Choose the best term from the box.

- rounding
- mental math
- sum
- tens
- difference
- regroup

1. In order to subtract 140 from 530, you need to _?_.

2. _?_ tells about how many or about how much.

3. When you subtract two numbers, the answer is the _?_.

4. When you add numbers together, you find the _?_.

Addition Facts

Find each sum.

5. $4 + 6$ **6.** $7 + 5$ **7.** $9 + 8$

8. $14 + 5$ **9.** $3 + 7$ **10.** $37 + 7$

11. $9 + 6$ **12.** $6 + 5$ **13.** $15 + 7$

14. $3 + 8$ **15.** $14 + 6$ **16.** $25 + 5$

Subtraction Facts

Find each difference.

17. $27 - 3$ **18.** $6 - 4$ **19.** $15 - 8$

20. $11 - 8$ **21.** $6 - 2$ **22.** $17 - 8$

23. $16 - 4$ **24.** $20 - 5$ **25.** $11 - 6$

26. $14 - 6$ **27.** $15 - 10$ **28.** $13 - 7$

© **29. Writing to Explain** Why does 843 round to 840 rather than to 850?

Topic Essential Questions
- How can sums and differences of whole numbers be estimated?
- What are standard procedures for adding and subtracting whole numbers?

Interactive Learning

Pose the problem. Start each lesson by working together to solve problems. It will help you make sense of math.

Applying Math Practices

- What am I asked to find?
- What else can I try?
- How are quantities related?
- How can I explain my work?
- How can I use math to model the problem?
- Can I use tools to help?
- Is my work precise?
- Why does this work?
- How can I generalize?

Lesson 4-1

ⓒ **Reason** Solve using mental math.

Luke collected 36 baseball cards and 34 football cards. What is the total number of cards in Luke's collection? Tell how you found the answer mentally.

Lesson 4-2

ⓒ **Reasonableness** Tell which estimate is more reasonable and explain why.

Vera went on a 3-day trip. Is 300 or 400 a more reasonable estimate for about how far she went on each of the three days? Explain.

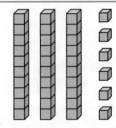

Vera's Trip

Day 1   336 miles
Day 2   423 miles
Day 3   357 miles

Lesson 4-3

ⓒ **Generalize** Use the data in the table. Solve any way you choose.

Three students brought bottles to a recycling center. How many bottles did they bring in all? Be sure to estimate the answer first. Explain how you found the estimate and the exact answer.

Student	Number of Bottles
Erica	219
Ana	142
Leon	436

Lesson 4-4

© **Generalize** Solve any way you choose.

During a gardening project, Ruben planted
168 seeds. Jana planted 191 seeds. How many
more seeds did Jana plant than Ruben? Be sure
to estimate the answer first. Explain how you
found the estimate and the exact answer.

Lesson 4-5

© **Generalize** Solve any way you choose.

How much taller is the Empire State Building
than the Citigroup Center? Show all of
your work.

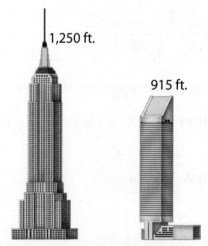

Empire State Building   Citigroup Center

Lesson 4-6

© **Model** Solve. Use the bar diagram at the
right to help choose which operation to use.

Marta's dog weighs 60 pounds. Suso's dog
weighs 43 pounds. How much more does
Marta's dog weigh than Suso's dog? Tell
which operation is needed and why.

60 pounds	
43	?

Common
Core

4.NBT.3 Use place value understanding to round multi-digit whole numbers to any place. Also **4.OA.3**

Using Mental Math to Add and Subtract

How can you use mental math to add and subtract?

Properties can sometimes help you add using mental math. How many years have Ms. Walston and Mr. Randall been teaching? What is the total number of years all of the teachers in the chart have been teaching?

Teacher	Years Teaching
Ms. Walston	12
Mr. Roy	5
Mr. Randall	30

Other Examples

Add using mental math.

Find 135 + 48.

?	
135	48

Use **breaking apart** to find a ten.

Adding 5 to 135 is easy. Break apart 48.

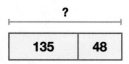

135 + 5 = 140
140 + 43 = 183
So, 135 + 48 = 183.

Use **compensation.**

135 + 48
135 + 50 = 185

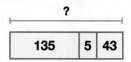 **Think** I added 2 too many, so I will subtract 2.

185 − 2 = 183
So, 135 + 48 = 183.

Subtract using mental math.

Find 400 − 165.

Use **counting on.**

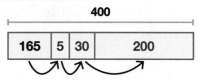

165 + 5 = 170
170 + 30 = 200
200 + 200 = 400

5 + 30 + 200 = 235
So, 400 − 165 = 235.

Use **compensation.**

Find 260 − 17.

It is easy to subtract 20.

260 − 20 = 240

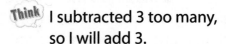 **Think** I subtracted 3 too many, so I will add 3.

240 + 3 = 243
So, 260 − 17 = 243.

Commutative Property of Addition

You can add two numbers in any order.

42

12	30

$$12 + 30 = 30 + 12$$

Ms. Walston and Mr. Randall have been teaching a combined total of 42 years.

Associative Property of Addition

You can change the grouping of addends.

47

12	30	5

$$(12 + 30) + 5 = 12 + (30 + 5)$$

The total number of years the three teachers have been teaching is 47 years.

Identity Property of Addition

Adding zero does not change the number.

$$12 + 0 = 12$$

Guided Practice*

 MATHEMATICAL PRACTICES

Do you know HOW?

In **1** through **6**, use mental math to add or subtract.

1. $86 + 25$
2. $497 + 0$
3. $566 - 359$
4. $169 - 48$
5. $239 + 509$
6. $(40 + 5) + 8$

Do you UNDERSTAND?

7. How could you use compensation to find $391 - 26$?

© 8. **Writing to Explain** Explain how you used mental math to find the answer to Exercise 4.

Independent Practice

Leveled Practice In **9** through **18**, use mental math to complete the calculation.

9. $400 - 227$

400

227	3	70	100

10. $500 - 89$

500

89	11	400

11. $906 - 289$

906

289	11	600	6

12. $7,000 + 2,130$

?

7,000	2,000	100	30

13. $583 + 317$

?

583	7	10	300

14. $125 + 28$

?

125	5	23

15. $1,700 - 315$

16. $2,000 + 4,996$

17. $438 - 129$

18. $0 + 284$

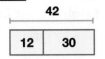 Animated Glossary
www.pearsonsuccessnet.com

For **19** through **21**, use the table to the right.

19. Which state has the greatest land area in square miles?

20. Which two states shown in the table have the smallest difference in land area?

21. Which two states shown in the table have the greatest difference in land area?

State	Total Square Miles
Alaska	571,951
Texas	261,797
California	155,959
Montana	145,552
New Mexico	121,356

22. Reasonableness Colin had 148 CDs in his collection. He traded 32 of them for 23 that he really wanted. How many CDs does Colin now have in his collection? Use mental math.

   A   106 CDs

   B   108 CDs

   C   116 CDs

   D   139 CDs

23. Ms. Gomez's class collected pencils for the community school supplies drive. Ethan's group brought in 143 pencils and Marcelina's group added 78 more. How many pencils did the groups contribute altogether?

   A   184 pencils   **C**   221 pencils

   B   204 pencils   **D**   245 pencils

24. Reason Is 881 − 262 more or less than 500? Explain how you can tell using mental math.

25. Writing to Explain How can you use mental math to subtract 158 − 29?

26. An adult human body has a total of 206 bones. There are 300 bones in a child's body because some of a child's bones fuse together as a child grows. How many more bones are in a child's body than in an adult's body?

300		
206	4	90

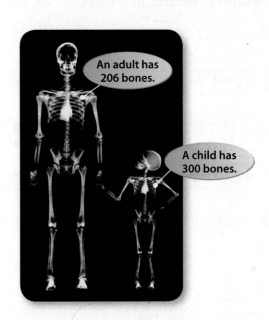

An adult has 206 bones.

A child has 300 bones.

27. Use Structure Write two numbers that have a 6 in the ones place and an 8 in the hundreds place.

Algebra Connections

Solving Number Sentences with Addition and Subtraction

A number sentence uses the equal sign (=) to show that two expressions have the same value.

Fill in the box or variable in each number sentence with the number that makes the number sentence true. Check your answers.

Example: $8 + \boxed{} = 35$

Think *What number plus 8 equals 35?*

When solving an addition number sentence, use subtraction to identify the missing number.

What is 35 minus 8?

Subtract 8 from 35.   Now, add 8 and 27.

$35 - 8 = 27$ $8 + 27 = 35$

Copy and complete each number sentence.

1. $7 + \boxed{} = 31$

2. $x + 6 = 21$

3. $26 - \boxed{} = 25$

4. $56 - \boxed{} = 38$

5. $\boxed{} - 47 = 12$

6. $66 + y = 85$

7. $\boxed{} - 98 = 1$

8. $103 - a = 72$

9. $10 + \boxed{} = 13$

10. $\boxed{} - 8 = 12$

11. $1 + \boxed{} = 7$

12. $744 - c = 327$

. . . .

ⓒ **Use Structure** For **13** through **16**, copy and complete the number sentence below each problem. Use it to help explain your answer.

13. Cheryl made 8 free-throw shots. She shot a total of 10 free-throw shots. How many free-throw shots did she miss?

$8 + \boxed{} = 10$

14. George delivered 118 newspapers in two days. He delivered 57 newspapers the first day. How many newspapers did George deliver the second day?

$57 + \boxed{} = 118$

15. 7 rabbits less than a certain number of rabbits is 13 rabbits. What is the missing number of rabbits, *r*?

$r - 7 = 13$

ⓒ **16. Be Precise** The cost of an apple is 39¢. Robert had 25¢ in his pocket. How much more money did Robert need to purchase the apple?

$25 + m = 39$

Lesson
4-2

Common
Core

4.NBT.3 Use place value
understanding to round
multi-digit whole numbers
to any place. Also 4.OA.3,
4.NBT.4

Estimating Sums and Differences of Whole Numbers

How can you estimate sums and differences of whole numbers?

The Empire State Building was completed in 1931. From ground to tip, it measures 1,250 feet. At the top of the building is a lightning rod which measures 204 feet. Estimate the total height of the structure.

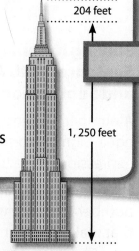

204 feet

1, 250 feet

Guided Practice*

MATHEMATICAL
PRACTICES

Do you know HOW?

In **1** through **6**, estimate each sum or difference.

1. $\begin{array}{r} 563 \rightarrow \boxed{}00 \\ + 375 \rightarrow \boxed{}00 \\ \hline \end{array}$

2. $\begin{array}{r} 288 \rightarrow \boxed{}0 \\ - 171 \rightarrow \boxed{}0 \\ \hline \end{array}$

3. 645 + 253

4. 262 − 132

5. 952 − 402

6. 398 + 121

Do you UNDERSTAND?

© **7. Writing to Explain** In the first example above, why can't you round both numbers to the nearest thousand?

8. The Statue of Liberty was completed in 1886. About how many years later was the Empire State Building completed than the Statue of Liberty?

Independent Practice

In **9** through **16**, estimate by rounding to the nearest ten.

9. $\begin{array}{r} 542 \\ + 27 \\ \hline \end{array}$

10. $\begin{array}{r} 281 \\ - 172 \\ \hline \end{array}$

11. $\begin{array}{r} 5,323 \\ - 2,611 \\ \hline \end{array}$

12. $\begin{array}{r} 6,324 \\ + 3,842 \\ \hline \end{array}$

13. 738 + 741

14. 895 − 305

15. 755 − 344

16. 586 + 278

In **17** through **24**, estimate by rounding to the nearest hundred.

17. $\begin{array}{r} 368 \\ + 137 \\ \hline \end{array}$

18. $\begin{array}{r} 918 \\ + 391 \\ \hline \end{array}$

19. $\begin{array}{r} 5,317 \\ + 1,734 \\ \hline \end{array}$

20. $\begin{array}{r} 778 \\ + 95 \\ \hline \end{array}$

21. 423 + 196

22. 891 + 223

23. 1,724 − 731

24. 551 − 249

For another example, see Set B on page 108.

Round each number to the nearest hundred.

The total height is about 1,500 feet.

$$
\begin{array}{r}
1{,}250 \longrightarrow 1{,}300 \\
+\ \ 204 \longrightarrow +\ \ 200 \\
\hline
1{,}500
\end{array}
$$

The answer is reasonable because the total height is greater than the height of the Empire State Building.

The Washington Monument was completed in 1884. About how many years after was the Empire State Building completed?

$$
\begin{array}{r}
1{,}931 \longrightarrow 1{,}930 \\
-\ 1{,}884 \longrightarrow -\ 1{,}880 \\
\hline
50
\end{array}
$$

Round each number to the nearest ten. Show rounding to subtract.

The Empire State Building was completed about 50 years later.

Problem Solving

MATHEMATICAL PRACTICES

25. Persevere Kala bought a board game for $24.75. She paid with a $20 bill and a $10 bill. What bills and coins did Kala get back in change?

26. Theo was born in the year 2004. One of his older sisters was born in 1992. Rounding to the nearest ten, about how many years younger is Theo?

27. This year, 35,658 people ran in a marathon. Last year, 8,683 fewer people ran. About how many people ran last year?

28. Reason During swimming practice, Juan swam 15 laps and Ted swam 9 laps. How many more laps did Juan swim than Ted?

29. The table below shows the number of students per grade. Estimate the total number of students in Grades 3, 4, and 5. About how many students are in Grades 4 and 5?

Grade	Number of Students
3	145
4	152
5	144
6	149

30. Use Structure Alex sold 86 tickets to a school talent show on Thursday and 103 tickets on Friday. About how many tickets to the talent show did Alex sell all together?

A About 100

B About 200

C About 300

D About 400

Lesson
4-3

Common
Core

4.NBT.4 Fluently add and
subtract multi-digit whole
numbers using the standard
algorithm.

Adding Whole Numbers

How do you add whole numbers?

A sports stadium with 24,595 seats is
increasing in size by 19,255 seats.
How many seats will there be in all?

New addition
19,255 seats

?

| 24,595 | 19,255 |

Original stadium
24,595 seats

Estimate: 25,000 + 19,000 = 44,000

Another Example How do you add more than two numbers?

Find the sum.
9,348 + 102 + 5,802 + 1,933

A 17,185   **C** 16,175

B 17,175   **D** 15,175

Estimate: 9,000 + 100 + 6,000 + 2,000 = 17,100

Step 1

Add the ones. Regroup
if necessary.

$$\begin{array}{r} \overset{1}{9{,}348} \\ 102 \\ 5{,}802 \\ + 1{,}933 \\ \hline 5 \end{array}$$

Step 2

Add the tens. Regroup
if necessary.

$$\begin{array}{r} \overset{1}{9{,}348} \\ 102 \\ 5{,}802 \\ + 1{,}933 \\ \hline 85 \end{array}$$

Step 3

Add the hundreds,
regroup, and then
add the thousands.

$$\begin{array}{r} \overset{2\ \ 1}{9{,}348} \\ 102 \\ 5{,}802 \\ + 1{,}933 \\ \hline 17{,}185 \end{array}$$

The correct answer is **A**.

Explain It

1. How are the ones regrouped in the example above?

© **2. Reasonableness** In Step 3 above, how can you tell
that the answer is reasonable?

Step 1

Add 24,595 + 19,255. Add the ones then the tens and then the hundreds. Regroup if necessary.

```
  1 1
 24,595
+  19,255
    850
```

Step 2

Add the thousands. Regroup if necessary.

```
  1   1 1
 24,595
+ 19,255
   3,850
```

Step 3

Add the ten thousands. Regroup if necessary.

```
  1   1 1
 24,595
+19,255
 43,850
```

The stadium will have 43,850 seats in all.

Other Examples

Adding larger numbers
Add 36,424 + 24,842.

Estimate:
36,000 + 25,000 = 61,000

```
  1 1
 36,424
+ 24,842
 61,266
```

The sum is reasonable because it is close to the estimate of 61,000.

Adding more than two numbers
Add 130,283 + 263,823 + 396,538.

Estimate:
130,000 + 264,000 + 397,000 = 791,000

```
 1 1 1 1 1
 130,283
 263,823
+ 396,538
 790,644
```

The sum is reasonable because it is close to the estimate of 791,000.

Guided Practice*

MATHEMATICAL PRACTICES

Do you know HOW?

In **1** through **6**, find each sum.

1. 821 + 4,543　　**2.** 14,926 + 3,832

3. 1,321 + 2,246　　**4.** 24,593 + 16,861

5.
```
   3,258
 + 1,761
```

6.
```
  16,018
 +   135
```

Do you UNDERSTAND?

7. Construct Arguments When adding 36,424 and 24,842 above, why is there no regrouping in the final step?

8. Volunteer teams identified 73 fish species, 30 corals, and 71 other invertebrates on the reef. How many species of fish, coral, and invertebrates were found in all?

In **9** through **24**, find each sum.

9.   78
  + 421

10.   617
  + 14,312

11.   873
  + 4,893

12. 38,911
  + 45,681

13.   327
  + 886

14.   295
  + 805

15. 3,751
  + 4,736

16.   623
  + 2,815

17. 4,231
  + 76,118

18.   265
  + 8,496

19. 9,634 + 2,958

20. 4,673 + 262

21. 7,845 + 509 + 3,746

22. 526 + 276 +1,086

23. 2,868 + 865

24. 15,891 + 527 + 1,086

Problem Solving

25. In 1972, the Apollo 16 lunar rover set the current lunar speed record at 11 miles per hour. In order to break free from Earth's orbit, Apollo missions had to go 24,989 miles per hour faster than the record speed of the lunar rover. How fast did the Apollo rockets travel?

© **26. Persevere** There were 10,453 items checked out of the public library one week. The next week, 12,975 items were checked out. A week later, 9,634 items were checked out. How many items were checked out in three weeks?

© **27. Model** Sandy read 235 pages of a book. She had 192 more pages to read before she was done. How many pages were there in the book?

?	
235	192

© **28. Model** Cheryl and Jason collect baseball cards. Cheryl has 315 cards, and Jason has 186 cards. How many cards do they have altogether?

?	
315	186

© **29. Reason** The sum of 86, 68, and 38 is 192. What do you also know about the sum of 68, 38, and 86?

© **30. Estimation** Maria added 45,273 and 35,687. Will her answer be greater or less than 80,000?

© **31. Persevere** The population of New City is 23,945. Eastdale has a population of 12,774. What is the total population of the two communities?

A 35,719   **B** 36,619   **C** 36,719   **D** 37,619

Find each sum. Estimate to check
if the answer is reasonable.

1.	4,572	2.	73,901	3.	3,468	4.	247
	+ 2,391		+ 5,799		+ 947		+ 312

5. 5,474 + 723   6. 47,090 + 2,910   7. 6,685 + 37

Find each sum or difference. Estimate to check
if the answer is reasonable.

8.	4,087	9.	8,354	10.	115	11.	6,000	12.	250
	+ 496		+ 2,568		− 76		+ 1,473		− 123

13. 399 − 88   14. 279 − 51   15. 832 − 801

Error Search Find each sum or difference that is not correct.
Write it correctly and explain the error.

16.	543	17.	6,043	18.	76,248	19.	394	20.	956
	+ 29		+ 972		+ 19,046		− 74		− 834
	562		7,025		95,294		320		122

Number Sense

MATHEMATICAL
PRACTICES

© **Reason** Write whether each statement is true or false.
Explain your answer.

21. The number 213,753 is ten thousand more than 223,753.

22. The sum of 6,823 and 1,339 is greater than 7,000
but less than 9,000.

23. The sum of 42,239 and 11,013 is less than 50,000.

24. The difference of 7,748 − 989 is greater than 7,000.

25. The sum of 596 + 325 is 4 less than 925.

26. The difference of 11,968 and 2,856 is closer
to 9,000 than 10,000.

Common
Core

4.NBT.4 Fluently add and
subtract multi-digit whole
numbers using the standard
algorithm.

Subtracting Whole Numbers

How do you subtract numbers?

Brenda has a total of 221 songs in her computer. Her sister, Susan, has a total of 186 songs in her computer. How many more songs does Brenda have in her computer than Susan?

Choose an Operation Subtract to find how many more songs.

221	
186	?

MATHEMATICAL
PRACTICES

Guided Practice*

Do you know HOW?

In **1** through **4**, subtract.

1.	527	2.	716
	− 338		− 254

3.	139	4.	1,268
	− 86		− 429

Do you UNDERSTAND?

ⓒ **5. Construct Arguments** In the example at the top, why was the 0 in the hundreds place not written in the answer?

6. Brenda would like to have 275 songs on her computer by next year. How many more songs does she need to download?

Independent Practice

In **7** through **26**, subtract.

7.	336	8.	693	9.	881	10.	479
	− 259		− 150		− 79		− 88

11.	1,931	12.	1,673	13.	2,173	14.	8,617
	− 509		− 849		− 108		− 3,909

15. 552 − 228   **16.** 3,711 − 1,683   **17.** 217 − 166   **18.** 562 − 199

19. 7,475 − 5,130   **20.** 5,831 − 1,156   **21.** 9,385 − 720   **22.** 1,111 − 589

23. 8,476 − 2,185   **24.** 6,251 − 964   **25.** 7,374 − 1,246   **26.** 8,327 − 3,796

Animated Glossary
www.pearsonsuccessnet.com

*For another example, see Set D on page 109.

Step 1	Step 2	Step 3

Step 1

Find 221 − 186.
Estimate: 220 − 190 = 30
Subtract the ones.

Regroup if necessary.

```
  1 11
  22̶1̶
− 186
─────
    5
```

Step 2

Subtract the tens.
Subtract the hundreds.

Regroup if necessary.

```
1 11 11
2̶ 2̶ 1̶
− 1 8 6
───────
    3 5
```

Step 3

Operations that undo each other are inverse operations. Addition and subtraction have an inverse relationship.

```
  1 1
  186      Add to check
+  35      your answer.
─────
  221
```

The answer checks.

Problem Solving

MATHEMATICAL PRACTICES

© 27. Reason A crayon company makes 17,491 green crayons and 15,063 red crayons. How many more green crayons are made than red crayons?

A 2,428   **C** 10,456

B 3,463   **D** 32,554

28. Angela hiked a trail that climbed 526 feet. Raul hiked a trail that climbed 319 feet. How many more feet did Angela climb than Raul?

526 feet

319	?

29. Jermaine and Linda collected aluminum cans for one month. Look at the chart below to see how many aluminum cans each student collected.

a Who collected more cans?

b Find the difference between the number of cans collected.

Data		
Jermaine	1,353 cans
Linda	1,328 cans

© 30. Persevere Mount Kilimanjaro is a mountain in Africa. A group of mountain climbers begin their descent from the peak. On Monday, the mountain climbers descended 3,499 feet. On Tuesday, they descended another 5,262 feet. How many feet have the mountain climbers descended?

Mount Kilimanjaro is 19,341 feet high.

© 31. Model Mike's team scored 63 points in the first half of a basketball game. His team won the game by a score of 124 to103. How many points did his team score in the second half?

Lesson
4-5

Common
Core

4.NBT.4 Fluently add and
subtract multi-digit whole
numbers using the standard
algorithm.

Subtracting Across Zeros

How do you subtract across zeros?

An airplane flight to Chicago has seats for 300 passengers. The airline sold 278 tickets for the flight. How many seats are still available for the flight?

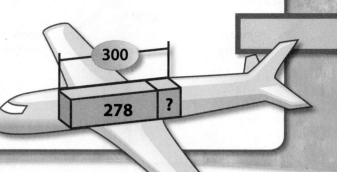

300

278   ?

Guided Practice*

MATHEMATICAL
PRACTICES

Do you know HOW?

In **1** through **6**, subtract.

1. 600
    − 177

2. 1,086
    − 728

3. 810 − 638

4. 3,304 − 1,137

5. 1,001 − 868

6. 4,000 − 1,698

Do you UNDERSTAND?

ⓒ **7. Use Structure** How would you check if the answer in the example above is correct?

8. One passenger flew from New York to Phoenix. The flight was 2,145 miles. Another passenger flew from Boston to Seattle. The flight was 2,496 miles. How many more miles was the flight to Seattle?

Independent Practice

In **9** through **28**, subtract.

9.   902
    − 883

10.   502
    − 380

11. 3,000
    − 673

12.   5,604
    − 1,717

13. 1,830
    − 722

14.   7,006
    − 3,529

15. 1,902
    − 903

16.   6,008
    − 4,879

17. 450 − 313

18. 5,025 − 178

19. 406 − 381

20. 1,001 − 35

21. 6,090 − 5,130

22. 2,700 − 1,699

23. 10,807 − 4,373

24. 504 − 319

25. 3,000 − 1,047

26. 5,001 − 368

27. 700 − 520

28. 900 − 406

For another example, see Set E on page 109.

One Way

Find 300 − 278.

Estimate: 300 − 280 = 20

Regroup hundreds to tens and tens to ones.

$$\begin{array}{r} \overset{9}{\cancel{2}\,\overset{10}{\cancel{10}}\,\overset{10}{\cancel{}}} \\ \cancel{3}\,\cancel{0}\,\cancel{0} \\ -\ 2\ 7\ 8 \\ \hline 2\ 2 \end{array}$$

3 hundreds =
2 hundreds + 9 tens +
10 ones

There are 22 seats available for the flight.

Another Way

Find 300 − 278.

Estimate: 300 − 280 = 20

Think of 300 as 30 tens and 0 ones.

$$\begin{array}{r} \overset{29}{}\ \overset{10}{} \\ \cancel{3}\,\cancel{0}\,\cancel{0} \\ -\ 2\ 7\ 8 \\ \hline 2\ 2 \end{array}$$

30 tens + 0 ones =
29 tens + 10 ones

There are 22 seats available for the flight.

Problem Solving

MATHEMATICAL PRACTICES

29. Shawn scored 10,830 points playing a video game. Miguel scored 9,645 points. How many more points did Shawn score than Miguel?

Ⓒ 30. Writing to Explain Will the difference between 4,041 and 3,876 be greater or less than 1,000? Explain your answer.

Ⓒ 31. Persevere Use the chart on the right. Music City sells CDs. Which of the following tells how many more Hip Hop CDs were sold than Latin CDs in April?

A 887   **C** 7,090

B 897   **D** 13,293

CDs Sold in April	
Music style	CDs sold in April
Rock	4,008
Hip Hop	7,090
Country	5,063
Latin	6,203

Data

Ⓒ 32. Model William drove from Atlanta, Georgia, to Portland, Oregon. The round trip was 5,601 miles. He traveled 2,603 miles to get to Portland, Oregon, but he decided to take a different route back. How many miles did he travel to get back to Atlanta?

33. On Thursday, 10,296 people attended a college basketball home game. The following week, 12,000 people attended an away game. How many more people attended the away game than the home game?

12,000 people in all

10,296	?

Ⓒ 34. Reason In a dart game, Casey scored 42 points, and Maggie scored 28 points. Jesse scored fewer points than Casey but more points than Maggie. Which is a possible score for Jesse?

A 50 points   **C** 34 points

B 46 points   **D** 26 points

Lesson
4-6

Common Core

4.NBT.4 Fluently add and subtract multi-digit whole numbers using the standard algorithm. Also 4.OA.3

Problem Solving

Draw a Picture and Write an Equation

The mass of a human brain is how much greater than the mass of a chimpanzee brain?

Average Masses of Brains	
House cat	30 grams
Chimpanzee	420 grams
Human	1,350 grams
Dolphin	1,500 grams

The human brain has a mass of 1,350 grams.

Guided Practice*

MATHEMATICAL PRACTICES

Do you know HOW?

Solve. Draw a picture to help you.

1. Sandy earned $36 from babysitting and $15 for doing her chores. Write an equation and find the total amount, t, that Sandy earned.

t	
$36	$15

Do you UNDERSTAND?

© 2. **Reasonableness** How can you show that 930 grams is a reasonable answer for the question asked above?

© 3. **Write a Problem** Write a problem using the table at the top.

Independent Practice

MATHEMATICAL PRACTICES

Solve. Draw a picture to help you.

4. Four cities are on the same road that runs east to west. Fleming is west of Bridgewater, but east of Clinton. Union is between Fleming and Bridgewater. It is 21 miles from Fleming to Union. It is 55 miles from Clinton to Union. How far is it from Clinton to Fleming?

5. Scott and his friends walk to school together. Scott leaves his home at 7:00 A.M. He meets Johnny and Zach at the end of the block. Next, they meet Paul, Tim, and Pete. Dan and Torey join them one block before the school. How many friends walk to school all together?

Applying Math Practices

- What am I asked to find?
- What else can I try?
- How are quantities related?
- How can I explain my work?
- How can I use math to model the problem?
- Can I use tools to help?
- Is my work precise?
- Why does this work?
- How can I generalize?

For another example, see Set F on page 109.

What do I know? The average mass of a chimpanzee brain is 420 grams. The average mass of a human brain is 1,350 grams.

What am I asked to find? The difference between the masses

Draw a picture.

1,350 grams	
420 grams	?

Write an equation. Use subtraction to solve.

$1,350 - 420 = \blacksquare$

The human brain has a mass that is 930 grams more than the chimpanzee brain.

ⓒ **6. Model** The American Kennel Club recognizes 17 breeds of herding dogs and 26 breeds of terriers. Draw a picture that could help find the total number of herding dogs and terriers.

ⓒ **7. Model** Using the information in Exercise 6, write an equation to find how many more breeds of terriers than herding dogs there are.

For **8** through **10**, use the table to the right.

8. There are about 200 more animals in the Minnesota Zoo than in the Phoenix Zoo. About how many animals are in the Minnesota Zoo?

9. About how many more animals are in the Indianapolis Zoo than the Phoenix Zoo?

10. How can you find the number of animals at the San Francisco Zoo?

Data

Name of Zoo	Approximate Number of Animals
Phoenix	200
Minnesota	
San Francisco	
Indianapolis	360
Total Animals	1,210

ⓒ **11. Persevere** A parking lot had a total of 243 cars in one day. By 6:00 A.M., there were 67 cars in the lot. In the next hour, 13 more cars joined these. How many more cars, *c*, would come to the lot by the end of the day?

243 cars in all

67	13	c

ⓒ **12. Use Tools** A shoe store sold 162 pairs of shoes. The goal was to sell 345 pairs. How many more pairs of shoes, *p*, did they need to sell to make their goal?

345 pairs of shoes

162	p

For **13** and **14**, use the table at the right.

© **13. Model** What equation can you write to help find the cost of the shoes and socks together?

© **14. Model** What equation can you write to help find the difference between the cost of the shirt and the shorts?

Cost of Gym Clothes	
Shirt	$12
Shorts	$19
Shoes	$42
Socks	$2
Hat	$15

15. Byron spent $7.75 on popcorn and a drink at the movie theater. The popcorn was $4.25. How much was the cost of the drink, d?

$7.75 in all	
$4.25	d

16. Each school day, Mikaela sold the same number of tickets to the school play. On Monday, she sold 4 tickets. How many tickets, t, did she sell all together in 5 days?

t				
4	4	4	4	4

↑
tickets sold
on one day

© **17. Writing to Explain** Ken makes 2 nametags in the time it takes Mary to make 5 nametags. When Mary has made 15 nametags, how many has Ken made?

18. Mr. Lee had 62 pencils at the beginning of the school year. At the end of the school year, he had 8 pencils left. How many pencils, g, were given out during the year?

62 pencils in all	
8	g

© **Think About the Structure**

19. Carlene bought a book for $13.58. She paid with a $10 bill and a $5 bill. Which expression would find the amount of change Carlene would receive?

A $15 − $13.58   **C** $10 + $5

B $15 − $1.42   **D** $13.58 + $1.42

20. Terrence rode 15 rides before lunch at the county fair. He rode 13 rides after lunch. Each ride requires 3 tickets. Which expression represents the number of rides he rode during the day?

A 15 − 13   **C** 15 − 3

B 15 + 13   **D** 13 − 3

Subtracting Money Using Place-Value Blocks

Use tools Place-Value Blocks to subtract 82¢ − 57¢.

Step 1 Go to the Place-Value Blocks eTool.
Select a two-part workspace.

Step 2 Using the arrow tool, select a flat place-value block, and click in the top workspace to display one flat.

In the Select Unit Block drop-down menu, select Flat to let this block represent one dollar.

$1 = 100¢

Use the hammer tool to break it into parts. Notice each strip is part of a flat.

Step 3 Select and break one of the strips. Notice that there are 10 small blocks in a strip and 100 small blocks in a flat.

Step 4 Show 82¢ with the place-value blocks. Use the erase tool to erase any blocks you don't need.

Step 5 Use the hammer tool to break one tens strip into 10 ones. Use the arrow tool to subtract 57¢ by taking away 7 ones and then 5 tens. Move them to the lower workspace. Look at the blocks that are left to find the difference.
82¢ − 57¢ = 25¢.

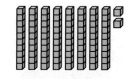

Practice

© **Use Tools** Solve.

1. 64¢ − 14¢   **2.** 27¢ − 13¢   **3.** 89¢ − 72¢   **4.** 93¢ − 27¢

5. 86¢ − 71¢   **6.** 38¢ − 19¢   **7.** 11¢ − 8¢   **8.** 35¢ − 21¢

9. 56¢ − 19¢   **10.** 74¢ − 49¢   **11.** 71¢ − 58¢   **12.** 85¢ − 38¢

Reteaching

Set A, pages 90–92

Add 155 + 83. Use mental math.

Use the breaking apart method.
Adding 5 to 155 is easy.

Break apart 83 into 5 and 78.

155 + 5 = 160

160 + 78 = 238

So, 155 + 83 = 238.

Remember that when you use compensation, you must adjust the sum or difference.

1. 53 + 88   **2.** 372 + 226

3. 5,342 + 1,826   **4.** 283 − 169

5. 676 − 521   **6.** 1,089 − 961

Set B, pages 94–95

Estimate   1,579
            +   1,248

Round each number to the nearest hundred.

1,579 rounds to 1,600.

1,248 rounds to 1,200.

Add   1,600
        + 1,200
           2,800

Remember you can round numbers to the nearest hundred or thousand when estimating sums and differences.

1. 473 + 465   **2.** 8,352 − 3,421

3. 586 − 483   **4.** 4,094 + 246

5. 1,440 − 933   **6.** 748 − 392

7. 981 + 193   **8.** 725 + 635

Set C, pages 96–98

Add 359 + 723.

Estimate: 400 + 700 = 1,100

Add the ones. Regroup if necessary.	Add the tens. Regroup if necessary.	Add the hundreds.
¹ 359 + 723 2	¹ 359 + 723 82	¹ 359 + 723 1,082

The answer is reasonable.

Remember to regroup if necessary when adding whole numbers.

1. 215 + 8,823   **2.** 14,296 + 444

3. 2,417 + 3,573   **4.** 572 + 941

5.   32,834   **6.**   14,382
       + 17,384   + 9,243

Find 831 − 796.

Estimate: 830 − 800 = 30

Subtract the ones. Regroup if necessary.	Subtract the tens. Subtract the hundreds.	Add to check your answer.
$\begin{array}{r} {}^{2\,11} \\ 8\,\cancel{3}\,\cancel{1} \\ -\ 7\,9\,6 \\ \hline 5 \end{array}$	$\begin{array}{r} {}^{7\ 12\,11} \\ \cancel{8}\,\cancel{3}\,\cancel{1} \\ -\ 7\,9\,6 \\ \hline 3\,5 \end{array}$	$\begin{array}{r} {}^{1\ 1} \\ 7\,9\,6 \\ +\ \ \ 3\,5 \\ \hline 8\,3\,1 \end{array}$

The answer is reasonable.

Remember you may need to regroup before you subtract.

1. 415 − 323   **2.** 4,978 − 2,766

3. 735 − 255   **4.** 4,558 − 2,613

5.   18,465   **6.**   651
    − 6,291   − 482

Find 609 − 547.

Estimate: 600 − 500 = 100

Subtract the ones. Regroup if necessary.	Subtract the tens. Subtract the hundreds.	Add to check your answer.
$\begin{array}{r} 6\,0\,9 \\ -\ 5\,4\,7 \\ \hline 2 \end{array}$	$\begin{array}{r} {}^{5\ 10} \\ \cancel{6}\,\cancel{0}\,9 \\ -\ 5\,4\,7 \\ \hline 6\,2 \end{array}$	$\begin{array}{r} {}^{1} \\ 5\,4\,7 \\ +\ \ \ 6\,2 \\ \hline 6\,0\,9 \end{array}$

The answer is reasonable.

Remember you can think of 100 as 10 tens or as 9 tens + 10 ones.

1. 400 − 256   **2.** 5,060 − 3,125

3. 805 − 125   **4.** 2,008 − 1,605

5.   20,305   **6.**   407
    − 5,213   − 239

Cathy spent $8 on lunch. She bought a sandwich, a fruit cup, and a milk at the snack bar. She spent a total of $6 on the sandwich and milk. How much did the fruit cup cost?

What do I know?
Cathy had $8. Cathy bought a sandwich, a milk, and a fruit cup. Cathy spent $6 on the sandwich and the milk.

What am I being asked to find?
The amount of money Cathy spent on the fruit cup

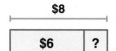

$8 − $6 = $2

Cathy spent $2 on the fruit cup.

Remember to draw a picture to help you solve a problem.

Draw a picture and write an equation to solve.

1. Doug saw 5 Agile wallabies and 9 Rock wallabies at the zoo. How many wallabies did Doug see?

2. Luz had collected 393 tokens from the games at Funland. To win a large stuffed animal, 500 tokens were needed. How many more tokens does Luz need to win the large stuffed animal?

1. Joe got 34,867 points playing a video game, and Carlos got 29,978 points. How many more points did Joe get than Carlos? (4-4)

A 14,889

B 4,999

C 4,989

D 4,889

2. The table shows tickets sold to the school play.

Tickets Sold	
Thursday	320
Friday	282
Saturday	375

Data

Which is the best estimate of the total tickets sold? (4-2)

A 1,100

B 1,000

C 900

D 800

3. David went to a sporting goods store with $400 and bought a set of golf clubs for $239 including the tax. How much money did David have left after his purchase? (4-5)

A $160

B $161

C $260

D $261

4. Manuel has 60 minutes to get to karate class. If it takes him 27 minutes to ride his bike to class and 10 minutes to change into his karate uniform, how much time does he have before he must leave his house? (4-6)

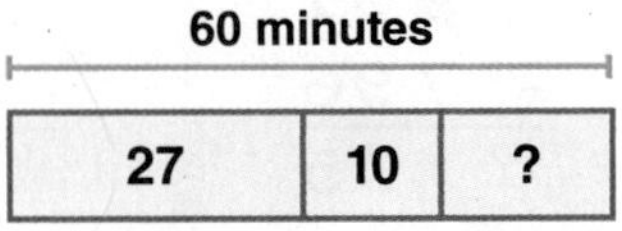

60 minutes		
27	10	?

A 20 minutes

B 21 minutes

C 23 minutes

D 97 minutes

5. To advertise for the school fun fair, 325 flyers were printed on Wednesday, 468 flyers were printed on Thursday, and 815 flyers were printed on Friday. How many flyers were printed in all? (4-3)

A 1,620

B 1,608

C 1,508

D 1,600

6. Garrett drove 239 miles on Saturday and 149 miles on Sunday. To find 239 + 149, Garrett made a multiple of ten, as shown below. What is the missing number? (4-1)

$239 + 149 = 240 + \boxed{} = 388$

A 129

B 130

C 147

D 148

7. A musical group made 8,000 copies of a CD. So far, they have sold 6,280 copies. How many copies are left? (4-5)

8. In April, 5,326 books were checked out of the library. In May, 3,294 books were checked out. How many books were checked out in all? (4-3)

9. What number makes the number sentence true? (4-1)

$$28 + 79 = \boxed{} + 28$$

10. Betty had 719 pennies in her piggy bank. If she gave her sister 239 pennies, how many pennies did Betty have left? (4-4)

11. The last total solar eclipse seen in Dallas, Texas was in 1623. The next one will not be seen until 2024. Write a number sentence that uses rounding to the tens place to estimate the number of years between the eclipses. (4-2)

12. Daria's book has 323 pages. She has read 141 pages. Use the diagram below to find the number of pages, p, she has left to read. (4-6)

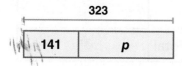

13. Find 5,000 − 2,898. (4-5)

14. Joe and Sara recorded the number of birds they saw in the park over the summer. How many more birds did they see in 2010 than 2011? (4-4)

Data	Birds	
	Summer 2010	458
	Summer 2011	397

15. In 2010, an animal shelter found adoption homes for 1,645 cats and dogs. If 1,218 of the adopted pets were dogs, how many cats, c, were adopted in 2010? (4-6)

1,645 cats and dogs

1,218	c

16. The average home attendance at a team's baseball games was 17,435. In a larger city, the average number was 46,491. Round to the nearest ten thousand. About how many more people attended games in the larger city? (4-2)

17. Toby and Quinn collected canned food for a food drive. Toby collected 38 cans and Quinn collected 44. How many cans did Toby and Quinn collect in all? Explain how you can use mental math to find the answer. (4-1)

A summer camp needs help planning transportation routes so that 25 campers have rides to camp every day. Van A, Van B, Van C, and Van D can each hold 5 campers. The minibus can hold 8 campers. The map below shows how many campers are in each town.

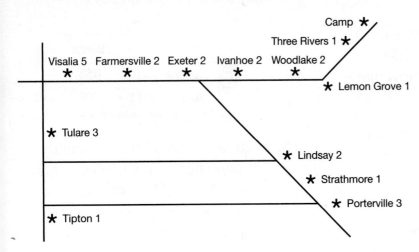

1. Plan a route for each vehicle.

2. Copy and complete the table below on a separate sheet of paper. Remember that all 25 campers need rides to camp. To fill in information about a vehicle, find the row for that vehicle. Then move across to the correct column and write down that information. The total seats column is done for you.

Vehicle Name	Total Seats	Unoccupied Seats	Occupied Seats
Van A	5		
Van B	5		
Van C	5		
Van D	5		
Minibus	8		
		Total	

3. Explain how you chose your routes.

4. The camp wants to replace the minibus with another van. Is it possible to pick up all the campers with 5 vans and no minibus? How would the routes change if you replaced the minibus with Van E, which also holds 5 campers?

Number Sense: Multiplying by 1-Digit Numbers

Topic **5**

▼ How many passengers can fit in 7 cabins on the London Eye Ferris Wheel? You will find out in Lesson 5-4.

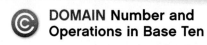

Review What You Know!

Vocabulary

Choose the best term from the box.

- multiples
- arrays
- factor
- product

1. When you multiply numbers, you find the _?_.

2. In the number sentence 8 × 6 = 48, 8 is a _?_ .

3. The numbers 5, 10, 15, and 20 are all _?_ of 5.

Multiplication Facts

Find each product.

4. 3 × 4   **5.** 7 × 3

6. 6 × 5   **7.** 2 × 8

8. 4 × 6   **9.** 9 × 5

10. 7 × 7   **11.** 8 × 9

Rounding

Round each number to the nearest ten.

12. 16   **13.** 82   **14.** 35

15. 53   **16.** 24   **17.** 49

18. 78   **19.** 73   **20.** 97

Round each number to the nearest hundred.

21. 868   **22.** 499   **23.** 625

24. 167   **25.** 341   **26.** 772

27. 919   **28.** 552   **29.** 809

30. Writing to Explain Explain how to round 745 to the hundreds place.

Topic Essential Questions
- How can some products be found mentally?
- How can products be estimated?

Interactive Learning

Pose the problem. Start each lesson by working together to solve problems. It will help you make sense of math.

Applying Math Practices

- What am I asked to find?
- What else can I try?
- How are quantities related?
- How can I explain my work?
- How can I use math to model the problem?
- Can I use tools to help?
- Is my work precise?
- Why does this work?
- How can I generalize?

Lesson 5-1

Ⓒ **Use Tools** Solve. Use place-value blocks or grid paper to help.

One section of bleachers in a tennis stadium holds 100 people. There are 6 sections like this in the stadium. How many seats are there all together?

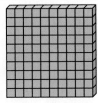

Lesson 5-2

Ⓒ **Use Structure** Find the products shown at the right using any method.

How did you find each product? Describe any patterns you observed.

$$\underline{3} \times \underline{4} = \underline{}$$

$$\underline{3} \times \underline{40} = \underline{}$$

$$\underline{3} \times \underline{400} = \underline{}$$

Lesson 5-3

© **Use Tools** Solve any way you choose. Use place-value blocks to help.

A parking lot has 4 rows with 23 spaces in each row. How many parking spaces are in the lot?

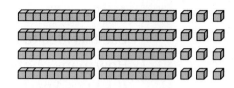

Lesson 5-4

© **Use Structure** Solve using mental math.

Suppose you ride your bicycle 27 miles each week. How many miles can you ride in 3 weeks? Explain how you found the product mentally.

Lesson 5-5

© **Use Structure** Solve. You only need an estimate.

Sarah earns $48 a week babysitting. She has saved all of her money for the past 6 weeks. About how much money has she saved? Explain how you found an estimate.

Lesson 5-6

© **Reasonableness** Solve any way you choose. Show all of your work.

Justin needs to buy 4 CDs that cost $11 each. He also wants to buy some notebooks that cost $4 each. Justin has $60 to spend. What is the greatest number of notebooks he can buy? Tell how you know your answer is reasonable.

Lesson
5-1

© Common Core

4.NBT.5 Multiply a whole number of up to four digits by a one-digit whole number, and multiply two two-digit numbers, using strategies based on place value and the properties of operations. Illustrate and explain the calculation by using equations, rectangular arrays, and/or area models.

Arrays and Multiplying by 10 and 100

10 buttons in each pack

How can you multiply by 10 and 100?

Addition and multiplication are related.

4×5 can be written as $5 + 5 + 5 + 5$.

Use this idea to multiply by 10 and 100.

How many photo buttons can Dara make if she buys 4 packs of 10 buttons?

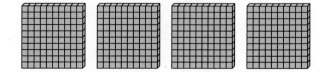

Guided Practice*

© MATHEMATICAL PRACTICES

Do you know HOW?

In **1** and **2**, find each product.

1. 5×10

2. 1×100

Do you UNDERSTAND?

© **3. Model** Which product is greater: 4×10 or 4×100? Draw a picture to show how you know.

4. How many photo buttons could Dara make if she bought five packs of 100 buttons?

Independent Practice

Leveled Practice For **5** through **8**, find each product.

5. 6×10

6. 3×100

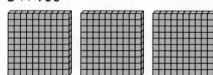

7. 2×10

8. 4×100

Find 4 × 10.

4 × 10 = 10 + 10 + 10 + 10

= 40

4 × 10 = 40

Dara can make 40 photo buttons.

Dara found a website that sells packs of 100 buttons. How many buttons will she have if she buys two packs of 100 buttons?

Find 2 × 100.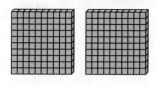

2 × 100 = 100 + 100

= 200

2 × 100 = 200

Dara will have 200 buttons.

For **9** through **12**, draw an array and find each product.

9. 9 × 10

10. 7 × 100

11. 8 × 10

12. 6 × 100

Problem Solving

MATHEMATICAL PRACTICES

Ⓒ **13. Look for Patterns** Give three whole number values for ▨ to solve the equation below.

▨ × 10 = ▨0

14. Cheryl has earned $37 babysitting. She needs $65 to buy a skateboard. How much more money does Cheryl need to earn?

Ⓒ **15. Construct Arguments** Miki has 6 bags of balloons with 8 balloons in each bag. Karen has 4 bags of balloons with 10 balloons in each bag. Who has more balloons? Explain how you know.

16. Luis has 4 rolls of pennies. There are 100 pennies in each roll. How many pennies does Luis have?

A 40

B 104

C 400

D 4,100

17. A sabal palm leaf can be up to 12 feet long and up to 6 feet wide. How many times as long can the leaf be as it is wide?

18. Jim is counting the number of sabal palms in his neighborhood. There are six neighbors who have 10 palms each and one neighbor with 7 palms. How many total palms are in Jim's neighborhood?

The sabal palm leaf can be up to 12 feet long.

Common Core

4.NBT.5 Multiply a whole number of up to four digits by a one-digit whole number, and multiply two two-digit numbers, using strategies based on place value and the properties of operations. Illustrate and explain the calculation by using equations, rectangular arrays, and/or area models.

Multiplying by Multiples of 10 and 100

What is the rule when you multiply by multiples of 10 and 100?

You can use basic multiplication facts to multiply by multiples of 10 and 100. Find 3×50.

150 in all

Guided Practice*

MATHEMATICAL PRACTICES

Do you know HOW?

In **1** through **6**, use basic facts to help you multiply.

1. 7×70

2. 2×700

3. 3×20

4. 9×800

5. 7×50

6. 8×500

Do you UNDERSTAND?

7. How many zeros will be in the product for 5×200? Explain how you know.

8. **Critique Reasoning** Peter said the product of 4×500 is 2,000. Bob said it is 200. Who is correct?

Independent Practice

Leveled Practice In **9** through **32**, find each product.

9. $3 \times 7 =$ ▨

$3 \times 70 =$ ▨

$3 \times 700 =$ ▨

10. $6 \times 4 =$ ▨

$6 \times 40 =$ ▨

$6 \times 400 =$ ▨

11. $8 \times 5 =$ ▨

$8 \times 50 =$ ▨

$8 \times 500 =$ ▨

12. $2 \times 8 =$ ▨

$2 \times 80 =$ ▨

$2 \times 800 =$ ▨

13. 4×20

14. 7×40

15. 70×2

16. 8×60

17. 3×40

18. 5×500

19. 3×600

20. 9×700

21. 600×6

22. 300×9

23. 5×40

24. 200×6

25. 9×50

26. 900×4

27. 80×3

28. 8×70

29. 2×90

30. 300×4

31. 7×600

32. 800×5

For another example, see Set B on page 130.

Find 3 × 50.

Multiply by the digit in the tens place.

Multiply:
3 × 5 = 15

Write one zero after 15.

3 × 5<u>0</u> = 15<u>0</u>
So, 3 × 50 = 150.

Find 3 × 500.

Multiply by the digit in the hundreds place.

Multiply:
3 × 5 = 15

Write two zeros after 15.

3 × 5<u>00</u> = 1,5<u>00</u>
So, 3 × 500 = 1,500.

When the product of a basic fact ends in zero, the answer will have an extra zero.

6 × 5 = 30

6 × 50 = 300

6 × 500 = 3,000

Problem Solving

In **33** and **34**, use the table to the right.

33. Tina visited Funland with her mom and a friend. They chose Plan C. How much did they save on the two children's tickets by buying combined tickets instead of buying separate tickets?

Funland Ticket Prices		
Plans	Adult	Child
Plan A Waterpark	$30	$20
Plan B Amusement Park	$40	$30
Plan C Combined A + B	$60	$40

34. Aimee's scout troop has 8 girls and 4 adults. How much did the troop pay for tickets to the amusement park?

35. **Science** A fourth grader breathes about 90 gallons of air per hour. Shana, a fourth grader, arrives at school at 8:00 A.M. and leaves at 3:00 P.M. How many gallons of air does she breathe at school?

© **36.** **Reason** Without calculating the answer, tell which has the greater product, 4 × 80 or 8 × 400. Explain how you know.

37. Last year, the fourth graders at Summit School collected 500 cans of food for the food drive. This year's fourth graders want to collect two times as many cans. How many cans do this year's fourth graders hope to collect?

A 250 cans C 1,000 cans

B 500 cans D 10,000 cans

© **38.** **Model** Ted, Jason, and Angelina are trying to raise 200 dollars for a local shelter. Ted raised 30 dollars. Jason raised 90 dollars. How much money does Angelina need to raise in order to reach their goal?

$200	
$30	$90

*For another ex

© Common Core

4.NBT.5 Multiply a whole number of up to four digits by a one-digit whole number, and multiply two two-digit numbers, using strategies based on place value and the properties of operations. Illustrate and explain the calculation by using equations, rectangular arrays, and/or area models.

Breaking Apart to Multiply

Hands-On place-value blocks

How can you use breaking apart to multiply with greater numbers?

A parking lot has the same number of spaces in each row. How many spaces are in the lot?

Choose an Operation Multiply to find the total for an array.

24 parking spaces in each row

4 rows

Other Example

Find 3×145.
Break apart 145 into 100, 40, and 5.

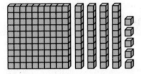 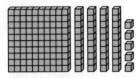 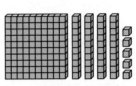

$$3 \times 145 = (3 \times 100) + (3 \times 40) + (3 \times 5)$$
$$= 300 + 120 + 15 \quad \text{Add the partial products.}$$
$$= 435$$

So, $3 \times 145 = 435$.

Guided Practice*

MATHEMATICAL PRACTICES

Do you know HOW?

In **1** and **2**, copy and complete. You may use place-value blocks or drawings to help.

1. 4×36
$$4 \times 30 = \blacksquare$$
$$4 \times 6 = \blacksquare$$
$$\blacksquare + \blacksquare = \blacksquare$$

2. 5×127
$$5 \times 100 = \blacksquare$$
$$5 \times 20 = \blacksquare$$
$$5 \times 7 = \blacksquare$$
$$\blacksquare + \blacksquare + \blacksquare = \blacksquare$$

Do you UNDERSTAND?

3. In the parking lot example above, what two groups is the array broken into?

4. The buses at a bus garage are parked in 4 equal rows. There are 29 buses in each row. How many buses are parked at the garage?

© **5.** **Use Structure** Why can you break apart numbers to multiply without changing the product?

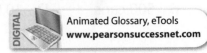
DIGITAL Animated Glossary, eTools
www.pearsonsuccessnet.com

...ample, see Set C on page 130.

Use an array to show 4 × 24.

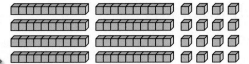

Break apart 24 into 20 and 4.

Think of 4 × 24 as

(4 × 20) + (4 × 4).

| |
80   16

Add each part to find the total.

80 + 16 = 96

80 and 16 are called partial products because they are parts of the product.

4 × 24 = 96

There are 96 spaces in the parking lot.

Independent Practice

In **6** through **15**, find each product. You may use place-value blocks or drawings to help.

6. 3 × 19   **7.** 4 × 131   **8.** 6 × 23   **9.** 5 × 325   **10.** 2 × 254

11. 3 × 49   **12.** 6 × 27   **13.** 5 × 143   **14.** 7 × 35   **15.** 4 × 462

Problem Solving

 MATHEMATICAL PRACTICES

16. Mia is buying two chairs that cost $46 each. The tax on each chair is $5. What is the total cost?

17. Reason Walt wants to buy shelves that cost $168 each. If he has $500, can he buy three shelves? Explain.

18. Use Structure Helen walked 5 miles every day for 37 days. Show breaking apart to find how many miles Helen walked in all.

19. Class A checks out 15 books from the school library each week. Class B checks out 8 fewer books than Class A each week. How many books do both Class A and Class B check out in 6 weeks?

20. **Science** The longest blue whale on record was about 18 scuba divers in length. Use breaking apart to estimate the length of the blue whale.

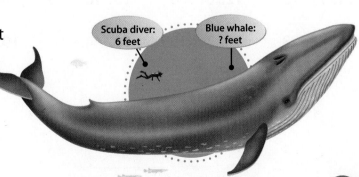

Scuba diver: 6 feet

Blue whale: ? feet

© Common Core

4.NBT.5 Multiply a whole number of up to four digits by a one-digit whole number, and multiply two two-digit numbers, using strategies based on place value and the properties of operations. Illustrate and explain the calculation by using equations, rectangular arrays, and/or area models. Also **4.NBT.3, 4.OA.3**

Using Mental Math to Multiply

What are some ways to multiply mentally?

Evan rode his bicycle for 18 miles each day for 3 days. How many miles did he ride his bicycle in all?

Find 3 × 18 mentally.

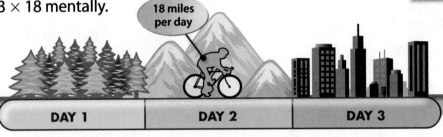

18 miles per day

DAY 1   DAY 2   DAY 3

 MATHEMATICAL PRACTICES

Guided Practice*

Do you know HOW?

In **1** through **4**, use compensation to find each product mentally.

1. 33 × 4   2. 9 × 83

3. 6 × 104   4. 2 × 394

Do you UNDERSTAND?

© 5. **Be Precise** Why were three groups of two subtracted instead of added in the example above?

6. Explain how to use mental math to multiply 4 × 56.

Independent Practice

Leveled Practice In **7** through **20**, use compensation to find each product.

7. 5 × 17   Substitute: 5 × ▢ = 100   Adjust: ▢ − 15 = ▢

8. 3 × 295   Substitute: 3 × ▢ = 900   Adjust: ▢ − 15 = ▢

9. 7 × 29   Substitute: 7 × ▢ = 210   Adjust: 210 − ▢ = ▢

10. 5 × 102   Substitute: 5 × ▢ = 500   Adjust: 500 + ▢ = ▢

11. 7 × 28   12. 61 × 8   13. 106 × 5   14. 64 × 3   15. 2 × 599

16. 4 × 23   17. 3 × 195   18. 44 × 6   19. 5 × 109   20. 9 × 52

DIGITAL   Animated Glossary
www.pearsonsuccessnet.com

*For another example, see Set D on page 131.

Use compensation to find 3 × 18.

Substitute a number for 18 that is easy to multiply.

3 × 18
↓
3 × 20 = 60

Now adjust. Subtract 3 groups of 2.
60 − 6 = 54   So, 3 × 18 = 54.

Evan rode his bicycle 54 miles in all.

With **compensation** you choose numbers close to the numbers in the problem to make the computation easier and then adjust the answer for the numbers chosen.

Evan rode his bicycle 405 miles each month for 3 months. How many miles did he ride in all?

Substitute a number for 405 that is easy to multiply.

3 × 405
↓
3 × 400 = 1,200

Now adjust. Add 3 groups of 5.

1,200 + 15 = 1,215   So, 3 × 405 = 1,215.

Evan rode his bicycle 1,215 miles in all.

Problem Solving

MATHEMATICAL PRACTICES

For **21** and **22**, use the table to the right.

© **21. Use Structure** To raise money, the high school band members sold items shown in the table. Use mental math to find how much money the band raised in all.

Item	Cost	Number Sold
Caps	$9	36
Mugs	$7	44
Pennants	$8	52

Data

© **22. Reason** How much more do 9 caps cost than 9 pennants?

© **23. Model** Ashley and 3 friends bought tickets to a musical. The cost of each ticket was 43 dollars. How much did the tickets cost in all? Explain how you found the answer.

? Total Cost

$43	$43	$43	$43

↑
Cost per person

24. A store clerk is stacking soup cans on shelves. If he puts 110 cans on each shelf, how many cans will be on 4 shelves?

A 106   **C** 444

B 440   **D** 510

25. Using the picture at the right, how many passengers can 7 cabins hold on the London Eye Ferris Wheel?

Each cabin can hold up to 25 people.

4.NBT.5 Multiply a whole number of up to four digits by a one-digit whole number, and multiply two two-digit numbers, using strategies based on place value and the properties of operations. Illustrate and explain the calculation by using equations, rectangular arrays, and/or area models. Also 4.NBT.3

Using Rounding to Estimate

How can you use rounding to estimate when you multiply?

Hoover School is holding a walk-a-thon. Any class that raises more than $500 earns a prize. Mr. Hector and Mrs. Alan both want to know if their class will earn a prize.

Class	Blocks Walked	Pledges per Block
Mr. Hector's	193	$4
Mrs. Alan's	115	$3

Guided Practice*

MATHEMATICAL
PRACTICES

Do you know HOW?

In **1** through **8**, estimate each product.

1. 6×125

2. 39×5

3. 538×3

4. 7×314

5. 2×97

6. 4×261

7. 63×6

8. 9×48

Do you UNDERSTAND?

© 9. Reason Is the estimate for Mr. Hector's class more or less than the actual answer? Explain how you know.

10. Mrs. Alan's class walked 70 more blocks. Estimate to see if her class will now get a prize.

Independent Practice

Leveled Practice In **11** through **34**, estimate each product.

11. 7×34 is close to $7 \times$ ___.

12. 6×291 is close to $6 \times$ ___.

13. 41×9 is close to ___ $\times 9$.

14. 814×3 is close to ___ $\times 3$.

15. 117×4

16. 3×86

17. 9×476

18. 34×6

19. 7×77

20. 52×9

21. 46×5

22. 3×287

23. 6×131

24. 602×9

25. 394×2

26. 77×8

27. 2×863

28. 44×8

29. 303×5

30. 486×7

31. 719×5

32. 6×609

33. 219×4

34. 54×8

For another example, see Set E on page 131.

Mr. Hector's Class
Estimate 4 × 193 using rounding.

4 × 193
↓ Round 193 to 200.
4 × 200 = 800

Mr. Hector's class raised more than 500 dollars.

His class has earned a prize.

Mrs. Alan's Class
Estimate 3 × 115 using rounding.

3 × 115
↓ Round 115 to 100.
3 × 100 = 300

Mrs. Alan's class has raised about 300 dollars.

This is not enough to earn a prize.

Problem Solving

MATHEMATICAL PRACTICES

35. Sam and his 2 brothers want to fly to Boston. One airline offers a round-trip fare of $319. Another airline has a round-trip fare of $389. About how much will Sam and his brothers save by buying the less expensive fare?

36. **Science** An adult female bald eagle has a wingspan that is about 7 feet long. If there are 12 inches in one foot, how long would you estimate a female bald eagle's wingspan is in inches?

© **37.** **Generalize** Ellie estimates that the product of 211 and 6 is 1,800. Is this estimate reasonable? Why or why not?

© **38.** **Reason** Which has more pencils, 3 packs with 40 pencils or 40 packs with 3 pencils? Explain.

In **39** through **41**, use the bar graph at the right.

© **39.** **Persevere** The students at Spring Elementary voted on a school mascot. Which mascot has about 4 times as many votes as the unicorn?

   A Lion   **C** Dragon

   B Owl   **D** Bear

40. Which mascot had the least number of votes?

© **41.** **Estimation** Explain how you could estimate the number of students who voted on a school mascot. Then give your estimate.

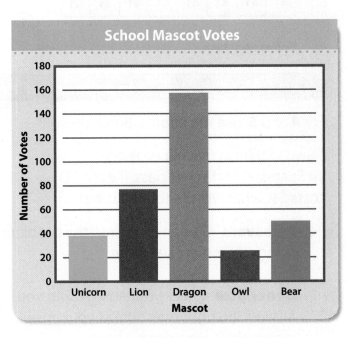

Common
Core

4.OA.3 Solve multistep word problems posed with whole numbers and having whole-number answers using the four operations, including problems in which remainders must be interpreted. Represent these problems using equations with a letter standing for the unknown quantity. Assess the reasonableness of answers using mental computation and estimation strategies including rounding. Also **4.NBT.3, 4.NBT.5**

Problem Solving

Reasonableness

Karen glued sequins onto her project. She used 7 rows with 28 sequins in each row. How many sequins did Karen glue in all?

After you solve a problem, check whether your answer is reasonable. Ask yourself: Did I answer the right question? Is the calculation reasonable?

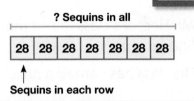

? Sequins in all

| 28 | 28 | 28 | 28 | 28 | 28 | 28 |

↑
Sequins in each row

Guided Practice*

MATHEMATICAL
PRACTICES

Do you know HOW?

Solve and make an estimate to show that your answer is reasonable.

1. A fish store has 8 empty tanks. After a delivery, the store put 41 fish in each tank. How many fish were in the delivery?

? Fish in all

| 41 | 41 | 41 | 41 | 41 | 41 | 41 | 41 |

↑
Fish in each tank

Do you UNDERSTAND?

2. How could Karen use mental math to multiply 7 and 28?

© **3. Write a Problem** Write and solve a problem that would have an answer near 80. Use an estimate to show that your answer is reasonable.

Independent Practice

MATHEMATICAL
PRACTICES

For **4** and **5**, use the information below.

Dawn's Spanish teacher ordered 20 Spanish CDs for her class. If each CD costs $9, what will the total cost be?

© **4. Persevere** Give an answer to the problem using a complete sentence.

© **5. Generalize** Check your answer. Did you answer the right question? Is your answer reasonable? How do you know?

Applying Math Practices

- What am I asked to find?
- What else can I try?
- How are quantities related?
- How can I explain my work?
- How can I use math to model the problem?
- Can I use tools to help?
- Is my work precise?
- Why does this work?
- How can I generalize?

Reasonable	Not reasonable
There were 196 sequins in all.	There were 140 sequins in all.
Estimate: $7 \times 30 = 210$	Estimate: $7 \times 20 = 140$
The answer is reasonable because 210 is close to 196.	The answer is not reasonable because 140 is not close to 196.
The right question was answered and the calculation is reasonable.	The right question was answered, but the calculation is not reasonable.

For **6** through **9**, use the data table at the right and the information below.

A plane increases its height at a rate of 400 feet per second.

6. How high will the plane be after 5 seconds?

7. What number sentence can you use to solve Problem 6?

8. Did you answer the right question?

© **9. Generalize** Is your answer reasonable? How do you know?

Elapsed Seconds	Increase in Height	Height
1 sec	400 ft	400 ft
2 sec	400 ft	800 ft
3 sec	400 ft	1,200 ft
4 sec	400 ft	1,600 ft
5 sec	400 ft	
6 sec	400 ft	2,400 ft

For **10** through **12**, use the data table at the right.

10. About how much money does an American family spend in 8 weeks to feed a child who is 11 years old?

© **11. Reason** In four weeks, about how much more money does a family spend to feed a child who is 8 years old than a child who is 3 years old?

© **12. Generalize** Is your answer for Problem 11 reasonable? How do you know?

Money Spent by an American Family to Feed a Child	
Age of Child	Weekly Amount
1–2 years	$27
3–5 years	$31
6–8 years	$42
9–11 years	$49

For **13** through **16**, use the chart at the right.

13. How many stickers does Mr. Richardson have on rolls?

© **14. Model** How many more stickers on sheets does Mr. Richardson have than stickers in boxes?

15. Is your calculation for Problem 14 reasonable? How do you know?

16. How many stickers does Mr. Richardson have in all?

Mr. Richardson's Stickers

On sheets	♥ ♥ ♥
On rolls	♥ ♥ ♥ ♥
In boxes	♥

Each ♥ = 10 stickers

For **17** through **20**, use the chart at the right.

17. How many miles does a police officer walk in 4 weeks?

18. How many miles does a nurse walk in 6 weeks?

19. How many miles does a mail carrier walk in 7 weeks?

20. How many miles does a doctor walk in 3 weeks?

Kind of Job	Distance Walked in 1 Week
Doctor	16 miles
Mail carrier	21 miles
Nurse	18 miles
Police officer	32 miles

© **Think About the Structure**

21. Which of the following uses the Distributive Property to solve 4×9?

A $4 \times 9 = (3 \times 3) + (1 \times 6)$

B $4 \times 9 = (4 \times 9) + (4 \times 9)$

C $4 \times 9 = (2 \times 9) + (2 \times 9)$

D $4 \times 9 = (2 \times 3) + (2 \times 6)$

22. Which of the following correctly uses compensation to solve 2×38?

A (2×40) and $80 - 2$

B (2×30) and $60 + 8$

C (2×40) and $80 - 4$

D (2×40) and $80 + 4$

Going Digital

Multiplying with Mental Math

Use 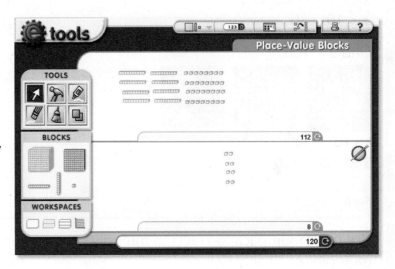 **tools** Place-Value Blocks.

Explain how to use compensation to find 4×28.

Step 1 Go to the Place-Value Blocks eTool. Select the two-part workspace.
30 is the closest number to 28 that is easy to multiply. Click on the horizontal long block. Then click in the top workspace to show 4 rows with 3 longs in each row, or 4×30.

Step 2 Click on the hammer tool icon. Then click on the last long in each row to break each into ten ones. Use the arrow tool to select two ones from the first group, and move them to the bottom workspace. Do the same for the last two ones in each row.

To find 4×28, find $4 \times 30 = 120$ and subtract $4 \times 2 = 8$.

So, $120 - 8 = 112$.

Practice

Use compensation to find each product mentally.

1. 3×19 **2.** 4×499 **3.** 2×67 **4.** 6×29

5. 4×38 **6.** 3×47 **7.** 3×29 **8.** 4×899

9. 2×49 **10.** 3×58 **11.** 4×109 **12.** 2×39

13. 3×107 **14.** 3×28 **15.** 4×47 **16.** 2×48

17. 4×37 **18.** 4×48 **19.** 3×57 **20.** 3×198

21. 2×47 **22.** 3×402 **23.** 4×67 **24.** 4×58

Set A, pages 116–117

Use arrays to multiply by 10 and 100.

Find 3 × 10.

$3 \times 10 = 10 + 10 + 10$
$3 \times 10 = 30$

Find 3 × 100.

$3 \times 100 = 100 + 100 + 100$
$3 \times 100 = 300$

Remember you can think of multiplication as repeated addition.

Find the product.

1. 5 × 10   **2.** 2 × 100

3. 6 × 100   **4.** 4 × 10

5. 7 × 10   **6.** 8 × 100

7. 9 × 100   **8.** 8 × 10

Set B, pages 118–119

Use basic multiplication facts to multiply by multiples of 10 and 100.

Find 4 × 60.   Find 4 × 600.

Multiply 4 × 6 = 24.   Multiply 4 × 6 = 24.

Write one zero after 24.   Write two zeros after 24.
$4 \times 60 = 240$ $4 \times 600 = 2,400$

Remember when the product of a basic fact ends in zero, the answer will have an extra zero.

Find the product.

1. 8 × 60   **2.** 3 × 40

3. 6 × 50   **4.** 5 × 300

5. 700 × 4   **6.** 2 × 900

7. 80 × 8   **8.** 400 × 5

Set C, pages 120–121

Use breaking apart to find 2 × 123.

Think of 123 as 100 + 20 + 3.
$2 \times 123 = (2 \times 100) + (2 \times 20) + (2 \times 3)$

$= 200 + 40 + 6$

$= 246$

Remember you can use place-value blocks or drawings to help you multiply.

Find the product.

1. 4 × 73   **2.** 2 × 59

3. 6 × 135   **4.** 3 × 281

5. 7 × 25   **6.** 5 × 146

7. 8 × 42   **8.** 5 × 354

Use compensation to find 2 × 297.

First substitute 300 for 297 and find 2 × 300 = 600.

Then adjust by subtracting 2 groups of 3.

600 − 6 = 594

So, 2 × 297 = 594.

Remember to check your answers for reasonableness.

Find the product.

1. 6 × 13   **2.** 3 × 46

3. 5 × 397   **4.** 6 × 72

5. 6 × 203   **6.** 4 × 499

Use rounding to estimate 9 × 83.

Round 83 to 80.

9 × 83

9 × 80 = 720

So, 9 × 83 is about 720.

Remember to round a two-digit number to the nearest ten and a three-digit number to the nearest hundred.

Estimate each product.

1. 8 × 76   **2.** 493 × 3

3. 96 × 5   **4.** 678 × 6

5. 707 × 4   **6.** 57 × 3

Ty is making centerpieces to place on tables. He will use 5 roses in each of 11 vases. Ty wants to buy 100 roses to make the centerpieces. Is this a reasonable number of roses to buy?

What do I know?	Ty wants to buy 100 roses.
	He will use 5 roses in each of 11 vases.
What am I asked to find?	Is it reasonable for Ty to buy 100 roses?

Estimate to determine reasonableness.

11 rounds to 10, and 10 × 5 = 50.

50 is not close to 100, so the number of roses Ty wants to buy is not reasonable.

Remember to use rounding to estimate.

Solve.

1. Mitch earned $88 delivering newspapers. He worked for 11 hours and earned $8 an hour. Is the amount Mitch earned reasonable? Explain.

2. Joan needs 9 packs of envelopes and each pack costs $4. She decided that she will need to spend a total of $72 on envelopes. Is her decision reasonable? Explain.

Multiple Choice

 ASSESSMENT

1. Mrs. Ortiz can make 50 tortillas out of one batch of dough. If she makes 4 batches of dough, how many tortillas can she make? (5-2)

   A 8

   B 20

   C 200

   D 2,000

2. There are 52 weeks in one year. If Jean turned 9 today, which is the best estimate of the number of weeks Jean has been alive? (5-5)

   A 600 weeks

   B 540 weeks

   C 530 weeks

   D 450 weeks

3. Which shows one way to use breaking apart to find 7×32? (5-3)

   A $(7 \times 30) + (7 \times 2)$

   B $(7 \times 30) - (5 \times 2)$

   C $(2 \times 30) + (3 \times 2)$

   D 30×7

4. A factory produces 295 cars in one week. How many cars does the factory produce in 4 weeks? (5-4)

   A 885

   B 1,180

   C 1,200

   D 1,220

5. Which shows another way to find $10 + 10 + 10$? (5-1)

   A $10 \times 10 \times 10$

   B 3×100

   C 3×10

   D 3×1

6. A bike loop is 8 miles long. Ed rode around the loop 18 times. He used compensation to find how far he rode. First, he multiplied $20 \times 8 = 160$. What should Ed do next? (5-4)

   A $160 + 8 = 168$

   B $160 - 8 = 152$

   C $160 + 16 = 176$

   D $160 - 16 = 144$

7. Susanna's school has 5 grades with an average of 48 students in each grade. Which is a reasonable number of students in Susanna's school? (5-6)

   A 205, because 5×48 is about $5 \times 40 = 200$

   B 240, because 5×48 is about $5 \times 50 = 250$

   C 285, because 5×48 is about $5 \times 60 = 300$

   D 315, because 5×48 is about $6 \times 50 = 300$

8. Ivan gets $22 a month for completing his chores. Use rounding to estimate the amount of money Ivan would have if he saved all the money for 6 months. Write a number sentence to show your work. (5-5)

9. Write a number sentence that shows another way to find 100 + 100 + 100 + 100. (5-1)

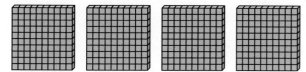

10. Mrs. Henderson bought 4 boxes of facial tissues. Each box has 174 tissues. Write a number sentence that uses rounding to estimate the total number of tissues. (5-5)

11. Write an expression that uses breaking apart to find 5 × 17. (5-3)

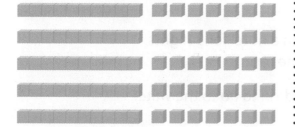

12. Ali ran for 19 minutes 7 days in a row. How many minutes did Ali run? (5-4)

13. Use breaking apart to find the product for 6 × 135. Show your work. (5-3)

14. A gallon of paint can cover about 400 square feet of wall space. About how many square feet of wall space will 3 gallons cover? (5-2)

15. Find the product for 7 × 10. (5-1)

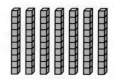

16. Judy has 5 rolls of stamps. There are 100 stamps in each roll. How many stamps does Judy have? (5-2)

17. Raul is buying 3 shirts that cost $29 each. How much will the 3 shirts cost in all? (5-3)

18. Ricky saves $7 each week. Use rounding to estimate the amount he will have saved after 1 year. Write a number sentence to show your work. (5-5)

Tip *There are 52 weeks in 1 year.*

19. Nia has 5 piles of paper clips. There are 79 paper clips in each pile. She says she has 3,995 paper clips in all. Is her answer reasonable? Explain why or why not. (5-6)

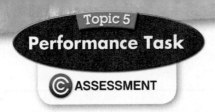

Mr. and Mrs. Swerdlow are planning a vacation for themselves and their two children.

The Swerdlows don't want to spend more than $2,000 on this vacation. Some of the information they are using to plan their trip is shown below. Use the information provided to solve **1** through **7** below.

Family Vacation Expenses

- A round-trip airline ticket costs $239.

- The hotel costs $200 a night.

- Amusement Park Tickets
  Adult: $42   Child: $29

- Water Park Tickets
  Adult: $25   Child: $15

1. Estimate the cost of airline tickets for everyone in the family. Will the actual cost be more or less than your estimate? How can you tell?

2. How would you use breaking apart to find the actual cost of the tickets?

3. How much will it cost the family to stay in a hotel for 3 nights, assuming they can all stay together in one room?

4. How much would it cost for the two children to go to the water park?

5. The entire family wants to go to the amusement park. What would that cost? Use compensation to solve.

6. The Swerdlow children are each saving their allowance so they will have spending money on their vacation. If they each save $4 per week for 20 weeks, how much will they save all together?

7. If the Swerdlows use the expenses that you found above, how much money will they have left for food and souvenirs? Explain how you decided.

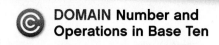

Topic 6

Developing Fluency: Multiplying by 1-Digit Numbers

▼ How many miles long is the Appalachian Trail? You will find out in Lesson 6-4.

Topic Essential Questions
- How can arrays be used to find products?
- What is a standard procedure for multiplying multi-digit numbers?

Review What You Know!

Vocabulary

Choose the best term from the box.

- product
- factor
- array
- rounding

1. You multiply numbers to find a _?_.

2. A(n) _?_ shows the number of objects in rows and columns.

3. When you estimate to the nearest 10 or 100, you may use _?_ .

Multiplication Facts

Find each product.

4. 4×8	**5.** 2×9
6. 9×5	**7.** 6×8
8. 6×4	**9.** 6×6
10. 8×5	**11.** 9×9

Rounding

Round each number to the nearest hundred.

12. 164	**13.** 8,263	**14.** 351
15. 527	**16.** 2,498	**17.** 9,634
18. 7,892	**19.** 472	**20.** 119

Round each number to the nearest thousand.

21. 8,685	**22.** 4,991	**23.** 62,549
24. 167,241	**25.** 77,268	**26.** 34,162
27. 1,372	**28.** 9,009	**29.** 919,263

© **30. Writing to Explain** Explain how to round 608,149 to the thousands place.

Interactive Learning Hands-On Minds-On

Pose the problem. Start each lesson by working together to solve problems. It will help you make sense of math.

Applying Math Practices

- What am I asked to find?
- What else can I try?
- How are quantities related?
- How can I explain my work?
- How can I use math to model the problem?
- Can I use tools to help?
- Is my work precise?
- Why does this work?
- How can I generalize?

Lesson 6-1

© **Use Tools** Solve. Use place-value blocks and build an array to find the answer.

A video store display shelf has videos stacked in 3 rows. There are 12 videos in each row. How many videos are on the shelf?

Lesson 6-2

© **Use Structure** Solve any way you choose. You may use place-value blocks or diagrams to help.

A large bus can seat 52 people. If 8 of these buses are fully loaded to take all students from one school to a high school graduation, how many students in all are on the buses?

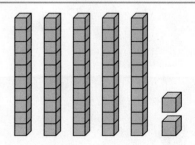

Lesson 6-3

© **Generalize** Solve any way you choose, but just use paper and pencil this time.

Suppose a school ordered 7 boxes of books. Each box contains the same number of books. How many books are there in all? How can you check that your answer is reasonable?

25 BOOKS

Lesson 6-4

© **Generalize** Solve. Use what you know about multiplying with smaller numbers.

Bonnie has 4 jars like the one at the right. How many pennies does she have all together? Tell how you know your answer is reasonable.

231 pennies

Lesson 6-5

© **Model** Use the skills you have learned to solve this problem.

A Cineplex contains 4 movie theaters. Each theater can seat the same number of people. How many people can this Cineplex seat in all? Tell how you know that your answer is reasonable.

THEATRE 1

Maximum Capacity
312 Persons

Lesson 6-6

© **Persevere** Solve. Is there any missing or extra information?

Ms. Silva was training for a race. She ran around a path 16 times in 1 week. How many miles did Ms. Silva run in all?

? miles

©
Common Core

4.NBT.5 Multiply a whole
number of up to four
digits by a one-digit whole
number, and multiply two
two-digit numbers, using
strategies based on place
value and the properties
of operations. Illustrate
and explain the calculation
by using equations,
rectangular arrays, and/or
area models.

Arrays and Using an Expanded Algorithm

Hands-On
place-value blocks

How can you record multiplication?

A store ordered 2 boxes of video games.
How many games did the store order?

Choose an Operation Multiply
to join equal groups.

Each box contains
16 video games.

Another Example How do you record multiplication when the product has three digits?

Gene played a game of checkers 23 times each day for 5 days.
How many times did he play checkers in 5 days?

A   18

B   28

C   115

D   145

Choose an Operation Since 5 equal groups of 23
are being joined, you will multiply. Find 5×23.

What You Show

What You Write

$$
\begin{array}{r}
23 \\
\times \quad 5 \\
\hline
15 \\
+ \ 100 \\
\hline
115 \\
\end{array}
$$

Gene played checkers 115 times in 5 days.
The correct choice is **C**.

Explain It

1. Explain how the partial products, 15 and 100, were found in the work above.

© **2. Generalize** How can an estimate help you eliminate choices above?

What You Show

Build an array to show 2 × 16.

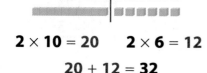

$2 \times 10 = 20$ $2 \times 6 = 12$

$20 + 12 = \mathbf{32}$

What You Write

Here is one way to record multiplication.

$$
\begin{array}{r}
16 \\
\times \quad 2 \\
\hline
12 \leftarrow \text{Partial} \\
+ \quad 20 \leftarrow \text{Products} \\
\hline
32
\end{array}
$$

The store ordered 32 games.

Guided Practice*

MATHEMATICAL
PRACTICES

Do you know HOW?

In **1** and **2**, use place-value blocks or draw pictures to build an array for each. Copy and complete the calculation.

1. $2 \times 34 =$ ▨

$$
\begin{array}{r}
34 \\
\times \quad 2 \\
\hline
\\
+ \quad \\
\hline
\\
\end{array}
$$

2. $3 \times 18 =$ ▨

$$
\begin{array}{r}
18 \\
\times \quad 3 \\
\hline
\\
+ \quad \\
\hline
\\
\end{array}
$$

Do you UNDERSTAND?

Use the array and the calculation shown for Problem 3.

$$
\begin{array}{r}
14 \\
\times \quad 3 \\
\hline
12 \\
+ \quad 30 \\
\hline
42
\end{array}
$$

3. Model What calculation was used to give the partial product 12? 30?

Independent Practice

Leveled Practice In **4** and **5**, use place-value blocks or draw pictures to build an array for each. Copy and complete the calculation.

4.

$$
\begin{array}{r}
27 \\
\times \quad 3 \\
\hline
\\
+ \quad \\
\hline
\\
\end{array}
$$

5.

$$
\begin{array}{r}
22 \\
\times \quad 4 \\
\hline
\\
+ \quad \\
\hline
\\
\end{array}
$$

eTools **Place-Value Blocks**
www.pearsonsuccessnet.com

*For another example, see Set A on page 158.

Lesson 6-1   **139**

Leveled Practice In **6** through **15**, copy and complete the calculation. Draw a picture to help.

6. 26
× 5
_____

7. 19
× 3
_____

8. 24
× 2
_____

9. 21
× 4
_____

10. 24
× 3
_____

+

11. 22
× 8
_____

12. 17
× 3
_____

13. 24
× 8
_____

14. 16
× 5
_____

15. 23
× 7
_____

Problem Solving

MATHEMATICAL
PRACTICES

Use the table at the right for **16** and **17**.

Ⓒ **16. Estimation** Emma wants to put 3 smiley stickers on each of her note cards. Use estimation to decide if one roll of smileys has enough stickers for 42 note cards.

Type of Sticker	Number of Stickers per Roll
★	50
🐕	75
😊	100
🌸	125

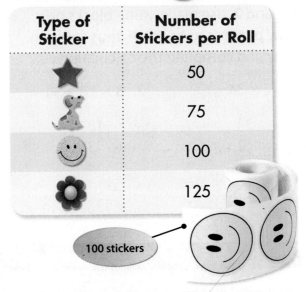
100 stickers

17. How many more stickers are in 3 rolls of dog stickers than in 3 rolls of star stickers?

A 50   **C** 100

B 75   **D** 150

18. Large tables in the library have 8 chairs and small tables have 4 chairs. How many students can sit at 3 large tables and 5 small tables if each seat is filled?

A 20 students   **C** 44 students

B 36 students   **D** 52 students

Ⓒ **19. Writing to Explain** Tim called 3×20 and 3×4 *simple calculations*. Explain what he meant.

20. 🔬 **Science** A jerboa can jump 25 times its body length. How many inches can this jerboa jump?

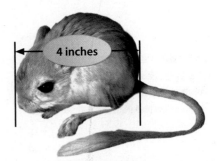
4 inches

Find the product.

1. 7×2 **2.** 4×5 **3.** 6×8 **4.** 9×7

5. 4×8 **6.** 0×1 **7.** 3×6 **8.** 8×8

9. 3×3 **10.** 6×7 **11.** 5×7 **12.** 9×4

Find the quotient.

13. $81 \div 9$ **14.** $4\overline{)12}$ **15.** $56 \div 7$ **16.** $2\overline{)10}$ **17.** $54 \div 6$

18. $5\overline{)20}$ **19.** $0 \div 8$ **20.** $3\overline{)21}$ **21.** $24 \div 6$ **22.** $9\overline{)27}$

23. $63 \div 9$ **24.** $8\overline{)64}$ **25.** $18 \div 3$ **26.** $5\overline{)5}$ **27.** $81 \div 9$

Error Search Find each product or quotient that is not correct. Write it correctly and explain the error.

28. $8 \div 1 = 8$ **29.** $4 \times 4 = 16$ **30.** $0 \div 5 = 5$ **31.** $9 \times 6 = 53$

32. $12 \div 2 = 6$ **33.** $25 \div 5 = 5$ **34.** $5 \times 3 = 15$ **35.** $24 \div 3 = 6$

36. $7 \times 7 = 42$ **37.** $18 \div 2 = 8$ **38.** $12 \div 6 = 2$ **39.** $28 \div 7 = 4$

Number Sense

© **Communicate** Write whether each statement is true or false. Explain your answer.

40. The product of 1 and 34,654 is 34,654.

41. The quotient of 8 divided by 0 is not possible.

42. The sum of 52,128 and 21,179 is less than 70,000.

43. The difference of $8,853 - 1,978$ is greater than 8,000.

44. The product of 2 and a number will always be even.

45. The product of 6 and 7 is 6 less than 36.

4.NBT.5 Multiply a whole number of up to four digits by a one-digit whole number, and multiply two two-digit numbers, using strategies based on place value and the properties of operations. Illustrate and explain the calculation by using equations, rectangular arrays, and/or area models. Also **4.OA.3**

Connecting the Expanded and Standard Algorithms

What is a common way to record multiplication?

A small school bus holds 24 passengers.
A small jet holds 4 times as many passengers.
How many passengers does the small jet hold?

Find 4 × 24.

? Passengers

| Small jet | 24 | 24 | 24 | 24 | ← 4 times as many |

| School bus | 24 |

Guided Practice*

© MATHEMATICAL PRACTICES

Do you know HOW?

In **1** through **6**, find each product two ways. First use the expanded algorithm, and then use the standard algorithm.

1. 5 × 17

2. 3 × 43

3. 4 × 56

4. 6 × 62

5. 29
    × 3

6. 88
    × 2

Do you UNDERSTAND?

© **7. Critique Reasoning** Mara used the expanded algorithm shown to the right. Is she correct? Explain.

```
   24
 ×  4
   80
 + 16
   96
```

8. A ferry can carry 16 cars. How many cars can the ferry carry in 5 trips?

Independent Practice

In **9** through **24**, find each product. Use either method.

9. 6 × 38

10. 4 × 47

11. 8 × 42

12. 5 × 64

13. 7 × 26

14. 9 × 33

15. 2 × 76

16. 4 × 29

17.   17
      × 9

18.   61
      × 3

19.   45
      × 7

20.   83
      × 5

21.   23
      × 5

22.   18
      × 8

23.   53
      × 3

24.   37
      × 7

For another example, see Set B on page 158.

Expanded Algorithm

Find the partial products.

$$
\begin{array}{r}
24 \\
\times\ 4 \\
\hline
16 \\
+\ 80 \\
\hline
96
\end{array}
$$

16 ← Partial
+ 80 ← Products

The jet can hold 96 passengers.

Standard Algorithm

First, multiply the ones. Regroup if needed.

$$
\begin{array}{r}
1 \\
24 \\
\times\ 4 \\
\hline
6
\end{array}
$$

4 × 4 ones = 16 ones
Regroup 16 ones as 1 ten 6 ones.

Then, multiply the tens. Add any extra tens.

$$
\begin{array}{r}
1 \\
24 \\
\times\ 4 \\
\hline
96
\end{array}
$$

4 × 2 tens = 8 tens
There is 1 extra ten.
8 tens + 1 ten = 9 tens

The jet can hold 96 passengers.

Problem Solving

MATHEMATICAL PRACTICES

25. A speedboat holds 12 adults and 6 children. How many people in all can go on 4 speedboat rides?

Ⓒ 26. Look for Patterns Vera created a design using 68 tiles. If she doubles her design and then doubles it again, how many tiles will she use in all?

Ⓒ 27. Estimation In 2008, a surfer set a world record for stand up paddle surfing. In 24 hours, he paddled 49 miles. About how far did he go each hour?

28. Luis recycles aluminum cans. His goal was to recycle 10,000 cans by May 1. He recycled 3,789 cans in March and 5,068 cans in April. How many cans is Luis over or under his goal? Explain how you found your answer.

29. 🌐 **Social Studies** In the Aztec calendar, each year has a number from 1 to 13. It also has one of four signs: house, rabbit, reed, or flint. It takes 4 × 13 years to go through one complete cycle of years. How many years are in one cycle?

30. Belle used 286 pages of newspaper to make a volcano of papier-mâché. What is this number rounded to the nearest hundred?

   A 200   **C** 290

   B 280   **D** 300

31. 🔍 **Science** Eucalyptus trees grow in Southern Florida. How much taller would a fast-growing eucalyptus tree be after 7 years?

A fast-growing eucalyptus can grow about 11 feet each year.

© Common Core

4.NBT.5 Multiply a whole number of up to four digits by a one-digit whole number, and multiply two two-digit numbers, using strategies based on place value and the properties of operations. Illustrate and explain the calculation by using equations, rectangular arrays, and/or area models. Also 4.OA.3

Multiplying 2-Digit by 1-Digit Numbers

What is a common way to record multiplication?

How many T-shirts with the saying, *and your point is...* are in 3 boxes?

Choose an Operation Multiply to join equal groups.

Saying on T-shirt	Number of T-shirts per Box
Trust Me	30 T-shirts
and your point is...	26 T-shirts
I'm the princess that's why 👑	24 T-shirts
Because I said so	12 T-shirts

Another Example **Does the common way to record multiplication work for larger products?**

Mrs. Stockton ordered 8 boxes of T-shirts with the saying, *I'm the princess that's why.* How many of the T-shirts did she order?

Choose an Operation Since you are joining 8 groups of 24, you will multiply. Find 8×24.

Step 1 Multiply the ones. Regroup if necessary.

$$\begin{array}{r} 3 \\ 24 \\ \times \quad 8 \\ \hline 2 \end{array}$$

$8 \times 4 = 32$ ones
Regroup 32 ones as 3 tens 2 ones.

Step 2 Multiply the tens. Add any extra tens.

$$\begin{array}{r} 3 \\ 24 \\ \times \quad 8 \\ \hline 192 \end{array}$$

8×2 tens $= 16$ tens
16 tens $+ 3$ tens $= 19$ tens
or 1 hundred 9 tens

Mrs. Stockton ordered 192 T-shirts.

Explain It

© 1. **Reasonableness** How can you use estimation to decide if 192 is a reasonable answer?

2. In the example above, do you multiply 8×2 or 8×20? Explain.

Step 1	Step 2	Step 3

Step 1

Multiply the ones. Regroup if needed.

$$\begin{array}{r} {\scriptstyle 1} \\ 26 \\ \times\ \ 3 \\ \hline 8 \end{array}$$

Step 2

Multiply the tens. Add any extra tens.

$$\begin{array}{r} {\scriptstyle 1} \\ 26 \\ \times\ \ 3 \\ \hline 78 \end{array}$$

There are 78 T-shirts in 3 boxes.

Step 3

Estimate to check reasonableness.

3×26 is about $3 \times 30 = 90$

The answer is reasonable because 78 is close to 90.

Guided Practice*

MATHEMATICAL PRACTICES

Do you know HOW?

In **1** through **8**, find each product. Estimate to check reasonableness.

1. $\begin{array}{r} 15 \\ \times\ 5 \\ \hline \end{array}$

2. $\begin{array}{r} 28 \\ \times\ 3 \\ \hline \end{array}$

3. $\begin{array}{r} 34 \\ \times\ 7 \\ \hline \end{array}$

4. $\begin{array}{r} 43 \\ \times\ 4 \\ \hline \end{array}$

5. 5×70

6. 5×78

7. 3×24

8. 3×79

Do you UNDERSTAND?

9. Explain how you would estimate the answer in Exercise 3.

10. Carrie bought 8 boxes of T-shirts with the saying *Because I said so.* How many T-shirts did Carrie buy?

© **11. Writing to Explain** Explain how the answer to Exercise 5 can be used to find the answer to Exercise 6.

Independent Practice

In **12** through **19**, find each product. Estimate to check reasonableness.

12. $\begin{array}{r} 12 \\ \times\ 6 \\ \hline \end{array}$

13. $\begin{array}{r} 18 \\ \times\ 7 \\ \hline \end{array}$

14. $\begin{array}{r} 72 \\ \times\ 5 \\ \hline \end{array}$

15. $\begin{array}{r} 49 \\ \times\ 8 \\ \hline \end{array}$

16. $\begin{array}{r} 31 \\ \times\ 4 \\ \hline \end{array}$

17. $\begin{array}{r} 52 \\ \times\ 6 \\ \hline \end{array}$

18. $\begin{array}{r} 79 \\ \times\ 7 \\ \hline \end{array}$

19. $\begin{array}{r} 87 \\ \times\ 7 \\ \hline \end{array}$

In **20** through **27**, find each product.
Estimate to check reasonableness.

20. 9×23 **21.** 6×51 **22.** 4×29 **23.** 8×42

24. 3×64 **25.** 5×56 **26.** 6×83 **27.** 4×47

Problem Solving

MATHEMATICAL PRACTICES

28. Use the diagram to the right. How many floors does the Purple-Tower Hotel have?

A 60   **B** 70   **C** 105   **D** 1,010

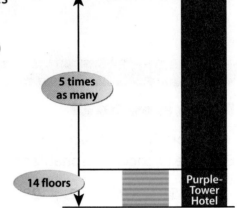

© 29. Estimation It takes 186 rolls of tape to make a car sculpture out of boxes. What is this number rounded to the nearest hundred?

A 100   **C** 200

B 180   **D** 280

© 30. Model Katie made 24 rag dolls. She gave away 8 of them as gifts. Which expression gives the number of rag dolls Katie had left?

A $24 + 8$ **C** $24 - 8$

B 24×8 **D** $24 \div 8$

31. A skateboard speed record of almost 63 miles per hour (about 92 feet per second) was set in 1998. At that speed, about how many feet would the skateboarder travel in 6 seconds?

? feet in all

| 92 | 92 | 92 | 92 | 92 | 92 |

↑
Feet traveled each second

For **32** and **33**, use the table to the right.

32. What is the average length fingernails will grow in one year?

A 60 mm   **C** 40 mm

B 50 mm   **D** 5 mm

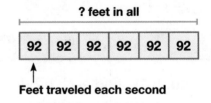

Average Rate of Growth in Millimeters per Month

Fingernails	5 mm
Hair	12 mm

33. How much longer will hair grow in six months than fingernails will grow in six months?

Algebra Connections

Multiplication and Number Sentences

Remember that a number sentence has two numbers or expressions connected by <, >, or =. Estimation or reasoning can help you tell if the left side or right side is greater.

Copy and complete. Write <, >, or = in the circle. Check your answers.

 Remember

   > *is greater than*   < *is less than*   = *is equal to*

> **Example:** 7×52 ◯ 7×60
>
> **Think** *Is 7 groups of 52 more than 7 groups of 60?*
>
> Since 52 is less than 60, the left side is less. Write "<".
>
> 7×52 ⦵ 7×60

1. 5×71 ◯ 5×70 **2.** 8×30 ◯ 8×35 **3.** 2×90 ◯ $89 + 89$

4. 4×56 ◯ 200 **5.** 6×37 ◯ 37×6 **6.** 190 ◯ 9×25

7. 3×33 ◯ 100 **8.** 80 ◯ 4×19 **9.** 10×10 ◯ 9×8

10. 1×67 ◯ $1 + 67$ **11.** $2 + 34$ ◯ 2×34 **12.** 6×18 ◯ 7×20

• •

For **13** and **14**, copy and complete the number sentence below each problem. Use it to help explain your answer.

13. A red tray holds 7 rows of oranges with 8 oranges in each row. A blue tray holds 8 rows of oranges with 5 oranges in each row. Which tray holds more oranges?

____ × ____ ◯ ____ × ____

14. Look at the hats below. Mr. Fox bought 2 brown hats. Mrs. Lee bought 3 green hats. Who paid more for their hats?

____ × ____ ◯ ____ × ____

Ⓒ **15.** **Write a Problem** Write a problem using the hats at the right.

4.NBT.5 Multiply a whole number of up to four digits by a one-digit whole number, and multiply two two-digit numbers, using strategies based on place value and the properties of operations. Illustrate and explain the calculation by using equations, rectangular arrays, and/or area models.

Multiplying 3- and 4-Digit by 1-Digit Numbers

How do you multiply larger numbers?

Juan guessed that the large bottle had 3 times as many pennies as the small bottle. What was Juan's guess?

Choose an Operation Multiply to find "3 times as many."

264 pennies

Other Examples

Find $3 \times 2{,}746$.

Step 1	**Step 2**	**Step 3**	**Step 4**
Multiply the ones. Regroup if necessary.	Multiply the tens. Add any extra tens. Regroup if necessary.	Multiply the hundreds. Add any extra hundreds. Regroup if necessary.	Multiply the thousands. Add any extra thousands. Regroup if necessary.
$\begin{array}{r} {\scriptstyle 1} \\ 2{,}746 \\ \times \quad 3 \\ \hline 8 \end{array}$	$\begin{array}{r} {\scriptstyle 1\,1} \\ 2{,}746 \\ \times \quad 3 \\ \hline 38 \end{array}$	$\begin{array}{r} {\scriptstyle 2\,1\,1} \\ 2{,}746 \\ \times \quad 3 \\ \hline 238 \end{array}$	$\begin{array}{r} {\scriptstyle 2\,1\,1} \\ 2{,}746 \\ \times \quad 3 \\ \hline 8{,}238 \end{array}$

Find $5 \times 3{,}138$

Step 1	**Step 2**	**Step 3**	**Step 4**
Multiply the ones. Regroup if necessary.	Multiply the tens. Add any extra tens. Regroup if necessary.	Multiply the hundreds. Add any extra hundreds. Regroup if necessary.	Multiply the thousands. Add any extra thousands. Regroup if necessary.
$\begin{array}{r} {\scriptstyle 4} \\ 3{,}138 \\ \times \quad 5 \\ \hline 0 \end{array}$	$\begin{array}{r} {\scriptstyle 1\,4} \\ 3{,}138 \\ \times \quad 5 \\ \hline 90 \end{array}$	$\begin{array}{r} {\scriptstyle 1\,4} \\ 3{,}138 \\ \times \quad 5 \\ \hline 690 \end{array}$	$\begin{array}{r} {\scriptstyle 1\,4} \\ 3{,}138 \\ \times \quad 5 \\ \hline 15{,}690 \end{array}$

Guided Practice*

MATHEMATICAL PRACTICES

Do you know HOW?

In **1** and **2**, find each product. Estimate to check for reasonableness.

1. $\begin{array}{r} 519 \\ \times \quad 4 \\ \hline \end{array}$

2. $\begin{array}{r} 3{,}378 \\ \times \quad 2 \\ \hline \end{array}$

Do you UNDERSTAND?

© **3. Reason** In the example at the top, 3×6 tens is how many tens?

4. A band performed 4 sold-out shows. All 2,428 seats were filled for each show. How many fans saw the 4 shows?

For another example, see Set D on page 159.

Step 1	Step 2	Step 3

Step 1
Multiply the ones. Regroup if needed.

$$\begin{array}{r} {}^{1} \\ 264 \\ \times\ \ 3 \\ \hline 2 \end{array}$$

3 × 4 ones = 12 ones
or 1 ten 2 ones

Step 2
Multiply the tens. Add any extra tens. Regroup if needed.

$$\begin{array}{r} {}^{1\,1} \\ 264 \\ \times\ \ 3 \\ \hline 92 \end{array}$$

(3 × 6 tens) + 1 ten = 19 tens
or 1 hundred 9 tens

Step 3
Multiply the hundreds. Add any extra hundreds.

$$\begin{array}{r} {}^{1\,1} \\ 264 \\ \times\ \ 3 \\ \hline 792 \end{array}$$

(3 × 2 hundreds) + 1 hundred
= 7 hundreds

Juan's guess was 792 pennies.

Independent Practice

In **5** through **12**, find each product. Estimate to check reasonableness.

5.
$$\begin{array}{r} 423 \\ \times\ \ 2 \\ \hline \end{array}$$

6.
$$\begin{array}{r} 3{,}942 \\ \times\ \ 4 \\ \hline \end{array}$$

7.
$$\begin{array}{r} 6{,}271 \\ \times\ \ 3 \\ \hline \end{array}$$

8.
$$\begin{array}{r} 159 \\ \times\ \ 5 \\ \hline \end{array}$$

9. 2 × 125

10. 3 × 3,196

11. 4 × 265

12. 5 × 4,129

Problem Solving

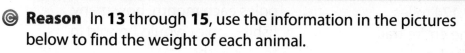

MATHEMATICAL
PRACTICES

© **Reason** In **13** through **15**, use the information in the pictures below to find the weight of each animal.

13. Horse   **14.** Rhino   **15.** Elephant

Bear:
Weighs 836 pounds

Horse:
Weighs 2 times as much as the bear

Rhino:
Weighs 5 times as much as the bear

Elephant:
Weighs 9 times as much as the bear

Use the table at the right for **16** through **21**.

Electronics Sale	
Mobile Phone	$135
Digital Camera	$295
Laptop Computer	$1,075
Flat-Screen TV	$1,650

Ⓒ **16. Estimation** About how much did Dr. Sims spend if he bought 3 flat-screen TVs for his office?

Ⓒ **17. Persevere** Which costs more—2 laptop computers or 4 digital cameras? Use number sense to decide.

Ⓒ **18. Model** Which tells how to find the total cost of a laptop computer and 5 digital cameras?

   A 5 × $295 × $1,075

   B $1,075 + (5 × $295)

   C $1,075 + $295

   D $295 + (5 × $1,075)

19. Larry is saving money to buy 2 mobile phones and a laptop computer. How much additional money will he need to save if he has already saved $400?

   A $675   **C** $945

   B $810   **D** $1,345

20. What did Mr. Sims buy at the electronics sale if (3 × $295) + $1,075 stands for the total price?

21. Mrs. Lee goes to the electronic sale with $3,275. Does she have enough money to buy 2 flat-screen TV's? Why or why not?

22. 🌐 **Social Studies** The Appalachian Trail is 2,174 miles long. If Andy hiked the entire trail one time, how many miles did he hike?

   A 1 mile

   B 1,087 miles

   C 2,174 miles

   D 4,348 miles

23. If Chuck's Sports sold 124 fishing poles each month, how many fishing poles would be sold in four months?

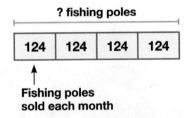

24. Renting a boat at a marina costs $118 a day. If the marina rented 8 boats in one day, how much money was earned from the rentals?

25. A manager at a fast food restaurant orders 8 packages of napkins. Each package contains 375 napkins. How many napkins did the manager order?

Find each product. Estimate to check
if the answer is reasonable.

1.	21 × 4	**2.**	843 × 6	**3.**	6,318 × 5	**4.**	528 × 9

5.	40 × 3	**6.**	17 × 8	**7.**	2,175 × 2	**8.**	796 × 7

9.	4,927 × 6	**10.**	1,234 × 9	**11.**	700 × 5	**12.**	99 × 9	**13.**	5,364 × 4

Find each difference. Estimate to check
if the answer is reasonable.

14. 3,427 − 648 **15.** 7,005 − 6,496 **16.** 502 − 89

Error Search Find each product that is not correct.
Write it correctly and explain the error.

17.	6,829 × 5 34,145	**18.**	438 × 9 3,872	**19.**	2,365 × 3 7,098	**20.**	45 × 4 49	**21.**	777 × 7 5,439

Number Sense

Estimating and Reasoning Write whether each
statement is true or false. Explain your answer.

22. The product of 6 and 39 is less than 240.

23. The sum of 3,721 and 1,273 is greater than 4,000 but less than 6,000.

24. The product of 5 and 286 is greater than 1,500.

25. The product of 4 and 3,123 is closer to 12,000 than 16,000.

26. The sum of 4,637 and 2,878 is greater than 8,000.

27. The quotient of 4 divided by 1 is 1.

Lesson
6-5

Common
Core

4.NBT.5 Multiply a whole
number of up to four
digits by a one-digit whole
number, and multiply two
two-digit numbers, using
strategies based on place
value and the properties
of operations. Illustrate
and explain the calculation
by using equations,
rectangular arrays, and/or
area models. Also 4.NBT.3,
4.OA.3

Multiplying by 1-Digit Numbers

What are the steps to record multiplication?

Paying for the damage to cars from potholes can be costly. The table shows some of the repair costs.

Repairs Due to Pothole Damage

Item	Cost
Shock Absorber	$69 each
Tires	$135 each
Paint	$1,450 per coat

Guided Practice*

Do you know HOW?

In **1** through **6**, find each product. Estimate to check reasonableness.

1. 5 × 188   **2.** 8 × 135

3. 6 × 276   **4.** 3 × 329

5. 1,450   **6.**   48
     ×   4   ×   9

Do you UNDERSTAND?

7. A road repair crew can usually fix 825 potholes each week. How many potholes can they fix in 6 weeks?

© **8. Writing to Explain** A tire shop sells 3 tires at $175 each and includes a fourth tire for free. Is this more or less expensive than buying 4 tires at $135 each? Explain.

Independent Practice

In **9** through **28**, find each product. Estimate to check reasonableness.

9. 6 × 77   **10.** 5 × 83   **11.** 4 × 62   **12.** 7 × 89

13. 3 × 245   **14.** 9 × 318   **15.** 2 × 736   **16.** 8 × 314

17. 4 × 4,347   **18.** 6 × 2,716   **19.** 7 × 1,287   **20.** 3 × 1,942

21.   195   **22.**   58   **23.**   426   **24.**   1,123
     ×   4   ×   7   ×   5   ×   3

25.   2,617   **26.**   985   **27.**   3,265   **28.**   2,134
     ×   6   ×   8   ×   4   ×   9

*For another example, see Set D on page 159.

What is the total cost for 3 new shock absorbers?	What is the total cost for 4 new tires?	What is the total cost for 2 coats of paint?

Estimate:
  3 × $69 is about
  3 × 70 = 210

$$\begin{array}{r} \overset{2}{69} \\ \times\ \ 3 \\ \hline 207 \end{array}$$

Three shocks cost $207.

Estimate:
  4 × $135 is about
  4 × 125 = 500

$$\begin{array}{r} \overset{1\,2}{135} \\ \times\ \ 4 \\ \hline 540 \end{array}$$

Four tires cost $540.

Estimate:
  2 × $1,450 is about
  2 × 1,500 = 3,000

$$\begin{array}{r} \overset{1}{1,450} \\ \times\ \ 2 \\ \hline 2,900 \end{array}$$

Two coats of paint cost $2,900.

Problem Solving

 **MATHEMATICAL PRACTICES**

29. Elaine rents a car for 5 days. It costs $44 a day to rent the car, $7 a day for insurance, and $35 to fill the car up with gas. How much does it cost Elaine to rent the car in all?

© **30. Estimation** A fundraiser was held at Ella School. The first day $188 was collected, $201 was collected the second day, and $79 was collected on the third day. About how much money was collected in all?

31. What is the perimeter of the rectangle below?

259 feet

346 feet

© **32. Construct Arguments** Mr. Tran would like to buy a new sofa that costs $934. He can pay the total all at once, or he can make a $125 payment each month for 8 months. Which plan costs less? Explain.

33. The first memory card was sold in 1998. How many images can seven 32-MB memory cards hold?

? images

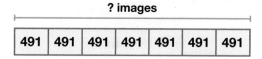

491	491	491	491	491	491	491

A 2,837   **C** 3,437

B 3,137   **D** 4,637

One 32-MB memory card can hold up to 491 images

Lesson
6-6

© **Common Core**

4.NBT.5 Multiply a whole number of up to four digits by a one-digit whole number, and multiply two two-digit numbers, using strategies based on place value and the properties of operations. Illustrate and explain the calculation by using equations, rectangular arrays, and/or area models. Also **4.OA.3**

Problem Solving

Missing or Extra Information

A pocket bike is smaller than an average-sized family car. The length of a pocket bike is 38 inches, the height is 19 inches, and the weight is 39 pounds. The length of the family car is five times the length of the pocket bike. How long is the family car?

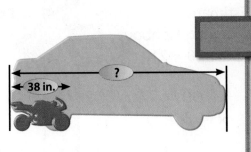

Guided Practice*

© **MATHEMATICAL PRACTICES**

Do you know HOW?

Solve. Tell if there is extra or missing information.

1. A sturdy dog crate weighs 29 pounds. It costs $68. Wendy has 3 dogs. How much will she spend on crates if she buys one for each dog?

Do you UNDERSTAND?

2. What operation was needed to solve Problem 1? Tell why.

© **3. Write a Problem** Write a problem that has extra or missing information.

Independent Practice

© **MATHEMATICAL PRACTICES**

For **4** through **6**, decide if each problem has extra or missing information. Solve if possible.

4. Niki is 3 months old and 21 inches tall. Her father Miles, who is 25 years old, is 3 times as tall as Niki. How tall is Miles?

5. A rectangular pool is 45 feet long. What is its perimeter?

6. Dry dog food comes in 6-pound bags that cost $15 each. How many pounds of food are there in 7 bags?

Applying Math Practices

- What am I asked to find?
- What else can I try?
- How are quantities related?
- How can I explain my work?
- How can I use math to model the problem?
- Can I use tools to help?
- Is my work precise?
- Why does this work?
- How can I generalize?

Draw a diagram to show what you know and what you want to find.

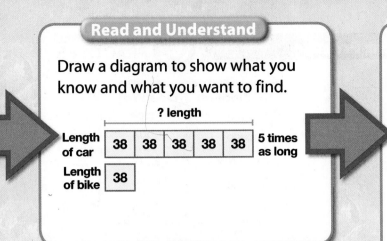

? length

| Length of car | 38 | 38 | 38 | 38 | 38 | 5 times as long |
| Length of bike | 38 | | | | | |

Is there extra information that is not needed to solve this problem?

Yes, the height and weight of the pocket bike are not needed.

Is there missing information that is needed to solve this problem?

No, all of the information I need is given in the problem.

$5 \times 38 = 190$

The average family car is 190 inches long.

---

7. In 1990, a high-school class in Indiana made a very large yo-yo. It weighed 6 times as much as a student who weighed 136 pounds. What was the weight of the yo-yo?

? pounds

| Yo-yo | 136 | 136 | 136 | 136 | 136 | 136 | 6 times as much |
| Student | 136 | | | | | | |

8. Yo-yos first appeared in the United States in 1866, but the name "yo-yo" was first used 50 years later. It is probably from a Filipino word for "come-come" or "to return." In what year did the toy get the "yo-yo" name?

? year

| 1866 | 50 |

For **9** and **10**, use the picture at the right.

9. What is the perimeter of the park?

© **10. Be Precise** If the length of the park was increased by 10 feet, what is the new perimeter?

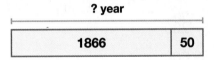

45 feet

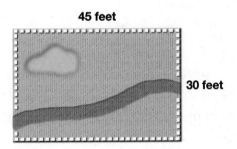

30 feet

11. At a large dog show, there were 45 entries for each of the breeds in the chart at the right. What is the total number of dogs in this show?

© **12. Persevere** A chihuahua weighs 6 pounds. The standard adult height of a Great Pyrenees is about 27 inches. What is the weight of the Great Pyrenees dog?

Breed of Dog

Hound

Working

Terrier

Gundog

Pastoral

Utility

Toy

Great Pyrenees Weighs 17 times as much

Chihuahua Weighs 6 pounds

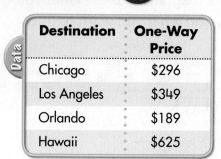

For **13** and **14**, use the table at the right.

13. What would the total cost be for 3 round-trip tickets to Hawaii?

Tip *The prices in the table are for one way!*

Destination	One-Way Price
Chicago	$296
Los Angeles	$349
Orlando	$189
Hawaii	$625

14. How much less does a one-way ticket to Orlando cost than a one-way ticket to Chicago?

For **15** and **16**, use the chart at the right.

15. Use the data to the right. How much more is a ton of dimes worth than a ton of pennies?

16. How much would three tons of pennies be worth?

   A $7,200

   B $9,800

   C $10,800

   D $12,800

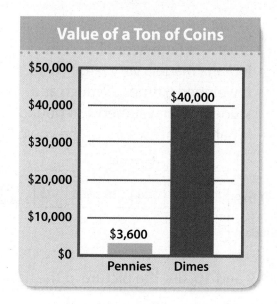

Value of a Ton of Coins

17. Persevere A food cart on an airplane has 6 slots. Each slot holds 2 food trays. How many trays are in 8 food carts?

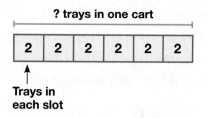

? trays in one cart

| 2 | 2 | 2 | 2 | 2 | 2 |

Trays in each slot

© **Think About the Structure**

18. A pocket bike costs 5 times as much as a 10-speed bicycle. If the bicycle costs $150, which expression gives the cost of the pocket bike?

   A 150 − 5   **C** 150 + 5

   B 150 × 5   **D** 150 ÷ 5

19. Tickets for a movie cost $10 for an adult and $6 for a child. Wally is buying tickets for 2 adults and 1 ticket for a child. Which expression can be used to find the total?

   A 10 + 10 + 10   **C** 10 + 6

   B 10 + 6 + 6   **D** 10 + 10 + 6

Operations on a Calculator

Jamie made 4 trips between Foster and Andersonville this summer. Each trip was 379 miles. How many miles were the 4 trips in all?

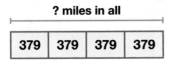 **Step 1** Draw a picture and choose an operation for the first question.

? miles in all

379	379	379	379

Multiply 4 × 379.

Step 2 Press: 4 [×] 379 [ENTER =]

Display: `1516`

Jamie's four trips were 1,516 miles in all.

In September, Jamie traveled 379 miles from Andersonville to Foster, 244 miles from Foster to Leyton, and 137 miles from Leyton back to Andersonville. How many miles did Jamie travel in September?

Step 1 Draw a picture and choose an operation for the second question.

? miles in all

379	244	137

Add 379 + 244 + 137.

Step 2 Press: 379 [+] 244 [+] 137 [ENTER =]

Display: `760`

Jamie traveled 760 miles in September.

Practice

For each problem, draw a picture, choose an operation, and solve.

1. How much farther did Jamie travel from Andersonville to Foster than from Foster to Leyton?

2. How many miles would Jamie travel if she went from Andersonville to Leyton and back to Andersonville?

Reteaching

Set A, pages 138–140

Find 6 × 22.

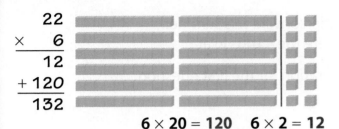

$$
\begin{array}{r}
22 \\
\times\ \ 6 \\
\hline
12 \\
+\ 120 \\
\hline
132
\end{array}
$$

6 × 20 = 120   6 × 2 = 12

120 + 12 = **132**

Remember to find the partial products.

Find each product using the expanded algorithm.

1.	28 × 6		**2.**	28 × 3
3.	75 × 5		**4.**	53 × 4
5.	88 × 2		**6.**	21 × 6

Set B, pages 142–143

A snack pack has 37 almonds in it. A can of nuts has 5 times as many almonds. How many almonds are in the can of nuts?

Find 5 × 37.

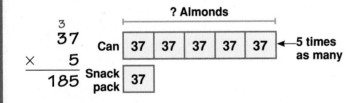

$$
\begin{array}{r}
\overset{3}{37} \\
\times\ \ 5 \\
\hline
185
\end{array}
$$

Remember to regroup when needed.

Find each product using the standard algorithm.

1.	14 × 7		**2.**	46 × 3
3.	51 × 2		**4.**	32 × 5
5.	19 × 2		**6.**	41 × 6

Set C, pages 144–146

Find 8 × 24.

Step 1

Multiply the ones. Regroup if needed.

$$
\begin{array}{r}
\overset{3}{24} \\
\times\ \ 8 \\
\hline
2
\end{array}
$$

Step 2

Multiply the tens. Add any extra tens.

$$
\begin{array}{r}
\overset{3}{24} \\
\times\ \ 8 \\
\hline
192
\end{array}
$$

Remember to check your answer with an estimate.

Find each product.

1.	18 × 2		**2.**	48 × 5
3.	33 × 6		**4.**	97 × 7

Find 768 × 6.

Step 1

Multiply the ones. Regroup if necessary.

$$
\begin{array}{r}
{\scriptstyle 4} \\
768 \\
\times \quad 6 \\
\hline
8
\end{array}
$$

Step 2

Multiply the tens. Add any extra tens. Regroup if necessary.

$$
\begin{array}{r}
{\scriptstyle 4\ 4} \\
768 \\
\times \quad 6 \\
\hline
08
\end{array}
$$

Step 3

Multiply the hundreds. Add any extra hundreds.

$$
\begin{array}{r}
{\scriptstyle 4\ 4} \\
768 \\
\times \quad 6 \\
\hline
4{,}608
\end{array}
$$

Remember to check your answer with an estimate.

Find each product.

1.
$$
\begin{array}{r}
239 \\
\times \quad 4 \\
\hline
\end{array}
$$

2.
$$
\begin{array}{r}
148 \\
\times \quad 5 \\
\hline
\end{array}
$$

3.
$$
\begin{array}{r}
4{,}233 \\
\times \quad 6 \\
\hline
\end{array}
$$

4.
$$
\begin{array}{r}
937 \\
\times \quad 7 \\
\hline
\end{array}
$$

5.
$$
\begin{array}{r}
3{,}261 \\
\times \quad 4 \\
\hline
\end{array}
$$

6.
$$
\begin{array}{r}
1{,}250 \\
\times \quad 8 \\
\hline
\end{array}
$$

An orchard has 3 times as many apple trees as cherry trees. If there are 63 pear trees and 52 cherry trees, how many apple trees are there?

What do I know?

There are 63 pear trees and 52 cherry trees. There are 3 times as many apple trees as cherry trees.

What am I being asked to find?

The number of apple trees

	? apple trees in all		
Number of apple trees	52	52	52

3 times as many

Number of cherry trees	52

Choose an Operation Multiply when you want to find "times as many."

$3 \times 52 = 156$

There are 156 apple trees.

The number of pear trees was extra information.

Remember some problems do not have enough information to solve.

Tell if there is extra information or if there is missing information. Solve if you have enough information.

1. Todd read 35 pages of his book on Saturday. He read for 10 minutes on Sunday. How many pages did Todd read over the weekend?

2. Molly bought 150 sheets of paper and 5 notebooks. She put 50 sheets in her math folder, 25 sheets in her science folder, 25 sheets in her social studies folder, and 40 sheets in her reading folder. How many sheets did Molly have left?

Multiple Choice

(C) ASSESSMENT

1. Part of the calculation for 3 × 26 is shown below. What is the missing partial product? (6-1)

   A 8
   B 18
   C 20
   D 60

   $$\begin{array}{r} 26 \\ \times\ \ 3 \\ \hline \blacksquare\blacksquare \\ +\ 60 \\ \hline 78 \end{array}$$

2. A factory produced 275 cars in one week. How many cars could the factory produce in 4 weeks? (6-4)

   A 880 cars
   B 1,000 cars
   C 1,100 cars
   D 8,300 cars

3. Denise bought four pairs of inline skates. Each pair cost $54. How much did Denise spend? (6-2)

   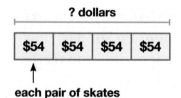

   ? dollars

   | $54 | $54 | $54 | $54 |

   ↑
   each pair of skates

   A $254
   B $216
   C $204
   D $162

4. A chain music store has 23 locations. If each location employs 5 clerks, how many clerks work for the chain store? (6-2)

   A 105
   B 108
   C 115
   D 155

5. There were 14 adults at the Jones family reunion. There were twice as many children as adults at the reunion. How many children attended the reunion? (6-3)

   A 14
   B 21
   C 24
   D 28

6. Which problem best describes the array modeled below? (6-1)

   A 30 + 12
   B 4 × 13
   C 3 × 14
   D 3 × 10

7. A country has 14 deepwater ports. Each port has 6 piers. How many piers are there in all? (6-2)

   A 184
   B 102
   C 84
   D 70

8. Kai owns a rental shop at a beach club. Last year, Kai bought 6 used water vehicles for $3,179 each. How much did Kai spend? (6-5)

9. The lighthouse is 76 feet tall and has 99 stairs. An ocean liner is 3 times as tall as the lighthouse. What is the extra information if you want to find the height of the ocean liner? (6-6)

10. Mr. Tyler lives in Miami, Florida. He travels to Richmond, Virginia, 4 times each month for business. The distance there and back is 2,658 kilometers. What is the total distance of Mr. Tyler's business trips each month? (6-4)

11. Seven students took a bus to the state park. The round-trip tickets cost $45 per student. They stayed for a few nights at a campground at a cost of $5 per student each night. Which missing information is needed to find the total amount each student spent on the camping trip? (6-6)

12. A construction company uses 1,020 nails for each house it builds. How many nails will be used to build 5 houses? How can you use estimation to check the reasonableness of your answer? (6-5)

13. In 1 day Sharla collected 36 cans to take to the recycling center. If she collects the same number of cans each day, how many will she collect in 7 days? (6-3)

14. A radio station played a new hit song 34 times a day for 4 days. What partial products would you use to find how many times the song was played in all? (6-1)

15. There are 1,576 seats in each section of a stadium. How many seats are there in 5 sections of the stadium? (6-5)

16. An office supply store sells 605 packages of paper each month. How many packages of paper are sold in 6 months? (6-4)

17. Liz drinks 28 liters of water each month. How many liters of water does Liz drink in 5 months? Explain each step you took to find your answer. (6-3)

18. Mr. Lee drove 8 miles from his house to Parkside. Parkside is 4 miles south of Springfield. From Parkside, he drove 3 miles to Springdale. Then he drove 20 miles from Springdale to Brookville. How far did Mr. Lee drive in all, from his house to Brookville? Identify the extra or missing information. Solve if possible. (6-6)

Mr. Lopez wants to buy 22 bicycle tires for the school racing team. He found three different stores that sell racing tires.

FRANK'S BIKE SHOP	Speed Bikes INC.	SUPER BIKES
Racing Tires: $9 each	Tire Sale: 2 for $16	Special on Tires! 5 for only $35

For Exercises 1–8, copy and complete the table below on a separate sheet of paper.

Store	Price per Tire	Estimated Price for 22 Tires	Actual Prices for 22 Tires
Frank's	$9		
Speed Bikes		$160	
Super Bikes	$7		

1. What is the estimated price for 22 tires at Frank's Bike Shop?

2. What is the actual price for 22 tires at Frank's Bike Shop?

3. How much does 1 tire cost at Speed Bikes INC.?

4. What is the actual price for 22 tires at Speed Bikes INC.?

5. What operation was used to calculate the price per tire at Super Bikes.

6. What is the estimated price for 22 tires at Super Bikes?

7. What is the actual price for 22 tires at Super Bikes?

8. How do the actual prices for 22 tires compare to the estimated prices?

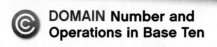

Topic **7**

Number Sense: Multiplying by 2-Digit Numbers

▼ How much water might you use while brushing your teeth? You will find out in Lesson 7-2.

Topic Essential Questions
• How can greater products be found mentally?
• How can greater products be estimated?

Review What You Know!

Vocabulary

Choose the best term from the box.

- equation
- product
- factors
- round

1. A(n) __?__ is another word for a number sentence.

2. One way to estimate a product is to __?__ each number.

3. A(n) __?__ is the answer to a multiplication problem.

4. In the equation $9 \times 5 = 45$, 9 and 5 are both __?__.

Multiplication Facts

Find each product.

5. 3×9 **6.** 5×6 **7.** 4×8

8. 6×9 **9.** 7×4 **10.** 9×8

Rounding

Round each number to the nearest hundred.

11. 864   **12.** 651   **13.** 348

14. 985   **15.** 451   **16.** 749

Multiplying Three Factors

© **Writing to Explain** Write an answer to the question.

17. Gina wants to multiply $9 \times 2 \times 5$. How can Gina group the factors to make it easier to multiply?

Pose the problem. Start each lesson by working together to solve problems. It will help you make sense of math.

Applying Math Practices

- What am I asked to find?
- What else can I try?
- How are quantities related?
- How can I explain my work?
- How can I use math to model the problem?
- Can I use tools to help?
- Is my work precise?
- Why does this work?
- How can I generalize?

Lesson 7-1

© **Reason** Solve. Use place-value blocks or a drawing to help.

There are 10 teams in a baseball league. Each team has 25 players on the roster. Use any way you can to find how many players are on the teams in all. Show your work.

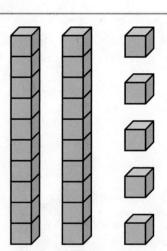

Lesson 7-2

© **Generalize** Solve. Look for patterns in the factors and products.

The principal of your school needs to order supplies for 20 new classrooms. He has made a list of how many desks, chairs, and pencils each classroom needs. How many of each item does the principal need to order for all 20 classrooms?

Each Classroom

20 desks

30 chairs

40 pencils

Lesson 7-3

© **Communicate** Solve. Use estimation to help.

To win a game, you need a product that is as close to 1,600 as possible. Select two factors from the numbers shown at the right. Which numbers can you select so that the product is closest to 1,600? Tell how you decided.

Number Choices			
18	42	56	81

Lesson 7-4

© **Persevere** Solve. Think of different ways you might estimate.

Remember the game you played during the last lesson? You needed a product that was as close to 1,600 as possible. This time you can choose two factors from a different set of numbers shown at the right. Which numbers can you select so that the product is closest to 1,600? Tell how you decided.

Number Choices			
24	32	61	78

Lesson 7-5

© **Model** Solve. Show how you found the answer.

Four friends bought a present for Joan. How much less would each friend pay if 6 friends shared the cost equally rather than 4?

$36

Lesson
7-1

© Common Core

4.NBT.5 Multiply a whole
number of up to four
digits by a one-digit whole
number, and multiply two
two-digit numbers, using
strategies based on place
value and the properties
of operations. Illustrate
and explain the calculation
by using equations,
rectangular arrays, and/or
area models.

Arrays and Multiplying 2-Digit Numbers by Multiples of 10

How can you use a model to multiply?

Max's Moving Company has boxes for packing books. If each box holds 24 books, how many books would fit into 10 boxes?

24 Books

Choose an Operation Multiply to join equal groups.

Another Example **What is another way to use a model to multiply?**

Mrs. Harrigan ordered 30 boxes of glasses for her restaurant. Each box holds 16 glasses. How many glasses did she order?

Step 1

To find 30×16, use a grid to draw a model. On the grid draw an array with 30 rows of 16. Break apart 16 into 10 and 6.

Step 2

Add to find the total.

$$\begin{array}{r} 300 \\ +\ 180 \\ \hline 480 \end{array}$$

$30 \times 16 = 480$

Mrs. Harrigan ordered 480 glasses.

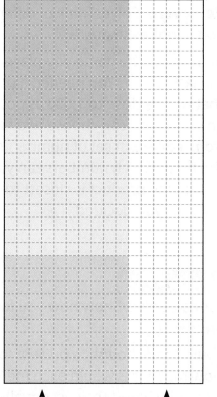

↑ 30 groups of 10 = 300   ↑ 30 groups of 6 = 180

Explain It

1. Explain how you found the product for 30 groups of 6.

2. Mrs. Harrigan also orders 30 boxes of plates. There are 25 plates in each box. How many plates did she order?

Use a model to find 10×24.

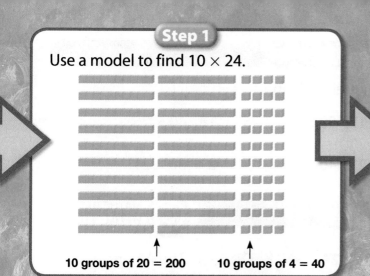

10 groups of 20 = 200   10 groups of 4 = 40

Add to find the total.

$$\begin{array}{r} 200 \\ +\quad 40 \\ \hline 240 \end{array}$$

$10 \times 24 = 240$

240 books will fit into 10 boxes.

Guided Practice*

MATHEMATICAL
PRACTICES

Do you know HOW?

For **1** through **6**, draw a model to find each product.

1. 10×18 **2.** 20×15

3. 10×27 **4.** 20×12

5. 20×23 **6.** 30×21

Do you UNDERSTAND?

7. Model Draw a model to show 40×16. Then use the model to find the product.

8. There are 30 boxes on one of Max's moving trucks. If each box weighs 36 pounds, how much do the boxes weigh all together?

Independent Practice

Leveled Practice In **9** through **14**, use models to find each product.

9. 10×22

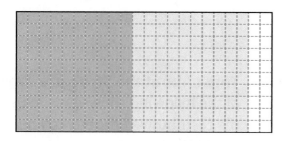

10. 10×13

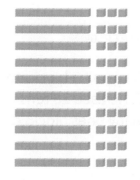

11. 20×35 **12.** 20×41 **13.** 30×29 **14.** 40×37

DIGITAL   eTools **Place-Value Blocks**
www.pearsonsuccessnet.com

In **15** through **22**, find each product. Use models to help.

15. 30 × 18   **16.** 40 × 22   **17.** 50 × 11   **18.** 40 × 25

19. 30 × 39   **20.** 50 × 15   **21.** 40 × 15   **22.** 60 × 21

Problem Solving

 MATHEMATICAL **PRACTICES**

© **23. Reason** In the first 3 months of the year, the electronics store sold 1,446 cameras. They sold 486 cameras in January and 385 cameras in February. How many cameras did they sell in March?

24. Science The American bison is the heaviest land mammal in North America. Bison live in groups of up to 20. How many bison could there be in 12 groups?

© **25. Critique Reasoning** Miranda says that 30 × 26 is greater than 20 × 36. Is she correct? Explain how you know.

© **26. Use Tools** Show how you can find 30 × 15 by drawing an array.

For **27**, use the picture at the right.

27. The 2001 record for balancing drinking glasses was 75 glasses. How many total fluid ounces could all of the glasses contain?

Each glass holds 20 fluid ounces.

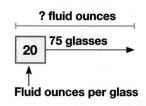

? fluid ounces

75 glasses

20

Fluid ounces per glass

28. Henry used place-value blocks to model 20 × 17. He used 20 tens blocks. How many ones blocks did he use?

   A   34

   B   37

   C 140

   D 170

© **29. Think About the Structure** Which of the following shows how to use the Distributive Property to find 3 × 46?

   A (3 × 40) + (3 × 6)

   B (3 × 46) + (3 × 46)

   C (1 × 4) + (2 × 6)

   D (3 × 4) + (3 × 6)

Going Digital

Perfect Squares

Use **tools** Counters.

The first three perfect square numbers are 1, 4, and 9. They are called perfect squares because they name square shaped arrays.

Use arrays to find the next perfect square.

$1 \times 1 = 1$ $2 \times 2 = 4$ $3 \times 3 = 9$

Step 1   Go to the Counters eTool. Select the array workspace icon. 🔲 Pull the resize button in the upper right corner of the rectangle to make an array that has 3 rows and 3 columns of counters. Increase the number of rows and columns until you see the next square shaped array, or perfect square. The total number of counters is shown in the odometer at the bottom of the page.

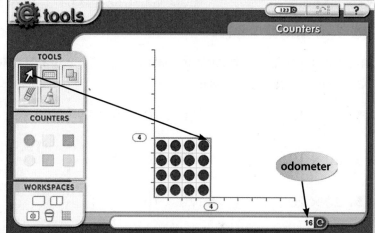

Step 2   The array shows that 16 is a perfect square.

Use the array to write the multiplication fact for the perfect square. There are 4 rows and 4 columns, which is 4×4.

Practice

© **Persevere** For **1** through **6**, find the multiplication fact for each perfect square.

1. 36   **2.** 64   **3.** 25

4. 100   **5.** 49   **6.** 81

4.NBT.5 Multiply a whole number of up to four digits by a one-digit whole number, and multiply two two-digit numbers, using strategies based on place value and the properties of operations. Illustrate and explain the calculation by using equations, rectangular arrays, and/or area models. Also **4.OA.3**

Using Mental Math to Multiply 2-Digit Numbers

How can you multiply by multiples of 10?

How many adults under 65 visit the Sunny Day Amusement Park in 20 days? How many children visit the park in 30 days? How many adults 65 and over visit the park in 50 days?

Average Number of Visitors Each Day

TICKET
Adults under 65: **60**

Adults 65 and over: **40**

Children: **80**

Guided Practice*

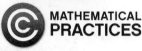

MATHEMATICAL PRACTICES

Do you know HOW?

In **1** through **8**, use basic facts and patterns to find the product.

1. 30×10 **2.** 50×10

3. 20×10 **4.** 60×20

5. 20×20 **6.** 70×10

7. 40×50 **8.** 80×50

Do you UNDERSTAND?

© **9. Reason** When you multiply 60×50, how many zeros are in the product?

10. In cold weather, fewer people go to Sunny Day Amusement Park. November has 30 days. If the park sells 30 tickets each day in November, how many would they sell for the whole month?

Independent Practice

For **11** through **34**, multiply using mental math.

11. 30×30 **12.** 10×60 **13.** 50×30 **14.** 80×40

15. 20×70 **16.** 70×90 **17.** 40×20 **18.** 40×30

19. 70×40 **20.** 20×30 **21.** 60×40 **22.** 60×90

23. 70×80 **24.** 30×80 **25.** 60×60 **26.** 70×30

27. 50×50 **28.** 30×90 **29.** 90×40 **30.** 30×60

31. 20×50 **32.** 80×30 **33.** 60×80 **34.** 50×90

For another example, see Set B on page 178.

Adults under 65 in 20 Days

To multiply 20 × 60, use a pattern.

2 × 6 = 12

20 × 6 = 120

20 × 60 = 1,200

1,200 adults under 65 visit the park in 20 days.

Children in 30 Days

The number of zeros in the product is the total number of zeros in both factors.

30 × 80 = 2,400

1 zero   1 zero   2 zeros

2,400 children visit the park in 30 days.

Adults 65 and over in 50 Days

If the product of a basic fact ends in zero, include that zero in the count.

5 × 4 = 20

50 × 40 = 2,000

2,000 adults 65 and over visit the park in 50 days.

Problem Solving

 MATHEMATICAL
PRACTICES

35. ♪ **Music** The world's fastest drummer can hit the drum 20 times in one second. How many times can the drummer hit the drum in 30 seconds?

© 36. **Construct Arguments** Explain why the product of 50 and 80 has three zeros when 50 has one zero and 80 has one zero.

© 37. **Model** Use the picture below. You might use about 2 gallons of water while brushing your teeth. How many cups of water might you use while brushing your teeth?

There are 16 cups in 1 gallon.

© 38. **Use Structure** Of every 30 minutes of television air time, about 8 minutes show TV commercials. If 90 minutes of television is aired, how many minutes of commercials will be played?

  A 8 minutes   **C** 38 minutes

  B 24 minutes   **D** 128 minutes

© 39. **Reason** If in one year a city recorded a total of 97 rainy days, how many of the days did it NOT rain?

365 days in one year

97	?

Lesson
7-3

Common
Core

4.NBT.3 Use place value understanding to round multi-digit whole numbers to any place. Also **4.OA.3**

Using Rounding to Estimate

How can you use rounding to estimate?

The workers at Mrs. Piper's apple grove picked 87 dozen apples. There are 12 apples in one dozen. About how many apples did the workers pick?

1 dozen apples

Guided Practice*

MATHEMATICAL
PRACTICES

Do you know HOW?

For **1** through **4**, estimate each product.

1. 24 × 18 rounds to ▢ × ▢ = ▢.

2. 33 × 31 is close to ▢ × ▢ = ▢.

3. 38 × 22   **4.** 45 × 48

Do you UNDERSTAND?

© **5. Writing to Explain** Sue said that 870 is a reasonable estimate for 87 × 12, and her teacher agreed. How could Sue get 870 as an estimate?

6. Howie used rounding to estimate the product of 35 × 42 and got 1,200. What did he do wrong?

Independent Practice

Leveled Practice For **7** through **24**, estimate each product.

7. 44 × 13 rounds to ▢ × ▢ = ▢.   **8.** 39 × 19 rounds to ▢ × ▢ = ▢.

9. 28 × 27 rounds to ▢ × ▢ = ▢.   **10.** 35 × 42 rounds to ▢ × ▢ = ▢.

11. 72 × 48 rounds to ▢ × ▢ = ▢.   **12.** 68 × 36 rounds to ▢ × ▢ = ▢.

13. 64 × 13   **14.** 24 × 28   **15.** 42 × 17   **16.** 82 × 36

17. 25 × 81   **18.** 15 × 38   **19.** 54 × 18   **20.** 66 × 41

21. 34 × 52   **22.** 74 × 34   **23.** 88 × 23   **24.** 57 × 49

For another example, see Set C on page 178.

Round both numbers in 87 × 12.

Round 87 to the nearest ten.
  7 > 5, so round 87 to 90.

Round 12 to the nearest ten.
  2 < 5, so round 12 to 10.

Estimate the product.

$$87 \times 12$$

$$90 \times 10 = 900$$

The workers picked about 900 apples.

Problem Solving

MATHEMATICAL PRACTICES

25. Julia worked about 18 hours last week making fruit baskets to sell as gifts. About how many minutes did she spend making fruit baskets?

Tip *There are 60 minutes in 1 hour.*

26. **Science** The world's smallest snake, the thread snake, can be 4 inches long. The world's largest snake, the anaconda, can be 60 times as long. How many inches long can an anaconda be?

Ⓒ **27. Critique Reasoning** Lenore uses rounding and estimates that the product of 52 × 38 is 1,500. Is this estimate reasonable? Why or why not?

Ⓒ **28. Use Structure** List the numbers from 50 to 60 that would make this number sentence true.

$$85 + 54 > \boxed{} + 85$$

Use the table at the right for **29** through **32**.

29. About how many Hamlin trees does Mr. Gonzalez have?

Ⓒ **30. Reason** Mr. Gonzalez has the same number of which two types of trees? Explain how you know.

Mr. Gonzalez' Trees		
Type of Orange Tree	Number of Rows	Number of Trees in Each Row
Hamlin	28	38
Temple	38	28
Valencia	31	46

Ⓒ **31. Writing to Explain** About how many more Valencia orange trees than Temple orange trees does Mr. Gonzalez have?

32. To the nearest hundred, about how many orange trees does Mr. Gonzalez have all together?

A 1,100   **C** 3,000

B 1,600   **D** 3,900

© Common Core

4.NBT.5 Multiply a whole number of up to four digits by a one-digit whole number, and multiply two two-digit numbers, using strategies based on place value and the properties of operations. Illustrate and explain the calculation by using equations, rectangular arrays, and/or area models. Also 4.NBT.3, 4.OA.3

Using Compatible Numbers to Estimate

How can you use compatible numbers to estimate?

Nolan set up an online blog for his friends to visit. Estimate the number of hits Nolan will have in 24 days.

Average number of hits per day: 41

Guided Practice*

 MATHEMATICAL PRACTICES

Do you know HOW?

In **1** through **3**, estimate to find each product.

1. 24 × 18
   24 is close to 25.
   18 is close to ▢.
   Multiply 25 × ▢ = ▢

2. 24 × 37   **3.** 52 × 27

Do you UNDERSTAND?

4. In the example above, suppose the average number of hits per day were 61. If you estimate 24 × 61 as 25 × 60, what is the estimate?

© **5. Writing to Explain** Rounding would give 20 × 60 as an estimate for 24 × 61. Why does 25 × 60 give a better estimate than 20 × 60?

Independent Practice

For **6** through **25**, estimate to find each product. When possible, use compatible numbers.

 Look for numbers near 25. Remember 2 × 25 = 50, 3 × 25 = 75, 4 × 25 = 100, 5 × 25 = 125, and so on.

6. 26 × 42   **7.** 31 × 46   **8.** 21 × 25   **9.** 58 × 12

10. 22 × 26   **11.** 78 × 21   **12.** 36 × 49   **13.** 66 × 31

14. 64 × 24   **15.** 21 × 19   **16.** 76 × 39   **17.** 32 × 24

18. 89 × 43   **19.** 79 × 79   **20.** 46 × 18   **21.** 86 × 37

22. 53 × 54   **23.** 68 × 39   **24.** 29 × 43   **25.** 48 × 16

Animated Glossary
www.pearsonsuccessnet.com

For another example, see Set D on page 179.

Estimate 24 × 41.

Rounding to the nearest ten gives 20 × 40 = 800 as an estimate.

However, you can get a closer estimate by using compatible numbers, which are numbers that are easy to compute mentally.

24 is close to 25
41 is close to 40

It is easy to find 25 × 40, since 25 and 40 are compatible numbers. Remember that 25 × 4 = 100. So 25 × 40 = 1,000.

Nolan will have about 1,000 hits in 24 days.

Notice that 24 is closer to 25 than to 20. So, 25 × 40 gives a better estimate than 20 × 40. However, either method can be used to find an estimate.

Problem Solving

MATHEMATICAL
PRACTICES

26. An electronics store sells about 45 computers a day. About how many computers could they sell in 4 weeks?

Tip *There are 7 days in 1 week.*

Ⓒ **27. Be Precise** Maya has the poster below on her wall. What is the perimeter of the poster?

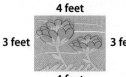

4 feet

3 feet   3 feet

4 feet

Ⓒ **28. Writing to Explain** Show how you would use estimation to decide which has the greater product, 39 × 21 or 32 × 32.

29. Mason swims about 55 minutes each day. Estimate the number of minutes he swims in 14 days.

30. A company ordered 28 cartons of tape. Each carton contained 24 rolls. What is the best estimate of the total number of rolls of tape ordered?

  A 280   **C** 750

  B 400   **D** 900

31. During her summer job at the local grocery store, Vivian earned $247 per week. If she worked for 6 weeks, how much money did she earn in all?

32. **Social Studies** In 1858, two ships connected a telegraph cable across the Atlantic Ocean for the first time. Using the diagram below, estimate the total distance of cable used.

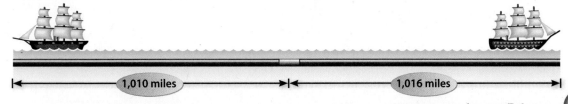

1,010 miles   1,016 miles

Common Core

4.NBT.5 Multiply a whole number of up to four digits by a one-digit whole number, and multiply two two-digit numbers, using strategies based on place value and the properties of operations. Illustrate and explain the calculation by using equations, rectangular arrays, and/or area models. Also **4.OA.3**

Problem Solving

Multiple-Step Problems

Paul and Libby sold some sock monkeys for a total of $72. Libby sold 5 monkeys from her collection. Paul sold 3 monkeys from his collection. If they sold each sock monkey for the same amount, how much did they sell each monkey for?

Paul sold 3 monkeys

Libby sold 5 monkeys

Guided Practice*

MATHEMATICAL PRACTICES

Do you know HOW?

Solve.

1. Adult admission to the town fair is $7. Child admission to the fair is $3. How much would it cost 2 adults and 4 children to enter the fair?

Do you UNDERSTAND?

2. What is the hidden question or questions from Problem 1?

© 3. **Write a Problem** Write a problem that contains a hidden question.

Independent Practice

MATHEMATICAL PRACTICES

Answer the hidden question or questions. Then solve the problem. Write your answer in a complete sentence.

4. Charlie and Lola like to walk around the perimeter of their town park. The perimeter is 2 miles long. Last week Charlie walked around the perimeter 4 times and Lola walked around it 5 times. How many more miles did Lola walk than Charlie last week?

5. Abby buys 15 sunflower plants and 12 petunia plants to plant in her garden. She plans to plant 3 flowers in each row. How many rows of flowers will Abby plant?

6. What is the hidden question in Problem 5?

Applying Math Practices

- What am I asked to find?
- What else can I try?
- How are quantities related?
- How can I explain my work?
- How can I use math to model the problem?
- Can I use tools to help?
- Is my work precise?
- Why does this work?
- How can I generalize?

Find the hidden question. How many monkeys did Paul and Libby sell in all?

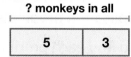

? monkeys in all

5	3

5 + 3 = 8 monkeys

They sold 8 sock monkeys.

Use the answer to the hidden question to solve the problem.

If they sold each sock monkey for the same amount, how much did they sell each sock monkey for?

$72

?	?	?	?	?	?	?	?

↑
Cost of
1 sock monkey

$72 ÷ 8 = 9

Paul and Libby sold each sock monkey for $9.

Ⓒ Model Use the data at the right for **7** through **9**.

7. Carlos's family bought 3 hamburgers and 2 salads from Diner Delight. They paid with a $20 bill. How much change did they receive?

8. Amber and her family bought 3 chicken sandwiches, 2 salads, and 1 baked potato. They spent $4 on drinks. How much did they spend in all?

9. Gene spent exactly $11 on lunch, including tax. He bought a chicken sandwich, a salad, and a baked potato. How much did Gene spend on tax?

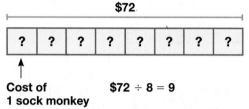

Diner Delight	
Hamburger	$4
Chicken Sandwich	$5
Baked Potato	$2
Salad	$3

Ⓒ Model For **10** through **12**, use the table to the right.

10. Terrence and Jennifer went to Al's Discount Music Store. Terrence bought 4 CDs and two 3-packs of blank CDs. Jennifer bought 8 DVDs, 3 CDs, and one 3-pack of blank CDs. Together, how much did they spend?

11. Give an example of a hidden question in Problem 10.

12. In one hour, Al's Discount Music Store sold 22 DVDs, 36 CDs, and six 3-packs of blank CDs. How much money did the store earn from these sales?

Al's Discount Music Store	
3-pack blank CDs	$7
DVDs	$5
CDs	$10

Set A, pages 166–168

Use a model to multiply 20 × 14.

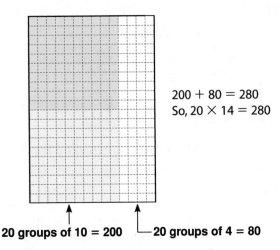

200 + 80 = 280
So, 20 × 14 = 280

20 groups of 10 = 200   20 groups of 4 = 80

Remember you can draw models to represent multiplication problems.

Draw a model to find each product.

1. 10 × 23	**2.** 20 × 34
3. 10 × 17	**4.** 30 × 15
5. 20 × 28	**6.** 40 × 33
7. 30 × 21	**8.** 20 × 16
9. 40 × 12	**10.** 30 × 18

Set B, pages 170–171

Use mental math to find 20 × 80.

Think about the pattern.

2 × 8 = 16

20 × 8 = 160

20 × 80 = 1,600

Remember when the product of a basic fact has a zero, there is one more zero in the answer.

Use a pattern to find each product.

1. 40 × 10	**2.** 60 × 20
3. 80 × 50	**4.** 30 × 90
5. 70 × 40	**6.** 20 × 50
7. 60 × 40	**8.** 30 × 40
9. 80 × 70	**10.** 60 × 60

Set C, pages 172–173

Use rounding to estimate 24 × 16.

Round each number to the nearest ten.

24 rounds to 20.
16 rounds to 20.

20 × 20

20 × 20 = 400
So, 24 × 16 is about 400.

Remember to check the digit to the right of the rounding place to decide how to round a number.

Estimate each product.

1. 27 × 21	**2.** 64 × 16
3. 53 × 32	**4.** 44 × 51
5. 35 × 42	**6.** 71 × 24

Use compatible numbers to estimate 28 × 19.

28 is about 25.
19 is about 20.

Remember, if 25 × 2 = 50, then 25 × 20 = 500.

25 × 20 = 500
So, 28 × 19 is about 500.

Remember compatible numbers are numbers that are easy to compute with mentally.

Estimate each product.

1. 26 × 32   **2.** 24 × 41

3. 29 × 31   **4.** 42 × 49

5. 73 × 18   **6.** 24 × 38

7. 19 × 31   **8.** 63 × 87

When you solve multiple-step problems you need to answer the hidden question or questions before you can solve the problem.

Maggie bought 3 puzzles and 4 games at a garage sale. The puzzles cost $3 each and the games cost $2 each. Maggie paid for the items with a $20 bill. How much change should she get back?

Hidden questions:
How much did the puzzles cost? 3 × $3 = $9
How much did the games cost?   4 × $2 = $8
What was the total cost? $9 + $8 = $17

Solve the problem:
$20 − $17 = $3

Maggie should get $3 back.

Remember to answer the hidden questions first.

Use the hidden question to solve each problem.

1. Gwen bought 4 dozen apples at the store. The apples were equally divided into 6 bags. How many apples were in each bag? (Hint: 1 dozen = 12)

2. Cindy has 35 pennies, and her brother has 37 pennies. They put all of their pennies together and placed them into 8 equal stacks. How many pennies are in each stack?

3. Keith's dad spent $28 buying movie tickets for himself and his 3 children. An adult ticket cost $10. How much did one child's ticket cost?

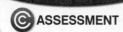
Multiple Choice

ⓒ ASSESSMENT

1. Don works 18 hours a week at the library. Which shows the best way to use rounding to estimate how many hours Don will work in 52 weeks? (7-3)

   A 10 × 50

   B 10 × 60

   C 20 × 50

   D 18 × 60

2. A Virginia opossum can have up to 21 babies at one time. Suppose 10 Virginia opossums had babies all at the same time. How many baby opossums could there be? (7-1)

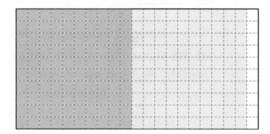

   A 320

   B 210

   C 110

   D 31

3. There are 24 rows in an auditorium. Each row has 42 seats. Which is the best estimate of the total number of seats? (7-4)

   A 70

   B 400

   C 500

   D 1,000

4. There are 24 schools competing in a cheerleading contest. There are 18 cheerleaders on each team. Which is the best way to use compatible numbers to estimate the number of cheerleaders that are competing? (7-4)

   A 20 × 10

   B 25 × 20

   C 30 × 10

   D 30 × 20

5. A movie theater sells 50 tickets for each showing of a movie. They showed the movie 40 times last week. How many tickets did they sell? (7-2)

   A 20,000

   B 2,000

   C 200

   D 20

6. Elaine is making 11 pinecone wreaths to sell at a fair. She needs 13 pinecones for each wreath. How many pinecones does she need in all? (7-1)

   A 24

   B 44

   C 143

   D 153

7. A tractor trailer has 18 wheels. How many more wheels are on 2 tractor trailers than on 5 cars? (7-5)

8. Mr. Hans bought 40 boxes of tiles for his kitchen floor. Each box of tiles cost $30. How much money did Mr. Hans pay for the tiles? (7-2)

9. Alex wants to use rounding to estimate 31 × 82. Write a number sentence that shows how Alex should round each factor and what the estimated product would be. (7-3)

10. A florist is making centerpieces for an event. He is putting 22 roses in each centerpiece. Use compatible numbers to estimate the number of roses he will need for 26 centerpieces. (7-4)

11. Complete the number sentence below. (7-2)

50 × 20 = ▮

12. Justine's plant stand has 6 shelves. Each shelf holds 4 plants. Justine has already placed 16 plants on her stand. How many more plants can fit on the plant stand? (7-5)

13. Felipe wants to keep his insect collection in display cases. Each case can hold 30 insects. How many insects will 20 full display cases hold? (7-2)

14. A school building is 32 feet tall. About how many inches tall is the building? (7-3)

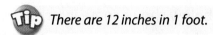 *There are 12 inches in 1 foot.*

15. Elizabeth is making 20 necklaces. Each necklace has 16 beads. How many beads does she need to make all of the necklaces? (7-1)

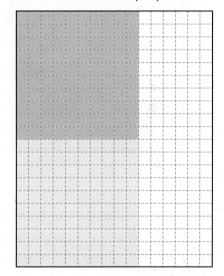

16. The local library places new books in a section with 31 shelves. Each shelf fits 18 books. Use compatible numbers to estimate the number of books that the library can fit on the shelves. (7-4)

17. Margo hikes 5 miles three times a week. Susan hikes 4 miles four times a week. Ralph hikes 2 miles seven times a week. How many miles do they hike in all? Explain your answer. (7-5)

Kelly works on one of the ferry boats that travel from Cape May, New Jersey, to Lewes, Delaware. She helps get the cars on and off the boat safely.

The sign below shows some information about the ferries. Use the information to answer the questions below.

Cape May–Lewes Ferry
- *10 trips leave from each city, every day.*
- *Each trip takes about 80 minutes.*
- *Each trip is 17 miles long.*
- *A ticket to walk onto the ferry costs $3.*
- *A ticket to drive your car onto the ferry costs $34.*

1. How many miles do the ferry boats travel all together each day? Write an equation to show how to solve the problem. Draw an array to help.

2. About how many minutes do all the boats spend traveling each day? Write an equation to show how to solve the problem.

3. It takes about 18 minutes to get the cars on the ferry. It takes about 18 minutes to get them off. Kelly worked on 25 trips last week. About how many minutes did she spend getting cars on and off the ferry? Explain how you solved the problem.

4. On one trip, 49 people drove their car onto the ferry and 52 people walked onto the ferry. About how much money did the ferry service collect for all the tickets? Explain how you solved the problem.

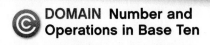
Topic 8

Developing Fluency: Multiplying by 2-Digit Numbers

▼ The Queen Mary 2 is as tall as a 23-story building. How many feet high is this above the water? You will find out in Lesson 8-4.

Review What You Know!

Vocabulary

Choose the best term from the box.

- rounding
- compatible
- Commutative Property
- Distributive Property

1. __?__ numbers are easy to compute mentally.

2. Breaking apart problems into two simpler problems is an example of the __?__ of Multiplication.

3. You can use __?__ when you do not need an exact answer.

Estimating Sums

Estimate each sum.

4. 16 + 13   **5.** 688 + 95

6. 1,511 + 269   **7.** 3,246 + 6,243

8. 283 + 178   **9.** 1,999 + 421

Multiplying by 1-Digit Numbers

Find each product.

10. 53 × 9   **11.** 172 × 7

12. 512 × 6   **13.** 711 × 4

14. 215 × 3   **15.** 914 × 5

Partial Products

© **16. Writing to Explain** Explain why the array shown below represents 3 × 21.

Topic Essential Questions
- How can arrays be used to find greater products?
- What is a standard procedure for multiplying multi-digit numbers?

Interactive Learning

Pose the problem. Start each lesson by working together to solve problems. It will help you make sense of math.

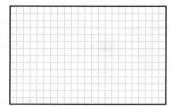

Applying Math Practices

- What am I asked to find?
- What else can I try?
- How are quantities related?
- How can I explain my work?
- How can I use math to model the problem?
- Can I use tools to help?
- Is my work precise?
- Why does this work?
- How can I generalize?

Lesson 8-1

© **Use Tools** Solve. Use grid paper to show an array and find the answer.

A theater has 14 rows of seats with 23 seats in each row. How many seats are in the theater?

Lesson 8-2

© **Use Tools** Use grid paper to show an array and find the answer. Record your work using numbers and multiplication.

There are 11 starters and 5 substitutes on a professional soccer team. How many players are there in all on 15 teams?

MATHEMATICAL
PRACTICES

Lesson 8-3

© **Generalize** Solve. Draw an array and then try to find a shortcut to solve the problem.

In January, Tim's aquarium had 23 guppies. A year later, he had 90 times as many guppies. How many guppies does Tim have?

Lesson 8-4

© **Model** Solve any way you choose. First, estimate the answer and then find the exact answer.

Ms. Silva has 12 weeks to practice for a running race. Over the course of one week, she plans to run 15 miles. How many miles will Ms. Silva run all together? Will she run more than 100 miles? Explain.

Running Practice	
Week 1	15 miles ✓
Week 2	15 miles
Week 3	15 miles
Week 4	15 miles

Lesson 8-5

© **Reason** Use the answer to the first problem to solve the second problem. Use the bar diagram to choose the needed operation for Problem 1.

Problem 1: Susan walked 3 miles and Maxine walked 2 miles to raise funds for a charity. How many miles did they walk in all?

Problem 2: A sponsor donated $50 for each mile they walked. How much did the sponsor donate?

? miles

2	3

Common Core

4.NBT.5 Multiply a whole number of up to four digits by a one-digit whole number, and multiply two two-digit numbers, using strategies based on place value and the properties of operations. Illustrate and explain the calculation by using equations, rectangular arrays, and/or area models.

Arrays and Multiplying 2-Digit Numbers

grid paper

How can you multiply using an array?

There are 13 bobble-head dogs in each row of the carnival booth. There are 24 equal rows. How many dogs are there?

Choose an Operation

Multiply to join equal groups.

13 dogs per row

Another Example **What is another way to multiply 2-digit numbers?**

There are 37 rows with 26 seats set up at the ring at the dog show. How many seats are there?

Find 37 × 26.

Step 1 Draw a table. Separate each factor into tens and ones. (30 + 7) × (20 + 6)

	20	6
30		
7		

Step 2 Multiply to find each product.

	20	6
30	600	180
7	140	42

Step 3 Add to find the product.

$$\begin{array}{r} 42 \\ 140 \\ 180 \\ + \ 600 \\ \hline 962 \end{array}$$

37 × 26 = 962

There are 962 seats at the dog show ring.

Explain It

1. How is breaking apart the problem 37 × 26 like solving four simpler problems?

Ⓒ 2. **Construct Arguments** Explain why the answer 962 is reasonable.

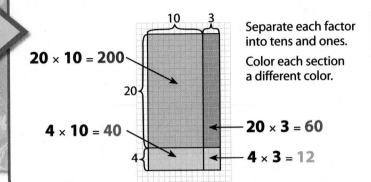

Step 1

Find 24 × 13.

Draw an array for 24 × 13.

10   3

Separate each factor into tens and ones.

Color each section a different color.

20 × 10 = 200

20

4 × 10 = 40

4

20 × 3 = 60

4 × 3 = 12

Step 2

Add the number of squares in each part of the array.

12
40
60
+ 200
312

In the booth, there are 312 bobble-head dogs.

Guided Practice*

Do you know HOW?

In **1** and **2**, use the grid or table to find the product.

1. 17 × 13

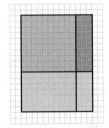

2. 24 × 16

```
      10    6
  20 |    |    |
   4 |    |    |
```

Do you UNDERSTAND?

3. In the example at the top, what four simpler multiplication problems were used to find 24 × 13?

4. Reason At the dog show, the first 2 rows are reserved. How many people can sit in the remaining 35 rows?

 There are 26 seats per row.

Independent Practice

Leveled Practice For **5** and **6**, find the product. Use grid paper to help.

 You can solve the simpler problems in any order.

5. 14 × 21

6. 14 × 12

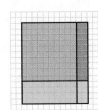

For **7** through **10**, find the product. Use grid paper to help.

7. 26 × 18

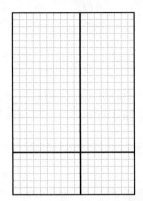

8. 19 × 27

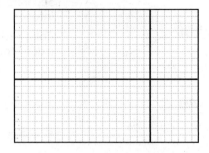

9. 11 × 16

10. 23 × 23

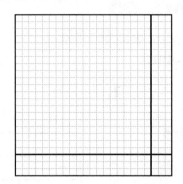

In **11** through **16**, copy and complete the table. Then find the total.

11. 18 × 25

	20	5
10		
8		

12. 12 × 28

	20	8
10		
2		

13. 17 × 68

	60	8
10		
7		

14. 13 × 31

	30	1
10		
3		

15. 16 × 27

	20	7
10		
6		

16. 22 × 88

	80	8
20		
2		

In **17** through **21**, find the product using either method.

17. 41
× 12

18. 38
× 27

19. 58
× 19

20. 29
× 15

21. 73
× 47

© **22. Writing to Explain** Why is the product of 15 × 32 equal to the sum of 10 × 32 and 5 × 32?

23. The flagpole in front of City Hall in Luis's town is 35 feet tall. How many inches tall is the flagpole?

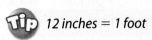 *12 inches = 1 foot*

24. The prices at Nolan's Novelties store are shown at the right. If 27 boxes of neon keychains and 35 boxes of glow-in-the-dark pens were purchased, what was the total cost?

Item	Price per box
Neon keychains	$15
Glow-in-the-dark pens	$10

25. A theatre has 1,918 seats in all. Section 200 has 27 rows with 14 seats in each row. How many seats are in Section 200?

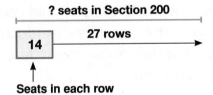

? seats in Section 200

27 rows

14

Seats in each row

© **26. Model** Elijah has *n* customers in his lawn-mowing business. He mows each lawn once a week. Which expression shows how many lawns he mows in 12 weeks?

A $n + 12$ **C** $12 - n$

B $n \times 12$ **D** $12 \div n$

For **27** and **28**, use the diagram to the right.

27. Maggie is making a balloon game for the school fair. Kids will throw darts to try to pop the balloons. How many balloons are needed to set up the game?

© **28. Think About the Structure** Maggie knows that she will have to completely refill the balloon board about 15 times a day. Which expression shows how to find the number of balloons she will need?

A 15×13 **C** $15 \times (13 \times 14)$

B 15×14 **D** $15 \times (13 + 14)$

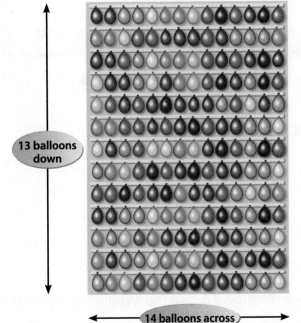

13 balloons down

14 balloons across

4.NBT.5 Multiply a whole number of up to four digits by a one-digit whole number, and multiply two two-digit numbers, using strategies based on place value and the properties of operations. Illustrate and explain the calculation by using equations, rectangular arrays, and/or area models.

Arrays and an Expanded Algorithm

How can you record multiplication?

Marcia picked oranges and put them in 12 mesh bags. Each bag had the same number of oranges. What is the total number of oranges Marcia picked?

Choose an Operation
Multiply to join equal groups.

15 oranges in each bag

Guided Practice*

MATHEMATICAL
PRACTICES

Do you know HOW?

In **1** and **2**, find all the partial products. Then add to find the product.

1.
```
    23
  × 14
```

2.
```
    41
  × 25
```

Do you UNDERSTAND?

3. In the example above, why do you find 2×10 rather than 2×1?

4. Writing to Explain Could you record the four partial products in the example above in a different order? Explain.

Independent Practice

Leveled Practice In **5** through **8**, find all the partial products. Then add to find the product.

5.
```
    34
  × 51
```

6.
```
    73
  × 81
```

7.
```
    64
  × 32
```

8.
```
    26
  × 53
```

In **9** through **16**, use the expanded algorithm to find each product.

9. 18×19

10. 42×16

11. 15×64

12. 27×51

*For another example, see Set B on page 198.

Find 12 × 15.

Use an array to model 12 × 15.

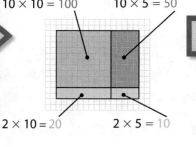

10 × 10 = 100   10 × 5 = 50

2 × 10 = 20   2 × 5 = 10

Step 1

Use the expanded algorithm to find 12 × 15.
Multiply the ones.

```
   15
×  12
───────
   10    2 × 5 = 10
   20    2 × 10 = 20
```

10 and 20 are partial products.

Step 2

Multiply the tens. Then add all the partial products.

```
     15
×    12
────────
     10
     20
     50    10 × 5 = 50
+  100    10 × 10 = 100
────────
    180
```

Marcia picked 180 oranges.

---

13. 17 × 38   **14.** 33 × 24   **15.** 43 × 19   **16.** 52 × 23

Problem Solving

MATHEMATICAL PRACTICES

17. Reason A pair of one type of shoes weighs 15 ounces. The shoebox they come in weighs 2 ounces. Which is the total weight of 15 pairs of these shoes, including the boxes?

   A 147 ounces   **C** 225 ounces

   B 155 ounces   **D** 255 ounces

18. A surveyor measures the length of two runways at an airport. The first runway, Runway 9, is 13,000 feet long. The second runway, Runway 12, is 9,354 feet long. How much shorter is Runway 12 than Runway 9?

19. Estimation Sara estimated 23 × 43 by using 20 × 40. Sam estimated 23 × 43 by using 25 × 40. Explain why Sam's method will give a closer estimate than Sara's method.

20. Construct Arguments A school has two large patios. One is rectangular and is 24 feet long by 18 feet wide. The other is square and each side is 21 feet long. Which patio has a greater perimeter? Explain.

21. The Castillo de San Marcos is a Spanish fortress that was built between 1672 and 1695. Rounded to the nearest ten thousand, how many pesos did it cost to build the fortress at that time?

It cost 138,375 pesos to build this fortress.

Lesson
8-3

Common
Core

4.NBT.5 Multiply a whole number of up to four digits by a one-digit whole number, and multiply two two-digit numbers, using strategies based on place value and the properties of operations. Illustrate and explain the calculation by using equations, rectangular arrays, and/or area models.

Multiplying 2-Digit Numbers by Multiples of 10

28 rocks per kit

How can you find the product?

Mr. Jeffrey buys 20 rock identification kits for his science classes. If each kit has 28 rocks, how many rocks are there in all?

Choose an Operation

Multiply to find the number of rocks.

Guided Practice*

 MATHEMATICAL PRACTICES

Do you know HOW?

In **1** through **6**, multiply to find each product.

1.
$$\begin{array}{r} 12 \\ \times\ 20 \\ \hline \blacksquare\blacksquare 0 \end{array}$$

2.
$$\begin{array}{r} 21 \\ \times\ 30 \\ \hline \blacksquare\blacksquare 0 \end{array}$$

3. 35×20

4. 63×20

5. 27×60

6. 66×40

Do you UNDERSTAND?

© 7. Writing to Explain Why is there a zero in the ones place when you multiply by 20 in the example above?

8. What multiplication problem can help you solve 38×70?

9. Each year, Mr. Jeffrey's school orders 100 rock kits. How many rocks are in all of the kits?

Independent Practice

Leveled Practice In **10** through **30**, multiply to find each product.

10.
$$\begin{array}{r} 12 \\ \times\ 30 \\ \hline \blacksquare\blacksquare 0 \end{array}$$

11.
$$\begin{array}{r} 24 \\ \times\ 50 \\ \hline \blacksquare,\blacksquare\blacksquare 0 \end{array}$$

12.
$$\begin{array}{r} 33 \\ \times\ 20 \\ \hline \blacksquare\blacksquare 0 \end{array}$$

13.
$$\begin{array}{r} 71 \\ \times\ 30 \\ \hline \blacksquare,\blacksquare\blacksquare 0 \end{array}$$

14.
$$\begin{array}{r} 63 \\ \times\ 40 \\ \hline \blacksquare,\blacksquare\blacksquare 0 \end{array}$$

15. 18×30

16. 20×51

17. 32×30

18. 40×22

19. 24×40

20. 34×50

21. 40×73

22. 88×30

23. 75×40

24. 22×60

25. 13×50

26. 60×23

27. 32×20

28. 82×80

29. 62×60

30. 52×50

For another example, see Set C on page 198.

One Way

Find 20 × 28.

Break 28 into tens and ones: **28** = **20** + **8**.

Use a grid to find the partial products.

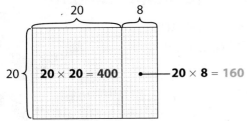

20 × 20 = 400   ·——— 20 × 8 = 160

Add the partial products to find the total.
400 + 160 = 560

Another Way

Find 20 × 28.

Multiply 2 tens × 28.

$$
\begin{array}{r}
1 \\
28 \\
\times\ 20 \\
\hline
560 \\
\end{array}
$$

Record a 0 in the ones place of the answer. This shows how many tens are in the answer.

There are 560 rocks in all.

Problem Solving

MATHEMATICAL
PRACTICES

31. Reason Rex's class raised frogs from tadpoles. The class has 21 students, and each raised 6 tadpoles. All but 6 of the tadpoles grew to be frogs. Write a number sentence to show how many frogs the class has.

32. Persevere How many fossil kits with 10 samples each have the same number of fossils as 30 fossil kits with 8 samples each?

A 20 **C** 200

B 24 **D** 240

33. It took Davina 45 minutes to clean her room. How many seconds did it take her?

Tip *There are 60 seconds in one minute.*

34. **Science** One family of Florida scrub jays inhabits about 25 acres of land. No other scrub jay families live within this area. How many acres of land do 24 families of Florida scrub jays need?

35. A roller coaster runs rides 50 times an hour and reaches speeds of 70 miles per hour. Using the picture at the right, how many people ride each hour?

A 160

B 1,500

C 1,600

D 2,240

8 rows of 4 people

Lesson
8-4

Common
Core

4.NBT.5 Multiply a whole
number of up to four
digits by a one-digit whole
number, and multiply two
two-digit numbers, using
strategies based on place
value and the properties
of operations. Illustrate
and explain the calculation
by using equations,
rectangular arrays, and/or
area models.

Multiplying 2-Digit by 2-Digit Numbers

What is a common way to record multiplication?

A ferry carried an average of 37 cars per trip on Saturday. If the ferry made 24 one-way trips, how many cars did it carry?

Choose an Operation Multiply to join equal groups.

37 cars per trip

Guided Practice*

MATHEMATICAL PRACTICES

Do you know HOW?

In **1** through **6**, find the product. Estimate to check for reasonableness.

1.
```
   41
×  23
   12
   20
    9
```

2.
```
   63
×  31
    3
   18
1,95
```

3. 27 × 12

4. 36 × 23

5. 18 × 42

6. 34 × 21

Do you UNDERSTAND?

7. Reasonableness In the example above, is 888 a reasonable answer for 37 × 24?

8. The ferry made 36 one-way trips on Sunday and carried an average of 21 cars on each trip.

a How many cars were ferried on Sunday?

b On which day were more cars ferried, Saturday or Sunday? Explain.

Independent Practice

Leveled Practice For **9** through **13**, find the product. Estimate to check for reasonableness.

9.
```
   33
×  18
    2
    0
    5
```

10.
```
   46
×  22
    2
    0
 ,
```

11.
```
   67
×  57
    9
 3
3,
```

12.
```
   45
×  16
    2
    0
```

13.
```
   35
×  29



 ,
```

*For another example, see Set D on page 199.

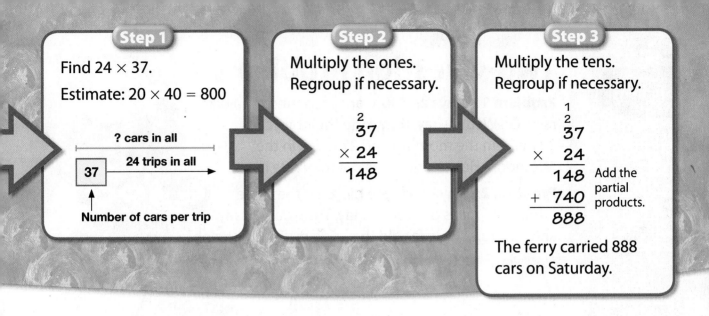

Find 24 × 37.

Estimate: 20 × 40 = 800

? cars in all

37   24 trips in all →

↑
Number of cars per trip

Step 2

Multiply the ones.
Regroup if necessary.

$$\begin{array}{r} \overset{2}{37} \\ \times\ 24 \\ \hline 148 \end{array}$$

Step 3

Multiply the tens.
Regroup if necessary.

$$\begin{array}{r} \overset{1}{\overset{2}{37}} \\ \times\ 24 \\ \hline 148 \\ +\ 740 \\ \hline 888 \end{array}$$ Add the partial products.

The ferry carried 888 cars on Saturday.

In **14** through **23**, find the product. Estimate to check for reasonableness.

14.   37
      × 21

15.   54
      × 37

16.   63
      × 22

17.   34
      × 41

18.   81
      × 17

19. 56 × 31   **20.** 53 × 17   **21.** 81 × 46   **22.** 15 × 16   **23.** 17 × 21

Problem Solving

 MATHEMATICAL
PRACTICES

© **24. Persevere** The *Queen Mary 2*'s height above the water is the same as a 23-story building. Use the diagram to the right. How high above the water is the *Queen Mary 2*?

Each story is 11 feet tall.

23-story building   *Queen Mary 2*

25. Mr. Morris bought sketch pads for 24 of his students. Each pad contained 50 sheets. How many sheets of paper were there all together?

? sheets in all

50   24 students →

↑
Sheets in each pad

© **26. Reasonableness** There are 52 weeks in one year. How many weeks are in 10 years?

A   62 weeks   **C**   520 weeks

B   120 weeks   **D**   620 weeks

27. In 2005, an ultra light airplane tracked Monarch butterflies migrating to Mexico. Over 13 days, how many miles did the butterflies travel?

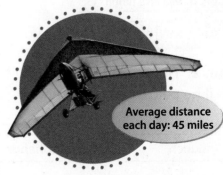

Average distance each day: 45 miles

Lesson 8-4 **195**

Lesson
8-5

Common Core

4.NBT.5 Multiply a whole number of up to four digits by a one-digit whole number, and multiply two two-digit numbers, using strategies based on place value and the properties of operations. Illustrate and explain the calculation by using equations, rectangular arrays, and/or area models. Also 4.OA.3

Problem Solving

Two-Question Problems

Problem 1: Maya and Jose are preparing for a bike race. On Wednesday, they rode their bicycles 32 miles in the morning and 22 miles in the afternoon. How many miles did they ride in all?

Problem 2: Maya and Jose bicycled the same number of miles on Wednesday, Thursday, Friday, and Saturday. How far did they ride during the week?

Rode the same distance 4 days in a row

Guided Practice*

MATHEMATICAL PRACTICES

Do you know HOW?

Solve.

1. **Problem 1:** Julia used 3 rolls of film to take pictures on her vacation. There were 24 pictures on each roll. How many pictures did Julia take?

   Problem 2: Julia had two copies made of each picture. How many copies were made?

Do you UNDERSTAND?

2. Why do you need to know how many pictures Julia took to solve Problem 2?

3. **Write a Problem** Solve Problem 1. Then write and solve a problem that uses the answer from Problem 1.
   Problem 1: Cal puts one vase on each of 5 tables. There are 6 flowers in each vase. How many flowers does Cal use?

Independent Practice

MATHEMATICAL PRACTICES

Solve.

4. **Problem 1:** Martin buys a sandwich for $4, an apple for $1, and a drink for $2. How much did he pay in all?

   ? Cost of Martin's lunch

$4	$1	$2

   Problem 2: How much change did Martin receive if he paid with a $20 bill?

   $20

Lunch	Change

Applying Math Practices

- What am I asked to find?
- What else can I try?
- How are quantities related?
- How can I explain my work?
- How can I use math to model the problem?
- Can I use tools to help?
- Is my work precise?
- Why does this work?
- How can I generalize?

For another example, see Set E on page 199.

Sometimes you have to answer one problem to solve another problem.

? miles bicycled on Wednesday

32	22

32 miles + 22 miles = 54 miles

Maya and Jose bicycled 54 miles on Wednesday.

Use the answer from Problem 1 to solve Problem 2.

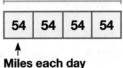

? miles bicycled during the week

54	54	54	54

↑
Miles each day

4 × 54 miles = 216 miles

Maya and Jose rode 216 miles during the week.

---

5. Problem 1: Sally and Byron mow their neighbors' lawns in the summer. Sally mows 5 lawns each week. Byron mows three times as many lawns as Sally. How many lawns does Byron mow each week?

? lawns mowed each week

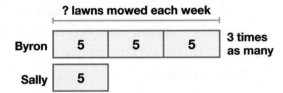

| Byron | 5 | 5 | 5 | 3 times as many |
| Sally | 5 | | | |

Problem 2: Byron gets paid $20 for each lawn he mows. How much does Byron get paid each week?

? Amount Byron gets paid each week

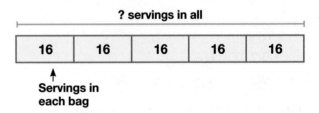

| 20 | 15 lawns → |

↑
Amount paid for each lawn

6. Problem 1: June's mom brought 3 bags of plain popcorn and 2 bags of caramel popcorn to the park. How many bags of popcorn did June's mom bring to the park?

? bags in all

3	2

Problem 2: Each bag of popcorn that June's mom brought to the park contained 16 servings. How many servings of popcorn did June's mom bring to the park?

? servings in all

16	16	16	16	16

↑
Servings in each bag

---

7. 🔍 **Science** The Florida panther is known to sleep about 18 hours a day. About how many hours would a Florida panther sleep in 3 weeks?

A 478 hours **C** 252 hours

B 378 hours **D** 54 hours

© 8 Persevere Dave plans to retile his porch floor. He wants to buy 25 black tiles and 23 white tiles. Each tile costs $2. How much money will it cost Dave to retile his porch floor?

Set A, pages 186–189

Find 14 × 12. Draw a 14 × 12 array.

Separate each factor into tens and ones.
Color each section a different color.
Add each part to find the product.

$10 \times 10 = 100$ $10 \times 2 = 20$

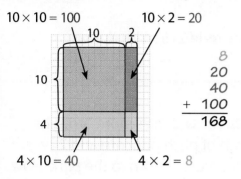

```
        8
       20
       40
   +  100
      168
```

$4 \times 10 = 40$ $4 \times 2 = 8$

Remember you can solve the simpler problems in any order and the answer will remain the same.

Find each product. Use grid paper to help.

1. 14 × 32   **2.** 64 × 12

3. 56 × 17   **4.** 72 × 15

5. 26 × 63   **6.** 47 × 27

Set B, pages 190–191

Find 16 × 35. List the partial products.

First multiply the ones:
```
    16
  × 35
    30    5 × 6
    50    5 × 10
```

Now multiply the tens:
```
    16
  × 35
    30
    50
   180    30 × 6
 + 300    30 × 10
```

Add: 30 + 50 + 180 + 300 = 560

Remember that to multiply two 2-digit factors, you must find four partial products. You can find them in any order. Be sure to use correct place value.

Multiply to find each product.

1. 18 × 34   **2.** 51 × 15

3. 53 × 17   **4.** 26 × 28

5. 22 × 66   **6.** 41 × 54

7. 64 × 86   **8.** 32 × 71

9. 93 × 44   **10.** 57 × 91

Set C, pages 192–193

Find 16 × 30.
Multiply 16 × 3 tens.

```
    1
   16
 × 30
  480
```
The 0 in the ones places shows how many tens are in the answer.

Remember to record a 0 in the ones place of the answer.

Multiply to find each product.

1. 39 × 10   **2.** 56 × 30

3. 41 × 20   **4.** 60 × 13

Use the standard algorithm to find 14×19.

Multiply the ones. Regroup if necessary.

$$\begin{array}{r} \overset{3}{19} \\ \times\, 14 \\ \hline 76 \end{array}$$

Multiply the tens. Regroup if necessary.

$$\begin{array}{r} 19 \\ \times\, 14 \\ \hline 76 \\ +\, 190 \\ \hline 266 \end{array}$$

Add the partial products.

Remember to regroup if necessary.

Find the product. Estimate to check for reasonableness.

1. $\begin{array}{r} 53 \\ \times\, 36 \\ \hline \end{array}$

2. $\begin{array}{r} 23 \\ \times\, 18 \\ \hline \end{array}$

3. $\begin{array}{r} 73 \\ \times\, 33 \\ \hline \end{array}$

4. $\begin{array}{r} 31 \\ \times\, 74 \\ \hline \end{array}$

5. 56×64

6. 39×82

When you solve two-question problems, solve the first problem. Then use that answer to help you solve the second problem.

Problem 1: It costs $3 for a ticket to the pool and $7 for a ticket to the water park. How much does it cost for 4 people to go to the pool and the water park?

Cost of 4 pool tickets:
$4 \times \$3 = \$12$

Cost of 4 water park tickets:
$4 \times \$7 = \$28$

Add the totals:
$\$12 + \$28 = \$40$

It costs $40 for 4 people to go to the pool and the water park.

Problem 2: How much more does it cost the group of 4 to go to the water park than to the pool?

$28 - 12 = 16$

It costs $16 more.

Remember to use the information from Problem 1 to answer Problem 2.

Solve.

1. **Problem 1:** Rose visited 14 cities on her vacation. She bought 3 souvenirs in each city to send to her friends. How many souvenirs did Rose buy on her vacation?

   Problem 2: Rose paid $2 in postage for each souvenir she sent. How much did it cost Rose to send all of the souvenirs that she bought on vacation?

2. **Problem 1:** Mrs. Conrath bought 9 packages of lead pencils for her classroom. Each package has 8 lead pencils. How many lead pencils did she buy?

   Problem 2: Mrs. Conrath saved 25 lead pencils for the Math Club. How many lead pencils were used for her classroom?

Multiple Choice

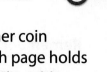 **ASSESSMENT**

1. Tess has 15 pages in her coin collector's album. Each page holds 32 coins. Tess is using the table below to find how many coins are in her album. Which number is missing from the table? (8-1)

   A 5

   B 150

   C 315

   D 480

	30	2
10	300	20
5	▨	10

2. What is 35 × 64? (8-4)

   A 1,240

   B 2,140

   C 2,240

   D 2,340

3. Which shows one correct way to use partial products to find 60 × 78? (8-3)

   A (60 × 70) + (60 × 8)

   B (60 × 70) + (60 × 780)

   C (60 × 70) + (60 × 80)

   D (30 × 70) + (30 × 8)

4. The librarian ordered 24 sets of sturdy bookmarks. Each set contained 20 bookmarks with different designs. How many bookmarks did the librarian order? (8-3)

   A 4,800

   B 2,420

   C 480

   D 240

5. Jonah bought 25 postcards that cost 17 cents each. He used partial products to find the total cost in cents. What is the missing partial product? (8-2)

   A 2

   B 20

   C 200

   D 425

   $$\begin{array}{r} 17 \\ \times\ 25 \\ \hline 35 \\ 50 \\ 140 \\ +\ \blacksquare\blacksquare\blacksquare \\ \hline \end{array}$$

6. What is 15 × 29? (8-1)

   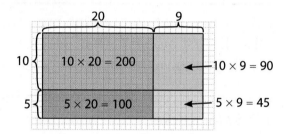

   A 335

   B 390

   C 435

   D 535

7. A school bought 28 new microscopes for its students to use. The price for each microscope was $87. How much did the microscopes cost in all? (8-4)

   A $1,436

   B $1,756

   C $2,336

   D $2,436

8. What partial products would be added to find 13 × 46? Add the partial products to solve. (8-2)

9. Tori's goal is to learn 15 new Spanish words each day. If Tori meets her goal, how many new Spanish words will she have learned after 40 days? (8-3)

10. Find the partial products for 78 × 49 and then solve. (8-1)

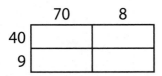

11. Sydney made 21 wooden penguins to sell at a fair. She used 5 pompoms and 4 beads to decorate each penguin. How many pompoms and beads did she use for the wooden penguins in all? (8-5)

12. A science museum presented a live exhibit that showed different butterflies. Each habitat held 48 butterflies. There were 12 different habitats. How many butterflies were in the live exhibit in all? (8-4)

13. A school bus can carry 35 passengers. How many passengers can 14 school buses carry? Multiply to find the partial products. Then add to find the product. (8-2)

14. At Washington Elementary school, no teacher has more than 20 students. If there are 37 teachers, what is the greatest number of students there could be? (8-3)

15. Problem 1: The longest book Toshi had read was 304 pages. She just finished *Kira-Kira* by Cynthia Kadohata, which is 256 pages. How much longer was the longest book Toshi read than *Kira-Kira*?

Problem 2: Toshi estimates that she needs 2 minutes to read one page. How many minutes longer did she spend reading the 304-page book than *Kira-Kira*? Explain how you found your answer. (8-5)

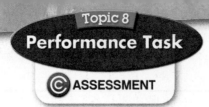
The table below shows sample costs of new textbooks for five school subjects. Use the data in the table to answer the questions that follow. For **1** through **3**, copy the table on a separate sheet and record your answers in the blank boxes.

Textbook Subject	Cost per Book	Students in Your Class	Total Cost per Subject
Language Arts	$39		
Mathematics	$42		
Science	$45		
Social Studies	$33		
Spelling	$27		
TOTAL			

1. Find the total cost of 1 new textbook from each subject.

2. Put a ✓ beside each kind of textbook your class uses. Write the number of books needed for each student in your class.

3. Find the cost for your class for each kind of textbook you checked. Then find the total cost.

4. Suppose your school orders new textbooks for your class as listed below. Find each total cost.

   a 45 language arts textbooks

   b 50 math textbooks

   c 30 science textbooks

   d 40 social studies textbooks

5. Which costs more, 33 spelling textbooks or 18 science textbooks? How much more? Explain.

6. A school received a $5,000 grant to buy new math textbooks for the fourth-grade classes. There are 3 fourth-grade classes with 33 students in each class. Is the grant money enough to buy new math textbooks for all the students? Explain how you know.

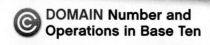
Topic
9

Number Sense: Dividing by 1-Digit Divisors

▼ How long does it take the International Space Station to orbit Earth one time? You will find out in Lesson 9-2.

Review What You Know!

Vocabulary

Choose the best term from the box.

- divisor
- quotient
- multiple
- product
- factor
- division

1. In the number sentence $9 \times 5 = 45$, 45 is the ? .

2. The number you divide by is the ? .

3. The answer in a division problem is the ? .

Multiplication Facts

Find each product.

4. 5×3 5. 7×2 6. 6×8

7. 8×0 8. 1×4 9. 2×8

10. 5×7 11. 3×6 12. 4×4

13. 4×5 14. 4×8 15. 2×6

Addition and Subtraction Facts

Write a subtraction fact for each addition fact.

16. $8 + 8 = 16$ 17. $4 + 7 = 11$

18. $6 + 6 = 12$ 19. $9 + 5 = 14$

20. Write a subtraction fact for the array below.

© 21. **Writing to Explain** Explain how you could subtract $146 - 51$ using mental math.

Topic Essential Questions
- What are different meanings of division?
- How can mental math and estimation be used to divide?

Interactive Learning

Pose the problem. Start each lesson by working together to solve problems. It will help you make sense of math.

Applying Math Practices

- What am I asked to find?
- What else can I try?
- How are quantities related?
- How can I explain my work?
- How can I use math to model the problem?
- Can I use tools to help?
- Is my work precise?
- Why does this work?
- How can I generalize?

Lesson 9-1

ⓒ **Use Structure** Solve using mental math.

José has 270 hockey cards to arrange in 9 boxes. Each box is to hold the same number of cards. How many cards should he place in each box? Explain how you found the answer mentally.

Lesson 9-2

ⓒ **Reasonableness** Solve. All you need is an estimate.

Three friends go to a video arcade and win 248 tickets all together. They decide to split the tickets equally. About how many tickets will each friend get? Explain how you found your estimate.

Arcade Tickets
248

Lesson 9-3

Ⓒ **Reason** Solve.

Jimi had 3,000 ride tickets for the school carnival. He is going to make and sell packages with 8 tickets in each. About how many packages will be made? Tell how you found your estimate.

Lesson 9-4

Ⓒ **Persevere** Solve any way you choose. Check that your answer is reasonable.

Jaycen has 14 trophies and 4 shelves. He wants to put the same number of trophies on each shelf. How many trophies will be on each shelf? How many trophies will be left over? Tell how you decided.

Lesson 9-5

Ⓒ **Model** Solve any way you choose.

Edith wants to buy lemonade for the fourth-grade picnic. There are 42 students in the fourth grade. If one quart of lemonade serves 5 students, how many quarts does she need? Show how you found the answer.

Lesson 9-6

Ⓒ **Model** Solve any way you choose. Use the bar diagram to help.

A present for Joan costs $30. How much less will each friend pay if 6 friends share the cost equally than if 5 friends share the cost? Show how you found the answer.

$30

© Common Core

4.NBT.6 Find whole-number quotients and remainders with up to four-digit dividends and one-digit divisors, using strategies based on place value, the properties of operations, and/or the relationship between multiplication and division. Illustrate and explain the calculation by using equations, rectangular arrays, and/or area models. Also 4.OA.3

Using Mental Math to Divide

How can you use patterns to help you divide mentally?

Mr. Díaz ordered a supply of 320 pastels. He needs to divide them equally among four art classes. How many pastels does each class get?

320 pastels

Choose an Operation
Division is used to make equal groups.

Guided Practice*

© MATHEMATICAL PRACTICES

Do you know HOW?

In **1** and **2**, use patterns to find each quotient.

1. $28 \div 7 =$ ▢
$280 \div 7 =$ ▢
$2,800 \div 7 =$ ▢

2. $64 \div 8 =$ ▢
$640 \div 8 =$ ▢
$6,400 \div 8 =$ ▢

Do you UNDERSTAND?

© **3. Reason** How is dividing 320 by 4 like dividing 32 by 4?

© **4. Communicate** José orders 240 binders and divides them equally among the 4 classes. How many binders will each class get? What basic fact did you use?

Independent Practice

In **5** through **8**, use patterns to find each quotient.

5. $36 \div 9 =$ ▢
$360 \div 9 =$ ▢
$3,600 \div 9 =$ ▢

6. $10 \div 2 =$ ▢
$100 \div 2 =$ ▢
$1,000 \div 2 =$ ▢

7. $45 \div 5 =$ ▢
$450 \div 5 =$ ▢
$4,500 \div 5 =$ ▢

8. $24 \div 8 =$ ▢
$240 \div 8 =$ ▢
$2,400 \div 8 =$ ▢

For **9** through **23**, use mental math to divide.

9. $200 \div 5$ **10.** $360 \div 4$ **11.** $540 \div 9$ **12.** $160 \div 4$ **13.** $160 \div 2$

14. $900 \div 3$ **15.** $320 \div 8$ **16.** $360 \div 6$ **17.** $180 \div 3$ **18.** $210 \div 7$

19. $720 \div 8$ **20.** $500 \div 5$ **21.** $350 \div 7$ **22.** $630 \div 9$ **23.** $480 \div 6$

For another example, see Set A on page 220.

Find 320 ÷ 4.

320 pastels

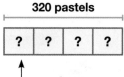

?	?	?	?

↑
pastels for each class

The basic fact is 32 ÷ 4 = 8.

32 tens ÷ 4 = 8 tens or 80.
320 ÷ 4 = 80

Each class will get 80 pastels.

Mr. Díaz wants to divide 400 erasers among 8 classes. How many erasers will each class get?

Find 400 ÷ 8.

The basic fact is 40 ÷ 8.

40 tens ÷ 8 = 5 tens or 50.
400 ÷ 8 = 50

Each class will get 50 erasers.

Problem Solving

© MATHEMATICAL PRACTICES

24. Selena used a basic fact to help solve 180 ÷ 6. What basic fact did Selena use?

25. There are 52 weeks in 1 year. How many years are equivalent to 520 weeks?

© **26. Use Structure** At the North American Solar Challenge, teams use up to 1,000 solar cells to design and build solar cars for a race. If there are 810 solar cells in 9 rows, how many solar cells are in each row?

9 rows of solar cells

27. A bakery produced 37 loaves of bread an hour. How many loaves were produced in 4 hours?

? loaves of bread

37	37	37	37

↑
loaves an hour

© **28. Model** On Saturday afternoon, 350 people attended a play. The seating was arranged in 7 equal rows. How many people sat in each row? How do you know?

350 people

?	?	?	?	?	?	?

↑
people in each row

29. Each row of seats in a stadium has 32 chairs. If the first 3 rows are completely filled, how many people are in the first 3 rows?

   A 9 people   **C** 96 people

   B 10 people   **D** 256 people

© **30. Writing to Explain** If you know that 20 ÷ 5 = 4, how does that fact help you find 200 ÷ 5?

Lesson 9-2

© Common Core

4.NBT.6 Find whole-number quotients and remainders with up to four-digit dividends and one-digit divisors, using strategies based on place value, the properties of operations, and/or the relationship between multiplication and division. Illustrate and explain the calculation by using equations, rectangular arrays, and/or area models. Also 4.OA.3

Estimating Quotients

When and how do you estimate quotients to solve problems?

Max wants to make 9 rubber-band balls. He bought a jar of 700 rubber bands. Estimate to find about how many rubber bands he can use for each ball.

700 rubber bands

Guided Practice*

MATHEMATICAL **PRACTICES**

Do you know HOW?

In **1** through **6**, estimate each quotient. Use multiplication or compatible numbers.

1. 48 ÷ 5

2. 235 ÷ 8

3. 547 ÷ 6

4. 192 ÷ 5

5. 662 ÷ 8

6. 362 ÷ 3

Do you UNDERSTAND?

© **7. Writing to Explain** Is an estimate or exact answer needed for the problem below?

Max bought two jars of rubber bands for $4.65 each. How much did he spend?

© **8. Reasonableness** Max decides to use the 700 rubber bands to make 8 balls. Is it reasonable to say that each ball would contain about 90 rubber bands?

Independent Practice

In **9** through **28**, estimate the quotient.

 Tip *First round to the nearest ten. Then try multiples of ten that are near the rounded number.*

9. 430 ÷ 9 **10.** 620 ÷ 7 **11.** 138 ÷ 5 **12.** 232 ÷ 6 **13.** 172 ÷ 3

14. 342 ÷ 8 **15.** 652 ÷ 6 **16.** 599 ÷ 9 **17.** 813 ÷ 8 **18.** 326 ÷ 4

19. 637 ÷ 6 **20.** 481 ÷ 4 **21.** 747 ÷ 8 **22.** 232 ÷ 9 **23.** 387 ÷ 4

24. 552 ÷ 7 **25.** 527 ÷ 5 **26.** 392 ÷ 2 **27.** 625 ÷ 3 **28.** 921 ÷ 3

*For another example, see Set B on page 220.

One Way

Use compatible numbers.

What number close to 700 is easily divided by 9?

Try multiples of ten near 700.

> 710 is not easily divided by 9.
>
> 720 is 72 tens and can be divided by 9.
>
> 720 ÷ 9 = 80

A good estimate is about 80 rubber bands for each ball.

A rounded solution is all that is needed. Max does not need to know the exact number of rubber bands to use for each ball.

Another Way

Use multiplication.

9 times what number is about 700?

9 × 8 = 72,
so 9 × 80 = 720.

700 ÷ 9 is about 80.

Problem Solving

 MATHEMATICAL PRACTICES

Use the chart at the right for **29** and **30**.

29. Ada sold her mugs in 3 weeks. About how many did she sell each week?

30. Ben sold his mugs in 4 weeks. About how many did he sell each week?

Mugs Sold in Fundraiser
Each Mug = 50 mugs

Ada

Ben

© **31. Use Structure** Tony's truck can safely carry 3,000 pounds. He has 21 televisions that he needs to deliver. Each television weighs 95 pounds.

  a Can Tony safely carry all of the televisions in his truck?

  b Is an exact answer needed or is an estimate needed? Explain.

© **32. Writing to Explain** Copy and complete by filling in the circle with > or <. Without dividing, explain how you know which quotient is greater.

930 ÷ 4 ◯ 762 ÷ 4

33. The International Space Station takes 644 minutes to orbit Earth 7 times. About how long does each orbit take?

  A 80 minutes

  B 90 minutes

  C 95 minutes

  D 100 minutes

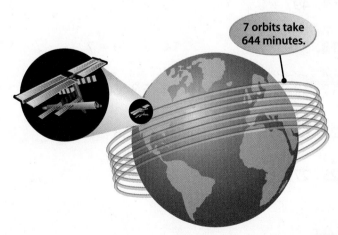

7 orbits take 644 minutes.

Cove Park

Garfield Park

Turtle Park

John's Park

Big Oak Park

Roosevelt Park

Springville's parks

Lesson 9-3

Common Core

4.NBT.6 Find whole-number quotients and remainders with up to four-digit dividends and one-digit divisors, using strategies based on place value, the properties of operations, and/or the relationship between multiplication and division. Illustrate and explain the calculation by using equations, rectangular arrays, and/or area models. Also 4.OA.3

Estimating Quotients for Greater Dividends

How do you estimate quotients using place value?

On a "Clean Up Your Town Day," 1,320 people volunteered to clean up the Springville parks. They were divided equally into teams to work in each of the town's parks. About how many people were in each team?

Guided Practice*

 MATHEMATICAL PRACTICES

Do you know HOW?

In **1** through **6**, use multiplication facts to help estimate each quotient.

1. 3,340 ÷ 8   **2.** 2,943 ÷ 7

3. 552 ÷ 9   **4.** 776 ÷ 4

5. 2,013 ÷ 5   **6.** 281 ÷ 3

Do you UNDERSTAND?

7. Reason What multiplication fact could you use to estimate the quotient 2,000 ÷ 4? How is this problem different from the others in this lesson?

8. When dividing a 4-digit number by a 1-digit number, how many digits can the quotient have?

Independent Practice

In **9** through **28**, estimate each quotient.

Tip *For numbers greater than 1,000, round to the nearest hundred. Then try multiples of one hundred that are near the rounded dividend.*

9. 497 ÷ 8   **10.** 4,971 ÷ 8   **11.** 3,051 ÷ 7   **12.** 305 ÷ 7

13. 779 ÷ 7   **14.** 7,779 ÷ 7   **15.** 3,688 ÷ 6   **16.** 423 ÷ 4

17. 5,684 ÷ 9   **18.** 5,346 ÷ 6   **19.** 508 ÷ 7   **20.** 2,120 ÷ 5

21. 647 ÷ 3   **22.** 3,958 ÷ 8   **23.** 224 ÷ 3   **24.** 915 ÷ 3

25. 279 ÷ 9   **26.** 2,449 ÷ 8   **27.** 3,124 ÷ 6   **28.** 4,519 ÷ 5

For another example, see Set B on page 220.

One Way

Use multiplication patterns.

6 times what number is about 1,320?

I know $6 \times 2 = 12$, so

$$6 \times 20 = 120 \text{ and}$$
$$6 \times 200 = 1,200.$$

1,200 is close enough to 1,320 for this estimate.

Another Way

Use estimation and division facts.

Estimate the quotient $1,320 \div 6$.

$$12 \div 6 = 2$$
$$120 \div 6 = 20$$
$$1,200 \div 6 = 200$$

$1,320 \div 6$ is about 200. Each team is made up of about 200 people.

Problem Solving

MATHEMATICAL
PRACTICES

In **29** through **34**, estimate each quotient.

29. In 1999, an 89-year-old woman walked 3,055 miles across the United States. She walked about 9 miles each day. About how many days did it take her to walk across the United States?

30. Casey is reading a book that has 169 pages. He reads about 9 pages a day. About how many days will it take for him to finish the book?

© **31. Reason** The students who run the school store ordered 1,440 pencils. They are putting them in packages of 6 pencils. About how many packages can they make? Will the exact answer be more or less than the estimate?

32. Ramon's older sister wants to buy a car that costs $7,993. She earns $9 for every hour she works. About how many hours must she work to earn enough money to buy the car?

    A 80 hours   **C** 800 hours

    B 90 hours   **D** 900 hours

© **33. Reasonableness** Eight students can fit at one cafeteria table. About how many tables are needed for 231 students? Does your answer make sense? How can you tell?

© **34. Persevere** Laura's dog eats 1 bag of dog food every 6 days. About how many bags will he eat in 1 year?

 1 year = 365 days

© **35. Writing to Explain** What is the first step when you estimate the answer to a division problem?

36. Andrea rides her bike 16 miles each week. How many miles will she ride her bike in 39 weeks?

Lesson
9-4

©
Common
Core

4.NBT.6 Find whole-number quotients and remainders with up to four-digit dividends and one-digit divisors, using strategies based on place value, the properties of operations, and/or the relationship between multiplication and division. Illustrate and explain the calculation by using equations, rectangular arrays, and/or area models.

Hands-On
counters

Dividing with Remainders
What happens when some are left?

Maria has 20 pepper plants to place in 3 rows. She has to plant the same number in each row. How many plants will go in each row? How many are left over?

3 rows of plants

Guided Practice*

© MATHEMATICAL PRACTICES

Do you know HOW?

In **1** through **4**, use counters or draw pictures. Tell how many items are in each group and how many are left over.

1. 26 pens
5 groups

2. 34 cars
7 boxes

3. 30 marbles
4 bags

4. 40 balls
6 bins

Do you UNDERSTAND?

© **5. Writing to Explain** When you divide a number by 6, what remainders are possible?

© **6. Use Structure** Tia is planting her garden with 15 plants. She wants them planted in equal groups of 4. How many groups of 4 can she make? How many plants will she have left over?

Independent Practice

In **7** through **14**, copy and then complete the calculations. Use counters or pictures to help.

 Tip *The remainder should always be less than the divisor.*

7. R
$8\overline{)35}$
$-$

8. R
$3\overline{)17}$
$-$

9. R
$9\overline{)51}$
$-$

10. R
$5\overline{)48}$
$-$

11. R
$6\overline{)47}$
$-$

12. R
$7\overline{)65}$
$-$

13. R
$9\overline{)77}$
$-$

14. R
$4\overline{)30}$
$-$

DIGITAL
Animated Glossary, eTools
www.pearsonsuccessnet.com

Divide 20 counters among 3 rows.

$3 \times 6 = 18$ counters

The part that is left after dividing is called the remainder.

There are 2 counters left over. This is not enough for another row, so the remainder is 2.

Check your answer.

$$\begin{array}{r} 6\,R2 \\ 3\overline{)20} \\ -18 \\ \hline 2 \end{array}$$

Divide: 3 groups of 6 in 20
Multiply: $3 \times 6 = 18$
Subtract: $20 - 18 = 2$
Compare: $2 < 3$

$3 \times 6 = 18$, and $18 + 2 = 20$

Maria can plant 6 plants in each row. She will have 2 plants left over.

In **15** through **29**, divide. You may use counters or pictures to help.

15. $3\overline{)29}$ **16.** $7\overline{)41}$ **17.** $9\overline{)55}$ **18.** $8\overline{)62}$ **19.** $5\overline{)37}$

20. $7\overline{)45}$ **21.** $4\overline{)22}$ **22.** $6\overline{)28}$ **23.** $8\overline{)33}$ **24.** $8\overline{)75}$

25. $9\overline{)86}$ **26.** $6\overline{)34}$ **27.** $7\overline{)39}$ **28.** $5\overline{)23}$ **29.** $8\overline{)61}$

Problem Solving

MATHEMATICAL PRACTICES

30. If $69 \div 9 = n$ R6, what is the value of n?

31. How many craft sticks are left if 9 friends equally share a package of 85 craft sticks?

32. Write a division sentence with a quotient of 7 and remainder of 3.

33. When you divide by 3, can the remainder be 5?

© **34. Reasonableness** Carl's teacher took 27 photos on their class trip. She wants to arrange them on the wall in 4 equal rows. Carl said if she does this, she will have 7 photos left over. Is this reasonable?

© **35. Writing to Explain** Jim has 46 compact discs. He wants to buy 5 cases that hold 8 discs. Explain why Jim needs to buy 6 cases to hold his 46 compact discs.

36. Jack helped Mrs. Sanchez pack 61 books in 7 boxes. Each box held 8 books. Which expression shows how to find how many books he had left?

A $61 - (7 + 8)$ **C** $61 + (7 \times 8)$

B $61 - (7 \times 8)$ **D** $61 + (7 + 8)$

© **37. Use Tools** At the school concert, there were 560 people seated in 8 rows. If there were no empty seats, how many people were in each row?

A 553 people **C** 70 people

B 480 people **D** 60 people

Lesson
9-5

Common
Core

4.NBT.6 Find whole-number quotients and remainders with up to four-digit dividends and one-digit divisors, using strategies based on place value, the properties of operations, and/or the relationship between multiplication and division. Illustrate and explain the calculation by using equations, rectangular arrays, and/or area models.
Also **4.NBT.5**

Multiplication and Division Stories

When should you multiply or divide?

Multiply when you want to combine equal groups. Divide when you want to find the number of groups or the number in each group.

Each canoe holds four people, how many people can sit in 14 canoes?

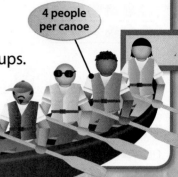

4 people per canoe

Another Example **How do you interpret a remainder?**

Ben has 55 dollars to buy helium balloons for the end-of-summer camp party.

The balloons cost 9 dollars per bunch.

Sometimes you ignore the remainder.	**Sometimes the remainder is the answer.**
How many bunches of balloons can Ben buy?	How much money will Ben have left?

$$\begin{array}{r} 6\,\text{R}1 \\ 9)\overline{55} \\ -54 \\ \hline 1 \end{array}$$

$$\begin{array}{r} 6\,\text{R}1 \\ 9)\overline{55} \\ -54 \\ \hline 1 \end{array}$$

Ben can buy 6 bunches of balloons.

Ben will have 1 dollar left.

Explain It

1. Why is the remainder the answer to how much money Ben will have left?

2. How could you check that you divided 55 ÷ 9 correctly?

3. If Ben wanted to buy another bunch of balloons, how much more money does he need?

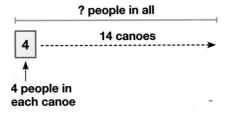

Find how many people can be seated in 14 canoes.

? people in all

4 ---- 14 canoes ---->

↑
4 people in each canoe

Multiply: $14 \times 4 = 56$

A total of 56 people can be seated in 14 canoes.

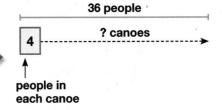

Find how many canoes will be needed for 36 people.

36 people

4 ---- ? canoes ---->

↑
people in each canoe

Divide: $36 \div 4 = 9$

A total of 9 canoes are needed for 36 people.

Guided Practice*

MATHEMATICAL PRACTICES

Do you know HOW?

Use the story below to solve **1** and **2**.

Ann is making costumes for a play. Each costume requires 3 yards of fabric.

1. How many yards of fabric are needed to make 12 costumes?

2. If Ann has 26 yards of fabric, how many costumes can she make?

Do you UNDERSTAND?

ⓒ 3. **Communicate** What does the remainder in Exercise 2 represent?

ⓒ 4. **Use Structure** On a canoe trip, 12 paddles are shared among 5 canoes. How many canoes get an extra paddle?

5. Ben ordered 15 pizzas. Each pizza had 8 slices. How many slices of pizza were there in all?

Independent Practice

In **6** through **9**, write a multiplication or division story for each number fact. Then solve.

6. 22×7 **7.** $63 \div 9$ **8.** $34 \div 7$ **9.** 13×12

Solve **10** through **11**. If it is a multiplication story, explain how you knew to multiply. If it is a division story, explain how you know to divide.

10. There are 50 people signed up for a boat trip. Each boat holds 6 people. How many boats are needed?

11. Admission to a museum is 6 dollars a person. If 38 students are visiting the museum, how much will it cost in all?

*For another example, see Set D on page 221.   Lesson 9-5   **215**

For **12** through **14**, use the table at the right.

12. Carl earns 23 tickets at the arcade. How many sticker packs can he get?

ⓒ **13. Writing to Explain** Carlos has 39 tickets. If he gets as many glitter gels as possible, will he have enough tickets left over to get a sticker pack?

FunTime Arcade	
Prize	**Tickets Needed**
Sticker packs	5
Glitter gel	8
Pencil case	14
Toy airplane	22

ⓒ **14. Reasonableness** Tim wants to buy 4 toy airplanes. How many tickets does he need?

? tickets needed

22	22	22	22

↑
tickets for each plane

15. Joel has 5 packets of seeds. Each packet holds 12 seeds. He wants to divide the seeds evenly among 10 rows of his garden. How many seeds can he plant in each row?

A 4 seeds   **C** 8 seeds

B 6 seeds   **D** 10 seeds

ⓒ **16. Model** Tina is making flag pins like the one shown below. How many of each color bead are needed to make 8 pins?

17. David is buying toys for a piñata. He wants to put 40 mini yo-yos in the piñata. Each bag has 8 yo-yos. If David spent 30 dollars on the yo-yos, how much did each bag cost?

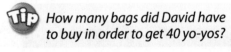 *How many bags did David have to buy in order to get 40 yo-yos?*

A $4   **B** $5   **C** $6   **D** $7

18. Maria is pouring glasses of juice for her friends. She pours 8 fluid ounces of juice into each glass. The container of juice is full and has 59 fluid ounces of juice. How many glasses of juice can Maria pour? How much juice is left?

19. Debbie has a collection of stickers. She puts her 12 stickers on each page of a book. Debbie has 35 pages full of stickers. How many stickers are on those pages in all?

Algebra Connections

Simplifying Number Expressions

In order to simplify a number expression you must follow the order of operations.

First, complete the operations inside the parentheses.

Then multiply and divide in order from left to right. Then add and subtract in order from left to right.

> **Example** $(5 + 3) \times 4$
>
> *Start with the operation inside the parentheses. What is 5 + 3?*
> $5 + 3 = 8$.
> *Then, multiply 8×4.*
> $8 \times 4 = 32$
> So, $(5 + 3) \times 4 = 32$

Simplify. Follow the order of operations.

1. $4 \times 8 - 6$

2. $12 + 8 \div 4$

3. $5 \times (8 - 2)$

4. $35 + (4 \times 6) - 7$

5. $5 \times 5 + 9$

6. $8 + 18 \div 3$

7. $6 + 4 + (12 \div 2)$

8. $(8 - 2) \div 3$

9. $(9 + 8) \times 2$

10. $10 + 4 \div (9 - 7)$

11. $(54 \div 9) + (6 \times 6)$

12. $(16 - 4) + (16 - 4)$

13. $(21 - 3) + 7$

14. $9 + 9 \div 3 \times 3$

15. $2 \div 2 + 2 - 1$

16. $3 \times 3 \div 3 + 6 - 3$

17. $5 + 4 \times 3 + 2 - 1$

18. $6 \div 3 \times 2 + 7 - 5$

· ·

© **Reason** For **19** through **24**, write the expression represented by each problem and then simplify the expression.

19. There are 2 teachers and 6 rows of 4 students in a classroom.

20. Three cartons of a dozen eggs each, with 4 eggs broken in each carton.

21. Two groups of 10 students are in a room. Four students leave the room.

22. Six rows of 5 small toys and 1 row of 7 large toys.

23. 4 baskets of 10 apples, with 2 bruised apples in each basket.

24. Five groups of 4 tulips, and 2 roses.

Lesson
9-6

Common
Core

4.NBT.6 Find whole-
number quotients and
remainders with up to
four-digit dividends and
one-digit divisors, using
strategies based on place
value, the properties of
operations, and/or the
relationship between
multiplication and division.
Illustrate and explain
the calculation by using
equations, rectangular
arrays, and/or area models.
Also **4.OA.2, 4.OA.3**

Problem Solving

Draw a Picture and Write an Equation

Ruben's scout troop is making 4 milk-jug
birdfeeders. Each birdfeeder will use the
same number of wooden dowels. If they
have 24 dowels in all, how many dowels
will be used for each feeder?

24 dowels

Guided Practice*

 MATHEMATICAL
PRACTICES

Do you know HOW?

Solve. Write an equation to help you.

1. Tina put 32 flowers into eight
   bouquets. How many flowers were
   in each bouquet if each had the
   same number of flowers?

   32 flowers in all

   | ? | ? | ? | ? | ? | ? | ? | ? |

   ↑
   **Flowers in
   each bouquet**

Do you UNDERSTAND?

© 2. **Model** How did the picture in
   Problem 1 help you to write an
   equation?

3. How many birdfeeders could
   Ruben's scout troop make with
   36 dowels?

© 4. **Write a Problem** Write a problem
   about sharing items that you can
   solve by drawing a picture.
   Then solve.

Independent Practice

 MATHEMATICAL
PRACTICES

Solve. Write an equation to help you.

5. Kylie bought a bag of 30 beads to make
   bracelets. Each bracelet requires 5 beads.
   How many bracelets can Kylie make?

   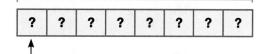

   30 beads

   | 5 | ? bracelets →

   ↑
   Beads on each bracelet

Applying Math Practices

- What am I asked to find?
- What else can I try?
- How are quantities related?
- How can I explain my work?
- How can I use math to model the
  problem?
- Can I use tools to help?
- Is my work precise?
- Why does this work?
- How can I generalize?

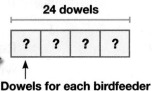

Read and Understand

What do I know? There are 24 dowels. There are 4 birdfeeders. Each birdfeeder has the same number of dowels.

What am I asked to find? The number of dowels for each birdfeeder

Plan and Solve

Draw a picture.

24 dowels

| ? | ? | ? | ? |

↑ Dowels for each birdfeeder

Write a number sentence.

Divide: 24 ÷ 4 = ▢

24 ÷ 4 = 6

There are 6 dowels for each birdfeeder.

Look Back and Check

Check the answer by multiplying.

Each birdfeeder has 6 dowels. There are 4 birdfeeders.

$4 \times 6 = 24$

The answer checks.

ⓒ **6. Reason** Sheena is packing 18 paperweights in boxes. She packs them in 6 boxes with the same number of paperweights in each box. How many paperweights are in each box?

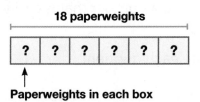

18 paperweights

| ? | ? | ? | ? | ? | ? |

↑ Paperweights in each box

ⓒ **7. Be Precise** Jodi is bundling newspapers. She has 54 newspapers and puts 6 newspapers in each bundle. How many bundles does Jodi make?

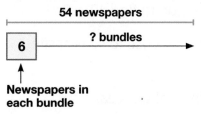

54 newspapers

| 6 | ? bundles →

↑ Newspapers in each bundle

Use the bar graph at the right for **8** and **9**.

8. How much more money did Katie save in September than in October?

9. Katie used the money she saved in November and December to buy her mother a present. How much did she spend?

Katie's Savings September–December

ⓒ **10. Model** Manny is going camping with friends. He packed 30 sandwiches. How many sandwiches can Manny and his friends eat each day if they go camping for 5 days and eat the same number of sandwiches each day?

11. Jenna bought 36 pencils to give to her friends before the first day of school. If each friend received 6 pencils, how many friends did Jenna buy pencils for?

Set A, pages 206–207

A class shares 270 pens equally among 3 groups of students.

270 pens

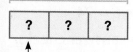

Pens for each
group of students

Find 270 ÷ 3.

The basic fact is 27 ÷ 3 = 9.
27 tens ÷ 3 = 9 tens or 90
So, 270 ÷ 3 = 90 pens.

Remember you can use patterns with zero to divide multiples of 10.

1. 250 ÷ 5   **2.** 810 ÷ 9

3. 3,200 ÷ 4   **4.** 4,200 ÷ 7

5. 1,000 ÷ 2   **6.** 240 ÷ 4

7. 450 ÷ 5   **8.** 720 ÷ 9

9. 3,600 ÷ 4   **10.** 4,900 ÷ 7

11. 2,000 ÷ 2   **12.** 280 ÷ 4

13. 2,100 ÷ 7   **14.** 560 ÷ 8

Set B, pages 208–211

Use estimation to find 42 ÷ 8.

What number close to 42 is easily divided by 8?

Try multiples of ten near 42:

40 is 4 tens and can be divided by 8.
40 ÷ 8 = 5

So, 42 ÷ 8 is about 5.

Use estimation to find 130 ÷ 7.

What number close to 130 is easily divided by 7?

Try multiples of ten near 130:

140 is 14 tens and can be divided by 7.
140 ÷ 7 = 20

So, 130 ÷ 7 is about 20.

Remember to try rounding the dividend to a number that is easily divided.

Estimate each quotient.

1. 718 ÷ 8   **2.** 156 ÷ 4

3. 482 ÷ 8   **4.** 28 ÷ 3

5. 843 ÷ 7   **6.** 321 ÷ 2

7. 428 ÷ 6   **8.** 811 ÷ 9

9. 561 ÷ 8   **10.** 723 ÷ 8

11. 632 ÷ 9   **12.** 362 ÷ 9

13. 57 ÷ 6   **14.** 1,222 ÷ 6

15. 2,511 ÷ 5   **16.** 362 ÷ 6

17. 4,940 ÷ 7   **18.** 9,312 ÷ 3

19. 331 ÷ 4   **20.** 174 ÷ 3

Find 56 ÷ 9.

$$
\begin{array}{r}
6\ \text{R}2 \\
9\overline{)56} \\
-\ 54 \\
\hline
2
\end{array}
$$

Divide: 9 groups of 6 in 56
Multiply: 9 × 6 = 54
Subtract: 56 − 54 = 2
Compare: 2 < 9

Check: 9 × 6 = 54 and 54 + 2 = 56

56 ÷ 9 = 6 R2

Remember that you can use pictures to help.

1. 8)41   2. 2)15

3. 7)59   4. 5)22

5. 3)28   6. 4)27

7. 7)69   8. 6)47

Joey wants to give 81 trading cards to 3 friends. If he gives each friend an equal amount, how many cards will each receive?

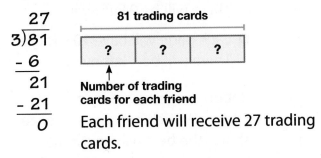

$$
\begin{array}{r}
27 \\
3\overline{)81} \\
-\ 6 \\
\hline
21 \\
-\ 21 \\
\hline
0
\end{array}
$$

81 trading cards

? ? ?

Number of trading cards for each friend

Each friend will receive 27 trading cards.

Remember to divide to find the number of equal groups.

Write a multiplication or division number story for each number fact.

1. 32 × 5   2. 6)54

3. 6)36   4. 19 × 4

5. 3 × $10   6. 7)49

What do I know?   Mrs. Collins has 36 pairs of scissors. She puts the same number of scissors in each of 6 drawers. How many pairs of scissors are in each drawer?

What am I being asked to find?   The number of scissors in each drawer

Draw a picture.

Divide to find the number of scissors in each drawer.

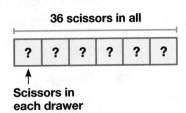

36 scissors in all

? ? ? ? ? ?

Scissors in each drawer

36 ÷ 6 = ▨

36 ÷ 6 = 6

There are 6 pairs of scissors in each drawer.

Remember to draw a picture to help you write an equation.

Draw a picture and write an equation to solve.

1. Winnie buys 20 bookmarks for herself and three of her friends. Each person received the same number of bookmarks. How many bookmarks did they each receive?

Multiple Choice

1. A stadium has 3,000 seats and 6 gates. How many seats are served by each gate if each gate serves the same number of seats? (9-1)

A 5

B 50

C 500

D 5,000

2. What is the quotient? (9-4)

A 3 R8

B 4 R2

C 4 R3

D 5 R2

3. A cyclist rides 2,823 miles in four weeks. He rides an equal distance each week. About how many miles does he ride each week? (9-3)

A 1,200

B 800

C 700

D 400

4. What is 38 ÷ 4? (9-4)

A 8 R2

B 8

C 9 R2

D 9

5. Philip has 54 new stickers. If he puts an equal number of stickers on each of 5 blank pages in his sticker book, how many stickers can he place on a page? (9-5)

A Each page will have 11 stickers. There will be 4 left over.

B Each page will have 11 stickers. There will be 0 left over.

C Each page will have 10 stickers. There will be 9 left over.

D Each page will have 10 stickers. There will be 4 left over.

6. Robert earned $196 by mowing 5 lawns. Which number sentence shows the best way to estimate the amount he earned for each lawn? (9-2)

A $200 ÷ 5 = $40

B $150 ÷ 5 = $30

C $200 ÷ 10 = $20

D 5 × $200 = $1,000

7. Eugenia bought 16 flowers. She used 3 flowers in each centerpiece. How many flowers were left over? (9-5)

A none

B 1 flower

C 2 flowers

D 6 flowers

8. Each costume requires 3 yards of material. How many costumes can Beth make out of 44 yards? How much material will she have left? (9-4)

9. Olivia has 36 daisies and 6 vases. Write a number sentence that shows how many daisies she can put in each vase if she puts the same number in each vase. (9-6)

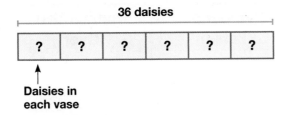

36 daisies

| ? | ? | ? | ? | ? | ? |

↑
Daisies in each vase

10. A case of plastic spoons has 4,800 spoons. There are 8 boxes of spoons in the case. How many spoons are in each box? (9-1)

11. Holly uses 7 sheets of tissue paper to make one flower. If she bought a package with 500 sheets of tissue paper, about how many tissue flowers will she be able to make? Use compatible numbers to find your answer. (9-2)

12. A mechanic replaced 36 tires. If he replaced all 4 tires on each car, then how many cars did he fix? (9-5)

13. Estimate the quotient $427 \div 7$. (9-3)

14. What number sentence comes next in the pattern? (9-1)

$48 \div 6 = 8$
$480 \div 6 = 80$
$4,800 \div 6 = 800$

15. There are 49 students on a tour. Each guide can take 5 students. How many guides are needed? Explain. (9-4)

16. The soccer club has one package of 360 paper cups to use in the concession stands. If they split the cups evenly between the 4 concession stands, how many cups would each stand have? (9-1)

17. Rory's older brother is saving to buy a used motorcycle that costs $3,550. He saves an equal amount of money each month for 6 months. About how much does he need to save each month to buy the motorcycle? (9-3)

18. Alex has 27 photos of her friends that she wants to display on 3 pages in her Friends Album. Write a number sentence that shows how many photos she can put on each page. (9-6)

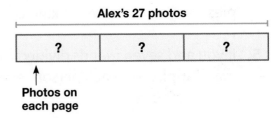

Alex's 27 photos

| ? | ? | ? |

↑
Photos on each page

You and five friends picked the apples shown in the table below. There are red, green, and yellow apples.

1. You and your friends decided to share each type of apple equally. Copy and complete the table to show how many of each type of apple each person will get. Don't forget to include yourself.

Kinds of Apples	Total Number	Number per Person	Number Left Over
Red apples	52		
Yellow apples	26		
Green apples	30		

Use the table to answer these questions.

2. How many apples will each person receive in all? Which color of apple has the greatest number left over? Did any color of apples have none left over?

3. How many apples in all are left over? Can these be shared equally with your group? Explain.

4. Suppose you make apple pies with your apples. It takes 6 apples for a green apple pie. It takes 9 apples for a deep dish apple pie made with red or yellow apples. How many pies can you make? What kind of pies will they be?

5. If you and seven friends divided the red apples equally, how many apples will each person receive? How many red apples will be left over?

Topic **10**

Developing Fluency: Dividing by 1-Digit Divisors

▼ Selenium is an element found in certain materials, such as these selenite crystals. It is often used to conduct electricity. Some of the tallest selenite crystals are found in Chihuahua, Mexico. Find out how many times taller they are than a 4-foot-tall fourth grader in Lesson 10-4.

Review What You Know!

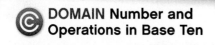

Vocabulary

Choose the best term from the box.

- array
- compatible numbers
- factors
- partial product

1. An arrangement of objects in rows and columns is called a(n) ? .

2. When multiplying a two-digit number by a two-digit number, a ? is found by multiplying the first factor by the ones of the second factor.

3. Numbers that are easy to compute mentally are called ? .

Division Facts

Divide.

4. 15 ÷ 3   **5.** 64 ÷ 8   **6.** 72 ÷ 8

7. 35 ÷ 7   **8.** 12 ÷ 4   **9.** 45 ÷ 9

Multiplying by 10 and 100

Find each product.

10. 62 × 10   **11.** 24 × 100   **12.** 65 × 100

13. 14 × 10   **14.** 35 × 100   **15.** 59 × 10

Arrays

16. Write a multiplication problem for the array at the right.

© **17. Writing to Explain** Is an array for 4 × 3 the same or different from the array shown above? Explain.

Topic Essential Questions
- How can repeated subtraction be used to model division?
- What is the standard procedure for dividing multi-digit numbers?

Interactive Learning

 Hands-On Minds-On

Pose the problem. Start each lesson by working together to solve problems. It will help you make sense of math.

Applying Math Practices

- What am I asked to find?
- What else can I try?
- How are quantities related?
- How can I explain my work?
- How can I use math to model the problem?
- Can I use tools to help?
- Is my work precise?
- Why does this work?
- How can I generalize?

Lesson 10-1

Ⓒ **Use Tools** Solve. Use counters if you want.

How many of the cans shown at the right are needed to hold 45 tennis balls? Show how you found the answer.

Lesson 10-2

Ⓒ **Reason** Solve this problem using only paper and pencil.

A certain bird feeder holds 6 cups of bird feed. How many times can this feeder be filled using a 72-cup bag of bird feed?

Lesson 10-3

Ⓒ **Use Tools** Solve. Use place-value blocks if you want.

Paulo has 39 patches from states he visited. He wants to arrange them on a board in 3 equal rows. How many patches will be in each row?

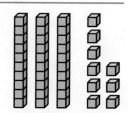

Lesson 10-4

Ⓒ **Generalize** Solve any way you choose.

Swati is packing T-shirts and shorts into boxes to put away for the winter. There are 42 items to pack. She packs the same number of items into 3 boxes. How many items does Swati pack in each box? Show how you found the answer.

Lesson 10-5

© **Generalize** Solve. Use what you learned in the previous lesson to help.

All 5 grades at the school shown at the right have the same number of students. How many students are in each grade? Show how you found the answer.

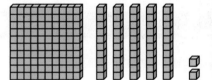

Lesson 10-6

© **Use Tools** Show 152 using place value blocks. Share the blocks to solve this problem.

Roberto is using craft sticks to make picture frames. He has 152 craft sticks. He uses 6 sticks for each frame. How many frames can he make? Tell what you did with the blocks to solve the problem.

Lesson 10-7

© **Reasonableness** Find two estimates for this problem. Tell how you found each.

A certain high school football stadium has 6 same-size sections. The stadium holds a total of 1,950 people. About how many people can be seated in each section? (a) Use estimation to give two multiples of 100 between which the exact quotient falls. (b) Then give a single number as an estimate of the quotient.

Lesson 10-8

© **Model** Solve any way you choose. Show your work.

Susan has $45. She spends $15 on a book for her father, $20 on candles for her mother, and $6 on a board game for her brother. Does Susan have enough money left to buy a box of markers for $5?

$45			
15	20	6	x

**Common
Core**

4.NBT.6 Find whole-number quotients and remainders with up to four-digit dividends and one-digit divisors, using strategies based on place value, the properties of operations, and/or the relationship between multiplication and division. Illustrate and explain the calculation by using equations, rectangular arrays, and/or area models.

Using Objects to Divide: Division as Repeated Subtraction

How can subtraction help you divide?

Su has 24 international postage stamps. She needs 2 of these stamps to send a postcard. How many postcards can she send using all of these stamps?

 24 stamps

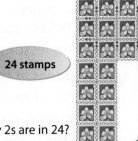

Think How many 2s are in 24?

Guided Practice*

MATHEMATICAL PRACTICES

Do you know HOW?

Use counters and repeated subtraction to divide. Record your work.

1. How many 3s are in 48?

2. How many 4s are in 60?

Do you UNDERSTAND?

© **3. Writing to Explain** Explain the shortcut this student used for solving the postcard problem above.

$24 - 10 = 14$ (5 groups of 2)
$14 - 10 = 4$ (5 more groups of 2)
 $4 - 4 = 0$ (2 more groups of 2)

12 postcards

Independent Practice

For **4** through **17** use counters and repeated subtraction to divide. Record your work.

4. How many 5s are in 35?

5. How many 4s are in 32?

6. How many 7s are in 84?

7. How many 6s are in 66?

8. How many 8s are in 72?

9. How many 3s are in 57?

10. $56 \div 7$

11. $54 \div 9$

12. $30 \div 2$

13. $84 \div 6$

14. $80 \div 5$

15. $112 \div 8$

16. $88 \div 8$

17. $117 \div 9$

For another example, see Set A on page 248.

Use counters to model 24 stamps. Take away 2 as many times as possible.

Take away 2.

$24 - 2 = 22$
$22 - 2 = 20$

Take away 2.

Continue to take away 2 as many times as possible. Record using symbols.

$20 - 2 = 18$	$10 - 2 = 8$
$18 - 2 = 16$	$8 - 2 = 6$
$16 - 2 = 14$	$6 - 2 = 4$
$14 - 2 = 12$	$4 - 2 = 2$
$12 - 2 = 10$	$2 - 2 = 0$

Since 2 was subtracted 12 times, Su can send 12 postcards.

Problem Solving

 MATHEMATICAL PRACTICES

18. Teams of 4 students will be formed for a scavenger hunt. How many teams will be formed if 52 students signed up?

19. Mary wants to share her collection of 42 marbles equally among 3 of her friends. How many marbles will each of her friends receive?

20. Billy is organizing his football cards into 3 equal stacks. How many cards should he put in each stack if he has a total of 75 football cards?

    A 15   **C** 25

    B 20   **D** 40

21. A pizza is cut into 12 pieces for 4 people to share equally. How many pieces will each person receive?

    A 3   **C** 1

    B 2   **D** 0

© **22. Critique Reasoning** Paul claims that when he organizes his collection of 70 marbles into 5 equal piles that there will be 15 marbles in each pile. Is Paul correct? Why or why not?

70 marbles in all

23. The 240 students at Cypress Elementary are taking a field trip. How many vans are needed to transport the students, if each van will hold 8 students?

24. Jeff buys a box of 30 apples. He eats 2 apples each day at lunch. How long will the apples last?

Lesson
10-2

Common
Core

4.NBT.6 Find whole-number quotients and remainders with up to four-digit dividends and one-digit divisors, using strategies based on place value, the properties of operations, and/or the relationship between multiplication and division. Illustrate and explain the calculation by using equations, rectangular arrays, and/or area models.

Division as Repeated Subtraction

How can you record division using repeated subtraction?

Each row on an airplane can seat 3 people. If there are 63 people waiting in line and each seat will be taken, how many rows of seats are needed?

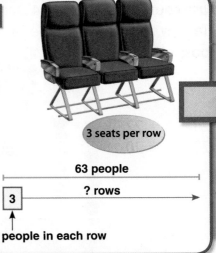

3 seats per row

 Think How many 3s are in 63?

63 people

3 | ? rows →

people in each row

Guided Practice*

 MATHEMATICAL PRACTICES

Do you know HOW?

Use repeated subtraction to divide. Record your work.

1. 48 ÷ 4

2. 75 ÷ 5

3. 153 ÷ 9

4. 65 ÷ 5

Do you UNDERSTAND?

Use repeated subtraction to divide. Record your work.

Ⓒ **5. Reason** Show one way of using repeated subtraction to solve. 69 ÷ 3.

Ⓒ **6. Reason** Show another way of using repeated subtraction to solve. 69 ÷ 3.

Independent Practice

For **7** through **14** use repeated subtraction to divide. Record your work.

7. 78 ÷ 6   **8.** 84 ÷ 7   **9.** 88 ÷ 8   **10.** 42 ÷ 3

11. 90 ÷ 6   **12.** 40 ÷ 2   **13.** 92 ÷ 4   **14.** 126 ÷ 7

Problem Solving

Ⓒ MATHEMATICAL PRACTICES

15. There are 5 players on a basketball team. How many teams can be formed from a list of 90 players?

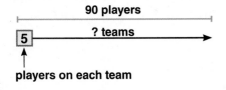

90 players

5 | ? teams →

players on each team

16. A collection of 64 stickers is being placed into 4 equal piles. How many stickers will be placed in each pile?

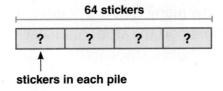

64 stickers

| ? | ? | ? | ? |

stickers in each pile

For another example, see Set B on page 248.

Here is one way to record the division problem 63 ÷ 3.

```
  63    Estimate: How many 3s are in 63? Try 10.
 -30    Multiply 10 × 3 and subtract.
  33    Estimate: How many 3s are in 33? Use 11.
 -33    Multiply 11 × 3 and subtract.
   0
```

10 + 11 = 21, so there are 21 3s in 63.

21 rows are needed to seat 63 people.

Here is another way to record the division problem.

```
  63    Estimate: How many 3s are in 63? Try 20.
 -60    Multiply 20 × 3 and subtract.
   3    Estimate: How many 3s are in 3? Use 1.
  -3    Multiply 1 × 3 and subtract.
   0
```

20 + 1 = 21, so there are 21 3s in 63.

21 rows are needed to seat 63 people.

17. Which statement below is the best estimate for the quotient 99 ÷ 3?

A between 0 and 10

B between 10 and 20

C between 20 and 30

D between 30 and 40

18. There are 2 dozen eggs in the kitchen. A chef is baking cookies for 3 birthday parties. For each party, the chef is using an equal number of eggs. How many eggs does the chef use for one party?

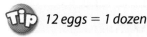 *12 eggs = 1 dozen*

© 19. Critique Reasoning Amanda thinks that she can separate her books into 7 equal piles. Amanda has a total of 42 books. Is Amanda's reasoning correct?

42 books

20. A photo album can hold 84 pictures. If 4 pictures are on each page, then how many pages are in the photo album?

A 25   **C** 20

B 21   **D** 16

© 21. Construct Arguments Ryan has a total of 85 pennies. Will he be able to give away his pennies equally to 4 of his friends? Explain your reasoning.

22. A local baker made 132 bagels one day. The baker sells bagels in packages of 6 bagels. He sold all of the bagels. How many packages of bagels did he sell?

© 23. Communicate How can you use repeated subtraction to divide 81 ÷ 3? Solve and explain your process.

24. A shoe store got a delivery of 104 pairs of shoes. There are 8 pairs of shoes in each case that was delivered. How many cases were delivered?

© Common Core

4.NBT.6 Find whole-number quotients and remainders with up to four-digit dividends and one-digit divisors, using strategies based on place value, the properties of operations, and/or the relationship between multiplication and division. Illustrate and explain the calculation by using equations, rectangular arrays, and/or area models. Also **4.NBT.1**

Using Objects to Divide: Division as Sharing

Hands-On
place-value blocks

57 student drawings

How can place value help you divide?

Mrs. Lynch displayed 57 student drawings on 3 walls in her art classroom. If she divided the drawings equally, how many drawings are on each wall?

Estimate: $60 \div 3 = 20$

drawings on each wall

Another Example How do you model remainders?

Helen has 55 postcards. As an art project, she plans to glue 4 postcards onto sheets of colored paper.

How many pieces of paper can she fill?

Step 1 Divide the tens.

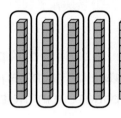

Division is used to find the number of equal groups.

$$\begin{array}{r} 1 \\ 4\overline{)55} \\ -\ 4 \\ \hline 1 \end{array}$$

There is 1 ten in each group and 1 ten left over.

Step 2 Regroup the 1 ten as 10 ones and divide.

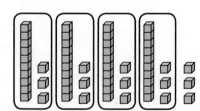

$$\begin{array}{r} 13\,R3 \\ 4\overline{)55} \\ -\ 4 \\ \hline 15 \\ -\ 12 \\ \hline 3 \end{array}$$

Trade the extra ten for ten ones.
The 1 ten and 5 ones make 15.
There are 3 ones in each group and 3 left over.

Helen will fill 13 pieces of colored paper.

Explain It

1. In the first step above, what does the 1 in the quotient represent?

© **2. Reasonableness** How can you check that the answer is correct?

Use place-value blocks to show 57.	Trade the extra tens for ones.	Divide the ones.

Use place-value blocks to show 57.

Divide the tens into three equal groups.

$$\begin{array}{r} 1 \\ 3\overline{)57} \\ -3 \end{array}$$ 3 tens used

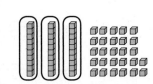

Trade the extra tens for ones.

$$\begin{array}{r} 1 \\ 3\overline{)57} \\ -3 \\ \hline 27 \end{array}$$ 3 tens used
27 ones left

Divide the ones.

$$\begin{array}{r} 19 \\ 3\overline{)57} \\ -3 \\ \hline 27 \\ -27 \\ \hline 0 \end{array}$$ 27 ones used

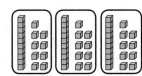

There are 19 drawings on each wall.

Guided Practice*

MATHEMATICAL PRACTICES

Do you know HOW?

I Know me

In **1** through **4**, use place-value blocks or draw pictures. Tell how many are in each group and how many are left over.

1. 76 magazines
5 boxes

2. 56 marbles
3 bags

3. 82 muffins
7 boxes

4. 72 photos
3 albums

Do you UNDERSTAND?

5. Use Tools Describe another way to show 57 using place-value blocks.

6. Mrs. Lynch displayed 48 paintings in 3 sets. If each set had the same number of paintings, how many were in each set?

Independent Practice

Leveled Practice In **7** through **10**, use the model to complete each division sentence.

7. 71 ÷ ▢ = ▢ R2

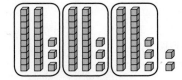

8. ▢ ÷ 4 = ▢

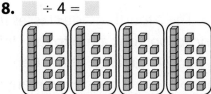

9. ▢ ÷ ▢ = ▢

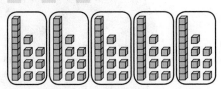

10. ▢ ÷ ▢ = ▢ R ▢

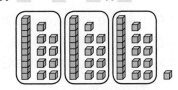

DIGITAL
eTools
www.pearsonsuccessnet.com

In **11** through **30**, use place-value blocks or draw pictures to solve.

11. 3)46   **12.** 8)96   **13.** 4)55   **14.** 2)51   **15.** 5)89

16. 6)76   **17.** 7)36   **18.** 3)72   **19.** 2)63   **20.** 4)92

21. 3)44   **22.** 4)67   **23.** 6)85   **24.** 3)56   **25.** 5)97

26. 2)39   **27.** 4)31   **28.** 5)87   **29.** 7)82   **30.** 5)22

Problem Solving

MATHEMATICAL
PRACTICES

31. Use Tools Maya used place-value blocks to divide 86. She made groups of 17 with 1 left over. Use place-value blocks or draw pictures to determine how many groups Maya made.

32. Writing to Explain Harold has 64 toy cars in 4 equal boxes. To find the number in each box, he divided 64 by 4. How many tens did he regroup as ones?

33. Think About the Structure Jake walks dogs and delivers papers to earn money. This month, he earned $52 delivering papers and $43 walking dogs. Each month, he puts half of his money into the bank. Which shows how much Jake saved this month?

A $(52 + 43) + 2$ **C** $(52 + 43) \div 2$

B $(52 + 43) \times 2$ **D** $(52 + 43) - 2$

34. Reason Tina has 50 berries. She wants to have some each day for lunch. How many berries can she have each day if she wants to eat them all in 5 days?

50 berries

?	?	?	?	?

↑
number of berries each day

35. Persevere The 4 fourth-grade classes from Jameson Elementary School took a trip to the United States Capitol. Each class had 24 students. At the Capitol, the students were divided into 6 equal groups. How many students were in each group?

36. A maximum of 40 people are allowed on a tour of the Capitol at one time. After 16 tours, how many people could have gone through the Capitol?

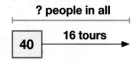

? people in all

40 | 16 tours →

Dividing by Multiples of 10

Patterns can be used when dividing by multiples of 10. It is easy to divide mentally using basic facts and place-value patterns.

Examples:

$7\overline{)21} = 3$

$7\overline{)210} = 30$

$7\overline{)2,100} = 300$

$7\overline{)21,000} = 3,000$

As the number of zeros in the dividend increases, the number of zeros in the quotient increases by the same amount.

$4\overline{)20} = 5$

$40\overline{)200} = 5$

$400\overline{)2,000} = 5$

$4,000\overline{)20,000} = 5$

The number of zeros in the dividend and divisor increase by the same amount, and the quotient remains the same as in the basic fact.

Practice

For **1** through **12**, divide. Use mental math.

1. $30\overline{)90}$

2. $90\overline{)6,300}$

3. $2\overline{)8,000}$

4. $900\overline{)4,500}$

5. $80\overline{)560}$

6. $8\overline{)7,200}$

7. $200\overline{)1,400}$

8. $70\overline{)4,200}$

9. $7\overline{)350}$

10. $20\overline{)120}$

11. $70\overline{)2,800}$

12. $400\overline{)1,600}$

Ⓒ **13. Reason** Write another division problem with the same answer as $90\overline{)3,600}$.

Ⓒ **14. Use Structure** How is dividing 490 by 7 like dividing 49,000 by 700?

15. A science museum has 2,400 gemstones displayed equally in 30 cases. How many gemstones are in each case?

16. Ryan has a collection of 1,800 stickers. He wants to put them in equal groups into 20 sticker albums. How many stickers will be in each album?

© Common Core

4.NBT.6 Find whole-number quotients and remainders with up to four-digit dividends and one-digit divisors, using strategies based on place value, the properties of operations, and/or the relationship between multiplication and division. Illustrate and explain the calculation by using equations, rectangular arrays, and/or area models.

Dividing 2-Digit by 1-Digit Numbers

76 cans of soup in all

What is a common way to record division?

At the school food drive, Al needs to put the same number of soup cans into four boxes. How many soup cans will go in each box?

Choose an Operation Divide to find the number in each group.

Another Example How do you divide with a remainder?

Al collects 58 cans of vegetables. He puts the same number of cans in four boxes. How many cans of vegetables will go in each box? How many cans will be left over?

A   14 cans, 2 cans left over

B   15 cans, 2 cans left over

C   16 cans, 2 cans left over

D   18 cans, 2 cans left over

Step 1

Divide the tens.

Regroup the remaining ten as 10 ones.

$$\begin{array}{r} 1 \\ 4\overline{)58} \\ -4 \\ \hline 1 \end{array}$$

Step 2

Divide the ones.

Subtract to find the remainder.

$$\begin{array}{r} 14 \\ 4\overline{)58} \\ -4 \\ \hline 18 \\ -16 \\ \hline 2 \end{array}$$

Step 3

Check: $14 \times 4 = 56$ and $56 + 2 = 58$.

There will be 14 cans of vegetables in each box and 2 cans left over.

The correct choice is **A**.

Explain It

© **1. Reasonableness** How can you use estimation to decide if 14 cans is reasonable?

2. Why is multiplication used to check division?

Divide the tens.

$$\frac{1}{4)\overline{76}}$$
$$-\ 4$$
$$\overline{\ \ 3}$$

Think There is **1** ten in each group and **3** tens left over.

Divide the ones.

$$\frac{19}{4)\overline{76}}$$
$$-4$$
$$\overline{36}$$
$$-36$$
$$\overline{\ \ 0}$$

Think Trade the 3 tens for 30 ones.

30 ones and 6 ones make **36** ones.

There will be 19 soup cans in each box.

Check by multiplying.

$$\frac{3}{19}$$
$$\times\ \ 4$$
$$\overline{76}$$

The answer checks.

Guided Practice*

MATHEMATICAL
PRACTICES

Do you know HOW?

In **1** and **2**, copy and complete each calculation.

1. $$\frac{4}{2)\overline{94}}$$
$$-\ \blacksquare$$
$$\overline{\ \ \blacksquare 4}$$
$$-\ 1\blacksquare$$
$$\overline{\ \ \ 0}$$

2. $$\frac{6R\blacksquare}{5)\overline{82}}$$
$$-\ 5$$
$$\overline{\ \ \blacksquare\blacksquare}$$
$$-\ \blacksquare\blacksquare$$
$$\overline{\ \ \ \blacksquare}$$

Do you UNDERSTAND?

© 3. **Communicate** Explain how you would estimate the answer in Exercise 2.

4. Al collects 85 cans of fruit. He puts the same number of fruit cans in 4 boxes. Will he have any cans left over? If so, how many cans?

Independent Practice

Leveled Practice In **5** through **8**, copy and complete each calculation. Estimate to check reasonableness.

5. $$\frac{\blacksquare\blacksquare}{7)\overline{84}}$$
$$-\ 7$$
$$\overline{\ \ \blacksquare 4}$$
$$-\ \blacksquare\blacksquare$$
$$\overline{\ \ \ 0}$$

6. $$\frac{6}{3)\overline{78}}$$
$$-\ \blacksquare$$
$$\overline{\ \ \blacksquare 8}$$
$$-\ 1\blacksquare$$
$$\overline{\ \ \ 0}$$

7. $$\frac{\blacksquare\blacksquare\ R\blacksquare}{4)\overline{93}}$$
$$-\ 8$$
$$\overline{\ \ \blacksquare\blacksquare}$$
$$-\ 1\blacksquare$$
$$\overline{\ \ \ 1}$$

8. $$\frac{1\blacksquare\ R\blacksquare}{6)\overline{80}}$$
$$-\ \blacksquare$$
$$\overline{\ \ \blacksquare\blacksquare}$$
$$-\ \blacksquare\blacksquare$$
$$\overline{\ \ \ \blacksquare}$$

For **9** through **18**, find each quotient. Use multiplication to check.

9. $3)\overline{63}$
10. $7)\overline{88}$
11. $6)\overline{96}$
12. $4)\overline{52}$
13. $5)\overline{73}$

14. $5)\overline{93}$
15. $3)\overline{87}$
16. $4)\overline{72}$
17. $6)\overline{77}$
18. $2)\overline{37}$

---

*For another example, see Set D on page 249.

Lesson 10-4

In **19** through **28**, find each quotient. Use multiplication to check.

19. $3\overline{)46}$ **20.** $7\overline{)65}$ **21.** $8\overline{)27}$ **22.** $9\overline{)86}$ **23.** $4\overline{)66}$

24. $8\overline{)59}$ **25.** $4\overline{)92}$ **26.** $3\overline{)74}$ **27.** $5\overline{)68}$ **28.** $2\overline{)89}$

MATHEMATICAL
PRACTICES

29. Reason Some of the tallest selenite crystals in a cave in Chihuahua, Mexico, are 50 feet tall. About how many times taller are the tallest crystals than a 4-foot-tall fourth grader?

30. Zelda has a piece of fabric that is 74 inches long. She wants to divide it into 2 equal pieces. What is the length of each piece?

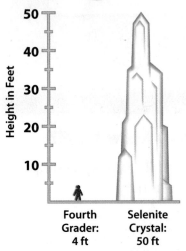

Fourth
Grader:
4 ft

Selenite
Crystal:
50 ft

Use the recipe at the right for **31** and **32**.

31. How many ounces of Tasty Trail Mix are made from the recipe?

32. Maggie is making trail mix. She makes 4 batches of the recipe shown. Then she divides it into 3 equal sized bags. How many ounces are in each bag?

Tasty Trail Mix	
Granola	8 oz
Nuts	5 oz
Raisins	2 oz
Cranberries	3 oz

33. Writing to Explain Why does $51 \div 4$ have two digits in the quotient, while $51 \div 6$ has only one digit in the quotient?

34. Write a Problem Write a problem that could be solved by dividing 78 by 5.

35. Persevere Paulo has 78 cattle on his ranch. He needs to divide them equally among 3 pastures. Which shows the best way to estimate the number of cattle in each pasture?

   A $60 \div 3$ **C** $75 \div 3$

   B $66 \div 3$ **D** $90 \div 3$

36. Every year, the city of San Marcos holds a Cinco de Mayo festival. If 60 students perform in 5 equal groups, how many students are in each group?

   A 10 students   **C** 25 students

   B 12 students   **D** 55 students

Venn Diagrams

A **Venn diagram** is a diagram that uses circles to show the relationships between groups of data. When the circles overlap, or **intersect**, the data belong to more than one group.

Example: Robin, Kevin, and Coreen are in the Math Club.

Sara, Callie, Mike, Brad, and Rachel are in the Science Club.

Gwen and Dan are in both clubs.

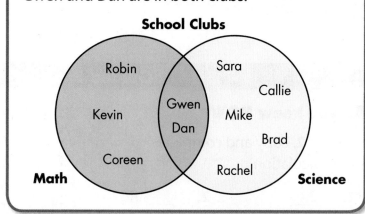

Practice

For **1** through **3**, use the Venn diagram to the right.

1. To which group does 24 belong?

2. Which numbers are multiples of both 3 and 5?

3. In which part of the Venn diagram would you place 48? 50? 60?

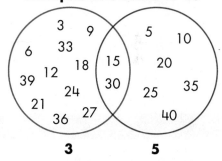

Multiples of 3 and 5 to 40

For **4** through **6**, use the Venn diagram to the right.

4. Which factors of 16 are also factors of 48?

5. Which factors of 48 are not factors of 16 and 40?

6. Which numbers are factors of 16, 40, and 48?

7. Make a Venn diagram that uses two circles.

8. Make a Venn diagram that uses three circles.

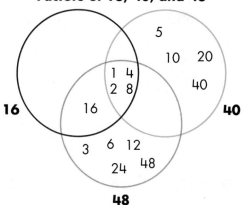

Factors of 16, 40, and 48

© Common Core

4.NBT.6 Find whole-number quotients and remainders with up to four-digit dividends and one-digit divisors, using strategies based on place value, the properties of operations, and/or the relationship between multiplication and division. Illustrate and explain the calculation by using equations, rectangular arrays, and/or area models.

Dividing 3-Digit by 1-Digit Numbers

How can you divide numbers in the hundreds?

A factory shipped 378 watches in 3 boxes. If the watches were equally divided, how many watches were there in each box?

Choose an Operation Divide to find the number in each group.

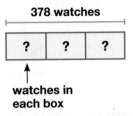

378 watches

| ? | ? | ? |

↑ watches in each box

Guided Practice*

© MATHEMATICAL PRACTICES

Do you know HOW?

In **1** and **2**, copy and complete each calculation.

1.
```
    3▮▮
2)658
 -▮
 ────
  ▮▮
 -▮▮
 ────
  ▮▮
 -▮▮
 ────
  ▮
```

2.
```
   ▮▮▮ R▮
4)954
 -8
 ────
  ▮▮
 -▮▮
 ────
  ▮▮
 -▮▮
 ────
  2
```

Do you UNDERSTAND?

© **3. Persevere** When you divide the hundreds in the problem above, what does the 1 in the quotient represent?

4. Jenny paid $195 to take violin lessons for 3 months. How much did 1 month of lessons cost?

$195

| ? | ? | ? |

↑ Cost for 1 month

Independent Practice

Leveled Practice In **5** through **13**, divide. You may draw a picture to help you.

5.
```
   1▮▮
5)595
 -▮
 ───
  ▮
 -▮
 ───
  4▮
 -▮▮
 ───
  ▮
```

6.
```
   ▮▮▮
2)832
 -▮
 ───
  3
 -▮
 ───
  2
 -▮▮
 ───
  ▮
```

7.
```
   2▮ R▮
3)866
 -▮
 ───
  ▮▮
 -▮▮
 ───
  ▮▮
 -▮▮
 ───
```

8.
```
   ▮▮▮ R▮
4)575
 -▮
 ───
  ▮▮
 -▮▮
 ───
  ▮▮
 -▮▮
 ───
```

9. 4)952 **10.** 3)761 **11.** 5)615 **12.** 2)871 **13.** 3)638

For another example, see Set E on page 250.

Estimate:

$360 \div 3 = 120$

Divide the hundreds.

$$\begin{array}{r} 1 \\ 3\overline{)378} \\ -3 \\ \hline 7 \end{array}$$

Divide the tens.

$$\begin{array}{r} 12 \\ 3\overline{)378} \\ -3 \\ \hline 7 \\ -6 \\ \hline 1 \end{array}$$

Divide the ones.

$$\begin{array}{r} 126 \\ 3\overline{)378} \\ -3 \\ \hline 7 \\ -6 \\ \hline 18 \\ -18 \\ \hline 0 \end{array}$$

There are 126 watches in each box.

The answer is reasonable because 126 is close to 120.

Problem Solving

MATHEMATICAL
PRACTICES

14. Reason The largest United States flag ever created was displayed at the Hoover Dam. The flag measures 255 feet by 505 feet. How many feet longer is the flag than it is wide?

Width: 255 feet

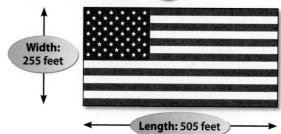

Length: 505 feet

For **15** and **16**, use the table at the right.

15. There are 848 people getting on board the *Memphis Belle.* How many seats are needed for every person to sit?

16. Writing to Explain If 793 people are on the *Natchez Willie,* how many seats are needed for each person to sit?

Data

Historic River Boat Tours	
Natchez Willie	6 riders per seat
Memphis Belle	4 riders per seat

17. If $698 \div 4 = 174$ R ☐ , what is the value of ☐ ?

18. The Galveston-Port Bolivar Ferry takes cars across Galveston Bay. One day, the ferry transported a total of 685 cars over a 5-hour period. If the ferry took the same number of cars each hour, how many cars did it take each hour?

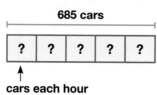

685 cars

?	?	?	?	?

cars each hour

19. Persevere Theo bought a T-shirt for $21 and a pair of shorts for $16. He paid with two $20 bills. How much money did Theo get back?

A $1

B $2

C $3

D $4

Lesson
10-6
ⓒ
Common Core

4.NBT.6 Find whole-number quotients and remainders with up to four-digit dividends and one-digit divisors, using strategies based on place value, the properties of operations, and/or the relationship between multiplication and division. Illustrate and explain the calculation by using equations, rectangular arrays, and/or area models.

Deciding Where to Start Dividing

What do you do when there aren't enough hundreds to divide?

Madison is making iguana key chains using pom-poms. She has 145 pink pom-poms. Are there enough pink pom-poms to make 36 key chains?

2 yellow pom-poms

4 pink pom-poms

7 blue pom-poms

31 green pom-poms

3 yards of plastic lace

4 pink
pom-poms

Guided Practice*

ⓒ MATHEMATICAL PRACTICES

Do you know HOW?

In **1** and **2**, copy and complete each calculation.

1.
```
      6▢
   7)455
  - ▢▢
  ─────
    ▢5
  - ▢▢
  ─────
    ▢
```

2.
```
     ▢▢ R▢
   5)319
  - 3
  ─────
    ▢▢
  - ▢▢
  ─────
    ▢
```

Do you UNDERSTAND?

3. Madison has 365 blue pom-poms. How many key chains can she make?

ⓒ **4. Communicate** Explain how an estimated quotient can help you decide where to start.

Independent Practice

Leveled Practice In **5** through **13**, divide. You may draw a picture to help you.

5.
```
      ▢▢
   6)444
  - ▢▢
  ─────
    ▢▢
  - ▢▢
  ─────
    ▢
```

6.
```
     1▢▢
   3)588
  - ▢
  ─────
     ▢8
  - ▢▢
  ─────
     ▢8
  - ▢▢
  ─────
     ▢
```

7.
```
      5▢ R▢
   8)417
  - ▢▢
  ─────
    ▢▢
  - ▢▢
  ─────
    ▢
```

8.
```
     ▢▢▢ R▢
   2)935
  - 8
  ─────
    ▢▢
  - ▢▢
  ─────
     ▢▢
  - ▢▢
  ─────
     ▢
```

9. 8)526

10. 5)690

11. 3)769

12. 4)923

13. 6)342

*For another example, see Set F on page 250.

There are not enough hundreds to put one in each group.	Divide the ones.	To check, multiply the quotient by the divisor and add the remainder.

There are not enough hundreds to put one in each group.

Start by dividing the tens.

$$\begin{array}{r} 3 \\ 4\overline{)145} \\ -12 \\ \hline 25 \end{array}$$

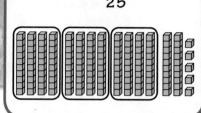

Divide the ones.

$$\begin{array}{r} 36\,R1 \\ 4\overline{)145} \\ -12 \\ \hline 25 \\ -\ 24 \\ \hline 1 \end{array}$$

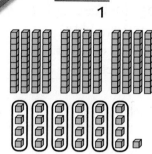

To check, multiply the quotient by the divisor and add the remainder.

$$\begin{array}{r} 2 \\ 36 \\ \times\ 4 \\ \hline 144 \end{array}$$

$144 + 1 = 145$

Madison has enough pink pom-poms to make 36 key chains.

In **14** through **23**, divide. Then check your answer.

14. $6\overline{)96}$ **15.** $5\overline{)295}$ **16.** $2\overline{)306}$ **17.** $9\overline{)517}$ **18.** $4\overline{)624}$

19. $7\overline{)430}$ **20.** $4\overline{)229}$ **21.** $5\overline{)655}$ **22.** $3\overline{)209}$ **23.** $6\overline{)438}$

Problem Solving

MATHEMATICAL PRACTICES

For **24** and **25**, use the bar graph at the right.

James is organizing his CDs. He plans to put them into stackable cubes that hold 8 CDs each.

24. How many cubes will James need for his entire collection?

25. If James decides to group his Rock and World music CDs together, how many cubes would he need for them?

© **26. Reason** How can you tell without dividing that $479 \div 6$ will have a 2-digit quotient?

© **27. Persevere** A family is going on a trip for 3 days. The total cost for the hotel is $336. They budgeted $100 a day for food. How much will each day of the trip cost?

    A $33   **B** $112   **C** $145   **D** $212

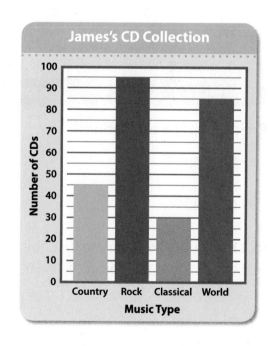

James's CD Collection

Number of CDs

Country Rock Classical World

Music Type

Lesson
10-7

Common
Core

4.NBT.6 Find whole-
number quotients and
remainders with up to
four-digit dividends and
one-digit divisors, using
strategies based on place
value, the properties of
operations, and/or the
relationship between
multiplication and division.
Illustrate and explain the
calculation by using
equations, rectangular
arrays, and/or area models.

Dividing 4-Digit by 1-Digit Numbers

How can you estimate larger quotients?

In all, 4,729 hot dogs were sold at a football game. If there are 8 hot dogs in a package, how many packages of hot dogs were sold?

4,729 hot dogs sold

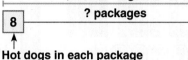

4,729 hot dogs in all

? packages

8

Hot dogs in each package

Guided Practice*

MATHEMATICAL PRACTICES

Do you know HOW?

Divide. Start by estimating.

1. $9\overline{)2,871}$

2. $4\overline{)2,486}$

3. $9\overline{)691}$

4. $4\overline{)1,140}$

Do you UNDERSTAND?

© **5. Reason** In the example above, how many hot dogs were left over in the extra package?

© **6. Writing to Explain** Vickie's estimated quotient was 80. The actual quotient she calculated was 48. Is her actual quotient reasonable? Explain.

Independent Practice

Divide. Start by estimating.

7. $8\overline{)3,248}$

8. $5\overline{)247}$

9. $6\overline{)1,380}$

10. $5\overline{)3,980}$

In **11** through **16**, estimate first. Tell if the answers are reasonable. If the answer is not reasonable, find the correct answer.

11. $6\overline{)367}$ 61 R1

12. $3\overline{)3,582}$ 911 R6

13. $5\overline{)247}$ 49 R2

14. $9\overline{)1,745}$ 93 R8

15. $7\overline{)375}$ 53 R4

16. $8\overline{)1,535}$ 91 R7

*For another example, see Set G on page 251.

Estimate. Decide where to start.

$$500 \times 8 = 4{,}000$$

The answer is more than 500.

$$600 \times 8 = 4{,}800$$

The answer is less than but close to 600.

Start dividing in the hundreds.

Divide.

```
      591 R1
  8)4,729
    -40
     72
    - 72
      09
    -  8
       1
```

47 hundreds ÷ 8 is about 5 hundreds
$8 \times 5 = 40$
72 tens ÷ 8 is 9 tens
$8 \times 9 = 72$
9 ones ÷ 8 is about 1 one
$8 \times 1 = 8$

591 complete packages were sold and 1 hot dog was sold from another package.

Problem Solving

MATHEMATICAL PRACTICES

Solve. Record your work.

17. A family of four drove from San Francisco to New York. They drove the same number of miles each day for 6 days. How many miles did they drive each day? What does the remainder mean?

2,906 miles

San Francisco

New York

18. **Reason** Without dividing, how can you tell that the quotient for 5,873 ÷ 8 is greater than 700? Is the quotient less than 800? Explain.

19. **Reason** Chose a value for x so that x ÷ 5 is between 400 and 500. Tell how you decided.

20. ♫ **Music** A square dance set is made up of 4 couples (8 dancers). Each couple stands on one of the four sides of a square. There are 150 people at a square dance. What is the greatest number of sets possible at the dance?

   A 18   **B** 19   **C** 37   **D** 38

21. Michelle traveled 498 miles from Lakeside to West Little River. She made 7 stops at equal intervals, including her final stop. Michelle estimated that she drove about 50 miles between stops. Is her estimate reasonable? Explain.

22. Mr. Girard sells fishing supplies. He traveled 527 miles from Jacksonville to Miami. He made 6 stops at equal intervals, including his final stop. About how many miles did he travel between stops?

23. Alycia has 164 treats to give to the 7 goats at the petting zoo. Each goat gets an equal share of the treats. How many treats will each goat get? How many treats will Alycia have left?

Common Core

4.OA.3 Solve multistep word problems posed with whole numbers and having whole-number answers using the four operations, including problems in which remainders must be interpreted. Represent these problems using equations with a letter standing for the unknown quantity. Assess the reasonableness of answers using mental computation and estimation strategies including rounding. Also **4.NBT.5**

Problem Solving

Multiple-Step Problems

Justine and her father are going on a fishing trip. The prices for supplies, including tax, are shown in the table. Justine and her father have $25. They bought 2 box lunches, 2 bottles of water, 5 hooks, and 5 sinkers. How many pounds of bait can they buy?

Captain Bob's Price List	
Bait	$3 per pound
Hooks	60¢ each
Sinkers	40¢ each
Bottled water	$1 each
Box lunch	$6 each

Guided Practice*

MATHEMATICAL
PRACTICES

Do you know HOW?

Solve.

1. Elsa babysits for the Smyth family. She earns $10 per hour on weekdays. She earns $15 per hour on the weekend. Last week, she worked 3 hours during the week and 4 hours on the weekend. How much did Elsa earn last week?

Do you UNDERSTAND?

2. What is the hidden question or questions in Problem 1?

Ⓒ 3. **Write a Problem** Write a problem that contains a hidden question.

Independent Practice

MATHEMATICAL
PRACTICES

Ⓒ **Persevere** Write the answer to the hidden question or questions. Then solve the problem. Write your answer in a complete sentence.

4. Gabriella buys lunch for herself and her friend. She buys 2 sandwiches and 2 drinks. Each sandwich costs $4. Each drink costs $1.50. How much did Gabriella spend on lunch?

5. Jamie is buying bowls for a school ice cream social. She buys 5 packages of red bowls, 3 packages of orange bowls, 4 packages of green bowls, and 7 packages of white bowls. Each package contains 8 bowls. How many bowls did she buy in all?

Applying Math Practices

- What am I asked to find?
- What else can I try?
- How are quantities related?
- How can I explain my work?
- How can I use math to model the problem?
- Can I use tools to help?
- Is my work precise?
- Why does this work?
- How can I generalize?

What do I know?

They bought:

2 lunches for $6 each
2 bottles of water for $1 each
5 hooks for 60¢ each
5 sinkers for 40¢ each

What am I asked to find?

The number of pounds of bait they can buy with the money they have left

Find the hidden question. How much money do Justine and her father have left?

The cost of lunches is	2 × $6	= $12
The cost of water is	2 × $1	= $2
The cost of hooks is	5 × 60¢	= $3
The cost of sinkers is	5 × 40¢	= $2
	The total is	$19

$25 − $19 = $6   They have $6 left.

Divide to find how many pounds of bait they can buy.

6 ÷ 3 = 2   They can buy 2 pounds of bait.

---

6. Kelly used 6 cups of apples, 4 cups of oranges, and 2 cups of grapes to make a fruit salad. She put an equal amount in each of 6 bowls. How many cups of fruit salad were in each bowl?

7. Muriel used the same recipe as Kelly to make her fruit salad. Muriel also added 1 cup of cherries and 1 cup of bananas. She put 2 cups of fruit salad into each bowl. How many bowls did Muriel need?

Use the data at the right for **8** through **11**.

8. The band needs to purchase 60 T-shirts. How much would it cost to purchase them from Shirt Shack?

9. How much would it cost the band to purchase 60 T-shirts from Just Jerseys?

© **10. Reason** How much more would it cost to buy 24 T-shirts at Just Jerseys than at Shirt Shack?

© **11. Construct Arguments** Would it be less expensive to buy one shirt from Just Jerseys or Shirt Shack? Explain.

Shirt Shack	
Number of shirts	**Price**
10	$90
20	$180
50	$450

Data

Just Jerseys	
Number of shirts	**Price**
8	$80
24	$240
48	$480

Data

© **12. Model** Each football practice is 45 minutes long. The team's next game is 6 practices away. How many minutes will they practice before the game?

A 135 minutes   **C** 243 minutes

B 270 minutes   **D** 2,430 minutes

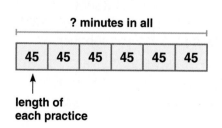

? minutes in all

45	45	45	45	45	45

length of each practice

Set A, pages 228–229

James is placing 4 photos on each page of a photo album. If he has a total of 32 photos, how many pages can James fill?

Use repeated subtraction to find the number of pages.

$32 - 4 = 28$
$28 - 4 = 24$
$24 - 4 = 20$
$20 - 4 = 16$
$16 - 4 = 12$ Subtract 4
$12 - 4 = 8$ eight times.
$8 - 4 = 4$
$4 - 4 = 0$

There are eight groups of 4 in 32.
$32 \div 4 = 8$
So, James can fill 8 pages.

Remember you can think about repeated subtraction to divide.

Use repeated subtraction to divide.

1. There are 24 students in 8 equal groups. How many students are in each group?

2. The hockey club has 35 hockey sticks for all the teams to share equally. If each team gets 5 hockey sticks, how many teams are there?

3. A chef uses 2 large eggs for each omelet. How many omelets are made if a total of 20 eggs are used?

4. A collection of 45 stickers is shared among 5 friends. How any stickers does each friend receive?

Set B, pages 230–231

Mary is mailing letters with 2 stamps on each letter. If she has a total of 30 stamps, how many letters can Mary send?

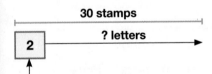

Stamps on each letter

Use repeated subtraction to find the number of letters.

$30 \div 2$

30 Estimate: How many 2s are in 30? Try 10.
$\underline{-20}$ Multiply 10×2 and subtract.
10 Estimate: How many 2s are in 10? Use 5.
$\underline{-10}$ Multiply 5×2 and subtract.
0

$10 + 5 = 15$ There are 15 2s in 30.

Mary can mail a total of 15 letters.

Remember you can think about sharing equally to divide.

Use the diagram to help you divide.

1. There are 15 chairs in 3 equal groups. How many chairs are in each group?

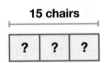

2. The soccer club has 28 balls for all the teams to share equally. If each team gets 7 balls, how many teams are there?

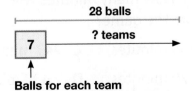

Balls for each team

Tom divides 54 pennies equally among 4 stacks. How many pennies are in each stack? How many are left over?

Use place-value blocks.

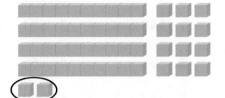

Each stack has 13 pennies.
Two pennies are left over.

Remember to divide the tens and then the ones.

Divide. You may use place-value blocks or pictures to help.

1. 38 CDs
5 stacks

2. 42 nickels
3 stacks

3. 62 dimes
4 stacks

4. 77 nickels
6 stacks

5. 53 stickers
8 stacks

6. 46 quarters
5 stacks

7. 65 marbles
9 piles

8. 81 pennies
9 stacks

9. 55 pencils
6 stacks

10. 75 pens
8 piles

Find $67 \div 4$.

$$
\begin{array}{r}
1 \\
4\overline{)67} \\
-4 \\
\hline
2
\end{array}
$$

Divide.
Multiply.
Subtract.

$$
\begin{array}{r}
16\ R3 \\
4\overline{)67} \\
-4\downarrow \\
\hline
27 \\
-24 \\
\hline
3
\end{array}
$$

Bring down the 7.
Divide.
Multiply.
Subtract.

Check:

$$
\begin{array}{r}
2 \\
16 \\
\times\ 4 \\
\hline
64
\end{array}
\qquad
\begin{array}{r}
64 \\
+\ 3 \\
\hline
67
\end{array}
$$

The answer checks.

Remember that the remainder must be less than the divisor.

Divide. Check your answer.

1. $43 \div 7$

2. $33 \div 2$

3. $19 \div 5$

4. $53 \div 2$

5. $86 \div 7$

6. $85 \div 3$

7. $94 \div 4$

8. $47 \div 3$

9. $46 \div 3$

10. $59 \div 4$

11. $88 \div 7$

12. $83 \div 5$

Set E, pages 240–241

Find 915 ÷ 6.

Estimate: 900 ÷ 6 = 150

The estimate is more than 100, so you can start dividing the hundreds.

```
     152 R3
  6)915        Divide the hundreds.
  - 6
  ————
    31          Divide the tens.
  - 30
  ————
    15          Divide the ones.
  -  12
  ————
     3          Include the remainder.
```

Remember to use an estimate to double-check your answers.

Divide. Check your answer.

1. 448 ÷ 4   **2.** 651 ÷ 5

3. 398 ÷ 3   **4.** 365 ÷ 3

5. 437 ÷ 2   **6.** 863 ÷ 4

7. 7)710   **8.** 5)572

9. 6)618   **10.** 7)814

11. 5)962   **12.** 2)735

13. 3)622   **14.** 8)839

15. 4)506   **16.** 9)926

17. 5)841   **18.** 8)910

Set F, pages 242–243

Find 566 ÷ 6.

```
    94 R2
 6)566         There are not enough
 - 0           hundreds to divide.
 ————
   56          Regroup the hundreds
 - 54          as tens and divide.
 ————
   26          Bring down the ones
 - 24          and divide.
 ————
    2
```

Remember to estimate the quotient to help you decide where to start dividing. Then divide.

Tell whether you will start dividing at the hundreds or the tens.

1. 710 ÷ 9   **2.** 601 ÷ 5

3. 398 ÷ 8   **4.** 429 ÷ 2

5. 628 ÷ 3   **6.** 255 ÷ 4

7. 470 ÷ 6   **8.** 739 ÷ 7

9. 409 ÷ 5   **10.** 110 ÷ 3

11. 603 ÷ 4   **12.** 727 ÷ 9

Find 4,849 ÷ 4. Estimate first. 4,800 ÷ 4 = 1,200.

```
      1,212 R1
   4)4,849
    - 4
      08
     - 8
      04
      - 4
       09
       - 8
        1
```

Check:
```
    1,212
  ×     4
    4,848
  +     1
    4,849
```

The quotient 1,212 R1 is close to the estimate, 1,200.

Remember that you can use your estimate to check that your answer is reasonable.

Divide.

1. 7,206 ÷ 6   **2.** 661 ÷ 3

3. 4)424   **4.** 3)9,143

5. 1,255 ÷ 3   **6.** 411 ÷ 8

7. 4)542   **8.** 6)9,232

Answer the hidden question first. Then solve the problem.

Brett and his family spent $21 for admission to the county fair. They bought 2 adult passes for $6 each and 3 children's passes for $3 each. How much more money did Brett's family spend on adult passes than children's passes?

$6 × 2 = $12 → Price of adult passes

$3 × 3 = $9 → Price of children's passes

Brett's family spent $12 on adult passes and $9 on children passes.

Use the hidden question to solve the problem.

How much more money did Brett's family spend on adult passes than children passes?

$12 − $9 = $3

Brett's family spent $3 more on adult passes.

Remember to find a hidden question to help you solve the problem.

1. Angelique works at a store at the mall. She earns a wage of $8 an hour and earns $10 an hour if she works on weekends and holidays. Last week, she worked 24 hours during the week and 16 hours during the weekend. How much did Angelique earn last week?

2. Brendan takes violin and guitar lessons. Each day, he practices 40 minutes on the violin and 25 minutes on the guitar. How many minutes does he practice his instruments in 5 days?

Multiple Choice

1. Three friends have 39 water balloons to share equally. How many water balloons will each friend get? (10-1)

A 9

B 12

C 13

D 15

2. For the division problem 589 ÷ 4, in what place will you start dividing? (10-6)

A thousands

B hundreds

C tens

D ones

3. Two boxes contain a total of 576 pencils. If each box has the same number of pencils, how many pencils are in each box? (10-5)

A 1,152

B 328

C 288

D 238

4. Tia has 15 metamorphic, 8 igneous, and 7 sedimentary rocks. She displays her rocks equally in 2 cases. Which shows how she found the number of rocks to put in each case? (10-8)

A 2 × 16

B 16 ÷ 2

C 2 × 30

D 30 ÷ 2

5. Nelly has 74 bricks to outline 5 different flower beds. How many bricks will she use for each flower bed if she uses the same number around each? (10-3)

A Each flower bed will use 10 bricks. There will be 4 left over.

B Each flower bed will use 13 bricks. There will be 9 left over.

C Each flower bed will use 14 bricks. There will be 0 left over.

D Each flower bed will use 14 bricks. There will be 4 left over.

6. What is 318 ÷ 4? (10-5)

A 78 R2

B 78

C 79 R2

D 79

7. Harold earned $1,468 by mowing lawns for 3 months in the summer. Which number sentence shows the best way to estimate the amount he earned for each month? (10-7)

A $1,500 ÷ 3 = $500

B $1,500 ÷ 5 = $300

C $2,000 ÷ 5 = $400

D 3 × $1,500 = $4,500

8. Mason bought a package of 20 wheels. Each model car needs 4 wheels. How many cars can he make? (10-2)

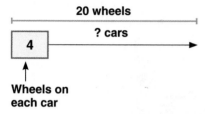

9. Each costume requires 2 yards of material. How many costumes can Sara make out of 35 yards? How much material will she have left? (10-4)

10. Tammy bought 24 apples to feed her horse. She wants to give her horse 2 apples a day. Tammy said that after 10 days she will have 4 apples left. Is Tammy correct? Explain your thinking. (10-2)

11. A biologist banded 3 birds in a week. If the biologist bands the same number of birds each week, how many weeks will it take her to band 42 birds? Use repeated subtraction. (10-1)

12. Ken has 78 pieces of wood for building birdhouses. Each birdhouse needs 6 pieces of wood. How many birdhouses can Ken make? (10-3)

13. A baker made 52 rolls. He put an equal amount in each of the 4 baskets in the display case. How many rolls did he put in each basket? (10-4)

14. Can you tell the number of digits that will be in the quotient for 427 ÷ 7 just by looking at the problem? Explain. (10-6)

15. A school has $1,016 for scholarships. The money was awarded equally to 8 students. Find the amount of money each student received. Show all of your work. (10-7)

16. Keith does work for his neighbors. When he does work outdoors he earns $12 an hour. When he works indoors he earns $8 an hour. Last month he did 18 hours of work outdoors and 16 hours of work indoors. How much did Keith earn last month? (10-8)

17. Tracey has 452 trading cards. She wants to put an equal number into each of 3 books to display them. How many cards will there be in each book? How many will be left over? (10-5)

18. There are 8,960 people who live in Springdale. The town is separated into 5 voting areas that each have the same number of people. How many people live in each voting area? (10-7)

The fourth-grade students at Skyview Elementary are studying poetry. They are trying to decide how to display their poems in the hallway. They want to put the poems in at least 2 rows, but not more than 5 rows.

Mr. Chang's class
45 Poems

Mrs. Steele's class
63 Poems

1. Mr. Chang's class wrote 45 poems. Can the students put the same number of poems in each row if they use 2 rows? Explain.

2. Describe two different ways that the students in Mr. Chang's class can display their 45 poems. For each display, tell how many poems would be in each row. There can be one row with fewer poems than the rest.

3. Mrs. Steele's class wrote 63 poems. How many poems would be in each row if the students use 3 rows? Explain.

4. Describe two different ways that the students in Mrs. Steele's class can display their 63 poems. For each display, tell how many poems would be in each row. There can be one row with fewer poems than the rest.

5. If both Mr. Chang's and Mrs. Steele's classes display their poems together, how might they be displayed? Describe two different ways.

6. The fourth-grade students ask all the students of Skyview Elementary to write one poem. If they collect 184 poems, can all of the poems be displayed in 7 equal rows? Can all of them be displayed in 8 equal rows? Explain.

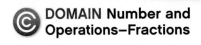

DOMAIN Number and Operations–Fractions

Topic 11

Fraction Equivalence and Ordering

▲ In 2005, the record for the world's largest pumpkin pie was set. How much did the pumpkin pie weigh? You will find out in Lesson 11-4.

Topic Essential Questions
- How can the same fractional amount be named using symbols in different ways?
- How can fractions be compared and ordered?

Review What You Know!

Vocabulary

Choose the best term from the box.

> - fraction
> - denominator
> - thirds
> - numerator

1. Three equal parts of a shape are called ? .

2. A ? can name a part of a whole.

3. The number below the fraction bar in a fraction is the ? .

Division

Divide.

4. 454 ÷ 5   **5.** 600 ÷ 3   **6.** 336 ÷ 4

7. 625 ÷ 5   **8.** 387 ÷ 3   **9.** 878 ÷ 7

10. 240 ÷ 8   **11.** 816 ÷ 2   **12.** 284 ÷ 4

13. 626 ÷ 6   **14.** 312 ÷ 3   **15.** 847 ÷ 9

Fraction Concepts

Name the number of equal parts in each figure.

16.   **17.**   **18.**

19.   **20.**   **21.**

© **22. Writing to Explain** Is $\frac{1}{4}$ of the figure below red? Why or why not?

Interactive Learning

Pose the problem. Start each lesson by working together to solve problems. It will help you make sense of math.

Applying Math Practices

- What am I asked to find?
- What else can I try?
- How are quantities related?
- How can I explain my work?
- How can I use math to model the problem?
- Can I use tools to help?
- Is my work precise?
- Why does this work?
- How can I generalize?

Lesson 11-1

© **Persevere** Solve any way you choose. Look for multiple solutions.

Jared has 12 flowers. He wants to plant them in equal rows in his garden with no leftovers. What are all the different ways he can arrange the flowers in equal rows?

Lesson 11-2

© **Use Tools** Solve. Use tiles to help.

Max has 2 red tiles, 3 blue tiles, 4 yellow tiles, and 8 green tiles. He is making 4 arrays, one in each color. Using all of a color's tiles, how many different arrays can he make from each color? Explain how you know that you found them all.

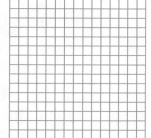

Lesson 11-3

© **Use Structure** Solve any way you choose.

There are 9 students in the chess club. The club wants to buy the same number of each item for each member. What number of items might the club buy? Can you give all possible answers? Explain.

Lesson 11-4

© **Reason** Solve. Use fraction strips to help.

How many fractions can you find that show an amount equal to $\frac{1}{3}$? Write each fraction and use drawings or words to explain your work.

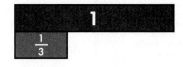

Lesson 11-5

© **Be Precise** Solve using number strips. Each strip represents the distance from 0 to 1 on the number line.

Can a point on the number line have more than one fraction name? Explain by showing examples with the number strips.

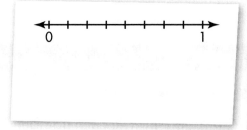

Lesson 11-6

© **Reason** Solve without using tools.

Juan read for $\frac{5}{6}$ of an hour. Larissa read for $\frac{1}{3}$ of an hour. Who read for a longer period of time? Explain.

Lesson 11-7

© **Generalize** Solve any way you choose.

Max skated $\frac{2}{5}$ mile, Carlos skated $\frac{3}{5}$ mile, and Pedro skated $\frac{1}{2}$ mile. Write these distances in order from least to greatest. Explain how you decided.

Lesson 11-8

© **Critique Reasoning** Tell whether the explanation at the right correctly answers the question below. If not, write another explanation in your own words.

Alicia wants to cut this board in four parts. She cut off the shaded part first. Did Alicia cut off $\frac{1}{4}$ of the board? Explain.

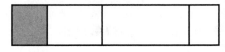

No. The parts are not equal.

4.OA.4 Find all factor pairs for a whole number in the range 1–100. Recognize that a whole number is a multiple of each of its factors. Determine whether a given whole number in the range 1–100 is a multiple of a given one-digit number. Determine whether a given whole number in the range 1–100 is prime or composite. Also **4.OA.5**

Factors

Hands-On
counters

How can you use multiplication to find all the factors of a number?

Jean has 16 action figures. She wants to arrange them in equal sized groupings around her room. What are the ways that Jean can arrange the action figures? Jean needs to think of all the factors of 16.

16 action figures

Guided Practice*

MATHEMATICAL PRACTICES

Do you know HOW?

In **1** through **4**, write each number as a product of two factors in two different ways.

1. 36   **2.** 42

3. 50   **4.** 64

In **5** through **8**, find all the factors of each number. Use counters to help.

5. 12   **6.** 20

7. 28   **8.** 54

Do you UNDERSTAND?

9. What factor does every even number have?

10. Writing to Explain Is 5 a factor of 16?

11. Jean got 2 more action figures. What are all the different equal groupings she can make now?

12. Jean's brother has 100 action figures. What are all of the factors for 100?

Independent Practice

In **13** through **32**, find all the factors of each number. Use counters to help.

Tip For even numbers, remember 2 is always a factor.

13. 6	**14.** 32	**15.** 45	**16.** 11	**17.** 36
18. 25	**19.** 63	**20.** 22	**21.** 51	**22.** 30
23. 14	**24.** 18	**25.** 27	**26.** 21	**27.** 40
28. 55	**29.** 39	**30.** 35	**31.** 29	**32.** 48

eTools
www.pearsonsuccessnet.com

$16 = 1 \times 16$

Jean can arrange
16 figures in 1 group
or
16 groups of 1 figure.

So, 1 and 16 are
factors of 16.

$16 = 2 \times 8$

Jean can arrange
2 figures in 8 groups
or
2 groups of 8 figures.

So, 2 and 8 are
factors of 16.

$16 = 4 \times 4$

Jean can arrange
4 figures in 4 groups.

4 is a factor of 16.

The factors of 16 are
1, 2, 4, 8, and 16.

Problem Solving

MATHEMATICAL
PRACTICES

33. As part of her science project, Shay is making a model of a wind farm. She wants to put 24 turbines in her model. What arrays can she make using 24 turbines?

4 is a factor of 24.

34. Anita wants to include an array of 15 photos on her web site. Describe the arrays that she can make.

35. Reasonableness Which lists all the factors of 38?

A 1, 38

C 1, 2, 38

B 1, 2, 14, 38

D 1, 2, 19, 38

36. Use Structure Any number that has 9 as a factor also has 3 as a factor. Why is this?

37. Reason Which is greater, 3×6 or 4×4?

38. The manatee is an endangered sea mammal. A mother manatee, pictured to the right, is three times as long as her baby. How long is the baby manatee?

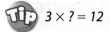 $3 \times ? = 12$

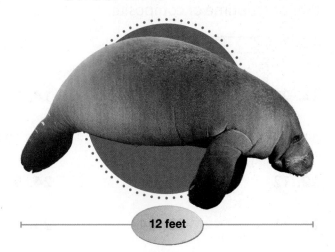

12 feet

4.OA.4 Find all factor pairs for a whole number in the range 1–100. Recognize that a whole number is a multiple of each of its factors. Determine whether a given whole number in the range 1–100 is a multiple of a given one-digit number. Determine whether a given whole number in the range 1–100 is prime or composite.

Prime and Composite Numbers

A **prime number** is a whole number greater than 1 that has exactly two factors, 1 and itself.

A **composite number** is a whole number greater than 1 that has more than two factors.

Numbers	Factors
2	1, 2
3	1, 3
4	1, 2, 4
5	1, 5
6	1, 2, 3, 6

Guided Practice*

MATHEMATICAL PRACTICES

Do you know HOW?

In **1** through **6**, tell whether each number is prime or composite.

1. 32   **2.** 41

3. 57   **4.** 21

5. 95   **6.** 103

Do you UNDERSTAND?

7. What is the only even prime number?

© **8. Writing to Explain** Give an example of an odd number that is not prime. What makes it a composite number?

9. Roger has 47 cars. Can he group the cars in more than 2 ways?

Independent Practice

Leveled Practice In **10** through **31**, write whether each number is prime or composite.

10. 7 ⬚⬚⬚⬚⬚⬚

11. 9 ⬚⬚⬚⬚⬚⬚⬚⬚⬚   ⬚⬚⬚/⬚⬚⬚/⬚⬚⬚

12. 23   **13.** 33   **14.** 56   **15.** 67   **16.** 38

17. 58   **18.** 75   **19.** 101   **20.** 51   **21.** 300

22. 12   **23.** 2   **24.** 97   **25.** 1,900   **26.** 37

27. 11   **28.** 44   **29.** 1,204   **30.** 10   **31.** 59

DIGITAL   Animated Glossary
www.pearsonsuccessnet.com

*For another example, see Set B on page 280.

Prime Numbers

The number 5 is a prime number. It has only two factors, 1 and itself.

 $1 \times 5 = 5$

Composite Numbers

The number 6 is a composite number. Its factors are 1, 2, 3, and 6.

 $1 \times 6 = 6$

$2 \times 3 = 6$

The number 1 is a special number. It is neither prime nor composite.

Problem Solving

© MATHEMATICAL PRACTICES

© **Use Tools** For **32** and **33**, use the pictograph at the right.

32. Which type of flower did a prime number of people vote for?

33. How many votes are represented by the pictograph?

Favorite Flowers

Daffodils	
Daisies	✿ ✿ ✿
Tulips	🌷 🌷 🌷 🌷 🌷

Key: Each flower icon equals 2 votes.

34. Which set of numbers below are all prime?

   A 1, 2, 7, 11, 25   **C** 3, 5, 13, 19

   B 1, 3, 5, 7, 9   **D** 15, 21, 27, 31

© **35. Critique Reasoning** Greta said that the product of two prime numbers must also be a prime number. Joan disagreed. Who is correct?

36. Use the following steps devised by the Greek mathematician Eratosthenes to create a list of prime numbers from 1 to 100. How many prime numbers are there between 1 and 100?

- Write all the numbers from 1 to 100.
- Draw a triangle around number 1; it is not prime nor composite.
- Circle 2 and cross out all other multiples of 2.
- Circle 3 and cross out all other multiples of 3.
- Circle 5, the next number that is not crossed out. Cross out other multiples of 5.
- Continue in the same way. When you have finished, the circled numbers are prime.

△1	②	③	⁴̸	⑤
6̸	⑦	8̸	9̸	1̸0̸
⑪	1̸2̸	⑬	1̸4̸	1̸5̸
1̸6̸	⑰	1̸8̸	⑲	2̸0̸
2̸1̸	2̸2̸	㉓	2̸4̸	2̸5̸
2̸6̸	2̸7̸	2̸8̸	㉙	3̸0̸
㉛	3̸2̸	3̸3̸	3̸4̸	3̸5̸
3̸6̸	㊲	3̸8̸	3̸9̸	4̸0̸

Common
Core

4.OA.4 Find all factor pairs for a whole number in the range 1–100. Recognize that a whole number is a multiple of each of its factors. Determine whether a given whole number in the range 1–100 is a multiple of a given one-digit number. Determine whether a given whole number in the range 1–100 is prime or composite. Also 4.OA.5

Multiples

How can you find multiples of a number?

It takes 8 minutes for Car A to make one full turn on the Ferris wheel. If the Ferris wheel continues to turn at the same speed for the next hour, at what times during the hour will Car A return to the starting point?

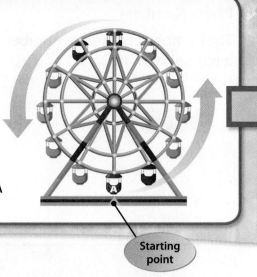

Starting point

Guided Practice*

MATHEMATICAL
PRACTICES

Do you know HOW?

In **1** through **4**, write five multiples of each number.

1. 2   **2.** 9

3. 3   **4.** 10

In **5** through **8**, tell whether the first number is a multiple of the second number.

5. 14, 2   **6.** 19, 3

7. 56, 9   **8.** 42, 7

Do you UNDERSTAND?

9. If the Ferris wheel in the example above continues to turn at the same speed, will Car A return to the starting point after 75 minutes? Explain.

10. Suppose the Ferris wheel speeds up so it makes one full turn in 6 minutes. When will Car A return to the starting point if the Ferris wheel continues to turn for one half hour?

11. Writing to Explain Is 9 a multiple of 3 or a factor of 3? Explain.

Independent Practice

In **12** through **15**, write five multiples of each number.

12. 7   **13.** 4   **14.** 6   **15.** 5

In **16** through **23**, tell whether the first number is a multiple of the second number.

16. 44, 6   **17.** 27, 3   **18.** 30, 6   **19.** 54, 9

20. 28, 3   **21.** 45, 5   **22.** 64, 7   **23.** 48, 8

*For another example, see Set C on page 281.

Step 1

You can use multiples of 8 to find when Car A reaches the starting point.

One full turn takes 8 minutes.

$$1 \times 8 = 8$$

Car A is back at the starting point after 8 minutes.

Step 2

Car A is at the starting point after another 8 minutes.

Second full turn:

$$2 \times 8 = 16$$

Two full turns take 16 minutes.

Car A is back to the starting point after 16 minutes.

Step 3

Car A is at the starting point every 8 minutes after that:

$$3 \times 8 = 24$$
$$4 \times 8 = 32$$
$$5 \times 8 = 40$$
$$6 \times 8 = 48$$
$$7 \times 8 = 56$$

During the hour, Car A returns to the starting point after 8, 16, 24, 32, 40, 48, and 56 minutes.

Problem Solving

MATHEMATICAL PRACTICES

© **Be Precise** For **24** and **25**, use the table at the right.

24. Which activities are scheduled to last more than 1 hour and 30 minutes?

25. Paulo's family arrived at the reunion at 8:30 A.M. How long do they have before the trip to Scenic Lake Park?

Suarez Family Reunion Schedule

Data

Trip to Scenic Lake Park	10:15 A.M. to 2:30 P.M.
Slide show	4:15 P.M. to 5:10 P.M.
Dinner	5:30 P.M. to 7:00 P.M.
Campfire	7:55 P.M. to 9:30 P.M.

26. Which is NOT a multiple of 7?

    A 20   **C** 35

    B 21   **D** 42

27. Jason's family went apple picking. They picked 5 bags of red apples and 1 bag of green apples. Write a fraction to represent the part of the bags containing green apples.

© 28. **Use Tools** Lisa made a Venn diagram showing five multiples of 3 and five multiples of 4. What does the shaded section in her diagram show?

Lisa's Venn Diagram

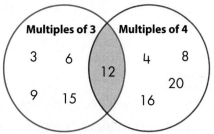

© 29. **Model** Name at least one number that is a multiple of 2 and a multiple of 5.

© 30. **Writing to Explain** Lindsay says that all numbers that are multiples of 4 have a factor of 2. Is Lindsay correct? Explain.

Common Core

4.NF.1 Explain why a fraction a/b is equivalent to a fraction (n × a)/(n × b) by using visual fraction models, with attention to how the number and size of the parts differ even though the two fractions themselves are the same size. Use this principle to recognize and generate equivalent fractions. Also **4.NF.2**

Equivalent Fractions

Hands-On
fraction strips

$\frac{1}{8}$

How can you find two ways to name the same part of a whole?

A fraction <u>describes one or more parts of a whole that is divided into equal parts</u>. Equivalent fractions <u>name the same part of a whole</u>.

Write a fraction that is equivalent to $\frac{1}{4}$.

Lee ate $\frac{1}{4}$ of a pizza.

Another Example **How can you divide to find an equivalent fraction?**

Sara ate $\frac{6}{8}$ of a small mushroom pizza. Which fraction is equivalent to $\frac{6}{8}$?

Divide the numerator and denominator by the same number to find an equivalent fraction.

$$\frac{6}{8} = \frac{3}{4}$$

÷ 2 ... ÷ 2

So, $\frac{3}{4}$ is equivalent to $\frac{6}{8}$.

Check your answer using fractions strips.

Find $\frac{6}{8}$ by counting 6 of the $\frac{1}{8}$ strips.

Find $\frac{3}{4}$ by counting 3 of the $\frac{1}{4}$ strips.

Both $\frac{6}{8}$ and $\frac{3}{4}$ name the same part of a whole.

1											
$\frac{1}{2}$						$\frac{1}{2}$					
$\frac{1}{3}$				$\frac{1}{3}$				$\frac{1}{3}$			
$\frac{1}{4}$			$\frac{1}{4}$			$\frac{1}{4}$			$\frac{1}{4}$		
$\frac{1}{5}$		$\frac{1}{5}$		$\frac{1}{5}$		$\frac{1}{5}$		$\frac{1}{5}$			
$\frac{1}{6}$		$\frac{1}{6}$		$\frac{1}{6}$		$\frac{1}{6}$		$\frac{1}{6}$		$\frac{1}{6}$	
$\frac{1}{8}$	$\frac{1}{8}$	$\frac{1}{8}$	$\frac{1}{8}$	$\frac{1}{8}$	$\frac{1}{8}$	$\frac{1}{8}$	$\frac{1}{8}$				
$\frac{1}{10}$	$\frac{1}{10}$	$\frac{1}{10}$	$\frac{1}{10}$	$\frac{1}{10}$	$\frac{1}{10}$	$\frac{1}{10}$	$\frac{1}{10}$	$\frac{1}{10}$	$\frac{1}{10}$		
$\frac{1}{12}$	$\frac{1}{12}$	$\frac{1}{12}$	$\frac{1}{12}$	$\frac{1}{12}$	$\frac{1}{12}$	$\frac{1}{12}$	$\frac{1}{12}$	$\frac{1}{12}$	$\frac{1}{12}$	$\frac{1}{12}$	

Explain It

1. Can you divide 6 and 8 by any number to find an equivalent fraction? Explain.

2. Using fraction strips, find two fractions that are equivalent to $\frac{9}{12}$.

One Way

The numerator <u>tells how many equal parts are described</u>. The denominator <u>tells how many equal parts in all</u>.

You can multiply the numerator and the denominator by the same number to find an equivalent fraction.

$$\overset{\times\,2}{\frac{1}{4} = \frac{2}{8}}_{\times\,2}$$

$$\frac{1}{4} = \frac{2}{8}$$

Another Way

Use fraction strips to find equivalent fractions.

Both $\frac{1}{4}$ and $\frac{2}{8}$ name the same part of a whole.

So, $\frac{1}{4}$ and $\frac{2}{8}$ are equivalent fractions.

Guided Practice*

 MATHEMATICAL PRACTICES

Do you know HOW?

In **1** through **6**, multiply or divide to find an equivalent fraction.

1. $\overset{\times\,3}{\frac{2}{3} = \frac{\blacksquare}{\blacksquare}}_{\times\,3}$

2. $\overset{\div\,5}{\frac{5}{10} = \frac{\blacksquare}{\blacksquare}}_{\div\,5}$

3. $\frac{5}{6} = \frac{\blacksquare}{12}$

4. $\frac{10}{12} = \frac{5}{\blacksquare}$

5. $\frac{3}{12} = \frac{\blacksquare}{4}$

6. $\frac{3}{4} = \frac{9}{\blacksquare}$

Do you UNDERSTAND?

7. Suppose Lee's pizza had 12 equal slices instead of 4. How many slices are gone if he ate $\frac{1}{4}$ of the pizza? Explain.

 8. Construct Arguments Josh, Lisa, and Vicki each ate $\frac{1}{2}$ of a pizza. The pizzas were the same size, but Josh ate 1 slice, Lisa ate 3 slices, and Vicki ate 4 slices. How is this possible?

Independent Practice

Leveled Practice For **9** through **16**, multiply or divide to find equivalent fractions.

Tip *You can check your answers using fraction strips.*

9. $\overset{\times\,5}{\frac{1}{2} = \frac{\blacksquare}{\blacksquare}}_{\times\,5}$

10. $\overset{\div\,3}{\frac{9}{12} = \frac{\blacksquare}{\blacksquare}}_{\div\,3}$

11. $\overset{\times\,2}{\frac{5}{6} = \frac{\blacksquare}{\blacksquare}}_{\times\,2}$

12. $\overset{\div\,2}{\frac{2}{4} = \frac{\blacksquare}{\blacksquare}}_{\div\,2}$

13. $\frac{10}{10} = \frac{1}{\blacksquare}$

14. $\frac{3}{4} = \frac{6}{\blacksquare}$

15. $\frac{1}{2} = \frac{\blacksquare}{4}$

16. $\frac{3}{5} = \frac{6}{\blacksquare}$

DIGITAL Animated Glossary, eTools
www.pearsonsuccessnet.com

In **17** through **26**, find an equivalent fraction for each.

17. $\frac{4}{6}$ **18.** $\frac{2}{10}$ **19.** $\frac{1}{3}$ **20.** $\frac{3}{5}$ **21.** $\frac{3}{9}$

22. $\frac{5}{10}$ **23.** $\frac{2}{8}$ **24.** $\frac{5}{6}$ **25.** $\frac{3}{12}$ **26.** $\frac{4}{10}$

Problem Solving

MATHEMATICAL
PRACTICES

For **27** and **28**, use the fraction strips at the right.

27. Name 10 pairs of equivalent fractions.

© **28. Reason** How can you show that $\frac{6}{8}$ and $\frac{9}{12}$ are equivalent by multiplying and dividing?

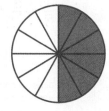 *First, divide the numerator and denominator of $\frac{9}{12}$ by 3. Then multiply.*

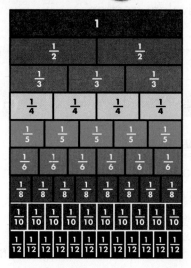

29. The world's largest pumpkin pie weighed 2,020 pounds. The pie was $12\frac{1}{3}$ feet across and $\frac{1}{3}$ foot thick. Write a fraction equivalent to $\frac{1}{3}$.

30. In a school poetry contest, 4 out of the 12 students who entered will win a small prize. Half of the remaining students receive a certificate. How many students get a certificate?

31. James has 18 mystery books and 12 sports books. Rich has twice as many mystery books and three times as many sports books. How many books does Rich have?

© **32. Communicate** In the United States, $\frac{2}{5}$ of all states start with the letters M, A, or N. How can you use equivalent fractions to find out how many states this is?

33. Look at the model. Name three equivalent fractions for the part of the circle that is red.

© **34. Persevere** Which shows $\frac{1}{2}$ and $\frac{1}{5}$ as fractions with the same denominator?

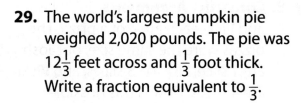

A $\frac{5}{10}$ and $\frac{2}{10}$

B $\frac{1}{10}$ and $\frac{2}{10}$

C $\frac{5}{10}$ and $\frac{1}{10}$

D $\frac{5}{10}$ and $\frac{3}{10}$

Going Digital

Equivalent Fractions

Use 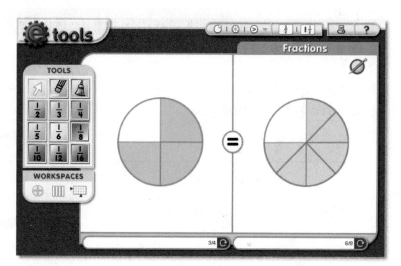 tools Fractions.

Find the numerator that makes the fractions equivalent. $\frac{3}{4} = \frac{\square}{8}$

Step 1 Go to the Fractions eTool. Select the equivalence workspace mode.

⊘ Select $\frac{1}{4}$ three times, to show $\frac{3}{4}$ in the first circle.

Step 2 Select the second circle by clicking on it. Select $\frac{1}{8}$ until the symbol changes from > to =. Read the fractions at the bottom of the workspace. $\frac{3}{4} = \frac{6}{8}$

Step 3 🧹 Use the Broom tool to clear the workspace before doing another problem.

Practice

Use the Fractions eTool to find the numerator that makes the fractions equivalent.

1. $\frac{1}{4} = \frac{\square}{8}$

2. $\frac{2}{5} = \frac{\square}{10}$

3. $\frac{4}{6} = \frac{\square}{3}$

4. $\frac{6}{12} = \frac{\square}{8}$

5. $\frac{1}{2} = \frac{\square}{6}$

6. $\frac{1}{3} = \frac{\square}{12}$

7. $\frac{8}{10} = \frac{\square}{5}$

8. $\frac{3}{12} = \frac{\square}{4}$

9. $\frac{3}{4} = \frac{\square}{12}$

10. $\frac{3}{5} = \frac{\square}{10}$

11. $\frac{3}{4} = \frac{\square}{12}$

12. $\frac{4}{8} = \frac{\square}{2}$

13. $\frac{1}{2} = \frac{\square}{12}$

14. $\frac{1}{2} = \frac{\square}{10}$

15. $\frac{5}{6} = \frac{\square}{12}$

16. $\frac{4}{5} = \frac{\square}{10}$

Common
Core

4.NF.1 Explain why a fraction *a/b* is equivalent to a fraction (*n* × *a*)/(*n* × *b*) by using visual fraction models, with attention to how the number and size of the parts differ even though the two fractions themselves are the same size. Use this principle to recognize and generate equivalent fractions. Also **4.NF.2**

Number Lines and Equivalent Fractions

How can you find equivalent fractions on a number line?

Sal rode his bike $\frac{3}{4}$ of a mile to school. What is another name for $\frac{3}{4}$?

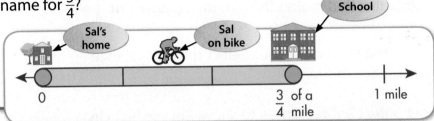

Guided Practice*

MATHEMATICAL
PRACTICES

Do you know HOW?

In **1** through **3**, find an equivalent fraction on the number line.

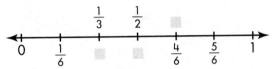

1. Name an equivalent fraction for $\frac{1}{3}$.

2. Name an equivalent fraction for $\frac{1}{2}$.

3. Name an equivalent fraction for $\frac{4}{6}$.

Do you UNDERSTAND?

4. A number line is divided into 12 equal parts to show twelfths. A point is labeled $\frac{1}{2}$. Name two equivalent fractions for the labeled point.

© 5. **Writing to Explain** Use the number line above to name an equivalent fraction for $\frac{1}{4}$. Why are they equivalent?

Independent Practice

MATHEMATICAL
PRACTICES

For **6** through **9**, use the number line to name equivalent fractions.

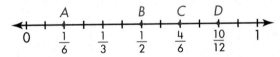

6. Which of the following names an equivalent fraction for point *A*?
   $\frac{3}{4}$ $\frac{2}{3}$ $\frac{2}{12}$ $\frac{1}{4}$

© 7. **Be Precise** Which of the following does NOT name an equivalent fraction for point *B*?
   $\frac{2}{4}$ $\frac{3}{6}$ $\frac{4}{10}$ $\frac{6}{12}$

8. Which of the following names an equivalent fraction for point *C*?
   $\frac{2}{6}$ $\frac{2}{3}$ $\frac{1}{2}$ $\frac{3}{4}$

9. Which of the following names an equivalent fraction for point *D*?
   $\frac{4}{6}$ $\frac{1}{2}$ $\frac{1}{10}$ $\frac{5}{6}$

*For another example, see Set E on page 282.

Show $\frac{3}{4}$ on a number line. Divide each fourth in half to show eighths. Find the fraction that names the same point as $\frac{3}{4}$.

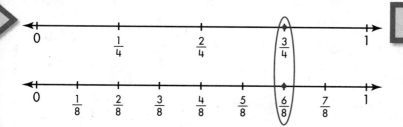

Since $\frac{3}{4}$ and $\frac{6}{8}$ name the same point on a number line, they are equivalent fractions.

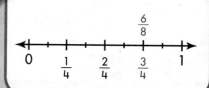

10. Draw a number line to show that $\frac{2}{5}$ and $\frac{4}{10}$ are equivalent fractions.

11. Draw a number line to show that $\frac{1}{3}$ and $\frac{4}{12}$ are equivalent fractions.

Problem Solving

12. Writing to Explain How can a number line be used to show that $\frac{2}{10} = \frac{1}{5}$?

13. Name two fractions that represent point Y.

14. In its entire lifetime, the average worker bee produces only $\frac{1}{2}$ of a teaspoon of honey. What is another fraction that names the same amount?

15. At the school fair, 147 tickets were sold. The tickets cost $3 each. The goal was to make $300 in ticket sales. By how much was the goal exceeded?

16. Be Precise Which of the following fractions does NOT name the same point on the number line?

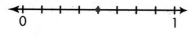

A $\frac{1}{2}$ **B** $\frac{3}{6}$ **C** $\frac{4}{8}$ **D** $\frac{3}{12}$

17. There are 267 students and 21 adults going on a school trip. An equal number of people will ride on each bus. If there are 9 buses, how many people will ride on each bus?

18. Use Structure Which of the following can help you find a fraction equivalent to $\frac{4}{6}$?

A Subtract the numerator from the denominator.

B Add the numerator and the denominator.

C Multiply the numerator and the denominator by the same number.

D Multiply the numerator by 4 and the denominator by 6.

4.NF.2 Compare two fractions with different numerators and different denominators... by comparing to a benchmark fraction such as $\frac{1}{2}$. Recognize that comparisons are valid only when the two fractions refer to the same whole. Record the results of comparisons with symbols >, =, or <, and justify the conclusions, e.g., by using a visual fraction model.

Comparing Fractions

Hands-On fraction strips

$\frac{1}{8}$

How can you compare fractions?

Isabella's father is building a model dinosaur with spare pieces of wood that measure $\frac{1}{4}$ of an inch and $\frac{5}{8}$ of an inch.

Which are longer, the $\frac{1}{4}$ inch pieces or the $\frac{5}{8}$ inch pieces?

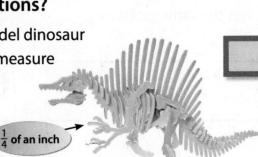

$\frac{1}{4}$ of an inch

Another Example **How can you compare fractions on a number line?**

Use equivalent fractions.

Which is greater, $\frac{4}{5}$ or $\frac{7}{10}$? Since $\frac{4}{5}$ is equivalent to $\frac{8}{10}$, you know that $\frac{4}{5} > \frac{7}{10}$.

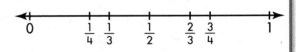

Use benchmark fractions.

A benchmark fraction is a fraction that is easy to visualize and use. Some benchmark fractions are $\frac{1}{4}, \frac{1}{3}, \frac{1}{2}, \frac{2}{3},$ and $\frac{3}{4}$.

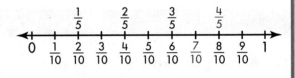

Which is greater, $\frac{5}{8}$ or $\frac{4}{10}$? Compare $\frac{5}{8}$ to the benchmark fraction $\frac{1}{2}$. Since $\frac{1}{2} = \frac{4}{8}$, you know $\frac{5}{8} > \frac{1}{2}$.

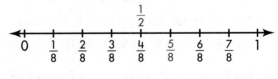

Now compare $\frac{4}{10}$ to $\frac{1}{2}$. Since $\frac{1}{2} = \frac{5}{10}$, you know $\frac{1}{2} > \frac{4}{10}$.

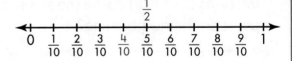

You know $\frac{5}{8} > \frac{1}{2}$ and $\frac{1}{2} > \frac{4}{10}$, so $\frac{5}{8} > \frac{4}{10}$.

Explain It

1. Which is greater $\frac{7}{8}$ or $\frac{3}{5}$? How do you know?

2. Can you use benchmark fractions to compare $\frac{2}{5}$ and $\frac{3}{8}$? Explain.

Use benchmark fractions.

Compare $\frac{1}{4}$ and $\frac{5}{8}$.

You can use fraction strips to compare both fractions to $\frac{1}{2}$.

$\frac{1}{4} < \frac{1}{2}$

$\frac{5}{8} > \frac{1}{2}$

So, $\frac{1}{4} < \frac{5}{8}$.

The $\frac{5}{8}$ inch pieces are longer.

Compare $\frac{1}{4}$ and $\frac{3}{4}$.

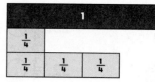

When the two fractions have the same denominators, you compare the numerators.

$3 > 1$

So, $\frac{3}{4} > \frac{1}{4}$.

Guided Practice*

 MATHEMATICAL PRACTICES

Do you know HOW?

Compare. Write >, <, or = for each ◯. Use fraction strips or drawings to help.

1. $\frac{3}{4}$ ◯ $\frac{6}{8}$ 2. $\frac{1}{4}$ ◯ $\frac{1}{10}$

3. $\frac{3}{5}$ ◯ $\frac{5}{10}$ 4. $\frac{1}{2}$ ◯ $\frac{4}{5}$

Do you UNDERSTAND?

© 5. **Writing to Explain** Mary says that $\frac{1}{8}$ is greater than $\frac{1}{4}$ because 8 is greater than 4. Is she right? Explain your answer.

6. Mr. Arnold used wood measuring $\frac{1}{2}$ foot, $\frac{1}{3}$ foot, and $\frac{3}{8}$ foot to build a birdhouse. Compare these lengths of wood.

Independent Practice

For **7** through **38**, compare. Then write >, <, or = for each ◯. Use fraction strips or benchmark fractions to help.

7. $\frac{5}{6}$ ◯ $\frac{10}{12}$ 8. $\frac{3}{10}$ ◯ $\frac{7}{8}$ 9. $\frac{5}{12}$ ◯ $\frac{1}{2}$ 10. $\frac{7}{8}$ ◯ $\frac{3}{4}$

11. $\frac{1}{3}$ ◯ $\frac{2}{8}$ 12. $\frac{1}{4}$ ◯ $\frac{2}{3}$ 13. $\frac{7}{12}$ ◯ $\frac{3}{4}$ 14. $\frac{2}{3}$ ◯ $\frac{2}{12}$

15. $\frac{3}{8}$ ◯ $\frac{2}{3}$ 16. $\frac{3}{4}$ ◯ $\frac{1}{8}$ 17. $\frac{2}{3}$ ◯ $\frac{5}{12}$ 18. $\frac{1}{2}$ ◯ $\frac{3}{4}$

19. $\frac{7}{10}$ ◯ $\frac{11}{12}$ 20. $\frac{7}{12}$ ◯ $\frac{4}{10}$ 21. $\frac{5}{12}$ ◯ $\frac{4}{5}$ 22. $\frac{2}{6}$ ◯ $\frac{3}{12}$

23. $\frac{8}{10}$ ◯ $\frac{3}{4}$ 24. $\frac{3}{8}$ ◯ $\frac{11}{12}$ 25. $\frac{2}{3}$ ◯ $\frac{10}{12}$ 26. $\frac{7}{8}$ ◯ $\frac{1}{6}$

 DIGITAL

eTools, Animated Glossary
www.pearsonsuccessnet.com

27. $\frac{3}{8} \bigcirc \frac{7}{8}$　　　28. $\frac{2}{4} \bigcirc \frac{4}{8}$　　　29. $\frac{6}{8} \bigcirc \frac{8}{12}$　　　30. $\frac{1}{3} \bigcirc \frac{4}{9}$

31. $\frac{6}{8} \bigcirc \frac{8}{10}$　　　32. $\frac{3}{5} \bigcirc \frac{3}{6}$　　　33. $\frac{2}{10} \bigcirc \frac{2}{12}$　　　34. $\frac{5}{6} \bigcirc \frac{4}{5}$

35. $\frac{4}{4} \bigcirc \frac{1}{1}$　　　36. $\frac{2}{4} \bigcirc \frac{8}{10}$　　　37. $\frac{7}{8} \bigcirc \frac{3}{5}$　　　38. $\frac{3}{9} \bigcirc \frac{1}{3}$

Problem Solving

MATHEMATICAL
PRACTICES

© 39. **Use Tools** Felicia drew the picture at the right to show that $\frac{3}{8}$ is greater than $\frac{3}{4}$. What was Felicia's mistake?

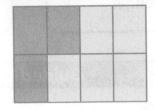

© 40. **Writing to Explain** Why can you compare two fractions with the same denominator by only comparing the numerators?

41. What can you conclude about $\frac{3}{5}$ and $\frac{12}{20}$ if you know that $\frac{3}{5} = \frac{6}{10}$ and that $\frac{6}{10} = \frac{12}{20}$?

© 42. **Be Precise** Which is longer, $\frac{1}{4}$ foot or $\frac{1}{4}$ yard? Explain.

43. If $34 \times 20 = 680$, then $34 \times 200 = $ ▨.

44. A melon was divided into 8 equal slices. Juan ate three slices. Tom and Stacy ate the remaining slices. What fraction of the melon did Tom and Stacy eat?

A $\frac{1}{4}$　　B $\frac{2}{8}$　　C $\frac{2}{3}$　　D $\frac{5}{8}$

45. Neil is setting up for a dinner party. He has 6 tables each seating 5 guests and another table seating the left over 3 guests. How many people are coming to Neil's dinner party?

© 46. **Reason** The numbers are missing from the graph at the right. Compare the bars to decide which farmer has about $\frac{1}{3}$ as many cows as Mr. Harris.

Cows Owned by Farmers

Number of Cows

Mr. Hall　Mr. Blake　Mr. Carr　Mr. Harris

Mixed Problem Solving

The Egyptians created a number system that used symbols, or hieroglyphs. The chart to the right shows the symbols and their equivalent numbers.

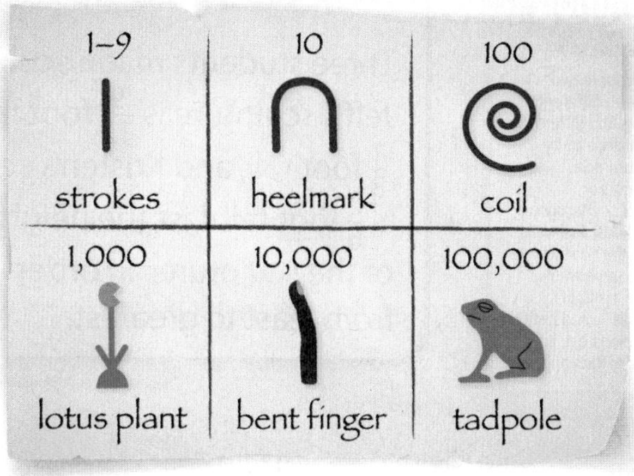

1–9	10	100
strokes	heelmark	coil
1,000	10,000	100,000
lotus plant	bent finger	tadpole

Data

Description	Symbol	Number
Hieroglyphs are drawn with the greater number in front of the lesser number.	 ∩∩∩I	31
Hieroglyphs can be read from left to right.		525
If the symbols are stacked, the greater number is on top.		214,419

1. Write 217 in word form and with hieroglyphs.

2. Use hieroglyphs to draw the greatest 5-digit number.

3. Which number will take less time to write with hieroglyphs, 9 or 100? Explain your answer.

4. Use hieroglyphs to draw the number one greater than 349.

5. It is believed that the Egyptian number system was created around 3000 B.C. Use hieroglyphs to represent this number.

6. Hieroglyphs can also be read from right to left. What number is represented by IIIII∩∩↓↓↓?

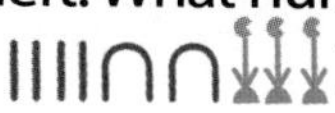

Common Core

4.NF.2 Compare two fractions with different numerators and different denominators, e.g., by creating common denominators or numerators …. Recognize that comparisons are valid only when the two fractions refer to the same whole. Record the results of comparisons … and justify the conclusions, e.g., by using a visual fraction model.

Ordering Fractions

Hands-On
fraction strips
$\frac{1}{8}$

How can you order fractions?

Three students made sculptures for a school project. Jeff's sculpture is $\frac{9}{12}$ foot tall, Scott's sculpture is $\frac{1}{3}$ foot tall, and Kristen's sculpture is $\frac{3}{6}$ foot tall. List the heights of the sculptures in order from least to greatest.

$\frac{9}{12}$ foot tall

Guided Practice*

MATHEMATICAL PRACTICES

Do you know HOW?

For **1** through **6**, order the fractions from least to greatest. Use fraction strips or drawings to help.

1. $\frac{2}{3}, \frac{1}{2}, \frac{5}{12}$

2. $\frac{5}{6}, \frac{1}{3}, \frac{1}{6}$

3. $\frac{7}{8}, \frac{3}{8}, \frac{3}{4}$

4. $\frac{2}{3}, \frac{3}{12}, \frac{3}{4}$

5. $\frac{7}{10}, \frac{1}{5}, \frac{4}{10}$

6. $\frac{2}{3}, \frac{1}{4}, \frac{1}{6}$

Do you UNDERSTAND?

7. **Use Structure** What denominator would you use to find equivalent fractions when comparing $\frac{2}{3}, \frac{2}{4}, \frac{2}{12}$?

8. Three other students made sculptures with these heights: $\frac{2}{3}$ foot, $\frac{5}{6}$ foot, and $\frac{2}{12}$ foot. Write these heights in order from least to greatest.

Independent Practice

For **9** through **20**, find equivalent fractions. Then order the fractions from least to greatest. Use drawings or fraction strips to help.

9. $\frac{1}{4}, \frac{1}{6}, \frac{1}{2}$

10. $\frac{2}{4}, \frac{2}{6}, \frac{2}{12}$

11. $\frac{2}{3}, \frac{5}{6}, \frac{7}{12}$

12. $\frac{5}{12}, \frac{2}{3}, \frac{1}{4}$

13. $\frac{3}{5}, \frac{4}{10}, \frac{1}{2}$

14. $\frac{1}{2}, \frac{3}{5}, \frac{2}{10}$

15. $\frac{5}{6}, \frac{3}{4}, \frac{8}{12}$

16. $\frac{8}{12}, \frac{1}{2}, \frac{3}{4}$

17. $\frac{6}{8}, \frac{1}{2}, \frac{3}{8}$

18. $\frac{2}{5}, \frac{3}{10}, \frac{3}{5}$

19. $\frac{10}{12}, \frac{1}{2}, \frac{3}{4}$

20. $\frac{2}{4}, \frac{3}{12}, \frac{2}{3}$

eTools
www.pearsonsuccessnet.com

For another example, see Set G on page 283.

Find equivalent fractions with a common denominator.

$$\frac{3}{6} = \frac{6}{12}$$

$$\frac{1}{3} = \frac{4}{12}$$

Compare the numerators.

$$\frac{4}{12} < \frac{6}{12} < \frac{9}{12}$$

So, $\frac{1}{3} < \frac{3}{6} < \frac{9}{12}$.

Order the fractions from least to greatest.

The heights of the sculptures in order from least to greatest are $\frac{1}{3}$ foot, $\frac{3}{6}$ foot, $\frac{9}{12}$ foot.

Problem Solving

MATHEMATICAL PRACTICES

© **21. Writing to Explain** Sandy's sculpture is taller than Jason's. Becca's sculpture is taller than Sandy's sculpture. If Sandy's sculpture is $\frac{2}{3}$ foot tall, how tall could Jason's and Becca's sculpture be?

© **22. Reason** The fraction $\frac{2}{3}$ is $\frac{1}{3}$ less than 1 whole. Without finding equivalent fractions, order the fractions $\frac{7}{8}, \frac{2}{3},$ and $\frac{5}{6}$ from least to greatest.

© **23. Persevere** The table at the right shows the number of pages four students read. Which lists the number of pages in order from least to greatest?

A 25, 69, 96, 64   **C** 64, 25, 69, 96

B 25, 64, 69, 96   **D** 25, 64, 96, 69

Students	Number of Pages
Francine	25
Ty	69
Greg	96
Vicki	64

© **24. Generalize** Find the missing numbers in the pattern below.

____ , 36, 54, ____ , ____ , 108, ____

25. Katie asked Kerry to name 3 fractions between 0 and 1. Kerry said $\frac{5}{12}, \frac{1}{4},$ and $\frac{2}{6}$. Order Kerry's fractions from least to greatest.

26. Geena had 6 pairs of earrings. Kiera had 3 times as many. How many pairs of earrings did Kiera have?

27. Each student in fourth grade had the same book to read. Charles read $\frac{2}{3}$ of the book, and Drew read $\frac{3}{5}$ of the book. Who read more?

©
Common Core

4.NF.2 Compare two fractions with different numerators and different denominators, e.g., by creating common denominators or numerators, or by comparing to a benchmark fraction such as $\frac{1}{2}$. Recognize that comparisons are valid only when the two fractions refer to the same whole. Record the results ... and justify the conclusions.... Also **4.NF.1**

Problem Solving

Writing to Explain

Jake found a piece of wood in the shape of an equilateral triangle. He cut off a section of the triangle as shown to the right.

Did Jake cut off $\frac{1}{3}$ of the triangle? Explain.

Section of wood cut off

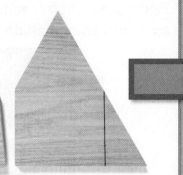

Another Example

Erin says that $\frac{1}{2}$ is always the same amount as $\frac{2}{4}$. Matthew says that $\frac{1}{2}$ and $\frac{2}{4}$ are equivalent fractions, but they could be different amounts. Which student is correct? Explain.

The circles are the same size.

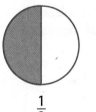 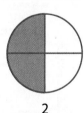

$\frac{1}{2}$ $\frac{2}{4}$

The amounts are the same.

The circles are not the same size.

$\frac{2}{4}$ $\frac{1}{2}$

The amounts are different.

Matthew is correct. $\frac{1}{2}$ and $\frac{2}{4}$ are equivalent fractions, but they could represent different amounts.

Explain It

©**1. Reasonableness** When will amounts of $\frac{1}{2}$ and $\frac{2}{4}$ be equal?

2. When are the fractional amounts $\frac{3}{6}$ and $\frac{2}{4}$ not equal?

What do I know? The triangle is an equilateral triangle. One piece is cut off.

What am I asked to find? Is the section that is cut off $\frac{1}{3}$ of the triangle?

Use words, pictures, numbers, or symbols to write a math explanation.

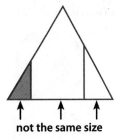

$\frac{1}{3}$ means that the whole has to be divided into 3 equal parts. The parts have to be the same size.

not the same size

The shaded section is not $\frac{1}{3}$ of the triangle.

Guided Practice*

 MATHEMATICAL PRACTICES

Do you know HOW?

1. A board is cut into 12 equal pieces. How many pieces together represent $\frac{3}{4}$ of the board? Explain how you arrived at your answer.

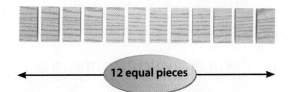

12 equal pieces

Do you UNDERSTAND?

2. Copy and draw the triangle above. Shade in $\frac{1}{3}$ of the triangle.

© 3. **Write a Problem** Write a problem that would use the figure below as part of its explanation.

Independent Practice

© MATHEMATICAL PRACTICES

Write to explain.

4. Devon and Amanda knit the same size scarf. Devon's scarf is $\frac{3}{5}$ yellow. Amanda's scarf is $\frac{3}{4}$ yellow. How can you use a picture to show whose scarf is more yellow?

5. The school newspaper has a total of 18 articles and ads. There are 6 more articles than ads. How many articles and ads are there? Explain how you found your answer.

Applying Math Practices

- What am I asked to find?
- What else can I try?
- How are quantities related?
- How can I explain my work?
- How can I use math to model the problem?
- Can I use tools to help?
- Is my work precise?
- Why does this work?
- How can I generalize?

6. Look at the cell pattern below. Explain how the number of cells changes as the number of divisions changes.

1 cell   1st division   2nd division   3rd division

© **7. Use Structure** Look at the number sentences below. What numbers replace ●, ▲, and ▧? Explain your answer.

▲ + ▧ = 18
● + ▲ = 20
▧ + ▧ = 14

8. At the bowling alley, there are 32 bowling balls. Of these, 8 are blue, 5 are pink, 6 are red, and the rest are black. How many of the bowling balls are black?

© **Reason** Use the data at the right for problems **9** and **10**.

9. How can you find the number of cards Linda has in her collection?

10. George has 100 rookie cards in his collection. How can you find the number of pictures in the pictograph that represent George's rookie cards?

Baseball Card Collections

George	🂠🂠🂠🂠🂠🂠🂠🂠🂠🂠🂠
Becky	🂠🂠🂠🂠🂠🂠🂠🂠🂠🂠
Trent	🂠🂠🂠🂠🂠🂠🂠🂠🂠🂠🂠🂠🂠
Linda	🂠🂠🂠🂠🂠🂠🂠🂠🂠🂠🂠

Each 🂠 = 25 cards

© **Think About the Structure**

11. Janet gets $25 a week to buy lunch at school. She spends $4 each day and saves the rest. Which expression can be used to find how much money Janet will save at the end of the 5 days?

  A $(4 \times 5) + 25$ **C** $(25 - 5) + 4$

  B $25 + (5 - 4)$ **D** $25 - (5 \times 4)$

12. During recess, Rachel played on the bars and swings. She spent 10 minutes on the bars and twice as long on the swings. Which expression can be used to find how much time she spent on the equipment?

  A $10 - (2 + 10)$ **C** $(10 + 2) - 10$

  B $10 + (2 \times 10)$ **D** $(10 \div 2) + 10$

Going Digital

Reasonableness of Sums

Estimate 2,968 + 983 + 5,442. Use a calculator to find the sum. Then, explain whether or not the sum you found is reasonable.

Step 1 Estimate 2,968 + 983 + 5,442.

3,000 + 1,000 + 5,000 = 9,000

Step 2 Use a calculator to add.

Press: 2,968 **+** 983 **+** 5,442

Display:

9393

Step 3 Explain whether or not the sum is reasonable.

Since 9,393 is close to the estimate of 9,000, the sum is reasonable.

Practice

Estimate each sum. Find the sum on a calculator.
Remember to check whether or not the sum is reasonable.

1. 956 + 1,495

2. 1,872 + 3,216

3. 4,857 + 5,679 + 3,298

4. 8,542 + 875 + 6,425

5. 1,978 + 7,435 + 2,986

6. 9,650 + 2,348 + 5,822

7. 2,726 + 1,247 + 3,476

8. 3,214 + 7,981 + 2,148 + 6,542

9. 872 + 2,729 + 221

10. 6,742 + 7,231

11. 8,792 + 3,864 + 298

12. 8,898 + 6,281

13. 1,372 + 6,261 + 204

14. 7,671 + 3,341

15. 3,634 + 8,916 + 192

16. 3,456 + 7,654 + 211

17. 101 + 3,561 + 41

18. 99 + 3,795 + 4,319

Find the factors of 12.

Start with 1 group of 12.
$12 = 1 \times 12$

Then 2 groups of 6.
$12 = 2 \times 6$

Then 3 groups of 4.
$12 = 3 \times 4$

Since the factor pairs have started to repeat, these are all the possible factors of 12: 1, 2, 3, 4, 6, 12.

Remember you can use counters to help find ways to multiply.

Write each number two different ways using multiplication.

1. 45   **2.** 40

3. 56   **4.** 63

5. 36   **6.** 16

7. 24   **8.** 64

Set B, pages 260–261

Is 49 prime or composite?

Find factors other than 1 and 49.

49 is composite because it is divisible by 7.

$49 = 7 \times 7$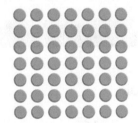

Is 31 prime or composite?

Find factors other than 1 and 31.

31 is prime because it has exactly two factors, 1 and itself.

$31 = 1 \times 31$

Remember that you can use an array to decide if a number is prime or composite.

Write whether each number is prime or composite.

1. 13   **2.** 25

3. 355   **4.** 2

5. 29   **6.** 32

7. 37   **8.** 72

9. 120   **10.** 2,232

Find three multiples of 8. Use multiplication.

$8 \times 1 = \mathbf{8}$ $8 \times 2 = \mathbf{16}$ $8 \times 3 = \mathbf{24}$

Three multiples of 8 are 8, 16, and 24.

Tell whether the first number is a multiple of the second number. Use multiplication facts.

32, 8

Yes because $8 \times 4 = 32$.

Remember to use multiplication and multiplication facts to find a multiple of a number.

Find five multiples of each number.

1. 3

2. 7

3. 4

4. 9

Tell whether the first number is a multiple of the second number.

5. 45, 9

6. 27, 4

7. 30, 4

8. 42, 7

Find an equivalent fraction for $\frac{2}{6}$ using multiplication.

Multiply the numerator and the denominator by the same number to find an equivalent fraction.

$$\frac{2}{6} = \frac{4}{12}$$

So, $\frac{2}{6}$ is equivalent to $\frac{4}{12}$.

Divide the numerator and denominator by 2.

$$\frac{2}{6} = \frac{1}{3} \qquad \frac{1}{3} = \frac{2}{6} = \frac{4}{12}$$

Remember to find an equivalent fraction you must multiply or divide the numerator and denominator by the same number.

Multiply or divide to find an equivalent fraction.

1. $\frac{8}{16} = \frac{\square}{8}$

2. $\frac{5}{6} = \frac{20}{\square}$

3. $\frac{12}{15} = \frac{4}{\square}$

4. $\frac{2}{9} = \frac{\square}{72}$

Find two equivalent forms for each fraction using multiplication and division.

5. $\frac{8}{12}$

6. $\frac{30}{40}$

7. $\frac{8}{72}$

8. $\frac{14}{22}$

9. $\frac{6}{8}$

10. $\frac{20}{25}$

Identify the fraction on the number line.

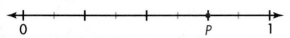

Point P could be called $\frac{3}{4}$, $\frac{6}{8}$, or any other equivalent fraction.

Remember to use equal parts on your number lines.

Draw a number line to show each fraction and an equivalent fraction.

1. $\frac{4}{8}$ **2.** $\frac{4}{6}$

3. $\frac{6}{10}$ **4.** $\frac{1}{3}$

5. $\frac{2}{8}$ **6.** $\frac{8}{10}$

Set F, pages 270–272

Compare $\frac{1}{6}$ and $\frac{3}{6}$.

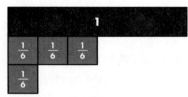

$1 < 3$

So, $\frac{1}{6} < \frac{3}{6}$.

Compare $\frac{4}{6}$ and $\frac{3}{4}$.

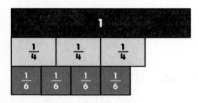

$\frac{4}{6}$ is less than $\frac{3}{4}$.

So, $\frac{4}{6} < \frac{3}{4}$.

Remember when comparing fractions with different denominators, you can use benchmark fractions such as $\frac{1}{4}$, $\frac{1}{3}$, $\frac{1}{2}$, $\frac{2}{3}$, and $\frac{3}{4}$.

Compare. Write $>$, $<$, or $=$ for each $\bigcirc$.

1. $\frac{5}{6} \bigcirc \frac{2}{3}$ **2.** $\frac{1}{3} \bigcirc \frac{3}{10}$

3. $\frac{5}{10} \bigcirc \frac{1}{2}$ **4.** $\frac{3}{4} \bigcirc \frac{5}{12}$

5. $\frac{3}{8} \bigcirc \frac{1}{3}$ **6.** $\frac{4}{10} \bigcirc \frac{3}{12}$

7. $\frac{7}{8} \bigcirc \frac{5}{8}$ **8.** $\frac{1}{5} \bigcirc \frac{2}{10}$

9. $\frac{2}{5} \bigcirc \frac{1}{4}$ **10.** $\frac{3}{6} \bigcirc \frac{3}{4}$

11. $\frac{2}{12} \bigcirc \frac{1}{6}$ **12.** $\frac{1}{8} \bigcirc \frac{8}{8}$

13. $\frac{9}{10} \bigcirc \frac{4}{5}$ **14.** $\frac{2}{6} \bigcirc \frac{2}{3}$

15. $\frac{2}{3} \bigcirc \frac{3}{4}$ **16.** $\frac{4}{5} \bigcirc \frac{1}{2}$

Order $\frac{5}{6}$, $\frac{2}{3}$, and $\frac{1}{2}$ from least to greatest.

Find equivalent fractions with a common denominator.

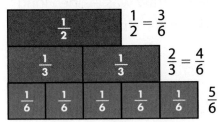

$\frac{1}{2} = \frac{3}{6}$

$\frac{2}{3} = \frac{4}{6}$

$\frac{5}{6}$

$\frac{3}{6} < \frac{4}{6} < \frac{5}{6}$ So, $\frac{1}{2}$, $\frac{2}{3}$, $\frac{5}{6}$.

Order $\frac{4}{6}$, $\frac{3}{4}$, and $\frac{1}{2}$ from least to greatest.

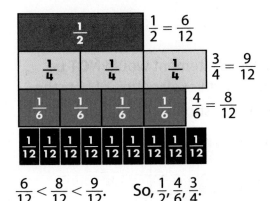

$\frac{1}{2} = \frac{6}{12}$

$\frac{3}{4} = \frac{9}{12}$

$\frac{4}{6} = \frac{8}{12}$

$\frac{6}{12} < \frac{8}{12} < \frac{9}{12}$.   So, $\frac{1}{2}$, $\frac{4}{6}$, $\frac{3}{4}$.

Remember you can use fraction strips to find equivalent fractions with common denominators.

Order from least to greatest.

1. $\frac{1}{2}$, $\frac{2}{3}$, $\frac{5}{12}$

2. $\frac{7}{8}$, $\frac{3}{8}$, $\frac{3}{4}$

3. $\frac{1}{3}$, $\frac{1}{6}$, $\frac{3}{6}$

4. $\frac{2}{5}$, $\frac{5}{6}$, $\frac{11}{12}$

5. $\frac{6}{8}$, $\frac{5}{8}$, $\frac{1}{2}$

6. $\frac{2}{5}$, $\frac{3}{10}$, $\frac{6}{10}$

Order from greatest to least.

7. $\frac{1}{3}$, $\frac{2}{3}$, $\frac{5}{6}$

8. $\frac{7}{8}$, $\frac{3}{4}$, $\frac{1}{1}$

9. $\frac{7}{10}$, $\frac{3}{12}$, $\frac{1}{3}$

10. $\frac{1}{4}$, $\frac{3}{8}$, $\frac{2}{6}$

11. $\frac{2}{8}$, $\frac{1}{3}$, $\frac{2}{4}$

12. $\frac{4}{5}$, $\frac{5}{6}$, $\frac{9}{12}$

Suppose a square is cut as shown. Is each section $\frac{1}{4}$ of the square?

What do I know?   The square is cut into 4 pieces.

What am I asked to find?   Do all the cuts represent $\frac{1}{4}$ of the square?

If each part is $\frac{1}{4}$ then the whole is divided into 4 equal parts.

The parts are not the same size. Each is not $\frac{1}{4}$ of the square.

Remember to explain your answer.

1. Peter says that $\frac{3}{4}$ of a pizza is always the same as $\frac{6}{8}$ of a pizza. Nadia says that while they are equivalent fractions, $\frac{3}{4}$ and $\frac{6}{8}$ of a pizza could represent different amounts. Who is correct?

2. David says you can have an unlimited number of equivalent fractions to any given fraction. Is he right?

Multiple Choice

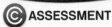 ASSESSMENT

1. Which statement is true? (11-2)

   A The only factors of 3 are 3 and 1.

   B The only factors of 4 are 4 and 1.

   C The only factors of 6 are 6 and 1.

   D The only factors of 8 are 8 and 1.

2. Which list shows only multiples of 6? (11-3)

   A 6, 12, 18, 24

   B 6, 16, 26, 36

   C 1, 2, 3, 6

   D 6, 16, 60, 66

3. What are two fractions that represent Point *P*? (11-5)

   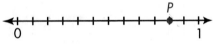

   A $\frac{5}{6}$ and $\frac{5}{10}$

   B $\frac{5}{6}$ and $\frac{10}{12}$

   C $\frac{5}{10}$ and $\frac{10}{12}$

   D $\frac{3}{4}$ and $\frac{9}{12}$

4. Which lists all the factors of 25? (11-1)

   A 1, 25

   B 1, 5, 25

   C 1, 10, 25

   D 1, 25, 50

5. Javier and Mark drew straws to see who went down the waterslide first. Javier's straw was $\frac{5}{12}$ inch long and Mark's was $\frac{7}{12}$ inch long. Which symbol makes the comparison true? (11-6)

   $\frac{5}{12} \bigcirc \frac{7}{12}$

   A $\times$

   B $=$

   C $<$

   D $>$

6. Which statement would **NOT** be used in an explanation of how the drawing shows that $\frac{2}{3} = \frac{4}{6}$? (11-8)

   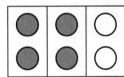

   A 2 of the 3 rectangles are filled with shaded circles.

   B 4 out of the 6 rectangles are shaded.

   C Both $\frac{2}{3}$ and $\frac{4}{6}$ describe the part that is shaded.

   D In the rectangles, 4 out of the 6 circles are shaded.

7. What number should go in the box to make the fractions equivalent? (11-4)

$\frac{3}{5} = \frac{6}{\blacksquare}$

8. Write all the factors of 24. (11-1)

9. Which of the following numbers is prime? (11-2)

88, 65, 51, 17

10. The student council ordered pizza for their meeting. Half of the members voted for cheese pizza, $\frac{1}{10}$ for hamburger, and $\frac{2}{5}$ for vegetable.

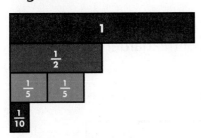

Write the fractions in order from least to greatest. (11-7)

11. Which of the following numbers is a multiple of 4? (11-3)

9, 15, 21, 40

12. What is the missing number that makes the fractions equivalent? (11-4)

$\frac{2}{3} = \frac{8}{\blacksquare}$

13. Mary bought $\frac{3}{4}$ pound of almonds. What point on the number line shows an equivalent fraction for $\frac{3}{4}$? (11-5)

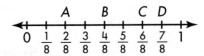

14. Write the fractions listed below in order from least to greatest. (11-7)

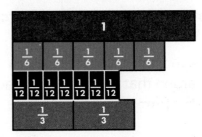

$\frac{5}{6}, \frac{7}{12}, \frac{2}{3}$

15. Sharon measured two apples. The green apple weighed $\frac{3}{8}$ pound. The red apple weighed $\frac{1}{3}$ pound. Which apple was heavier? Write an inequality to show how their weights compare. (11-6)

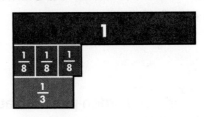

16. Josh says that $\frac{2}{3}$ is always the same as $\frac{4}{6}$. Meghan says that $\frac{2}{3}$ and $\frac{4}{6}$ are equivalent fractions, but they could be different amounts. Which student is correct? Explain. (11-8)

The Garden Club recently planted their garden. Each student has a small plot. The layout of the garden is shown below. Each part shows the name of the gardener and the vegetable planted in the plot.

The Garden Club

Pedro	Christina	David	Greg	Hillary	Kim
Carrots	**Peas**	**Squash**	**Carrots**	**Peas**	**Corn**
Rosa	Daisy	Lauren	Juan	Sheri	Anna
Carrots	**Potatoes**	**Carrots**	**Corn**	**Corn**	**Carrots**

1. List each vegetable in the garden. Then write the fractional part of the garden that is taken up by each vegetable. Write each fraction in simplest form.

2. Write two statements describing the fractional parts of the garden.

3. Sally plants $\frac{1}{3}$ of her plot with peas as shown to the right. About what fractional part of the plot is planted with corn?

Peas
Corn

4. Plan your own garden plot with at least two different vegetables.

   Describe what fraction of your plot you would plant with each vegetable. Draw your garden on a separate sheet of paper.

Topic 11

Topic 12

Adding and Subtracting Fractions and Mixed Numbers with Like Denominators

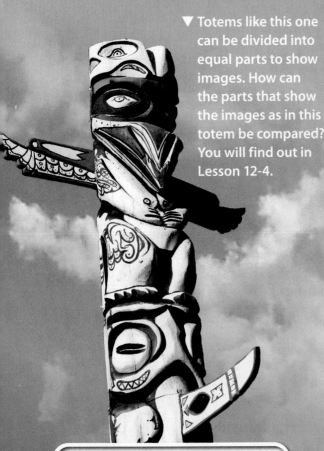

▼ Totems like this one can be divided into equal parts to show images. How can the parts that show the images as in this totem be compared? You will find out in Lesson 12-4.

Review What You Know!

Vocabulary

Choose the best term from the box.

- denominator
- factor
- product
- numerator

1. In the fraction $\frac{2}{3}$, the number 2 is the __?__ of the fraction and 3 is the __?__ of the fraction.

2. You multiply one __?__ by another to find a __?__.

Equivalent Fractions

Write the missing values to show pairs of equivalent fractions.

3. $\frac{2}{3} = \frac{?}{6}$

4. $\frac{?}{4} = \frac{3}{12}$

5. $\frac{6}{5} = \frac{?}{10}$

6. $\frac{1}{2} = \frac{50}{?}$

7. $\frac{1}{5} = \frac{?}{10}$

8. $\frac{3}{?} = \frac{30}{100}$

Models for Fractions

Tell what fraction is represented by each model.

9.

10.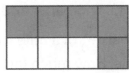

11. Writing to Explain Draw two ways to model $\frac{5}{6}$. Explain why there can be more than one way to model a fraction.

Topic Essential Questions

- What does it mean to add and subtract fractions and mixed numbers with like denominators?
- What is a standard procedure for adding and subtracting fractions and mixed numbers with like denominators?
- How can fractions and mixed numbers be added nnd subtracted on a number line?

Interactive Learning

Pose the problem. Start each lesson by working together to solve problems. It will help you make sense of math.

Lesson 12-1

ⓒ **Use Tools** Solve using fraction strips.

Megan is working on a community mural. She paints $\frac{3}{8}$ of her wall green and $\frac{4}{8}$ purple. How much of the wall has she painted so far? Show how you solved the problem.

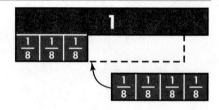

Lesson 12-2

ⓒ **Generalize** Solve using paper and pencil.

Mark is baking banana bread and muffins for a neighborhood party. He uses $\frac{2}{5}$ bag of walnuts for the banana bread and $\frac{1}{5}$ bag for the muffins. How much of the bag of walnuts does Mark use all together?

Lesson 12-3

ⓒ **Use Tools** Solve using fraction strips.

You use $\frac{4}{6}$ of a sheet of construction paper to make decorations. How much of the sheet is left? Show how you solved the problem.

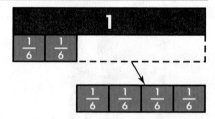

Lesson 12-4

ⓒ **Generalize** Solve using paper and pencil.

Kwami wants to walk $\frac{8}{10}$ of a mile to the park. He has already walked $\frac{5}{10}$ of a mile. How much farther does he have to walk?

Lesson 12-5

ⓒ **Use Tools** Solve. Use a number line to help.

Sammy has $\frac{6}{8}$ jar of red paint. He uses $\frac{2}{8}$ jar of the paint on a model airplane. What fraction of the jar does Sammy have left?

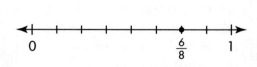

MATHEMATICAL PRACTICES

Lesson 12-6

Ⓒ **Use Structure** Solve. Use what you know about fractions less than one to help.

Albert took $1\frac{1}{3}$ granola bars with him on a bicycle ride. How can you write $1\frac{1}{3}$ as a fraction? Tell how you decided.

Lesson 12-7

Ⓒ **Use Tools** Solve. Use fraction strips to help.

Tory is cutting bread loaves into fourths. She needs to wrap up $3\frac{3}{4}$ loaves to take to a potluck supper and $1\frac{2}{4}$ loaves for a bake sale. How many loaves does Tory need to wrap in all for the potluck supper and the bake sale?

Lesson 12-8

Ⓒ **Use Tools** Solve any way you choose. Record your work on paper.

Joaquin used $1\frac{3}{6}$ cups of whole-wheat flour and $1\frac{4}{6}$ cups of buckwheat flour in a recipe. How much flour did he use in all?

Lesson 12-9

Ⓒ **Use Tools** Solve any way you choose. Record your work on paper.

Evan is walking $2\frac{1}{8}$ miles to his aunt's house. He has already walked $\frac{6}{8}$ mile. How much farther does he have to go?

Lesson 12-10

Ⓒ **Use Structure** Solve. Find as many answers as you can.

Karyn had $\frac{7}{8}$ of a pound of oatmeal to put into three bowls. How much could she put into each bowl, if the oatmeal did not have to be divided evenly among the bowls?

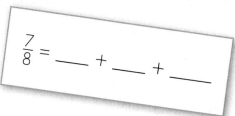

Lesson 12-11

Ⓒ **Model** Solve. Draw a bar diagram to help choose an appropriate operation.

Michelle rode her bike $\frac{3}{4}$ mile on Thursday, $\frac{3}{4}$ mile on Friday, and $\frac{2}{4}$ mile on Saturday. How far did she ride her bike in all?

Common Core

4.NF.3 Understand a fraction $\frac{a}{b}$ with $a > 1$ as a sum of fractions $\frac{1}{b}$.
Also **4.NF.3.a**

Modeling Addition of Fractions

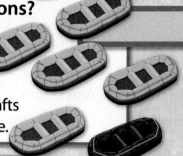

Hands-On
fraction strips

$\frac{1}{8}$

How can you use fraction strips to add fractions?

Ten whitewater rafting teams are racing downriver. Two teams have red rafts and one team has a blue raft. What fraction of the rafts are either red or blue?

Choose an Operation Add the fraction of the total rafts that are red to the fraction of the total rafts that are blue.

Guided Practice*

MATHEMATICAL **PRACTICES**

Do you know HOW?

In **1** through **6**, use fraction strips to add fractions. Simplify, if possible.

1. $\frac{1}{3} + \frac{1}{3}$　　　　2. $\frac{1}{6} + \frac{1}{6}$

3. $\frac{2}{5} + \frac{1}{5}$　　　　4. $\frac{2}{6} + \frac{2}{6}$

5. $\frac{1}{4} + \frac{2}{4}$　　　　6. $\frac{1}{5} + \frac{3}{5}$

Do you UNDERSTAND?

© 7. **Reason** In the problem above, what fraction of the rafts are yellow? What two fractions would you add to find the part of the rafts that are either red or yellow?

8. What two fractions are being added below? What is the sum?

| $\frac{1}{6}$ | $\frac{1}{6}$ |

| $\frac{1}{6}$ | $\frac{1}{6}$ | $\frac{1}{6}$ |

Independent Practice

In **9** through **23**, find each sum. Simplify, if possible. You may use fraction strips.

9. $\frac{1}{3} + \frac{1}{3}$　　　10. $\frac{4}{10} + \frac{1}{10}$　　　11. $\frac{2}{12} + \frac{4}{12}$

12. $\frac{1}{6} + \frac{2}{6} + \frac{3}{6}$　　　13. $\frac{3}{12} + \frac{4}{12}$　　　14. $\frac{4}{10} + \frac{3}{10}$

15. $\frac{5}{8} + \frac{1}{8}$　　　16. $\frac{3}{4} + \frac{1}{4}$　　　17. $\frac{4}{12} + \frac{2}{12}$

18. $\frac{1}{4} + \frac{1}{4}$　　　19. $\frac{2}{10} + \frac{3}{10}$　　　20. $\frac{1}{10} + \frac{2}{10} + \frac{1}{10}$

21. $\frac{4}{6} + \frac{1}{6}$　　　22. $\frac{2}{3} + \frac{1}{3}$　　　23. $\frac{1}{8} + \frac{5}{8} + \frac{1}{8}$

For another example, see Set A on page 320.

DIGITAL

eTools
www.pearsonsuccessnet.com

<table>
<tr><td colspan="2">

What You Show

$\frac{2}{10}$ of the rafts are red and $\frac{1}{10}$ of the rafts are blue. Use two $\frac{1}{10}$ strips to show $\frac{2}{10}$ and one $\frac{1}{10}$ strip to show $\frac{1}{10}$.

Three $\frac{1}{10}$ strips are needed.

</td>
<td>

What You Write

Add the numerators. Write the sum over the common denominator.

$$\frac{2}{10} + \frac{1}{10} = \frac{3}{10}$$

Three out of ten or $\frac{3}{10}$ of the total rafts are either red or blue.

</td></tr>
</table>

Problem Solving

MATHEMATICAL
PRACTICES

24. Model A pizza is divided into 6 equal pieces. Draw a picture to show that $\frac{1}{6} + \frac{2}{6} = \frac{3}{6}$ or $\frac{1}{2}$.

25. Tomika wants to give 125 stickers to 5 of her friends. If she divides the stickers equally among her friends, how many stickers will each friend receive?

26. Reason Suppose two different fractions with the same denominators are both less than 1. Can their sum equal 1? Can their sum be greater than 1?

27. A chicken farm produces an average of 75 dozen eggs per week. There are 12 eggs in a dozen. How many eggs does the farm produce in an average week?

28. Writing to Explain Sophia walked $\frac{1}{4}$ mile to Sheila's house, and they both walked $\frac{2}{4}$ mile to the pool. How far did Sophia walk? Explain how you found your answer.

29. Model When does the sum of two fractions equal 1?

30. Find the missing value in the equation.

$$\frac{1}{10} + \frac{\square}{10} + \frac{3}{10} = \frac{9}{10}$$

A 2 **C** 4

B 3 **D** 5

31. Think About the Structure Maribel had 8 stickers. She bought 4 more. Then she gave her sister 5 stickers.

What numerical expression shows how many stickers Maribel has now?

A $(8 + 4) - 5$ **C** $8 - (4 + 5)$

B $(8 \times 4) \div 5$ **D** $8 - (4 - 5)$

Lesson
12-2

Common
Core

4.NF.3.a Understand
addition and subtraction
of fractions as joining and
separating parts referring
to the same whole. Also
4.NF.3.d

Adding Fractions with Like Denominators

How can you add fractions with like denominators?

The table shows the results of a fifth-grade class survey. What fraction of the class chose soccer or basketball as their favorite sport?

Choose an Operation Add the fractions for soccer and basketball to find the results.

Favorite Sport	
	$\frac{2}{12}$
	$\frac{1}{12}$
	$\frac{4}{12}$
	$\frac{5}{12}$

Guided Practice*

 MATHEMATICAL PRACTICES

Do you know HOW?

For **1** through **6**, add the fractions. Simplify, if possible.

1. $\frac{2}{4} + \frac{1}{4}$ **2.** $\frac{1}{3} + \frac{2}{3}$

3. $\frac{2}{12} + \frac{4}{12}$ **4.** $\frac{1}{10} + \frac{4}{10}$

5. $\frac{1}{5} + \frac{3}{5}$ **6.** $\frac{3}{6} + \frac{1}{6}$

Do you UNDERSTAND?

7. Communicate In the survey above, what do the numerators stand for? The denominators?

8. Using the survey above, what fraction of the class chose either roller skating or biking?

Independent Practice

In **9** through **26**, add the fractions. Simplify, if possible.

9. $\frac{2}{6} + \frac{2}{6}$ **10.** $\frac{3}{5} + \frac{2}{5}$ **11.** $\frac{2}{4} + \frac{1}{4}$

12. $\frac{3}{8} + \frac{5}{8}$ **13.** $\frac{5}{10} + \frac{3}{10}$ **14.** $\frac{5}{12} + \frac{4}{12}$

15. $\frac{3}{10} + \frac{2}{10}$ **16.** $\frac{1}{12} + \frac{3}{12}$ **17.** $\frac{2}{8} + \frac{4}{8}$

18. $\frac{2}{6} + \frac{1}{6}$ **19.** $\frac{2}{12} + \frac{6}{12}$ **20.** $\frac{3}{10} + \frac{2}{10} + \frac{4}{10}$

21. $\frac{3}{5} + \frac{2}{5}$ **22.** $\frac{30}{100} + \frac{40}{100}$ **23.** $\frac{3}{6} + \frac{1}{6}$

24. $\frac{4}{12} + \frac{6}{12}$ **25.** $\frac{14}{100} + \frac{6}{100}$ **26.** $\frac{25}{100} + \frac{75}{100}$

For another example, see Set B on page 320.

Step 1

?

| $\frac{1}{12}$ | $\frac{5}{12}$ |

Write the sum of the fractions.

$$\frac{1}{12} + \frac{5}{12}$$

Step 2

Add the numerators. Write the sum over the common denominator.

$$\frac{1}{12} + \frac{5}{12} = \frac{6}{12}$$

Step 3

Write the sum in simplest form, if possible.

$$\frac{6 \div 6}{12 \div 6} = \frac{1}{2}$$

One half $\left(\frac{1}{2}\right)$ of the students chose soccer or basketball as their favorite sport.

Problem Solving

 MATHEMATICAL PRACTICES

27. Maria swam in a race that was 35 lengths of a pool. If one length of the pool is 25 meters, then how many meters did Maria swim?

A 725 meters

B 775 meters

C 855 meters

D 875 meters

28. Perimeter is the distance around the outside of any polygon. If a side of a square is $\frac{1}{2}$ foot long, what is the perimeter of the square?

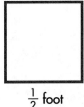

$\frac{1}{2}$ foot

Ⓒ **29. Model** Using the survey in the example at the top of the page, find two activities that have a sum of $\frac{5}{12}$. Write your answer as an expression.

30. If a painter poured $\frac{1}{4}$ gallon of yellow paint and $\frac{1}{4}$ gallon of red paint into a bucket, how much paint is in the bucket?

Ⓒ **31. Reason** One brand of socks is on sale at 3 pairs for $6. Another brand is on sale at 5 pairs for $9. Which is the better buy?

32. Michael's family lives at 13450 Oak Street. What is the expanded form of 13,450?

Ⓒ **33. Use Structure** Find the missing numerator in each equation.

a $\frac{4}{9} + \frac{\square}{9} = \frac{8}{9}$ **c** $\frac{2}{7} + \frac{\square}{7} = \frac{5}{7}$

b $\frac{\square}{10} + \frac{3}{10} = \frac{9}{10}$ **d** $\frac{4}{12} + \frac{\square}{12} = \frac{7}{12}$

Ⓒ **34. Persevere** Jorgé bought $\frac{3}{8}$ of a yard of fabric. He already had $\frac{1}{8}$ of a yard of the same cloth. What are 3 equivalent fractions for how much fabric Jorgé has now?

Lesson
12-3

Common
Core

4.NF.3.a Understand
addition and subtraction
of fractions as joining and
separating parts referring
to the same whole.
Also 4.NF.3.d

Hands-On
fraction strips

$\frac{1}{8}$

Modeling Subtraction of Fractions

How can you use fraction strips to subtract fractions?

A garden plot is divided into twelve equal sections. If two sections are used to grow hot peppers, what fraction is left to grow other crops?

Choose an Operation Take away a part from the whole to find the difference.

Guided Practice*

MATHEMATICAL PRACTICES

Do you know HOW?

For **1** through **6**, use fraction strips to subtract. Simplify, if possible.

1. $\frac{4}{4} - \frac{1}{4}$ 2. $\frac{4}{5} - \frac{2}{5}$

3. $\frac{7}{8} - \frac{5}{8}$ 4. $\frac{9}{10} - \frac{3}{10}$

5. $\frac{7}{12} - \frac{3}{12}$ 6. $\frac{7}{8} - \frac{1}{8}$

Do you UNDERSTAND?

7. **Generalize** In the problem above, what part of the garden is represented by each fraction strip?

8. In the example above, if 4 sections are used to grow hot peppers, what fraction is left to grow other crops? How did you find your answer?

Independent Practice

In **9** through **26**, use fraction strips to subtract. Simplify, if possible.

9. $\frac{2}{3} - \frac{1}{3}$ 10. $\frac{3}{5} - \frac{2}{5}$ 11. $\frac{6}{10} - \frac{2}{10}$

12. $\frac{11}{12} - \frac{5}{12}$ 13. $\frac{2}{2} - \frac{1}{2}$ 14. $\frac{3}{4} - \frac{1}{4}$

15. $\frac{5}{6} - \frac{2}{6}$ 16. $\frac{6}{8} - \frac{2}{8}$ 17. $\frac{4}{12} - \frac{1}{12}$

18. $\frac{4}{6} - \frac{1}{6}$ 19. $\frac{5}{8} - \frac{2}{8}$ 20. $\frac{7}{10} - \frac{4}{10}$

21. $\frac{8}{10} - \frac{2}{10}$ 22. $\frac{3}{5} - \frac{1}{5}$ 23. $\frac{5}{6} - \frac{4}{6}$

24. $\frac{4}{5} - \frac{4}{5}$ 25. $\frac{8}{10} - \frac{4}{10}$ 26. $\frac{1}{3} - \frac{1}{3}$

DIGITAL
eTools
www.pearsonsuccessnet.com

For another example, see Set C on page 320.

What You Show

Use twelve $\frac{1}{12}$ fraction strips to represent the whole garden.

| 1 |
| $\frac{1}{12}$ $\frac{1}{12}$ $\frac{1}{12}$ $\frac{1}{12}$ $\frac{1}{12}$ $\frac{1}{12}$ $\frac{1}{12}$ $\frac{1}{12}$ $\frac{1}{12}$ $\frac{1}{12}$ | → $\frac{1}{12}$ $\frac{1}{12}$ |

Take two strips away.

Ten strips are left. So $\frac{10}{12}$ of the garden is used for other crops.

What You Write

Write the part taken away over the common denominator. Subtract the numerators.

$$\frac{12}{12} - \frac{2}{12} = \frac{10}{12}$$

Write in simplest form, if possible.

$$\frac{10}{12} = \frac{5}{6}$$

Problem Solving

MATHEMATICAL PRACTICES

© **27. Model** Draw a model of the garden plot according to the data table below. The plot is divided into 12 sections. What fraction of the plot will be flowers?

Class Garden Plot

Crop	Number of Sections
Strawberries	1
Hot Peppers	2
Corn	2
Tomatoes	4
Flowers	the rest

© **28. Persevere** A quilt is divided into 8 equal panels. Seven panels are blue. Two blue panels are removed to be repaired. Which equation shows the blue part of the quilt that remains after two parts are removed?

A $\frac{7}{8} - \frac{2}{8} = \frac{5}{16}$ **C** $\frac{7}{8} - \frac{2}{8} = \frac{5}{8}$

B $\frac{1}{8} - \frac{6}{8} = \frac{3}{8}$ **D** $\frac{7}{8} - \frac{2}{8} = \frac{9}{16}$

29. What fraction of the circle is the orange part? What fraction of the circle is not orange?

30. Clare had $\frac{5}{6}$ of a pound of almonds. She used $\frac{3}{6}$ of a pound to make a cake. How many pounds of almonds were left? Simplify, if possible.

31. **Science** To avoid predators, ghost crabs usually stay in burrows during the day and feed mostly at night. Suppose a ghost crab eats $\frac{1}{8}$ of its food before 10:00 P.M. By midnight, it has eaten $\frac{5}{8}$ of its food. How much of its food did it eat between 10:00 P.M. and midnight?

Lesson
12-4

Common
Core

4.NF.3.a Understand
addition and subtraction
of fractions as joining and
separating parts referring
to the same whole. Also
4.NF.3.d

Subtracting Fractions with Like Denominators

How do you subtract fractions when the denominators are the same?

A recipe for pancakes calls for $\frac{7}{8}$ of a cup of milk. Lori only has $\frac{3}{8}$ of a cup. How much more milk does she need to make the pancakes?

Choose an Operation Subtract the fractions to find the difference.

$\frac{3}{8}$ cup

Guided Practice*

MATHEMATICAL
PRACTICES

Do you know HOW?

For **1** through **6**, subtract the fractions. Simplify, if possible.

1. $\frac{2}{3} - \frac{1}{3}$
2. $\frac{3}{4} - \frac{2}{4}$
3. $\frac{5}{6} - \frac{2}{6}$
4. $\frac{9}{12} - \frac{3}{12}$
5. $\frac{7}{8} - \frac{3}{8}$
6. $\frac{7}{10} - \frac{1}{10}$

Do you UNDERSTAND?

7. **Writing to Explain** A pancake recipe calls for $\frac{3}{5}$ cup of flour and Lori has 1 cup. Does she have enough flour to make 2 batches of pancakes? Explain.

8. In the example above, if Lori's neighbor gave her $\frac{6}{8}$ cup of milk, would she then have enough milk to make her recipe?

Independent Practice

In **9** through **29**, subtract the fractions. Simplify, if possible.

9. $\frac{11}{12} - \frac{1}{12}$
10. $\frac{7}{10} - \frac{1}{10}$
11. $\frac{6}{8} - \frac{3}{8}$

12. $\frac{4}{4} - \frac{1}{4} - \frac{1}{4}$
13. $\frac{4}{6} - \frac{1}{6}$
14. $\frac{8}{100} - \frac{3}{100}$

15. $\frac{5}{6} - \frac{1}{6}$
16. $\frac{5}{8} - \frac{2}{8} - \frac{3}{8}$
17. $\frac{6}{8} - \frac{4}{8}$

18. $\frac{3}{4} - \frac{1}{4}$
19. $\frac{9}{12} - \frac{8}{12}$
20. $\frac{11}{12} - \frac{2}{12} - \frac{1}{12}$

21. $\frac{8}{10} - \frac{5}{10}$
22. $\frac{5}{6} - \frac{4}{6}$
23. $\frac{3}{8} - \frac{1}{8}$

24. $\frac{7}{12} - \frac{2}{12}$
25. $\frac{80}{100} - \frac{40}{100}$
26. $\frac{9}{10} - \frac{8}{10}$

27. $\frac{30}{100} - \frac{10}{100}$
28. $\frac{5}{8} - \frac{1}{8}$
29. $\frac{9}{12} - \frac{1}{12}$

For another example, see Set D on page 321.

Step 1

$\frac{7}{8}$ cup

$\frac{3}{8}$ cup	?

Write the difference of the fractions.

$$\frac{7}{8} - \frac{3}{8}$$

Step 2

Subtract the numerators. Write the difference over the common denominator.

$$\frac{7}{8} - \frac{3}{8} = \frac{4}{8}$$

Step 3

Write the difference in simplest form, if possible.

$$\frac{4}{8} = \frac{1}{2}$$

Lori needs another $\frac{1}{2}$ cup of milk to make pancakes.

Problem Solving

MATHEMATICAL PRACTICES

30. The Screaming Eagle roller coaster has $\frac{9}{12}$ of the cars full. What fraction of the cars are empty?

A $\frac{9}{12}$ **C** $\frac{1}{3}$

B $\frac{4}{12}$ **D** $\frac{1}{4}$

31. 🔍 **Science** A giraffe's neck is approximately $\frac{1}{3}$ of its height. What fraction of the giraffe's height is not the neck?

32. There are 12 colored marbles in a bag: $\frac{4}{12}$ of the marbles are green, $\frac{3}{12}$ yellow, and $\frac{5}{12}$ blue. Emmanuel has already picked $\frac{2}{12}$ of the marbles. What fraction of marbles are left in the bag?

© 33. Model Chris mowed $\frac{1}{4}$ of the yard in the morning and $\frac{2}{4}$ before football practice. How much of the yard does Chris have left to mow that night? Explain how you found your answer.

34. If $\frac{34}{100}$ of the children on a spinning swing ride are girls, what fraction of the children on the ride are boys?

© 35. Reason Micah is thinking of a 2-digit number. It is a multiple of 6 and 12. It is a factor of 108. The sum of its digits is 9. What number is Micah thinking of?

36. The totem shown at the right is divided into equal parts that represent different animals. How much more of the totem is devoted to bears than to whales? Write your answer as a fraction.

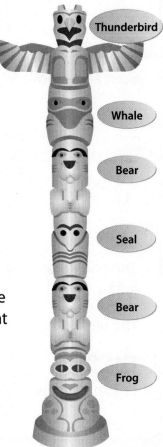

Thunderbird

Whale

Bear

Seal

Bear

Frog

© Common Core

4.NF.3.d Solve word problems involving addition and subtraction of fractions referring to the same whole and having like denominators, e.g., by using visual fraction models and equations to represent the problem. Also **4.NF.3.a**

Adding and Subtracting on the Number Line

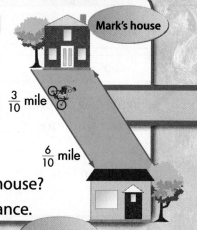

Mark's house

How do you use a number line to solve fraction problems?

Mark starts to ride his bike to Juan's house. After $\frac{3}{10}$ mile, he gets a flat tire and must walk $\frac{6}{10}$ mile. What is the distance from Mark's house to Juan's house?

$\frac{3}{10}$ mile

$\frac{6}{10}$ mile

Choose an Operation Add to find the total distance.

Juan's house

Another Example **How do you subtract fractions on a number line?**

A board is $\frac{11}{12}$ foot in length. Then $\frac{5}{12}$ foot is cut from the board. How long is the remaining board?

Step 1

Draw a number line for twelfths.

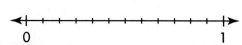

0   1

Step 2

Start at $\frac{11}{12}$. Move 5 spaces to the left to show subtracting $\frac{5}{12}$.

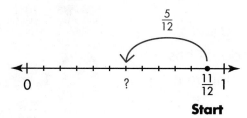

$\frac{5}{12}$

0   ? $\frac{11}{12}$ 1

Start

Step 3

The ending point is $\frac{6}{12}$ or $\frac{1}{2}$. The equation shown on the number line is $\frac{11}{12} - \frac{5}{12} = \frac{1}{2}$.

The remaining board is $\frac{1}{2}$ foot long.

Explain It

1. Explain how you can find $\frac{5}{12} - \frac{1}{12}$ on the number line above.

Draw a number line for tenths. Start at 0. Move 3 spaces to show adding $\frac{3}{10}$. Then move 6 more spaces to show adding $\frac{6}{10}$.

Think What fraction names the ending point on the number line?

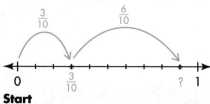

The equation shown on the number line is $\frac{3}{10} + \frac{6}{10} = \frac{9}{10}$.

Find $\frac{3}{10} + \frac{6}{10}$.

Add the numerators.

$\frac{3}{10} + \frac{6}{10} = \frac{9}{10}$

The distance from Mark's house to Juan's house is $\frac{9}{10}$ mile.

Guided Practice*

MATHEMATICAL
PRACTICES

Do you know HOW?

For **1** and **2**, write the equation shown on the number line. Write your answer. Simplify, if possible.

1.

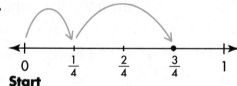

2.

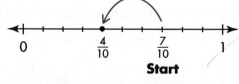

Do you UNDERSTAND?

© **3. Writing to Explain** In the example above, how is the denominator illustrated on the number line? The numerator?

4. In the example above, if the distance between the houses were $\frac{4}{12}$ of a mile, how far would Mark have to go if he wanted to walk from his house to Juan's and then back home?

© **5. Model** Draw a number line to represent $\frac{3}{12} + \frac{5}{12}$. Simplify the sum, if possible.

Independent Practice

In **6** through **9** write the equation shown by each number line. Write your answer. Simplify, if possible.

Tip Arrows to the right show addition. Arrows to the left show subtraction.

6.

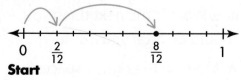

7.

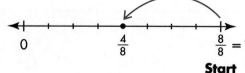

8.

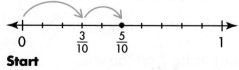

9.

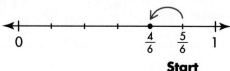

*For another example, see Set E on page 321.

For **10** through **15**, find each answer and simplify, if possible.
Remember that you can draw or use a number line.

10. $\frac{3}{8} + \frac{4}{8}$

11. $\frac{7}{10} - \frac{3}{10}$

12. $\frac{1}{12} + \frac{3}{12}$

13. $\frac{1}{4} + \frac{1}{4} + \frac{1}{4}$

14. $\frac{5}{6} - \frac{4}{6} + \frac{3}{6}$

15. $\frac{8}{12} + \frac{3}{12} - \frac{2}{12}$

Problem Solving

MATHEMATICAL
PRACTICES

16. Find the missing numerator in each equation.

a $\frac{\blacksquare}{5} + \frac{2}{5} = \frac{4}{5}$

b $\frac{8}{10} - \frac{\blacksquare}{10} = \frac{3}{10}$

c $\frac{3}{12} + \frac{\blacksquare}{12} = \frac{11}{12}$

© **17. Be Precise** Luis filled his gallon fish tank before vacation. When he came back, only $\frac{5}{8}$ of the water remained. How much water evaporated? Use a number line to show how you found your answer.

© **18. Reasonableness** A box of fruit contains 2 peaches, 3 bananas, 4 strawberries, and 3 plums. What fraction of the fruit in the box is either peaches or plums?

A $\frac{4}{12}$

B $\frac{5}{12}$

C $\frac{5}{8}$

D $\frac{6}{10}$

© **19. Model** Rodolfo and Aarron are having a turtle race. Rodolfo's turtle reached the finish line, while Aarron's turtle crawled $\frac{4}{6}$ of the way, and then stopped for a nap. Show the turtles' finishing positions on a number line. How much farther did Aarron's turtle have to go to finish? Be sure to label your answer.

© **20. Estimation** Ethan started his hike at the trailhead, has reached the picnic area, and is headed toward the lookout tower. According to the map, how much farther does Ethan have to hike? Estimate the distance.

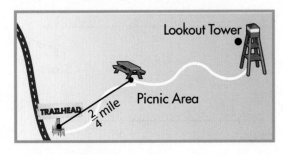

© **21. Reason** How do you know the quotient of $427 \div 4$ is greater than 100 before you actually divide?

© **22. Think About the Structure** You want to show $\frac{7}{8} - \frac{2}{8} = \frac{5}{8}$ on a number line. What is the next thing you should do after you locate $\frac{7}{8}$?

A Move to the right 2 spaces.

B Move to the left 2 spaces.

C Mark the ending point $\frac{5}{8}$.

D Locate $\frac{2}{8}$ on the line.

Algebra Connections

Fractions and Equations

Remember that an equation uses an equal sign to show that two expressions have the same value.

$$\frac{1}{3} + \frac{1}{3} = \frac{2}{3}$$

Example

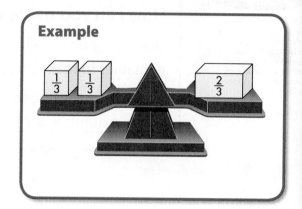

In **1** through **12**, complete each equation by filling in the missing value(s). Check your answers by making sure both sides of each equation are equal.

1. $\frac{3}{8} + \frac{\square}{\square} = \frac{5}{8}$

2. $\frac{\square}{\square} - \frac{1}{5} = \frac{1}{5}$

3. $\frac{7}{\square} + \frac{4}{\square} = \frac{11}{12}$

4. $\frac{8}{10} - \frac{3}{\square} = \frac{5}{\square}$

5. $\frac{\square}{4} + \frac{\square}{4} = \frac{3}{4}$

6. $\frac{5}{6} - \frac{\square}{\square} = \frac{2}{6}$

7. $\frac{\square}{\square} - \frac{7}{12} = \frac{3}{12}$

8. $\frac{4}{6} + \frac{\square}{\square} = \frac{5}{6}$

9. $\frac{1}{2} - \frac{\square}{\square} = 0$

10. $\frac{1}{3} + \frac{\square}{\square} = \frac{2}{3}$

11. $\frac{1}{4} + \frac{\square}{\square} + \frac{1}{4} = \frac{3}{4}$

12. $\frac{8}{10} - \frac{\square}{\square} - \frac{1}{10} = \frac{6}{10}$

. . . .

For **13** through **18**, use the number line below to write and solve each equation. Simplify, if possible. The distance between points represents twelfths.

```
◄──┼──┼──┼──┼──┼──┼──┼──┼──┼──┼──┼──►
   0  A  B  C  D  E  F  G  H  I  J  K  1
```

Example: $B + B = \frac{2}{12} + \frac{2}{12} = \frac{4}{12} = \frac{1}{3}$

13. $A + A = \square$

14. $K - A = \square$

15. $B + D = \square$

16. $F - B = \square$

17. $H + A = \square$

18. $I - C = \square$

19. Write a word problem using one of the equations in **13** through **18**.

Lesson
12-6

ⓒ
**Common
Core**

4.NF.3.c Add and subtract mixed numbers with like denominators, e.g., by replacing each mixed number with an equivalent fraction, and/or by using properties of operations and the relationship between addition and subtraction. Also **4.NF.3.b**

Improper Fractions and Mixed Numbers

Hands-On
fraction strips

$\frac{1}{8}$

How can you name an amount in two different ways?

How many times will Matt need to fill his $\frac{1}{4}$ cup container to make $2\frac{1}{4}$ cups of punch?

$2\frac{1}{4}$ is a mixed number. A mixed number <u>has a whole number part and a fraction part.</u>

$2\frac{1}{4}$ cups

Another Example **How can you write an improper fraction as a mixed number or whole number?**

Jack used $\frac{10}{3}$ cups of water to make lemonade. Write $\frac{10}{3}$ as a mixed number.

   A $10\frac{1}{3}$ cups

   B $3\frac{1}{3}$ cups

   C $3\frac{1}{10}$ cups

   D $\frac{3}{3}$ cups

Use a model. Show $\frac{10}{3}$ or 10 thirds.

There are 3 wholes shaded and $\frac{1}{3}$ of another whole shaded.

So, $\frac{10}{3} = 3\frac{1}{3}$.

Jack made $3\frac{1}{3}$ cups of lemonade.

The correct answer choice is **B**.

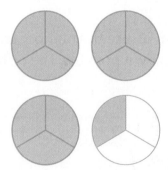

Explain It

1. Explain why $\frac{6}{3} = 2$. Draw a model to help you.

2. Jacquelyn made punch using $\frac{7}{2}$ cups of water. Write $\frac{7}{2}$ as a mixed number.

Use a model to write $2\frac{1}{4}$ as an improper fraction.

An improper fraction <u>has a numerator greater than or equal to its denominator.</u>

Count the shaded fourths.

There are 9 fourths or $\frac{9}{4}$ shaded. So, $2\frac{1}{4} = \frac{9}{4}$.
$\frac{9}{4}$ is an improper fraction.

Matt needs to fill the $\frac{1}{4}$-cup container 9 times.

Use fraction strips.

1			
$\frac{1}{4}$	$\frac{1}{4}$	$\frac{1}{4}$	$\frac{1}{4}$
$\frac{1}{4}$	$\frac{1}{4}$	$\frac{1}{4}$	$\frac{1}{4}$
$\frac{1}{4}$			

So, $2\frac{1}{4} = \frac{9}{4}$.

Guided Practice*

MATHEMATICAL PRACTICES

Do you know HOW?

Write each mixed number as an improper fraction. Write each improper fraction as a mixed number or whole number. Use models to help you.

1. $1\frac{3}{8}$

2. $\frac{4}{3}$

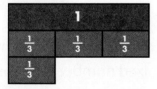

Do you UNDERSTAND?

3. Reason How else could you model $2\frac{1}{4}$ using fraction strips?

4. If Matt filled a $2\frac{1}{5}$ cup container, how many $\frac{1}{5}$ cups would he need to use?

5. Nancy bought $7\frac{1}{2}$ gallons of milk for the school cafeteria. She bought only half-gallon containers. How many half-gallon containers did she buy?

Independent Practice

For **6** through **8**, write each number as a mixed number or improper fraction.

6. $1\frac{3}{4}$

1			
$\frac{1}{4}$	$\frac{1}{4}$	$\frac{1}{4}$	$\frac{1}{4}$
$\frac{1}{4}$	$\frac{1}{4}$	$\frac{1}{4}$	

7. $\frac{7}{3}$

1		
$\frac{1}{3}$	$\frac{1}{3}$	$\frac{1}{3}$
$\frac{1}{3}$	$\frac{1}{3}$	$\frac{1}{3}$
$\frac{1}{3}$		

8. $3\frac{1}{5}$

1				
$\frac{1}{5}$	$\frac{1}{5}$	$\frac{1}{5}$	$\frac{1}{5}$	$\frac{1}{5}$
$\frac{1}{5}$	$\frac{1}{5}$	$\frac{1}{5}$	$\frac{1}{5}$	$\frac{1}{5}$
$\frac{1}{5}$	$\frac{1}{5}$	$\frac{1}{5}$	$\frac{1}{5}$	$\frac{1}{5}$
$\frac{1}{5}$				

Animated Glossary, eTools
www.pearsonsuccessnet.com

DIGITAL

For **9** through **11**, write each number as a mixed number or improper fraction.

9. $4\frac{2}{3}$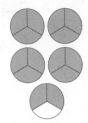

10. $\frac{10}{3}$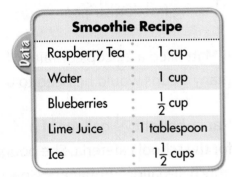

11. $1\frac{1}{2}$

Problem Solving

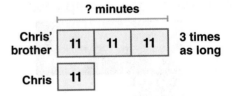

MATHEMATICAL PRACTICES

12. Jeremy used this recipe to make a smoothie. How many $\frac{1}{2}$-cups of ice does Jeremy need?

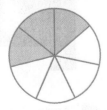

Smoothie Recipe	
Raspberry Tea	1 cup
Water	1 cup
Blueberries	$\frac{1}{2}$ cup
Lime Juice	1 tablespoon
Ice	$1\frac{1}{2}$ cups

© 13. Use Tools Chris finished eating his lunch in 11 minutes. His brother took 3 times as long. How many minutes did it take his brother to finish his lunch?

14. Sara bought a box of 6 granola bars. The total weight was $7\frac{1}{3}$ ounces. Write $7\frac{1}{3}$ as an improper fraction.

© 15. Critique Reasoning Kathy wrote the mixed number for $\frac{35}{5}$ as $\frac{7}{5}$. Is she correct? Why or why not?

16. Julia bought $3\frac{1}{4}$ yards of fabric. How many $\frac{1}{4}$-yards of fabric did Julia buy?

17. In one week, Nate drank $\frac{17}{3}$ cups of milk. Write $\frac{17}{3}$ as a mixed number.

18. What fraction or mixed number does this model show?

© 19. Persevere The average milk cow produces $4\frac{1}{2}$ gallons of milk a day. How much milk is this amount as an improper fraction?

A $\frac{11}{9}$ gallons   C $\frac{9}{2}$ gallons

B $\frac{19}{9}$ gallons   D $\frac{19}{2}$ gallon

Mixed Problem Solving

Artists frequently mix base colors together to create different hues of paint for use in paintings. They begin with three primary colors: blue, red, and yellow. The colors that are produced depend upon the fractions of paints that are combined.

Mr. McCrory is mixing paints together to create colors to use in some oil paintings. The chart at the right shows the fraction of a tube of paint he used to make each color.

Paint 1	$\frac{1}{4}$ blue	$\frac{1}{6}$ red	$\frac{5}{6}$ yellow
Paint 2	$\frac{3}{4}$ red	$\frac{1}{3}$ yellow	$\frac{5}{8}$ blue
Color	Purple	Orange	Green

1. Use fraction strips to compare the fractions of color paint that were used to make purple. Then compare the fractions used to make orange. Write the fractions from *greatest* to *least*.

2. Use benchmark fractions to compare the fractions of paint used to make green. Write the fractions from *least* to *greatest*.

3. Jared painted on a canvas using different colored paint. The chart at the right shows the fractional amount of each tube of paint that was used. Order each fraction from *least* to *greatest*.

Color of paint	Blue	Red	Yellow	White
Amount used	$\frac{2}{3}$	$\frac{6}{12}$	$\frac{3}{4}$	$\frac{4}{10}$

4. Elsie took a course on making stained glass at the community art center. She made a sun catcher that was $\frac{2}{6}$ green-colored glass, $\frac{1}{2}$ yellow-colored glass, and $\frac{1}{6}$ red-colored glass. Was more of her sun catcher made up of green or yellow colored glass? Draw a model to show your answer.

5. A flag is made up of fractional colors. $\frac{1}{2}$ of the flag is blue, and $\frac{1}{4}$ is white. The rest of the flag is made up of $\frac{2}{12}$ red and $\frac{1}{12}$ green. Order the fractions of color from *least* to *greatest*.

Common
Core

4.NF.3.c Add and subtract
mixed numbers with like
denominators, e.g., by
replacing each mixed
number with an equivalent
fraction, and/or by using
properties of operations
and the relationship
between addition and
subtraction. Also 4.NF.3.b

Modeling Addition and Subtraction of Mixed Numbers

Hands-On
fraction strips

$\frac{1}{8}$

How can you model addition of mixed numbers?

Jill has 2 boards she will use to make picture frames. What is the total length of the boards Jill has to make picture frames?

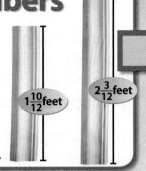

$1\frac{10}{12}$feet $2\frac{3}{12}$feet

Choose an Operation Add to find the total length.

Another Example How can you model subtraction of mixed numbers?

Find $2\frac{3}{8} - 1\frac{7}{8}$.

Step 1

Model the number you are subtracting from, $2\frac{3}{8}$.

If the fraction you will be subtracting is greater than the fraction of the number you model, rename 1 whole.

Since $\frac{7}{8} > \frac{3}{8}$, rename 1 whole as $\frac{8}{8}$.

Step 2

Use your renamed model to cross out the number that you are subtracting, $1\frac{7}{8}$.

There are $\frac{4}{8}$ left.

So, $2\frac{3}{8} - 1\frac{7}{8} = \frac{4}{8}$.

Simplify: $\frac{4}{8} = \frac{1}{2}$

Explain It

1. In the example above, why is $2\frac{3}{8}$ renamed as $1\frac{11}{8}$?

Guided Practice*

Do you know HOW?

Use fraction strips to find each sum or difference. Simplify, if possible.

1. $2\frac{3}{5} + 1\frac{4}{5}$ **2.** $4\frac{1}{4} - 3\frac{3}{4}$

3. $5\frac{1}{6} - 3\frac{3}{6}$ **4.** $3\frac{2}{3} + 2\frac{2}{3}$

Do you UNDERSTAND?

5. How is renaming to add mixed numbers different from regrouping to add whole numbers?

6. When adding two mixed numbers is it always necessary to rename the fractional sum? Explain.

306   *For another example, see Set G on page 322.

Model the addends and add the fractional parts.

$2\frac{3}{12}$

$+ 1\frac{10}{12}$

$\frac{13}{12}$

Rename $\frac{13}{12}$ as $1\frac{1}{12}$.

Now add the whole numbers, including the renamed fraction.

$2 + 1 + 1 = 4$

So, $2\frac{3}{12} + 1\frac{10}{12} = 4\frac{1}{12}$.

The total length of the boards is $4\frac{1}{12}$ feet.

Independent Practice

MATHEMATICAL PRACTICES

In **7** and **8**, use each model to find the sum or difference. Simplify if possible.

7. Charles used $1\frac{1}{3}$ cups of blueberries and $2\frac{1}{3}$ cups of cranberries to make breakfast bread. How many cups of blueberries and cranberries did he use in all?

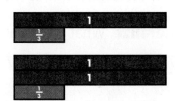

8. Eva ran to her friend's apartment in $2\frac{4}{6}$ minutes. It took Eva $4\frac{3}{6}$ minutes to go back home. How much more time did Eva take to get home?

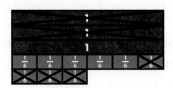

© **Use Tools** In **9** through **16**, use fraction strips to find each sum or difference. Simplify if possible.

9. $5\frac{3}{6} - 2\frac{4}{6}$

10. $2\frac{2}{5} + 3\frac{4}{5}$

11. $4\frac{9}{10} + 3\frac{7}{10}$

12. $1\frac{1}{3} + 3\frac{2}{3}$

13. $1\frac{3}{4} + 2\frac{2}{4}$

14. $12\frac{3}{8} - 9\frac{5}{8}$

15. $2\frac{5}{12} + 4\frac{7}{12}$

16. $13\frac{7}{9} - 10\frac{8}{9}$

eTools
www.pearsonsuccessnet.com

For **17** and **18**, use fraction strips to solve. Simplify, if possible.

17. Jim said, "On summer vacation, I spent $1\frac{3}{4}$ months with my grandma and $\frac{3}{4}$ month with my aunt."

    a How many months is that in all?

    b How many months longer did Jim spend with his grandmother than with his aunt?

18. Ethan used $1\frac{2}{3}$ gallons of yellow paint for the ceiling and $3\frac{2}{3}$ gallons of blue paint for the walls of his kitchen.

    a How much paint did Ethan use in all?

    b How much more blue paint did Ethan use than yellow paint?

For **19** through **21**, use the table at the right.

19. Sarah is making costumes for the school play. Write the amount of material for a peasant blouse as a mixed number.

20. Which costume requires the most fabric?

21. Which costume requires the least fabric?

Costume Shopping List	
Costume	**Yards**
Peasant skirt	$\frac{12}{3}$
Peasant vest	$\frac{9}{8}$
Peasant blouse	$\frac{9}{4}$

© **22. Generalize** What is the value of the underlined digit in 627?

    A 7 ten thousands   **B** 7 thousands   **C** 7 tens   **D** 7 ones

For **23** and **24**, use the table at the right.

23. Science How many inches longer is a Hercules beetle than a ladybug?

24. What is the difference between the largest and the smallest stag beetles? What is the sum of their lengths?

Beetles by Length	
Beetle	**Length in inches**
Hercules beetle	$6\frac{3}{4}$
Ladybug	$\frac{1}{4}$
Stag beetle	$1\frac{1}{8}$ to $2\frac{4}{8}$

25. Nicole, Tasha, Maria, and Joan ran a relay race. Nicole ran the first leg of the race in $1\frac{5}{6}$ minutes. Tasha ran the second leg in $2\frac{1}{6}$ minutes. Maria ran the third leg in $1\frac{5}{6}$ minutes. Joan ran the last leg in $2\frac{1}{6}$ minutes to finish the race.

    © **a Reason** How can you find how much faster Maria ran than Joan?

    b The team wanted to run the race in less than six minutes. Did they meet their goal? Explain.

Mixed Problem Solving

♪ **Music**

Different musical instruments make different sounds. The shape of an instrument can affect how it sounds. Use the table at the right to answer **1–4**.

1. Which instrument is made up of a long, narrow rectangular prism and a short cylinder?

2. Which of the percussion instruments has a cylinder shape?

3. Which instrument has the shape of a 3-sided figure?

4. What solid does the recorder look like?

5. The instrument that makes the sound with the greatest number of decibels is the loudest. Which instrument in the table below can make the loudest sound?

Data	Instrument	Maximum Loudness (in decibels)
	Trumpet	95
	Cymbal	110
	Bass drum	115
	Piano	100

Musical Instruments

Name of Instrument	Group of Instruments
Banjo	String
Drum	Percussion
Recorder	Woodwind
Triangle	Percussion

© 6. **Persevere** Solve. Use the strategy Work Backward.

Elian plays three instruments. The drum weighs 5 pounds more than the guitar. The trumpet weighs 5 pounds less than the guitar. The trumpet weighs 3 pounds. How many pounds does the drum weigh?

Common
Core

4.NF.3.c Add and subtract mixed numbers with like denominators, e.g., by replacing each mixed number with an equivalent fraction, and/or by using properties of operations and the relationship between addition and subtraction.

Adding Mixed Numbers

How can you add mixed numbers?

Brenda mixes sand with $2\frac{7}{8}$ cups of potting mixture to prepare soil for her plants. After mixing them together, how many cups of soil does Brenda have?

Choose an Operation Add to find the total amount of soil.

$1\frac{3}{8}$ cups

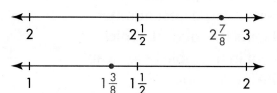 **Another Example** How can you check for reasonableness?

You just found that the sum of $2\frac{7}{8}$ and $1\frac{3}{8}$ is $4\frac{1}{4}$. You can use estimation to check that a sum is reasonable.

Estimate $2\frac{7}{8} + 1\frac{3}{8}$.

A number line can help you replace mixed numbers with the nearest one-half or whole unit.

$2\frac{7}{8}$ is close to 3.

$1\frac{3}{8}$ is close to $1\frac{1}{2}$.

Add: $3 + 1\frac{1}{2} = 4\frac{1}{2}$

Since both of the addends were replaced with larger numbers for the estimate, the actual answer will be less.

The actual sum, $4\frac{1}{4}$, is reasonable because it is close to the estimate, $4\frac{1}{2}$.

 **Guided Practice*** | **MATHEMATICAL PRACTICES**

Do you know HOW?

Find each sum. Simplify, if possible. Estimate to check for reasonableness.

1. $1\frac{7}{8}$
    $+ 1\frac{2}{8}$

2. $2\frac{4}{10}$
    $+ 5\frac{5}{10}$

3. $4\frac{2}{3} + 1\frac{2}{3}$

4. $6\frac{5}{12} + 4\frac{11}{12}$

Do you UNDERSTAND?

© **5. Reason** How is adding mixed numbers like adding fractions and whole numbers?

© **6. Writing to Explain** Alan used 9 as an estimate for $3\frac{7}{10} + 5\frac{4}{10}$. He added and got $9\frac{1}{10}$ for the actual sum. Is his answer reasonable?

For another example, see Set H on page 322.

Step 1

Find $2\frac{7}{8} + 1\frac{3}{8}$. Add the fractions.

$2\frac{7}{8}$ | $\frac{1}{8}$ $\frac{1}{8}$ $\frac{1}{8}$ $\frac{1}{8}$ $\frac{1}{8}$ $\frac{1}{8}$ $\frac{1}{8}$

$+1\frac{3}{8}$ | $\frac{1}{8}$ $\frac{1}{8}$ $\frac{1}{8}$

$\frac{10}{8}$ | $\frac{1}{8}$ $\frac{1}{8}$ $\frac{1}{8}$ $\frac{1}{8}$ $\frac{1}{8}$ $\frac{1}{8}$ $\frac{1}{8}$ $\frac{1}{8}$ $\frac{1}{8}$ $\frac{1}{8}$

Step 2

Add the whole numbers. Simplify the sum if possible.

$2\frac{7}{8}$

$+1\frac{3}{8}$

$3\frac{10}{8}$

$3\frac{10}{8} = 4\frac{2}{8} = 4\frac{1}{4}$

Brenda prepared $4\frac{1}{4}$ cups of soil.

Independent Practice

Leveled Practice For **7** through **18**, find each sum and simplify, if possible. Check for reasonableness.

7. $\quad 2\frac{5}{6}$

$\quad +5\frac{4}{6}$

8. $\quad 11\frac{7}{10}$

$\quad +10\frac{9}{10}$

9. $\quad 9\frac{7}{8}$

$\quad +7\frac{5}{8}$

10. $\quad 5\frac{7}{8}$

$\quad +8\frac{1}{8}$

11. $4\frac{1}{10} + 6\frac{5}{10}$

12. $9\frac{7}{12} + 4\frac{9}{12}$

13. $5 + 3\frac{1}{8}$

14. $8\frac{3}{4} + 7\frac{3}{4}$

15. $2\frac{4}{5} + 7\frac{3}{5}$

16. $3\frac{2}{6} + 8\frac{5}{6}$

17. $1\frac{7}{12} + 2\frac{10}{12}$

18. $3\frac{6}{8} + 9\frac{3}{8}$

Problem Solving

MATHEMATICAL
PRACTICES

ⓒ 19. Persevere Joe biked $1\frac{9}{12}$ miles from home to the lake, then went $1\frac{3}{12}$ miles around the lake, and then back home. How many miles did he bike?

A $2\frac{1}{12}$ miles

B $3\frac{1}{12}$ miles

C $4\frac{3}{4}$ miles

D $4\frac{5}{12}$ miles

20. a Use the map below to find the distance from the start of the trail to the end.

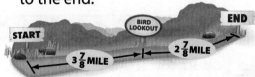

b Linda walked from the start of the trail to the bird lookout and back. Did she walk more or less than if she had walked from the start of the trail to the end?

21. The length of a male Parson's chameleon can be up to $23\frac{2}{4}$ inches. It can extend its tongue up to $35\frac{1}{4}$ inches to catch its food. What is the total length of a male Parson's chameleon when its tongue is fully extended?

©
Common
Core

4.NF.3.c Add and subtract mixed numbers with like denominators, e.g., by replacing each mixed number with an equivalent fraction, and/or by using properties of operations and the relationship between addition and subtraction.

Subtracting Mixed Numbers

How can you subtract mixed numbers?

A golf ball measures about $1\frac{4}{6}$ inches across the center. What is the difference between the distance across the center of a tennis ball and the golf ball?

Choose an Operation Subtract to find the difference.

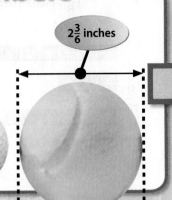

$2\frac{3}{6}$ inches

Another Example **How can you check for reasonableness?**

You just found that the difference of $2\frac{3}{6}$ and $1\frac{4}{6}$ is $\frac{5}{6}$. You can use estimation to check that a difference is reasonable.

Estimate $2\frac{3}{6} - 1\frac{4}{6}$.

$2\frac{3}{6}$ is the same as $2\frac{1}{2}$.

$1\frac{4}{6}$ is close to $1\frac{1}{2}$.

Subtract: $2\frac{1}{2} - 1\frac{1}{2} = 1$.

The actual difference, $\frac{5}{6}$, is reasonable because it is close to the estimate, 1.

Guided Practice*

MATHEMATICAL
PRACTICES

Do you know HOW?

Find each difference and simplify, if possible. Check for reasonableness.

1. $7\frac{3}{8} = 6\frac{\square}{8}$

   $-\ 2\frac{4}{8} = 2\frac{\square}{8}$

2. $5\ \ \ = \ \ \frac{\square}{4}$

   $-\ 2\frac{3}{4} = \ \ 2\frac{3}{4}$

3. $6\frac{3}{10} - 1\frac{8}{10}$

4. $9\frac{4}{12} - 4\frac{9}{12}$

Do you UNDERSTAND?

5. In Exercise 2, why do you need to rename the 5?

© 6. **Reasonableness** Could two golf balls fall into a hole that is $3\frac{3}{6}$ inches across at the same time? Explain your reasoning.

For another example, see Set I on page 322.

Subtract the smaller number from the larger number.

$2\frac{3}{6}$
$-1\frac{4}{6}$

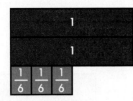

 Tip You cannot subtract $\frac{4}{6}$ from $\frac{3}{6}$.

Rename $2\frac{3}{6}$ to show more sixths.

$2\frac{3}{6} = 1\frac{9}{6}$
$-\ 1\frac{4}{6} = 1\frac{4}{6}$

Tip $1 = \frac{6}{6}$

Subtract the fractions. Then subtract the whole numbers.

$2\frac{3}{6} = 1\frac{9}{6}$
$-\ 1\frac{4}{6} = 1\frac{4}{6}$
$\overline{\phantom{-1\frac{4}{6}=1}\frac{5}{6}}$

The tennis ball is $\frac{5}{6}$ inch wider.

Independent Practice

Leveled Practice For **7** through **18**, find each difference and simplify, if possible. Check for reasonableness.

7. $8\frac{2}{8} = 7\frac{}{8}$
　　$-\ 2\frac{7}{8} = 2\frac{}{8}$

8. $4\frac{5}{10} = 3\frac{}{10}$
　　$-\ 1\frac{9}{10} = 1\frac{}{10}$

9. $4\frac{1}{8}$
　　$-\ 1\frac{4}{8}$

10. 6
　　$-\ 2\frac{4}{5}$

11. $6\frac{1}{3} - 5\frac{2}{3}$

12. $9\frac{2}{4} - 6\frac{3}{4}$

13. $8\frac{3}{8} - 3\frac{5}{8}$

14. $7 - 3\frac{1}{2}$

15. $15\frac{1}{6} - 4\frac{5}{6}$

16. $13\frac{1}{12} - 8\frac{3}{12}$

17. $6\frac{2}{5} - 2\frac{3}{5}$

18. $10\frac{5}{10} - 4\frac{7}{10}$

Problem Solving

 MATHEMATICAL PRACTICES

19. The average weight of a basketball is $21\frac{1}{8}$ ounces. The average weight of a baseball is $5\frac{2}{8}$ ounces. How many more ounces does the basketball weigh?

　　A $15\frac{1}{8}$　　**B** $15\frac{7}{8}$　　**C** $16\frac{1}{8}$　　**D** $16\frac{7}{8}$

© **20. Reason** As of 2008, the world's shortest horse is Thumbelina. She is $17\frac{1}{4}$ inches tall. The second shortest horse, Black Beauty, is $18\frac{2}{4}$ inches tall. How much shorter is Thumbelina than Black Beauty?

21. The smallest mammals on Earth are the bumblebee bat and the Etruscan pygmy shrew. The length of a bumblebee bat is $1\frac{1}{5}$ inches. The length of an Etruscan pygmy shrew is $1\frac{2}{5}$ inches. How much smaller is the bat than the shrew?

© **22. Writing to Explain** How are the parallelogram and the rectangle alike? How are they different?

Lesson
12-10

Ⓒ
Common
Core

4.NF.3.b Decompose a
fraction into a sum of
fractions with the same
denominator in more
than one way, recording
each decomposition by
an equation. Justify
decompositions, e.g., by
using a visual fraction
model. Also 4.NF.3.d

Decomposing and Composing Fractions

How can you use addition to represent a fraction in a variety of ways?

Charlene wants to leave $\frac{1}{6}$ of her garden empty. What are some different ways she can plant the rest of her garden?

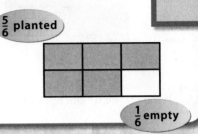

$\frac{5}{6}$ planted

$\frac{1}{6}$ empty

Another Example **How can you use addition to show a mixed number in a variety of ways?**

Jeanie had $3\frac{1}{8}$ sections of a garden to divide equally. How can you use addition to show $3\frac{1}{8}$ as a composition of fractions?

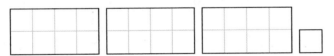

Each whole can be shown as eight equal parts.

$3\frac{1}{8} = \frac{8}{8} + \frac{8}{8} + \frac{8}{8} + \frac{1}{8}$

Guided Practice*

Ⓒ MATHEMATICAL
PRACTICES

Do you know HOW?

Write each of the following fractions or mixed numbers as a sum of two or three fractions in two different ways.

1. $\frac{3}{5} = \blacksquare + \blacksquare$ $\frac{3}{5} = \blacksquare + \blacksquare + \blacksquare$

2. $1\frac{3}{4} = \blacksquare + \blacksquare$ $1\frac{3}{4} = \blacksquare + \blacksquare + \blacksquare$

Do you UNDERSTAND?

3. Draw a picture to show why both of these equations are true.

$\frac{5}{6} = \frac{3}{6} + \frac{2}{6}$ $\frac{5}{6} = \frac{1}{6} + \frac{2}{6} + \frac{2}{6}$

Ⓒ **4. Critique Reasoning** Remegio said that the sum for $\frac{1}{10} + \frac{7}{10} + \frac{4}{10}$ is the same as $\frac{5}{10} + \frac{5}{10} + \frac{2}{10}$. Is he correct? Explain.

She could plant 4 sections of blue flowers and 1 section of red peppers.

$\frac{5}{6}$ planted

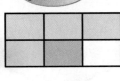

$\frac{1}{6}$ empty

$$\frac{5}{6} = \frac{4}{6} + \frac{1}{6}$$

She could plant 1 section of green beans, 1 section of yellow squash, 1 section of red peppers, and 2 sections of blue flowers.

$\frac{5}{6}$ planted

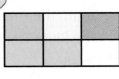

$\frac{1}{6}$ empty

$$\frac{5}{6} = \frac{1}{6} + \frac{1}{6} + \frac{1}{6} + \frac{2}{6}$$

Independent Practice

For **5** through **12** find the sum. Then write another addition problem that has the same sum and uses two or more fractions.

5. $\frac{1}{4} + \frac{3}{4} + \frac{3}{4}$

6. $\frac{3}{5} + \frac{3}{5} + \frac{1}{5}$

7. $\frac{3}{10} + \frac{3}{10} + \frac{2}{10}$

8. $\frac{2}{3} + \frac{2}{3} + \frac{1}{3}$

9. $1\frac{1}{2} + \frac{1}{2} + 2\frac{1}{2}$

10. $\frac{3}{6} + \frac{1}{6} + \frac{1}{6}$

11. $\frac{5}{8} + \frac{7}{8} + \frac{3}{8}$

12. $\frac{4}{12} + \frac{6}{12} + \frac{1}{12}$

Problem Solving

MATHEMATICAL PRACTICES

13. DeAnna walked $\frac{1}{8}$ mile to the park, then $\frac{4}{8}$ mile to the store, and finally $\frac{2}{8}$ mile home. How far did DeAnna walk in all?

A $\frac{5}{8}$ mile

C $\frac{7}{8}$ mile

B $\frac{6}{8}$ mile

D $1\frac{1}{8}$ miles

14. Justin read $\frac{2}{6}$ of his book on Monday, $\frac{1}{6}$ of his book on Tuesday, and $\frac{2}{6}$ of his book on Saturday. How much of his book did Justin read in all?

A $\frac{3}{6}$

C $1\frac{5}{6}$

B $\frac{5}{6}$

D $2\frac{2}{6}$

ⓒ **15. Persevere** Serena is wrapping presents, she has $\frac{3}{4}$ yard of red ribbons for wrapping. If she used $\frac{1}{4}$ yard of red ribbon to wrap a present and $\frac{1}{4}$ yard of red ribbon to decorate a card, what fraction amount of ribbon is left?

A $\frac{1}{4}$ yard

C $\frac{3}{4}$ yard

B $\frac{2}{4}$ yard

D $1\frac{1}{4}$ yards

ⓒ **16. Model** At the first stop, a bus picks up $\frac{2}{5}$ of the number of passengers it can carry. At the second stop, it picks up $\frac{3}{5}$ of the number of passengers it can carry. If the bus drops off $\frac{1}{5}$ of its passengers on the third stop, what fraction of the total number of passengers will be left? Use fraction strips to model.

Ⓒ
Common
Core

4.NF.3.d Solve word problems involving addition and subtraction of fractions referring to the same whole and having like denominators, e.g., by using visual fraction models and equations to represent the problem. Also **4.NF.3.a**

Problem Solving

Draw a Picture and Write an Equation

Marie and her mother hiked three trails, the Ansel Trail, The Briar Trail, and the River Trail. How far did they walk in all?

Ansel Trail	$\frac{7}{8}$	Mile
Briar Trail	$\frac{3}{8}$	Mile
River Trail	$\frac{5}{8}$	Mile

Another Example Regina and Don are hiking a trail. They have already hiked $\frac{1}{12}$ of a mile. How much farther do they have to travel to reach the $\frac{11}{12}$-mile mark?

Write an equation and subtract the fractions.

Let x = how much farther they have to travel.

$\frac{11}{12}$ = the total distance of the hike

$\frac{1}{12}$ = the distance already hiked

$\frac{11}{12} - \frac{1}{12} = x$

$x = \frac{10}{12} = \frac{5}{6}$

$\frac{11}{12}$ of a mile in all

$\frac{1}{12}$	x

Regina and Don need to hike $\frac{5}{6}$ of a mile farther to reach the $\frac{11}{12}$-mile mark.

Explain It

1. How could you find how much farther Regina and Don will have to hike to reach one mile?

Ⓒ 2. **Reason** If Regina and Don turn around and hike back $\frac{1}{12}$ of a mile, how can you find the difference between the total length they traveled and $\frac{11}{12}$ of a mile?

What do I know?

Marie and her mother hiked 3 trails.

Ansel Trail = $\frac{7}{8}$ mi

Briar Trail = $\frac{3}{8}$ mi

River Trail = $\frac{5}{8}$ mi

What am I asked to find?

How far did Marie and her mother walk in all?

Let x = total miles hiked

x miles in all

$\frac{7}{8}$	$\frac{3}{8}$	$\frac{5}{8}$

Write an equation and add the fractions.

$x = \frac{7}{8} + \frac{3}{8} + \frac{5}{8} = \frac{15}{8}$ or $1\frac{7}{8}$ miles

Marie and her mother walked $1\frac{7}{8}$ miles in all.

Guided Practice*

MATHEMATICAL PRACTICES

Do you know HOW?

Draw a picture and write an equation to solve.

1. Heather ran $\frac{2}{6}$ of a mile. Rick ran $\frac{1}{6}$ of a mile. How much farther did Heather run than Rick?

Do you UNDERSTAND?

2. Writing to Explain If you were asked to find how far Marie and her mother walked on the Briar and River Trails alone, would the model be different?

3. Write a Problem Write a problem that you can solve by drawing a picture and writing an equation.

Independent Practice

MATHEMATICAL PRACTICES

Model Draw a picture and write an equation to solve.

4. Barb connected a wire extension that is $\frac{7}{12}$ foot long to another wire that is $\frac{11}{12}$ foot long. How long is the wire with the extension?

x feet

$\frac{7}{12}$	$\frac{11}{12}$

5. The smallest female spider measures about $\frac{5}{10}$ millimeter (mm) in length. The smallest male spider measures about $\frac{4}{10}$ mm in length. How much longer is the female spider than the male spider?

$\frac{5}{10}$ mm long

$\frac{4}{10}$	x

Applying Math Practices

- What am I asked to find?
- What else can I try?
- How are quantities related?
- How can I explain my work?
- How can I use math to model the problem?
- Can I use tools to help?
- Is my work precise?
- Why does this work?
- How can I generalize?

For another example, see Set K on page 323.

6. A recipe calls for 3 times as many carrots as peas. If Clara used 2 cups of peas, how many cups of carrots will she use?

x cups of carrots

| Carrots | 2 | 2 | 2 | ← 3 times as many |

| Peas | 2 |

© 7. Use Tools Freddie bought $\frac{5}{6}$ pound of peanuts. He ate $\frac{3}{6}$ pound of the peanuts with his friends. How much did Freddie have left?

$\frac{5}{6}$ pound of peanuts

| $\frac{3}{6}$ | *x* |

8. Buck's dog has a square pen. The length of one side of the pen is 7 feet. What is the perimeter of the pen?

9. Daryll has 9 books about space and 3 books about trains. His brother says $\frac{3}{4}$ of his books are about space. Terrence says that $\frac{9}{12}$ of his books are about space. Who is correct? Explain your answer.

© 10. Writing to Explain If the perimeter of the parallelogram below is 56 inches, and you know one side is 8 inches, will you be able to find the length of the other 3 sides? Why or why not?

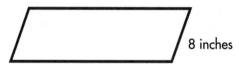
8 inches

11. A banana bread recipe calls for $\frac{6}{8}$ cup of mashed bananas and $\frac{1}{8}$ cup of pecans. Draw a picture and write an equation to find the total amount of bananas and pecans added to the recipe.

© Think About the Structure

12. Four relay team members skate an equal part of an 8-kilometer race. Which equation shows how far each member skates?

  A $4 + 2 = 6$ **C** $2 + 2 + 2 = 6$

  B $8 ÷ 4 = 2$ **D** $8 + 4 = 12$

13. Janie took a handful of jellybeans from a jar. She had 3 green, 4 red, and 4 licorice jellybeans. Which equation tells how many of Janie's jellybeans were not licorice?

  A $4 - 3 = 1$ **C** $3 + 4 + 4 = 11$

  B $11 - 4 = 7$ **D** $7 × 4 = 28$

Algebra Connections

What's the Conversion Rule?

How can you use tables to find out how two units are related?

The rules for converting one unit into another are not always given. Sometimes it is necessary to compare two different units.

A dram is a small customary unit of weight.

How many drams are there in an ounce?

Ounces	Drams
2	32
4	64
5	

Think How are these units related?

2×16 drams per ounce = 32 drams
4×16 drams per ounce = 64 drams
So, there are 16 drams in 1 ounce.

How many drams are there in 5 ounces?
$5 \times 16 = 80$ drams

In **1** through **4**, complete the tables and find a rule of conversion.

1.

Dash	Teaspoon
8	1
16	2
24	
32	

8 dashes per teaspoon

2.

Hogshead	Gallon
1	63
2	
4	252
5	

63 gallons per hogshead

3.

Quart	Peck
16	2
24	3
40	5
56	

8 quarts per peck

4.

Bushel	Peck
	8
4	16
6	
7	28

4 pecks per bushel

5. A "stone" is an old unit of weight used in Ireland and England to measure potatoes. A stone is 14 pounds, and 160 stones make up a "long ton." How many pounds is a long ton?

6. A furlong is a unit of length still used today in racing and agriculture. A race that is 8 furlongs is 1 mile. A furlong is 660 feet. How many feet are in 1 mile?

7. A famous novel by Jules Verne is titled *20,000 Leagues Under the Sea*. A league is a nautical measurement equal to 3 miles. The deepest point in the ocean is about 6.84 miles. About how many leagues deep can you actually go?

8. Neil is reading a sign of old measures of volume from England. He sees that there are 2 pecks in 1 kenning. There are 2 kennings in 1 bushel. There are 2 bushels in 1 strike. There are 4 strikes in 1 quarter. There are 4 quarters in 1 chaldron. Write a number sentence to show the number of pecks in a chaldron.

Set A, pages 290–291

While Ricardo's family was bird watching, they spotted eight loons. There were five in the water, one in the air, and two walking on land. What fraction of the loons did they see in the water or on land?

Add the fraction of the total loons that were in the water to the fraction of the total loons that were on land. Use fraction strips.

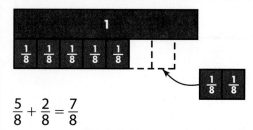

$$\frac{5}{8} + \frac{2}{8} = \frac{7}{8}$$

Remember that you can use fraction strips to model addition of fractions.

Add. Simplify if possible.

1. $\frac{2}{4} + \frac{2}{4}$

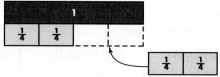

2. $\frac{3}{6} + \frac{2}{6}$

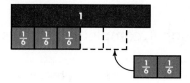

Set B, pages 292–293

Add $\frac{4}{12} + \frac{5}{12}$. Write in simplest form.

Step 1

Add the numerators; keep the denominator.

$$\frac{4}{12} + \frac{5}{12} = \frac{9}{12}$$

Step 2

Simplify the sum if possible.

$$\frac{9 \div 3}{12 \div 3} = \frac{3}{4}$$

Remember to add the numerators when denominators are the same.

Add. Simplify if possible.

1. $\frac{2}{5} + \frac{2}{5}$ 2. $\frac{1}{4} + \frac{1}{4}$

3. $\frac{3}{8} + \frac{4}{8}$ 4. $\frac{4}{10} + \frac{2}{10}$

Set C, pages 294–295

Use fraction strips to subtract $\frac{5}{8} - \frac{2}{8}$.

Use five $\frac{1}{8}$ strips to model $\frac{5}{8}$. Take two strips away.

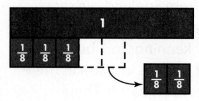

Three strips are left.

$$\frac{5}{8} - \frac{2}{8} = \frac{3}{8}$$

Remember that you can use fraction strips to model subtraction of fractions.

Subtract. Simplify if possible.

1. $\frac{3}{3} - \frac{1}{3}$

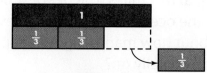

2. $\frac{3}{4} - \frac{2}{4}$

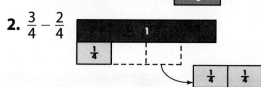

Subtract $\frac{7}{8} - \frac{5}{8}$. Write in simplest form.

Step 1

Subtract the numerators; keep the denominator.

$\frac{7}{8} - \frac{5}{8} = \frac{2}{8}$

Step 2

Simplify the difference if possible.

$\frac{2 \div 2}{8 \div 2} = \frac{1}{4}$

Remember that you can subtract the numerators when the denominators are the same.

Subtract the fractions. Write in simplest form, if possible.

1. $\frac{7}{10} - \frac{1}{10}$ 2. $\frac{10}{12} - \frac{3}{12}$

3. $\frac{4}{4} - \frac{2}{4}$ 4. $\frac{5}{6} - \frac{1}{6}$

5. $\frac{4}{8} - \frac{2}{8}$ 6. $\frac{4}{5} - \frac{1}{5}$

Find the sum or difference shown on the number line. Write in simplest form, if possible.

$\frac{2}{10} + \frac{4}{10} = \frac{6}{10} = \frac{3}{5}$

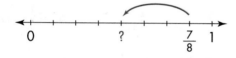

$\frac{7}{8} - \frac{3}{8} = \frac{4}{8} = \frac{1}{2}$

Remember when adding or subtracting fractions with like denominators on a number line, the denominator does not change.

Find the sum or difference shown on the number line. Write in simplest form, if possible.

1.

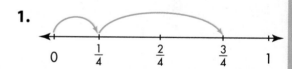

2.

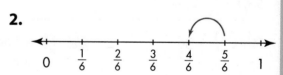

Write $\frac{7}{4}$ as a mixed number.

Use fraction strips.

1			
$\frac{1}{4}$	$\frac{1}{4}$	$\frac{1}{4}$	$\frac{1}{4}$

4 fourths in one whole

$\frac{1}{4}$	$\frac{1}{4}$	$\frac{1}{4}$

3 fourths

So, $\frac{7}{4} = 1\frac{3}{4}$

Remember you can use fraction strips to write a mixed number as an improper fraction.

Write each number as a mixed number or an improper fraction.

1. $2\frac{2}{5}$ 2. $\frac{9}{4}$

Set G, pages 306–308

Find $2\frac{1}{6} - 1\frac{5}{6}$.

Step 1 Model the number you are subtracting from and rename 1 whole if necessary to subtract.

Step 2 Use your renamed model to cross out the number you are subtracting.

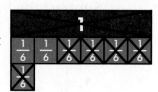

$$2\frac{1}{6} - 1\frac{5}{6} = \frac{2}{6}$$

Step 3 Write the answer in simplest form: $\frac{2}{6} = \frac{1}{3}$

Remember that when you use a model to add mixed numbers, you should rename improper fractions in the sum.

Use a model to find each sum or difference. Simplify, if possible.

1. $2\frac{1}{4} + 3\frac{3}{4}$ 2. $6\frac{2}{3} + 5\frac{2}{3}$

3. $7\frac{5}{8} + 8\frac{7}{8}$ 4. $12\frac{1}{4} - 7\frac{2}{4}$

5. $15\frac{3}{5} - 3\frac{4}{5}$ 6. $5\frac{5}{8} - 3\frac{1}{8}$

Set H, pages 310–311

Find $1\frac{7}{8} + 2\frac{3}{8}$.

$$1\frac{7}{8}$$
$$+ 2\frac{3}{8}$$
$$\overline{3\frac{10}{8}} = 4\frac{2}{8} = 4\frac{1}{4}$$

Step 1 Add the fractions.

Step 2 Add the whole numbers.

Step 3 Rename improper fractions and simplify the sum, if possible.

Remember that mixed numbers are added the same way whole numbers and fractions are added.

Find each sum. Simplify, if possible.

1. $5\frac{4}{8} + 2\frac{1}{8}$ 2. $3\frac{3}{6} + 1\frac{5}{6}$

3. $5\frac{7}{10} + 4\frac{4}{10}$ 4. $7\frac{3}{5} + 6\frac{3}{5}$

5. $8\frac{2}{3} + 9\frac{1}{3}$ 6. $2\frac{5}{12} + 3\frac{9}{12}$

Set I, pages 312–313

Find $5\frac{1}{5} - 3\frac{3}{5}$.

$$5\frac{1}{5} = 4\frac{6}{5}$$
$$- 3\frac{3}{5} = 3\frac{3}{5}$$
$$\overline{\qquad 1\frac{3}{5}}$$

Step 1 Rename $5\frac{1}{5}$ to show more fifths.

Step 2 Subtract the fractions.

Step 3 Subtract the whole numbers. Simplify the difference, if possible.

Remember that subtracting mixed numbers may require renaming.

Find each difference. Simplify, if possible.

1. $7\frac{5}{6} - 3\frac{4}{6}$ 2. $2\frac{6}{10} - 1\frac{5}{10}$

3. $5\frac{4}{6} - 4\frac{5}{6}$ 4. $9 - 3\frac{3}{8}$

5. $3\frac{1}{3} - 1\frac{2}{3}$ 6. $6\frac{1}{5} - 3\frac{2}{5}$

7. $9\frac{2}{8} - 2\frac{5}{8}$ 8. $4 - 1\frac{2}{5}$

A zoo wants to keep $\frac{1}{8}$ of its habitat sections empty. Show two different ways they could fill the remaining habitat sections with monkeys, giraffes, and elephants.

$\frac{7}{8}$ of habitat sections occupied

The zoo could put monkeys in $\frac{2}{8}$ of the habitat, giraffes in $\frac{3}{8}$, and elephants in $\frac{2}{8}$.

$\frac{2}{8} + \frac{3}{8} + \frac{2}{8} = \frac{7}{8}$

Or, they could put elephants in $\frac{4}{8}$ of the habitat, giraffes in $\frac{2}{8}$, and monkeys in $\frac{1}{8}$.

$\frac{4}{8} + \frac{2}{8} + \frac{1}{8} = \frac{7}{8}$

Remember You can use fraction strips to add fractions with like denominators.

Find the sum of the fractions or mixed numbers. Simplify, if possible.

1. $\frac{1}{3} + \frac{2}{3} + \frac{1}{3}$

2. $\frac{3}{8} + \frac{1}{8} + \frac{2}{8}$

3. $2\frac{3}{4} + 1\frac{2}{4}$

4. $\frac{4}{6} + \frac{4}{6}$

5. $\frac{5}{12} + \frac{6}{12} + \frac{7}{12}$

6. $4\frac{1}{2} + 2\frac{1}{2} + 1\frac{1}{2}$

Add the fractions and then show another way the sum could be shown.

7. $\frac{1}{10} + \frac{1}{10} + \frac{9}{10}$

8. $\frac{1}{5} + \frac{2}{5} + \frac{3}{5}$

Tina and Andy are building a model airplane. Tina built $\frac{6}{10}$ of the model, and Andy built $\frac{4}{10}$. How much more has Tina built than Andy?

Tina	$\frac{6}{10}$	
Andy	$\frac{4}{10}$	x

Find a common denominator and subtract.

So, $x = \frac{6}{10} - \frac{4}{10} = \frac{2}{10}$ or $\frac{1}{5}$

Tina built $\frac{1}{5}$ more of the model than Andy.

Remember to use a picture to help you write an equation.

1. Bonnie ran $\frac{2}{8}$ of a mile. Olga ran $\frac{1}{8}$ of a mile. How much farther did Bonnie run than Olga?

2. Linda's plant was $\frac{9}{12}$ foot tall. Macy's plant was $\frac{8}{12}$ foot tall. How much taller is Linda's plant than Macy's?

Multiple Choice

1. Paul found that $\frac{2}{8} + \frac{5}{8} = \frac{7}{8}$. Which of the following is another way to show $\frac{7}{8}$? (12-10)

A $\quad \frac{3}{8} + \frac{3}{8}$

B $\quad \frac{1}{8} + \frac{5}{8} + \frac{2}{8}$

C $\quad \frac{3}{3} + \frac{4}{5}$

D $\quad \frac{1}{8} + \frac{1}{8} + \frac{1}{8} + \frac{1}{8} + \frac{1}{8} + \frac{1}{8} + \frac{1}{8}$

2. On Friday, $\frac{3}{12}$ of the students in class were absent. What fraction of the students attended class? (12-3)

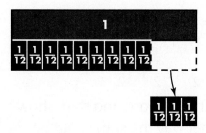

A $\quad \frac{12}{12}$

B $\quad \frac{9}{12}$

C $\quad \frac{8}{12}$

D $\quad \frac{3}{12}$

3. Rick made a paper football that was $\frac{7}{8}$ inch long. Carly made one that is $\frac{5}{8}$ inch long. How many inches longer is Rick's paper football than Carly's? (12-4)

A $\quad \frac{1}{4}$ inch

B $\quad \frac{1}{2}$ inch

C $\quad \frac{3}{4}$ inch

D $\quad \frac{3}{2}$ inches

4. What is the sum of $4\frac{5}{6} + 3\frac{5}{6}$? (12-8)

A $\quad 8\frac{5}{6}$ C $\quad 7\frac{5}{6}$

B $\quad 8\frac{4}{6}$ D $\quad 7\frac{1}{6}$

5. Which equation is represented on the number line below? (12-5)

A $\quad \frac{6}{10} - \frac{2}{10} = \frac{4}{10}$

B $\quad \frac{6}{10} + \frac{2}{10} = \frac{8}{10}$

C $\quad \frac{6}{6} + \frac{2}{2} = \frac{8}{8}$

D $\quad \frac{10}{10} - \frac{10}{10} = \frac{2}{10}$

6. Manny used the computer for $\frac{2}{10}$ of his time before school, and $\frac{3}{10}$ of his time after school. Which of the following can be used to find how much of his time was spent on the computer? (12-2)

A Add 10 + 10, and write the sum over 2 + 3 to get $\frac{20}{5}$. Simplify $\frac{20}{5}$ to $\frac{4}{1}$.

B Add 2 + 3, and write the sum over 10 + 10 to get $\frac{5}{20}$. Simplify $\frac{5}{20}$ to $\frac{1}{5}$.

C Add 2 + 3, and write the sum over 10 to get $\frac{5}{10}$. Simplify $\frac{5}{10}$ to $\frac{1}{2}$.

D Add 2 + 3 and write the sum over 10 − 10 to get $\frac{5}{0}$.

7. Sean made a ribbon that was $3\frac{1}{6}$ inches long. Fran made one $1\frac{5}{6}$ of an inch long. How much longer was Sean's ribbon than Fran's? (12-9)

8. The Jacobys went on a 600-mile trip. On the first day they drove $5\frac{3}{4}$ hours and on the second day they drove $4\frac{3}{4}$ hours. How many hours did they drive during the first two days? (12-8)

9. The average length of an adult Rough Green snake is $\frac{5}{6}$ yard. The length for an Eastern Garter snake is $\frac{4}{6}$ yard. How much longer is a Rough Green snake than an Eastern Garter snake? (12-4)

10. Max is earning money to pay for his new trumpet. He earned $\frac{2}{5}$ of the money he needed last week and $\frac{1}{5}$ of the money this week. What fraction of the money has he earned? (12-1)

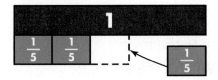

11. Roger and Su were finding ways to show the mixed number $1\frac{1}{6}$ as an addition of fractions. Roger wrote $\frac{1}{6} + \frac{1}{6} + \frac{2}{6} + \frac{3}{6}$. Su wrote $\frac{3}{6} + \frac{4}{6}$. Who was right? Explain. (12-10)

12. Yao drank $\frac{11}{4}$ bottles of water during a soccer game. What is this number written as a mixed number? (12-6)

13. Marie needs $2\frac{2}{8}$ yards of fabric. She already has $1\frac{3}{8}$ yards of fabric. How many more yards of fabric does she need? (12-9)

14. What is the sum of $1\frac{7}{8} + 2\frac{3}{8}$? (12-7)

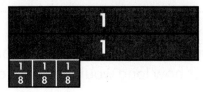

15. Tracey is at school for $7\frac{1}{4}$ hours each day. One day the school lets out early. She is at school for $3\frac{3}{4}$ hours that day. How much longer is a regular school day? Simplify, if possible. (12-7)

16. Rhys is kayaking down a $2\frac{3}{5}$-mile stream. He has already traveled $1\frac{1}{5}$ miles. How much farther does he need to travel? Draw a picture and write an equation to solve. (12-11)

Lia and Paul each have a length of rope.

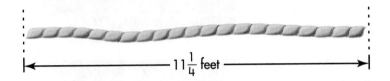

Lia's rope

Paul's rope

$10\frac{3}{4}$ feet

1. Lia untied the knot in her rope. The full length of the rope is shown below. How much rope did the knot use?

$11\frac{1}{4}$ feet

2. **Estimate** If Lia laid her untied rope end-to-end with Paul's rope, about how long would the two ropes be? Explain whether the actual length would be more or less than your estimate.

3. Lia and Paul tied their two ropes together with a square knot. The knot used $1\frac{3}{4}$ feet of rope. How long is their rope? Explain.

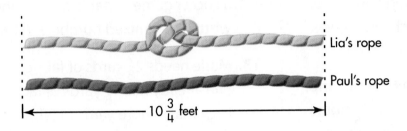

4. Toni had a rope measuring $9\frac{1}{4}$ feet. She tied her rope to the rope from **3** with another square knot that uses $1\frac{3}{4}$ feet. What is the total length of the rope with the 2 square knots? Show your work.

5. How would your answer to **4** change if Lia, Paul, and Toni laid their ropes end-to-end without knots? Explain how you found your answer.

Topic
13

Extending Fraction Concepts

▼ According to the Greek mathematician, Zeno, who lived in the fourth century B.C., this ball will never stop bouncing. You will find out why in Lesson 13-5.

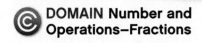

Review What You Know!

Vocabulary

Choose the best term from the box.

> • greater   • place value
> • digits   • number line

1. A ? is a line that shows numbers in order using a scale.

2. 245 is made up of the ? "2," "4," and "5."

3. In 738, the ? of the 7 is "hundreds."

4. The number 3,704 is ? than the number 3,407.

Comparing Numbers

Compare. Write >, <, or = for each ◯.

5. 1,909 ◯ 1,990

6. 43,627 ◯ 43,167

7. 629,348 ◯ 629,348

8. 455,311 ◯ 455,331

9. 101,101 ◯ 101,011

10. 95,559 ◯ 95,555

Ordering Numbers

Order the numbers from greatest to least.

11. 3,687   3,867   3,678   3,768

12. 41,101   41,011   41,110   41,001

13. 4,593   4,395   4,595   4,359

© **14. Writing to Explain** How would you order the numbers below from least to greatest? Explain.

15,420   154,200   1,542

Topic Essential Questions
• How is decimal numeration related to whole number numeration?
• How can decimals be compared and ordered?
• How are fractions and decimals related?

Interactive Learning

Pose the problem. Start each lesson by working together to solve problems. It will help you make sense of math.

Lesson 13-1

ⓒ **Use Structure** Write an explanation.

Kalil and Mara were working on their math homework. Mara had written $\frac{3}{4}$ as $\frac{1}{4} + \frac{1}{4} + \frac{1}{4}$. Kalil looked at it and said, "I think you could use multiplication to rewrite that." Is Kalil's observation correct? Explain.

$\frac{1}{4}$	$\frac{1}{4}$	$\frac{1}{4}$

Lesson 13-2

ⓒ **Use Structure** Solve any way you choose. Show your work.

How much tomato juice is needed for a group of 4 people if each person gets $\frac{1}{3}$ of a cup of juice? How much is needed if they each get $\frac{2}{3}$ of a cup of juice?

Lesson 13-3

ⓒ **Persevere** Solve. Use what you learned in the previous two lessons.

How much orange juice does it take to make 8 gallons of fruit punch if each gallon needs $\frac{3}{4}$ of a cup of orange juice?

Lesson 13-4

ⓒ **Use Structure** Solve.

In Allan's neighborhood, 2 out of 10 boys have a basketball hoop on their driveway. How can you write $\frac{2}{10}$ as a decimal? Explain.

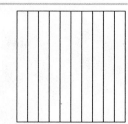

Lesson 13-5

ⓒ **Use Tools** Solve. Use the number line at the right to help.

Jacob jogged $\frac{3}{5}$ of a mile and walked $\frac{3}{10}$ of a mile to get to the park. Where would each of these fractions be shown on the number line? Tell how you decided.

Lesson 13-6

© **Communicate** Write an explanation.

Three fourths of the students in Mr. Brown's class have a younger brother or sister. How would you write $\frac{3}{4}$ as a decimal? Tell how you decided.

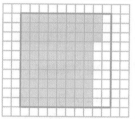
A good explanation should be:
- correct
- simple
- complete
- easy to understand

Lesson 13-7

© **Use Tools** Use the drawing at the right to complete this task.

Juan is competing in a game show. Every time he answers a question correctly, a bulb lights up. The board at the right shows how he did. How could you describe Juan's score?

Lesson 13-8

© **Reason** Use what you know about place value to complete this task.

Write the decimals 0.67, 0.66, and 0.7 in order from least to greatest. Tell how you decided.

Hundreds	Tens	Ones	.	Tenths	Hundredths

Lesson 13-9

© **Persevere** Solve any way you choose.

Suppose you have $3.45. How many ways can you find to show this amount using coins and bills? Which way uses the fewest of each kind of bill or coin?

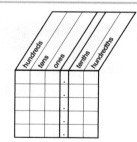

Lesson 13-10

© **Be Precise** Solve. Copy and use the diagram at the right.

Olivia is making a drawing of a bike path. She made a mark for 0.2 mile because that is the location of a shelter. There is a water fountain at 0.6 mile. Where should Olivia show the mark for 0.6 mile? Tell how you decided.

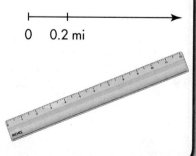

0   0.2 mi

Common
Core

4.NF.4.a Understand a
fraction $\frac{a}{b}$ as a multiple
of $\frac{1}{b}$.

Fractions as Multiples of Unit Fractions: Using Models

Hands-On
fraction strips

How can you describe a fraction using a unit fraction?

A unit fraction is a fraction that describes one part of the whole. Unit fractions always have a numerator of 1.

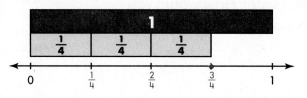

Guided Practice*

MATHEMATICAL PRACTICES

Do you know HOW?

For **1** through **4**, write the fraction as a multiple of a unit fraction. Use fraction strips to help.

1. $\frac{2}{3} = \boxed{} \times \frac{1}{3}$

2. $\frac{5}{6} = 5 \times \frac{1}{\boxed{}}$

3. $\frac{3}{2} = \boxed{}$

4. $\frac{6}{5} = \boxed{}$

Do you UNDERSTAND?

5. **Use Structure** Draw a picture to explain why $\frac{8}{5} = 8 \times \frac{1}{5}$.

6. Write the multiplication equation to show each part of the following story. Mark's family ate $\frac{6}{4}$ chicken pot pies for dinner. There are 6 people in Mark's family. Each family member ate $\frac{1}{4}$ of a pie.

Independent Practice

Leveled Practice For **7** through **22**, write the fraction as a multiple of a unit fraction. Use fraction strips to help.

7. $\frac{3}{4} = \boxed{} \times \frac{1}{4}$

8. $\frac{3}{6} = 3 \times \frac{1}{\boxed{}}$

9. $\frac{2}{5} = \boxed{} \times \frac{1}{5}$

10. $\frac{8}{12} = 8 \times \frac{1}{\boxed{}}$

11. $\frac{7}{10} = \boxed{}$

12. $\frac{8}{8} = \boxed{}$

13. $\frac{5}{12} = \boxed{}$

14. $\frac{6}{6} = \boxed{}$

15. $\frac{6}{4} = \boxed{}$

16. $\frac{9}{6} = \boxed{}$

17. $\frac{8}{5} = \boxed{}$

18. $\frac{9}{8} = \boxed{}$

19. $\frac{7}{8} = \boxed{}$

20. $\frac{9}{4} = \boxed{}$

21. $\frac{8}{6} = \boxed{}$

22. $\frac{35}{100} = \boxed{}$

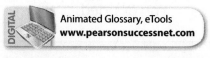

DIGITAL
Animated Glossary, eTools
www.pearsonsuccessnet.com

For another example, see Set A on page 356.

When a whole is divided into four equal parts, each part is described as $\frac{1}{4}$.

Three of those parts are described as $\frac{3}{4}$.

Multiplication and a unit fraction also can be used to describe $\frac{3}{4}$.

$\frac{3}{4} = 3 \times \frac{1}{4}$, or three $\frac{1}{4}$ parts.

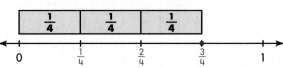

Three $\frac{1}{4}$ parts make $\frac{3}{4}$.

$$\frac{3}{4} = 3 \times \frac{1}{4}$$

So, $\frac{3}{4}$ is a multiple of $\frac{1}{4}$.

A multiple is the result of multiplying a number by a whole number.

Problem Solving

23. Model Write an equation that describes the picture below. Show your answer as a multiplication equation with a unit fraction as a factor.

24. Write a Problem Look at the picture. Write and solve a problem for it. Show your answer as a multiplication equation with $\frac{1}{2}$ as a factor.

25. Leslie is baking bread. The recipe calls for $1\frac{3}{4}$ cups of all-purpose flour and $1\frac{1}{4}$ cups of whole wheat flour. How many cups of flour does Leslie need in all?

A $\frac{1}{2}$

B 2

C 3

D $3\frac{1}{4}$

26. Mari is packing oranges into bags. She packs the same number of oranges in each bag. The table below shows the number of oranges she packs for different numbers of bags. How many oranges does Mari need to pack 9 bags?

Number of Bags	3	5	7	9	11
Number of Oranges	9	15	21		33

27. Use Structure Kevin is baking cookies. Each batch of cookies uses $\frac{1}{8}$ pound of butter. Kevin has $1\frac{3}{8}$ pounds of butter. How many batches of cookies can he make? Show your answer as a multiplication equation with $\frac{1}{8}$ as a factor.

28. Use Structure Kobe drinks $\frac{1}{3}$ cup of grapefruit juice each morning. He has $2\frac{1}{3}$ cups of juice left. For how many mornings will it last? Show your answer as a multiplication equation with $\frac{1}{3}$ as a factor. (Hint: Write $2\frac{1}{3}$ as an improper fraction.)

Lesson
13-2

Common
Core

4.NF.4.b Understand a
multiple of $\frac{a}{b}$ as a multiple
of $\frac{1}{b}$, and use this
understanding to multiply
a fraction by a whole
number. Also 4.NF.4

Multiplying a Fraction by a Whole Number: Using Models

How can you find the product of a fraction multiplied by a whole number?

Doris lives $\frac{1}{4}$ of a mile from school. If she walks to and from school each day, how far does she walk during a school week?

Distance Walked (in miles)					
	Mon	Tues	Wed	Thurs	Fri
To School	$\frac{1}{4}$	$\frac{1}{4}$	$\frac{1}{4}$	$\frac{1}{4}$	$\frac{1}{4}$
From School	$\frac{1}{4}$	$\frac{1}{4}$	$\frac{1}{4}$	$\frac{1}{4}$	$\frac{1}{4}$

Another Example

Show a picture of Doris's walk in another way. Show 5 days of $\frac{2}{4}$ mile walks.

$\frac{1}{4}$	$\frac{1}{4}$	$\frac{1}{4}$	$\frac{1}{4}$	$\frac{1}{4}$	$\frac{1}{4}$	$\frac{1}{4}$	$\frac{1}{4}$	$\frac{1}{4}$	$\frac{1}{4}$
$\frac{2}{4}$		$\frac{2}{4}$		$\frac{2}{4}$		$\frac{2}{4}$		$\frac{2}{4}$	

You can show the total she walks with addition.

$$\frac{2}{4} + \frac{2}{4} + \frac{2}{4} + \frac{2}{4} + \frac{2}{4} = \frac{10}{4} = 2\frac{1}{2}$$

Doris walks $2\frac{1}{2}$ miles each week.

You can also show the total with multiplication.

$$5 \times \frac{2}{4} = 5 \times \left(2 \times \frac{1}{4}\right)$$
$$= (5 \times 2) \times \frac{1}{4}$$
$$= 10 \times \frac{1}{4}$$
$$= \frac{10}{4} \text{ or } 2\frac{2}{4} = 2\frac{1}{2} \text{ miles}$$

Guided Practice*

MATHEMATICAL
PRACTICES

Do you know HOW?

In **1** and **2**, write a multiplication equation with a whole number and a fraction for each picture.

1.

2.
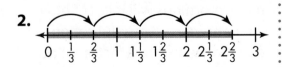

Do you UNDERSTAND?

3. **Reason** In the example at the top of the page, explain why the total distance Doris walks to school each week can also be found using multiplication.

4. Draw a picture to explain why $3 \times \frac{2}{5} = \frac{(3 \times 2)}{5} = \frac{6}{5}$.

5. **Reason** What property of multiplication is used to write $5 \times (2 \times \frac{1}{4}) = (5 \times 2) \times \frac{1}{4}$? How does this help you multiply?

Draw a picture to show the distance Doris walks.

$\frac{1}{4}$	$\frac{1}{4}$	$\frac{1}{4}$	$\frac{1}{4}$	$\frac{1}{4}$	$\frac{1}{4}$	$\frac{1}{4}$	$\frac{1}{4}$	$\frac{1}{4}$	$\frac{1}{4}$

0   1   2

$$\frac{1}{4} + \frac{1}{4} + \frac{1}{4} + \frac{1}{4} + \frac{1}{4} + \frac{1}{4} + \frac{1}{4} + \frac{1}{4} + \frac{1}{4} + \frac{1}{4} = \frac{10}{4}$$

Simplify $\frac{10}{4}$.

$$\frac{10}{4} = 2\frac{2}{4} = 2\frac{1}{2}$$

Ten $\frac{1}{4}$ miles added together makes $\frac{10}{4}$ miles, or $2\frac{1}{2}$ miles.

Multiplication can also be used to join equal parts.

$$10 \times \frac{1}{4} = \frac{10}{4} = 2\frac{2}{4} = 2\frac{1}{2}$$

Doris walks $2\frac{1}{2}$ miles to and from school each week.

Independent Practice

In **6** and **7**, write a multiplication equation with a whole number and a fraction for each picture.

6.

$\frac{1}{8}$ mi	$\frac{1}{8}$ mi	$\frac{1}{8}$ mi	$\frac{1}{8}$ mi	$\frac{1}{8}$ mi

7.

$\frac{2}{10}$ $\frac{2}{10}$ $\frac{2}{10}$

Problem Solving

MATHEMATICAL PRACTICES

© **8. Reason** Kiona fills a measuring cup with $\frac{3}{4}$ cup of juice 3 times. Write and solve a multiplication equation with a whole number and a fraction to show the total amount of juice she uses.

© **9. Model** Each lap around a track is $\frac{3}{10}$ kilometer. Eliot walked around the track 4 times. How far did Eliot walk in all?

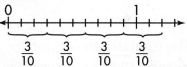

0   1

$\frac{3}{10}$ $\frac{3}{10}$ $\frac{3}{10}$ $\frac{3}{10}$

A $\frac{2}{5}$ kilometer   **C** $1\frac{1}{5}$ kilometer

B $\frac{7}{10}$ kilometer   **D** $1\frac{2}{5}$ kilometer

© **10. Persevere** Wendy sliced a loaf of bread into 12 equal slices. She used 4 of the slices to make sandwiches. What fraction of the loaf of bread was left?

11. A pan of lasagna is cut into 6 equal pieces. The chef serves 5 pieces of the lasagna. Write and solve a multiplication equation to show how much of the lasagna is served.

© **12. Communicate** Zach made trail mix using $\frac{1}{8}$ pound of each of the following: walnuts, raisins, almonds, peanuts, sunflower seeds, and dates. What is the total weight of the trail mix? Explain by drawing a picture and writing an equation.

Common Core

4.NF.4.c Solve word problems involving multiplication of a fraction by a whole number, e.g., by using visual fraction models and equations to represent the problem.
Also 4.NF.4, 4.NF.4.b

Multiplying a Fraction by a Whole Number: Using Symbols

When can you use the product of a fraction and a whole number to solve a problem?

At his job at the ice cream counter, Stanley makes large ice cream sundaes that contain $\frac{3}{4}$ pint of ice cream. Today, Stanley made 5 of these sundaes. How much ice cream did he use?

$\frac{3}{4}$ pt of ice cream in each sundae

Guided Practice*

MATHEMATICAL PRACTICES

Do you know HOW?

For **1–4**, multiply.

1. $8 \times \frac{1}{2} = $ ▨

2. $13 \times \frac{3}{4} = $ ▨

3. $7 \times \frac{2}{3} = $ ▨

4. $9 \times \frac{1}{8} = $ ▨

For **5** and **6**, write a multiplication equation for each situation.

5. Medicine taken in 10 days if the dose is $\frac{3}{4}$ ounce per day.

6. The total length needed to decorate 9 boxes if each box uses $\frac{2}{3}$ yard of ribbon.

Do you UNDERSTAND?

Write a number sentence that describes each situation.

© 7. Model Sarah has $\frac{1}{2}$ of a granola bar. Her friend has 5 times as many granola bars. How many granola bars does Sarah's friend have?

© 8. Model Sue needs $\frac{5}{6}$ cup of cocoa to make one batch of chocolate pudding. She wants to make 4 batches of pudding to take to a party. Write and solve an equation to show how much cocoa Sue will need for all 4 batches of pudding.

Independent Practice

For **9–17**, multiply. Write the product in simplest form.

9. $4 \times \frac{1}{3} = $ ▨

10. $6 \times \frac{3}{8} = $ ▨

11. $8 \times \frac{2}{5} = $ ▨

12. $12 \times \frac{5}{6} = $ ▨

13. $11 \times \frac{2}{3} = $ ▨

14. $5 \times \frac{7}{8} = $ ▨

15. $7 \times \frac{3}{4} = $ ▨

16. $9 \times \frac{3}{5} = $ ▨

17. $4 \times \frac{5}{8} = $ ▨

For another example, see Set B on page 356.

I am joining 5 groups of $\frac{3}{4}$ of a pint.

$\frac{3}{4} + \frac{3}{4} + \frac{3}{4} + \frac{3}{4} + \frac{3}{4}$

Joining equal-sized groups can be shown with multiplication.

Find $5 \times \frac{3}{4}$.

$5 \times \frac{3}{4} = \frac{(5 \times 3)}{4}$

$= \frac{15}{4}$

$= 3\frac{3}{4}$

Stanley needs $3\frac{3}{4}$ pints of ice cream to make 5 sundaes.

For **18** and **19**, write a number sentence for each situation and find the answer.

18. The total distance Mary runs in one week if she runs $\frac{7}{8}$ mile each day.

19. The length of 5 pieces of ribbon laid end to end if each piece is $\frac{2}{3}$ yard long.

Problem Solving

MATHEMATICAL PRACTICES

© **20. Model** Malik swims $\frac{9}{10}$ of a mile each day. How many miles will he swim in 8 days? Write a number sentence and solve.

21. Sean is making picture frames. Each frame uses $\frac{4}{5}$ yard of wood. What is the total length of wood Sean will need to make 12 frames?

© **22. Persevere** Sun is making 7 fruit tarts. Each tart needs $\frac{3}{4}$ cup of strawberries and $\frac{1}{4}$ cup of blueberries. What is the total amount of fruit that Sun needs for her tarts?

© **23. Writing to Explain** Lydia is making 4 loaves of rye bread and 3 loaves of wheat bread. Each loaf takes $\frac{3}{4}$ cup of sugar. What is the total amount of sugar Lydia will need? Explain.

24. Write a story to go along with the multiplication sentence $3 \times \frac{3}{10}$. Then, solve your problem.

26. It takes Mario $\frac{1}{4}$ hour to mow Mr. Harris's lawn. It takes him 3 times as long to mow Mrs. Carter's lawn. How long does it take Mario to mow Mrs. Carter's lawn?

© **25. Reason** Olivia is doing her math homework. For each problem, she uses $\frac{3}{4}$ of a sheet of paper. How many sheets of paper will she need to complete 20 problems?

A 4 sheets   **C** 15 sheets

B $5\frac{3}{4}$ sheets   **D** $20\frac{3}{4}$ sheets

Lesson
13-4

Common
Core

4.NF.6 Use decimal
notation for fractions with
denominators 10 or 100.
Also 4.NF.5

Fractions and Decimals

Hands-On
grid paper

How can you write a fraction as a decimal and a decimal as a fraction?

On Kelsey Street, six out of 10 homes have swing sets in their backyards.

Write $\frac{6}{10}$ as a decimal.

6 of 10 houses
have swing sets.

Other Examples

A tenth <u>is one of 10 equal parts of a whole</u>.

0.1

A hundredth <u>is one of 100 equal parts of a whole</u>.

0.01

Guided Practice*

MATHEMATICAL
PRACTICES

Do you know HOW?

For **1** and **2**, write a decimal and a fraction in simplest form for the part of each grid that is shaded.

1.   2.

Do you UNDERSTAND?

© 3. Writing to Explain Why is the fraction $\frac{6}{10}$ not written 0.06?

© 4. Model On Kelsey Street, what fraction of homes do **NOT** have swings? Write your answer as a fraction and a decimal.

Independent Practice

For **5** through **9**, write a decimal and a fraction in simplest form for the part of each grid that is shaded.

5.   6.   7.   8.   9.

For another example, see Set C on page 357.

Write $\frac{6}{10}$ as a decimal.

$\frac{6}{10}$ is six tenths, or 0.6.

$$\frac{6}{10} = 0.6$$

So, 0.6 of the houses have swing sets.

In Rolling Hills, 0.75 of the houses are two-story homes.

Write 0.75 as a fraction.

0.75 is seventy-five hundredths, or $\frac{75}{100}$.

$$0.75 = \frac{75}{100}$$

So, $\frac{75}{100}$, or $\frac{3}{4}$, of the houses are two-story homes.

For **10** through **19**, write each fraction as an equivalent decimal, and write each decimal as a fraction or a mixed number in simplest form.

10. $9\frac{4}{10}$ **11.** $\frac{21}{100}$ **12.** 11.6   **13.** $1\frac{81}{100}$ **14.** 0.65

15. $\frac{50}{100}$ **16.** 0.48   **17.** $4\frac{7}{10}$ **18.** $\frac{20}{200}$ **19.** 1.45

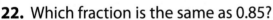

Problem Solving

MATHEMATICAL PRACTICES

ⓒ **20. Estimation** About what fraction of the rectangle to the right is shaded green?

ⓒ **21. Use Structure** The arena of the Colosseum in Rome was about $\frac{3}{20}$ of the entire Colosseum. Write this amount as a decimal.

Tip $\frac{1}{20} = \frac{5}{100}$

The arena is $\frac{3}{20}$ of the Colosseum.

22. Which fraction is the same as 0.85?

A $\frac{85}{1,000}$ **C** $\frac{85}{1}$

B $\frac{85}{100}$ **D** $\frac{85}{10}$

ⓒ **23. Reason** James, Vicki, Jaime, and Jill are in line for tickets for the basketball game. Jaime is first. Vicki is behind Jill. Jill is not last. James is in front of Jill. How are they ordered?

24. Find the missing numbers in the pattern below.

■, 18, 27, ■, ■, 54, ■

Animated Glossary, eTools
www.pearsonsuccessnet.com

DIGITAL

Common Core

4.NF.5 Express a fraction with a denominator 10 as an equivalent fraction with denominator 100, and use this technique to add two fractions with respective denominators 10 and 100. Also **4.NF.6**

Fractions and Decimals On the Number Line

How can you locate points on a number line?

In short-track speed skating, each lap is $\frac{1}{9}$ kilometer.

In long-track speed skating, each lap is 0.4 kilometer.

How can you use a number line to show these distances?

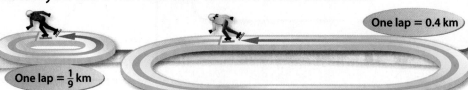

One lap = 0.4 km

One lap = $\frac{1}{9}$ km

Another Example How can you add $\frac{4}{10}$ and $\frac{43}{100}$?

Find $\frac{4}{10}$ on a number line

$$0 \quad \frac{1}{10} \quad \frac{2}{10} \quad \frac{3}{10} \quad \frac{4}{10} \quad \frac{5}{10} \quad \frac{6}{10} \quad \frac{7}{10} \quad \frac{8}{10} \quad \frac{9}{10} \quad 1$$

There are 10 equal parts between 0 and 1.

There are 4 equal parts between 0 and $\frac{4}{10}$.

Find $\frac{43}{100}$ on a number line

$\frac{43}{100}$ will be between $\frac{4}{10}$ and $\frac{5}{10}$ because $\frac{4}{10}$ is equivalent to $\frac{40}{100}$ and $\frac{5}{10}$ is equivalent to $\frac{50}{100}$.

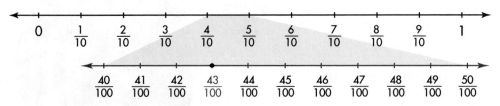

We can add fractions with like denominators.

$$\frac{40}{100} + \frac{43}{100} = \frac{83}{100}$$

Explain It

1. Reasonableness Describe where you would place $\frac{55}{100}$ on a number line that shows only tenths.

2. What number is at point *R*?

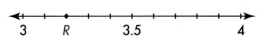

$$3 \qquad R \qquad 3.5 \qquad\qquad 4$$

Locate $\frac{1}{9}$ on a number line.

Draw a number line, and label 0 and 1. Divide the distance from 0 to 1 into 9 equal parts.

Draw a point at $\frac{1}{9}$.

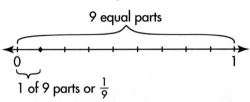

9 equal parts

0   1

1 of 9 parts or $\frac{1}{9}$

Locate 0.4 on a number line.

Draw a number line, and divide the distance from 0 to 1 into 10 equal parts to show tenths.

Draw a point at 0.4.

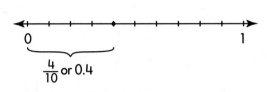

0   1

$\frac{4}{10}$ or 0.4

Guided Practice*

MATHEMATICAL PRACTICES

Do you know HOW?

For **1** and **2**, use the number line below to name the fraction.

1. A   **2.** B

A   C   B

0   1

For **3** and **4**, name the point on the number line for each decimal.

3. 1.33   **4.** 1.39

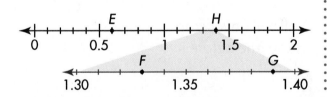

E   H

0   0.5   1   1.5   2

F   G

1.30   1.35   1.40

Do you UNDERSTAND?

5. Where would you locate 0.46 on the number line at the top?

6. Model Use the number line for Exercises 1 and 2. What fraction is located at point *C*?

7. A 1,500-meter speed-skating race is 13.5 laps around a short track. Show 13.5 on a number line.

8. Model Use the number line for Exercises 3 and 4. What point is at $\frac{6}{10}$?

Independent Practice

For **9** through **13**, use the number line below to name the decimal.

9. J   **10.** K   **11.** L   **12.** M   **13.** N

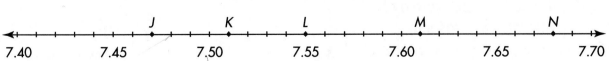

J   K   L   M   N

7.40   7.45   7.50   7.55   7.60   7.65   7.70

For **14** through **18**, name the fraction that should be written at each point.

14. *V*   **15.** *Z*   **16.** *X*   **17.** *W*   **18.** *Y*

```
         V    W              X              Y              Z
←+----+----+----+----+----+----+----+----+----+----+----→
 0    1/10                  6/10                          1
```

For **19** through **23**, name the point for each decimal.

19. 10.1   **20.** 10.28   **21.** 10.25   **22.** 9.6   **23.** 10.0

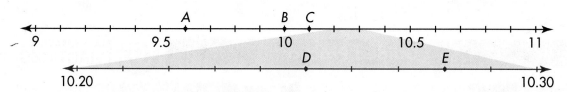

```
                        A         B  C
←+----+----+----+----+----+----+----+----+----+----+----→
 9              9.5        10         10.5        11
          10.20         D         E
←+----+----+----+----+----+----+----+----+----+----+----→
      10.20                                   10.30
```

MATHEMATICAL
PRACTICES

24. Which two points on the number line to the right represent the same point?

```
←+----+----+----+----+----+----+----+→
 8              8.5        Z    9
   ←+----+----+----+----+----+----+→
        8.70         X         Y
```

ⓒ **25.** **Use Structure** Jack walked $\frac{4}{5}$ mile to the library. What is this distance as a decimal?

26. Write an expression that tells how to find the perimeter of a triangle with each side 2 inches long.

Use the diagram below for **27** and **28**.

According to the Greek mathematician Zeno, a ball will never stop bouncing because each bounce is half as high as the one before it.

ⓒ **27.** **Look for Patterns** What fraction should be written at point *D*?

ⓒ **28.** **Writing to Explain** Do you think it would be possible for the ball to reach zero by moving halfway closer at every step? Why or why not?

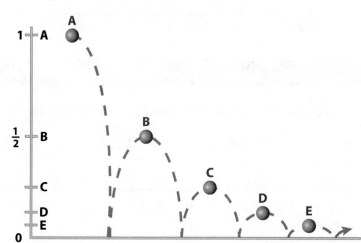

Find the quotient. Estimate to check
if the answer is reasonable.

1. 480 ÷ 8   **2.** 29 ÷ 3   **3.** 749 ÷ 8   **4.** 304 ÷ 3

5. 4)$\overline{608}$ **6.** 5)$\overline{528}$ **7.** 515 ÷ 3   **8.** 6)$\overline{87}$

9. 95 ÷ 5   **10.** 888 ÷ 9   **11.** 54 ÷ 4   **12.** 210 ÷ 3

13. 8)$\overline{807}$ **14.** 465 ÷ 2   **15.** 5)$\overline{64}$ **16.** 964 ÷ 4

Find the sum. Estimate to check if the answer is reasonable.

17. 46,037   **18.**   9,979   **19.**   73,678   **20.**   2,873   **21.**   21,165
   + 12,750   + 2,956   + 26,321   +   49   + 15,375

22. 54,893 + 3,746   **23.** 23,963 + 12 + 3,987   **24.** 48 + 40,287 + 834

© **Be Precise** Find each quotient that is not correct.
Write it correctly and explain the error.

25. 19 ÷ 2 = 9 R1   **26.** 808 ÷ 4 = 22   **27.** 354 ÷ 5 = 70 R4

28. 74 ÷ 6 = 12 R2   **29.** 377 ÷ 3 = 125   **30.** 940 ÷ 7 = 140

Number Sense

Write whether each statement is true or false. Explain your answer.

31. The quotient of 398 ÷ 4 is closer to 100 than 90.

32. The product of 9 and 32 is greater than the product of 3 and 92.

33. The quotient of 154 ÷ 5 is less than 30.

34. The quotient of 1,500 ÷ 30 is 30.

35. The difference of 4,321 − 2,028 is less than 1,000.

36. The sum of 2,243 and 5,809 is greater than 7,000 but less than 9,000.

Lesson
13-6

Common Core

4.NF.6 Use decimal notation for fractions with denominators 10 or 100. Also **4.NF.5**

Equivalent Fractions and Decimals

How can you use equivalent fractions to change a fraction to a decimal?

A pan of cornbread was divided into 12 equal pieces, and 6 out of 12 pieces or $\frac{6}{12}$ of the cornbread remains. Write a fraction equivalent to $\frac{6}{12}$, and then change the fraction to a decimal.

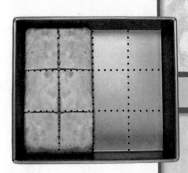

Other Examples

Write $\frac{3}{12}$ as a decimal.

In simplest form $\frac{3}{12}$ is $\frac{1}{4}$.

Find an equivalent fraction with a denominator of 100.

Think 4 times what number equals 100?

$$\times 25$$
$$\frac{1}{4} = \frac{25}{100}$$
$$\times 25$$

$\frac{25}{100}$ is twenty-five hundredths, or 0.25.

So, $\frac{3}{12}$ = 0.25.

Write 0.8 as a fraction in simplest form.

0.8 is eight tenths, or $\frac{8}{10}$.

Simplify the fraction $\frac{8}{10}$.

Think 8 and 10 are multiples of what number?

$$\div 2$$
$$\frac{8}{10} = \frac{4}{5}$$
$$\div 2$$

0.8 is eight tenths, or $\frac{4}{5}$.

So, 0.8 = $\frac{4}{5}$.

Explain It

© **1. Reason** Why is the fraction $\frac{1}{2}$ not written as 0.12?

2. What steps would you take to rename $\frac{2}{4}$ as an equivalent fraction with a denominator of 100?

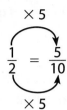

In simplest form $\frac{6}{12}$ is $\frac{1}{2}$. Find an equivalent fraction with a denominator of 10.

Think 2 times what number equals 10?

$$\begin{array}{c} \times 5 \\ \frac{1}{2} = \frac{5}{10} \\ \times 5 \end{array}$$

$\frac{1}{2} = \frac{5}{10}$

$\frac{5}{10}$ is five tenths, or 0.5.

So, 0.5 of the cornbread remains.

Write $\frac{3}{4}$ as a decimal.

Multiply to find an equivalent fraction with a denominator of 100.

Think 4 times what number equals 100?

$$\begin{array}{c} \times 25 \\ \frac{3}{4} = \frac{75}{100} \\ \times 25 \end{array}$$

$\frac{3}{4} = \frac{75}{100}$ $\times 25$

$\frac{75}{100}$ is seventy-five hundredths, or 0.75.

Guided Practice*

 MATHEMATICAL PRACTICES

Do you know HOW?

For **1** through **6**, write each fraction as a decimal.

1. $\frac{3}{5} = \frac{}{10}$ **2.** $\frac{2}{4} = \frac{50}{}$

3. $\frac{1}{5}$ **4.** $\frac{3}{12}$

5. $\frac{2}{8}$ **6.** $\frac{3}{5}$

Do you UNDERSTAND?

7. Write a fraction and an equivalent decimal to show the part of the cornbread that has been eaten.

© **8. Writing to Explain** When you write a fraction as a decimal, why do you need to rename the fraction as an equivalent fraction with a denominator of 10 or 100?

Independent Practice

In **9** through **18**, write each fraction as a decimal.

9. $\frac{2}{5} = \frac{}{10}$ **10.** $\frac{4}{5} = \frac{}{10}$ **11.** $\frac{4}{5} = \frac{8}{}$ **12.** $\frac{2}{8} = \frac{}{100}$ **13.** $\frac{7}{100} = \frac{}{100}$

14. $\frac{3}{12}$ **15.** $\frac{6}{10}$ **16.** $\frac{4}{10}$ **17.** $\frac{1}{5}$ **18.** $\frac{35}{100}$

In **19** through **30**, tell whether each pair shows equivalent numbers.

19. $\frac{4}{8}$, 0.5   **20.** $\frac{1}{5}$, 0.15   **21.** $\frac{65}{100}$, 0.65   **22.** $\frac{2}{4}$, 0.35

23. $\frac{4}{8}$, 0.08   **24.** $\frac{6}{12}$, 0.6   **25.** $\frac{4}{8}$, 0.5   **26.** $\frac{8}{100}$, 0.08

27. $\frac{3}{12}$, 0.25   **28.** $\frac{3}{10}$, 0.03   **29.** $\frac{4}{5}$, 0.8   **30.** $\frac{1}{2}$, 0.05

For another example, see Set E on page 358.

31. Roger got 24 hits out of 100 times at bat. What is his batting average as a fraction in simplest form? Then write an equivalent decimal.

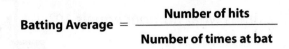

$$\text{Batting Average} = \frac{\text{Number of hits}}{\text{Number of times at bat}}$$

© **32. Critique Reasoning** The model below represents 1 whole. Maura says that the shaded part of the model shows that $\frac{70}{100} = 0.07$. Is Maura correct? Explain why or why not.

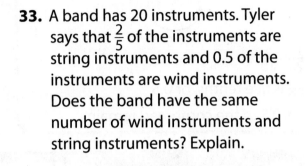

33. A band has 20 instruments. Tyler says that $\frac{2}{5}$ of the instruments are string instruments and 0.5 of the instruments are wind instruments. Does the band have the same number of wind instruments and string instruments? Explain.

34. Gina wrote a 4-digit number. She used each of the digits 1, 3, 5, and 7 once. How many different 4-digit numbers can Gina write?

© **35. Writing to Explain** Which is greater, $\frac{3}{4}$ or 0.75? Explain your answer.

© **36. Reason** The cell phone was invented in Sweden in 1979. How many years ago was the cell phone invented?

37. Write a fraction in simplest form and an equivalent decimal to show what part of a dollar 5 cents represents. (Hint: 1 dollar = 100 cents.)

For **38**, use the diagram at the right.

38. Kwan has 37 customers on his paper route. He delivers newspapers every day. How many newspapers does he deliver in one week?

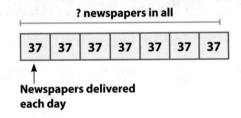

? newspapers in all

| 37 | 37 | 37 | 37 | 37 | 37 | 37 |

Newspapers delivered each day

© **39. Reasonableness** Betty's score on a 5-point quiz was 4 out of 5, or $\frac{4}{5}$. What is $\frac{4}{5}$ written as a decimal?

A 0.4

B 0.45

C 0.6

D 0.8

40. Nine of the 12 students in the school play are fourth graders. Which decimal represents the part of the students that are fourth graders?

A 0.25

B 0.6

C 0.75

D 0.9

Solve each equation for z.

1. $z + 22 = 24$ **2.** $z - 19 = 24$ **3.** $z \times 4 = 32$

4. $z \div 9 = 4$ **5.** $15 + z = 24$ **6.** $z - 22 = 22$

7. $6 \times z = 6$ **8.** $z \div 5 = 1$ **9.** $3 \times z = 18$

Round each decimal to the nearest tenth.

10. 9.64   **11.** 1.05   **12.** 3.52   **13.** 16.67   **14.** 87.24

Find the sum. Estimate to check if the answer is reasonable.

15. $9 + 3,529 + 27 + 621$ **16.** $17,868 + 913 + 2,781$

17. $475 + 25 + 5,350 + 25,275$ **18.** $2 + 129 + 56 + 374$

© **Reason** Find each value of w that is not correct.
Write it correctly, and explain the error.

19. $20 + w = 68$ **20.** $w - 12 = 50$ **21.** $w \div 2 = 9$ **22.** $w \times 6 = 42$
$w = 88$ $w = 62$ $w = 11$ $w = 8$

Number Sense

© **Construct Arguments** Write whether each
statement is true or false. Explain your answer.

23. The expression $101 - 25$ equals 76.

24. The product of 4 and 682 is closer to 2,400 than 2,800.

25. The sum of 251 and 173 is less than 400.

26. The quotient of 0 divided by 1 is 1.

27. The product of 5 and 45 is 25 more than 200.

28. The difference of 844 and 172 is greater than 600.

Common Core

4.NF.7 Compare two decimals to hundredths by reasoning about their size. Recognize that comparisons are valid only when the two decimals refer to the same whole. Record the results of the comparisons with the symbols >, =, or <, and justify the conclusions, e.g., by using a visual model.

Decimal Place Value

What are some ways to represent decimals?

A squirrel can weigh 1.64 pounds. There are different ways to represent 1.64.

1.64 pounds

Guided Practice*

MATHEMATICAL PRACTICES

Do you know HOW?

For **1** and **2**, write the expanded form for each number.

1. 3.91   **2.** 6.87

In **3** and **4**, draw and shade a grid for each number. Then, write the word form for each number.

3. 1.06   **4.** 2.36

Do you UNDERSTAND?

5. Use Structure In Exercise 1, what digit is in the tenths place? in the hundredths place?

6. At the end of a basketball game, there are 3.29 seconds left on the clock. How would the referee say this number?

Tip *When you read a number or write a number in word form, replace the decimal point with the word and.*

Independent Practice

In **7** through **9**, write the decimal for each shaded part.

7.

8.

9.

In **10** through **15**, write the number in standard form.

10. four and thirty-six hundredths

11. 5 + 0.2 + 0.08

12. 2 + 0.01

13. six and nineteen hundredths

14. 3 + 0.7 + 0.04

15. 1 + 0.5 + 0.07

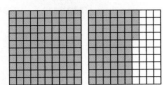

One Way

Use a decimal model.

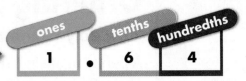

Another Way

Use a place-value model.

ones . tenths hundredths

| 1 | . | 6 | 4 |

Expanded form: 1 + 0.6 + 0.04
Standard form: 1.64
Word form: one and sixty-four hundredths

Expanded form: 1 + 0.6 + 0.04
Standard form: 1.64
Word form: one and sixty-four hundredths

In **16** through **20**, write the number in word form and give the value of the red digit for each number.

16. 2.47   **17.** 23.79   **18.** 1.85   **19.** 14.12   **20.** 9.05

In **21** through **25**, write each number in expanded form.

21. 3.19   **22.** 13.62   **23.** 0.78   **24.** 8.07   **25.** 17.2

Problem Solving

MATHEMATICAL
PRACTICES

26. Reason Write a number that has a 4 in the tens place and a 6 in the hundredths place.

27. Mr. Cooper has 6 gallons of gas in his car. His car can hold 15 gallons in its gas tank. Will Mr. Cooper need more or less than 10 gallons to fill his tank?

28. Tisha wrote this amount: Five dollars and nine cents.

   a What is the decimal word form for this amount?

   b What is the decimal number?

29. Model Write three numbers between 4.1 and 4.2.

 Use hundredths grids or money to help.

30. Writing to Explain Use the decimal model below to explain why 0.08 is less than 0.1.

31. Persevere What is the value of the 5 in 43.51?

   A five hundredths

   B five tenths

   C fifty-one hundredths

   D five

©
**Common
Core**

4.NF.7 Compare two
decimals to hundredths by
reasoning about their size.
Recognize that comparisons
are valid only when the two
decimals refer to the same
whole. Record the results of
the comparisons with the
symbols >, =, or <, and
justify the conclusions, e.g.,
by using a visual model.

Comparing and Ordering Decimals

How do you compare decimals?

A penny made in 1982 weighs
about 0.11 ounce. A penny made
in 2006 weighs about 0.09 ounce.
Which penny weighs more,
a 1982 penny or a 2006 penny?

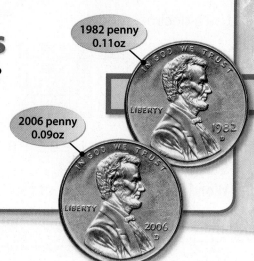

1982 penny
0.11oz

2006 penny
0.09oz

Another Example ## How do you order decimals?

Patrick has a 1982 penny, a 2006 penny, and a dime
in his pocket. Order the weights of the coins from
least to greatest.

Dime
0.10 oz

First compare the tenths place.

0.1̲1

0.0̲9

0.1̲0

The least number is 0.09 because it has a 0 in the tenths place.

Compare the remaining numbers.
First compare the tenths. Both
decimals have a 1 in the tenths place.

0.1̲0

0.1̲1

Compare the hundredths place.

0.10̲

0.11̲

1 > 0, so 0.11 is the greatest decimal.

The order from least to greatest is 0.09, 0.10, 0.11.

Explain It

1. Order the numbers above from greatest to least.

2. Which place did you use to compare 0.10 and 0.11?

One Way

Use hundredths grids.

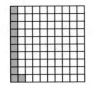

11 hundredths > 9 hundredths

0.11 > 0.09

Another Way

Use place value.

Start at the left. Look for the first place where the digits are different.

0.11   0.09

1 tenth > 0 tenths

0.11 > 0.09

A penny made in 1982 weighs more than a penny made in 2006.

Guided Practice*

MATHEMATICAL PRACTICES

Do you know HOW?

In **1** through **4**, write >, <, or = for each ◯. Use grids to help.

1. 0.7 ◯ 0.57

2. 0.23 ◯ 0.32

3. 1.01 ◯ 0.98

4. 0.2 ◯ 0.20

In **5** and **6**, order the numbers from least to greatest.

5. 0.65 0.6 0.71

6. 1.21 1.01 1.2

Do you UNDERSTAND?

ⓒ **7. Reason** Which is greater, 2.02 or 0.22? Explain.

ⓒ **8. Model** Maria told Patrick that her quarter weighs less than what a nickel weighs because 0.2 has fewer digits than 0.18. How can Patrick show Maria that 0.2 is greater than 0.18?

Quarter 0.2oz   Nickel 0.18oz

Independent Practice

For **9** through **16**, compare. Write >, <, or = for each ◯. Use grids to help.

9. 0.01 ◯ 0.1

10. 7.31 ◯ 7.29

11. 6.56 ◯ 5.98

12. 1.1 ◯ 1.10

13. 3.22 ◯ 4.44

14. 9.01 ◯ 9.1

15. 2.01 ◯ 1.7

16. 0.01 ◯ 1.02

For **17** through **22**, order the numbers from least to greatest.

17. 1.2, 1.23, 1.1

18. 0.56, 4.56, 0.65

19. 0.21, 0.12, 0.22

20. 3.8, 0.38, 3.08

21. 0.71, 0.07, 1.7

22. 0.5, 0.25, 1.05

© **23. Use Structure** A bag of 500 nickels weighs 5.5 pounds. A bag of 200 half dollars weighs 5 pounds. Which bag weighs more?

© **24. Writing to Explain** Evan said the numbers 7.37, 7.36, 2.59, and 2.95 were in order from greatest to least. Is he correct?

25. Which numbers are **NOT** in order from least to greatest?

A 0.3, 0.7, 0.9

B 0.04, 0.09, 0.12

C 0.15, 0.19, 0.23

D 0.24, 0.09, 0.18

26. Which number is **NOT** greater than 0.64?

A 6.4

B 4.6

C 0.46

D 0.66

For **27** and **28**, use the clocks at the right.

27. Which clock shows the earliest time?

28. Order the clock times from latest to earliest.

29. Tell which coin is worth more.
  a 1 quarter or 1 half dollar

  b 1 dime or 1 penny

  c 1 dollar or 1 penny

© **30. Reason** Ms. Alvarez has $0.83 in her change purse. She has 7 coins. She has the same number of pennies as quarters. What coins does she have?

31. Which number has a 3 in the ten-thousands place?

A 23,604   **C** 593,100

B 32,671   **D** 694,392

32. Which number is between 6.7 and 7.3?

A 6.07   **C** 6.83

B 6.26   **D** 7.4

33. Fishing lures are sold by weight. A yellow minnow lure weighs 0.63 ounce and a green minnow lure weighs 0.5 ounce. Which lure weighs more?

© **34. Persevere** Tom has one $10 bill, one $5 bill, four $1 bills, 3 quarters, and 2 dimes. Janet has three $5 bills, three $1 bills, and 8 quarters. Who has more money?

Algebra Connections

Number Patterns

Number patterns can help you predict the next number or numbers that follow.

Example: 10, 20, 30, 40, ▨

Think *How is each number in the number pattern related?*

Compare 10 and 20.

10 + <u>10</u> = 20

Now, compare 20 and 30.

20 + <u>10</u> = 30

The pattern that best describes the list of numbers is: <u>add 10</u>.

The missing number in the number pattern is represented by a shaded box. Use the number pattern to find the missing number.

40 + <u>10</u> = 50

The missing number is 50.

Fill in each shaded box with the number that best completes the number pattern. Then, tell how you completed the pattern.

1. 2, 4, 6, 8, ▨

2. 5, 10, 15, 20, ▨

3. 5, 8, 11, 14, ▨

4. 1, 3, 5, ▨, 9

5. 5, 15, ▨, 35, 45

6. 30, 23, ▨, 9, 2

7. 28, ▨, 18, 13, 8

8. 32, 36, ▨, 44, 48, ▨

9. 47, 56, ▨, 74, ▨, 92

10. 98, 91, ▨, 77, ▨

11. 75, 59, 43, ▨, ▨

12. 3, 5, 4, 6, 5, 7, 6, ▨

. . . .

13. What are the missing numbers in the number pattern? Describe the number pattern.

48, ▨, ▨, 33, 28, 23

14. Complete the table. Describe the pattern.

A	B	C
4	6	10
5	8	13
6		16
	11	19
15		30
20	14	

© **15. Write a Problem** Write a problem using one of the number patterns in Exercises 1 to 12.

Lesson
13-9

Common Core

4.MD.2 Use the four operations to solve word problems involving … money, including problems involving … decimals, and problems that require expressing measurements given in a larger unit in terms of a smaller unit…. Also 4.NF.7

Using Money to Understand Decimals

How are decimals related to money?

 Hands-On money

A dime is one tenth of a dollar.

 **0.1**

A penny is one hundredth of a dollar.

  0.01

Guided Practice*  **MATHEMATICAL PRACTICES**

Do you know HOW?

In **1** and **2**, copy and complete.

1. $9.75 = ☐ dollars + ☐ dimes + ☐ pennies

9.75 = ☐ ones + ☐ tenths + ☐ hundredths

2. $3.62 = ☐ dollars + ☐ pennies

3.62 = ☐ ones + ☐ hundredths

Do you UNDERSTAND?

3. Writing to Explain How many hundredths are in one tenth? Explain using pennies and a dime.

4. How many pennies are equal to 6 dimes?

5. Use Tools Gina's allowance is $2.50. How much is this in dollars and dimes?

 Remember, the number of dimes is the same as the number of tenths.

Independent Practice

In **6** through **9**, copy and complete.

6. $5.83 = ☐ dollars + ☐ pennies

5.83 = ☐ ones + ☐ hundredths

7. $7.14 = ☐ dollars + ☐ pennies

7.14 = ☐ ones + ☐ hundredths

8. $2.19 = ☐ dollars + ☐ dime + ☐ pennies

2.19 = ☐ ones + ☐ tenth + ☐ hundredths

9. $3.24 = ☐ dollars + ☐ dimes + ☐ pennies

3.24 = ☐ ones + ☐ tenths + ☐ hundredths

 Animated Glossary, eTools www.pearsonsuccessnet.com

For another example, see Set H on page 359.

One Way

You can use a place-value chart to show the decimal value of money.

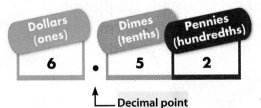

Dollars (ones) | Dimes (tenths) | Pennies (hundredths)

6 . 5 2

↑ Decimal point

Read: six dollars *and* fifty-two cents.

Another Way

You can show $6.52 several ways.

$6.52 = 6 dollars + 5 dimes + 2 pennies

= 6 ones + 5 tenths + 2 hundredths

$6.52 = 6 dollars + 52 pennies

= 6 ones + 52 hundredths

In **10** through **13**, write the amount with a dollar sign and decimal point.

10. 6 dollars + 9 dimes + 3 pennies

11. 5 dollars + 8 pennies

12. 7 dollars + 3 dimes + 4 pennies

13. 4 dollars + 7 dimes

Problem Solving

Ⓒ **MATHEMATICAL PRACTICES**

14. Make a place-value chart to show the value of 5 dollars, 1 dime, and 3 pennies.

Ⓒ **15. Writing to Explain** Why do you only need to look at the number of dollars to know that $5.12 is greater than $4.82?

16. Pablo saves $1.20 each week. How much has he saved, in dollars and dimes, after one week? two weeks? three weeks?

Ⓒ **17. Reason** Which is more?

a 4 dimes and 6 pennies or 6 dimes and 4 pennies?

b 5 dimes or 45 pennies?

In **18** and **19**, use the information at the right.

18. How could you use only dollars, dimes, and pennies to buy the bubble blower?

19. How could you use only dollars, dimes, and pennies to buy the snow globe?

$9.29

$4.59

bubble blower   snow globe

Ⓒ **20. Persevere** Which is equal to 6 dollars, 3 dimes, and 4 pennies?

A $3.46   B $3.64   C $6.34   D $6.43

Common Core

4.NF.6 Use decimal notation for fractions with denominators 10 or 100. Also 4.MD.1, 4.MD.2

Problem Solving

Draw a Picture

A hiking path is being planned for the local park. The planner started marking the drawing of the path with distances, but stopped. Where should the 1-mile mark be placed?

0   0.4 miles

Guided Practice*

MATHEMATICAL PRACTICES

Do you know HOW?

Solve.

1. Look at the hiking path below. Carla begins at the starting point and walks 0.8 miles. Where on the drawing would Carla end her walk?

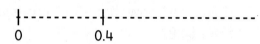

0   0.4

Do you UNDERSTAND?

2. **Reason** How are the numbers 0.4 and 0.8 related? How can this help you to find where 0.8 is located on the drawing?

3. **Write a Problem** Write a problem that uses the drawing below to solve.

0   0.3

Independent Practice

MATHEMATICAL PRACTICES

Solve.

4. Look at the line below. How can you use the mark on the line to find where 1.0 should be located?

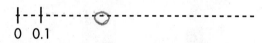

0   0.1

5. Copy the line segment from Problem 4. Find 1.0.

Applying Math Practices

- What am I asked to find?
- What else can I try?
- How are quantities related?
- How can I explain my work?
- How can I use math to model the problem?
- Can I use tools to help?
- Is my work precise?
- Why does this work?
- How can I generalize?

What do I know? The hiking path must be 1 mile long. The marker for 0.4 mile is located on the drawing.

What am I asked to find? Where the 1-mile mark should be located on the drawing

Double the distance from 0 to 0.4 to get 0.8.

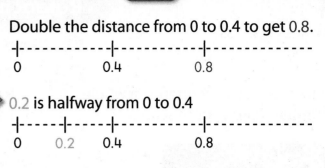

0   0.4   0.8

0.2 is halfway from 0 to 0.4

0   0.2   0.4   0.8

Move 0.2 to the right of 0.8 and get to 1.

0   0.2   0.4   0.8   1.0

---

6. Allie needed to design a banner for field day. She wanted her banner to be 2 feet long. Allie marked 0.5 feet on her drawing. How can she use this distance to find 2 feet?

Allie's drawing

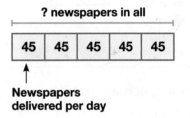

0   0.5

7. Dawn has 45 customers on her paper route. She delivers newspapers every day. How many newspapers does she deliver in five days?

? newspapers in all

| 45 | 45 | 45 | 45 | 45 |

↑ Newspapers delivered per day

© 8. Writing to Explain Blake jogged 1.7 miles one morning. His sister jogged $1\frac{3}{4}$ miles that same day. Who jogged farther? Explain your answer.

9. What would a good estimate for point G be on the drawing below?

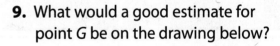

0   0.4   G   1.0

A 0.3 **B** 0.5 **C** 0.7 **D** 0.8

10. Shawn marked 0.8 feet on the chalkboard. How can Shawn use this distance to find 2 feet?

Shawn's drawing

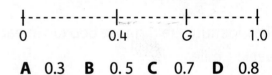

0   0.8

© 11. Model John has twice as many brothers as Bob. If Bob has *b* brothers, how many brothers does John have?

© 12. Persevere Nick wrote a four-digit number. He used the digits 2, 4, 6, and 8, and he used each digit only once. How many four-digit numbers could Nick have written?

13. Mary has 3 coin purses with 58 coins in each. How many coins does Mary have?

Set A, pages 330–331

A fraction can be written as a whole number times a unit fraction.

This model shows $\frac{5}{8}$.

It shows fraction strips that are each $\frac{1}{8}$.

There are five $\frac{1}{8}$ fraction strips, so you can write a multiplication equation with a unit fraction that describes the fraction.

$$\frac{5}{8} = 5 \times \frac{1}{8}$$

Remember that a unit fraction is a fraction with 1 as the numerator.

Write a multiplication equation with a unit fraction that describes the fraction shown.

1. 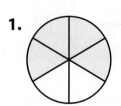 **2.**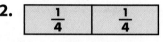

Find each of the missing values.

3. $\frac{4}{5} = \blacksquare \times \dfrac{\ \ }{\blacksquare}$ **4.** $\frac{7}{12} = \blacksquare \times \dfrac{\ \ }{\blacksquare}$

Set B, pages 332–335

Bob runs $\frac{3}{5}$ mile each week. How far does he run after 2 weeks?

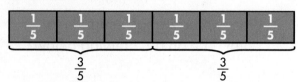

First, identify the distance Bob ran in each week: $\frac{3}{5}$ mile.

Next, identify the number of weeks Bob ran: 2 weeks.

There are 2 groups of $\frac{3}{5}$.

The product $2 \times \frac{3}{5}$ goes with the picture.

Multiply the whole number by the numerator of the fraction and write the product above the denominator of the fraction.

$$2 \times \frac{3}{5} = \frac{(2 \times 3)}{5} = \frac{6}{5}$$

So, Bob ran $\frac{6}{5}$ or $1\frac{1}{5}$ miles.

Remember you can show repeated addition.

Write a multiplication equation of a whole number and fraction to go with each picture.

1.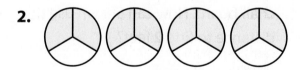

2. ⊕ ⊕ ⊕ ⊕

3. Adrian uses $\frac{3}{4}$ cup of milk in each bowl of cereal he eats. He eats one bowl of cereal each day. How many cups of milk does Adrian use for cereal in one week? Write your answer in simplest form.

Write $\frac{37}{100}$ as a decimal.

$\frac{37}{100}$ is thirty-seven hundredths, or 0.37.

Write 1.7 as a mixed number.

Since $0.7 = \frac{7}{10}$,
$1.7 = 1\frac{7}{10}$.

Remember you can write a decimal and a fraction for the shaded part of each grid.

1.   **2.**

3.   **4.**

5.

Show $6\frac{1}{4}$ on a number line.

Divide the distance from 6 to 7 into 4 equal lengths. Label the tick marks and draw a point at $6\frac{1}{4}$.

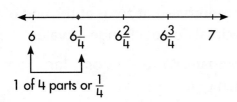

Show 7.7 on a number line.
Divide the distance from 7 to 8 into 10 equal lengths.

Label the tick marks, and draw a point at 7.7.

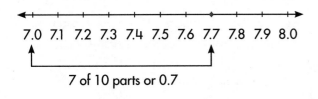

Remember each tick mark is set evenly apart.

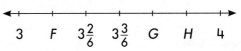

Name the fraction at each point.

1. *G* **2.** *F* **3.** *H*

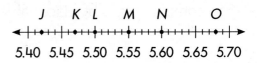

Name the decimal at each point.

4. *K* **5.** *M* **6.** *O*

Identify the point on the number line for each number.

7. $5\frac{3}{5}$ **8.** $5\frac{1}{2}$ **9.** 5.42

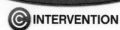
Set E, pages 342–344

Write $\frac{6}{15}$ as a decimal.

Write $\frac{6}{15}$ in simplest form: $\frac{6}{15} = \frac{2}{5}$

Find an equivalent fraction
with a denominator of 10.

$\frac{4}{10}$ is four tenths, or 0.4

Remember you can multiply or divide to
find an equivalent fraction.

Write each fraction as a decimal.

1. $\frac{3}{6}$ **2.** $\frac{1}{25}$ **3.** $\frac{3}{50}$

4. $\frac{9}{12}$ **5.** $\frac{2}{10}$ **6.** $\frac{19}{50}$

Set F, pages 346–347

Write the decimal shown in expanded,
standard, and word form.

ones	tenths	hundredths
2 .	0	1

Expanded form: 2 + 0.01

Standard form: 2.01

Word form: Two and one hundredth

Remember to use the word *and* for
the decimal point when you write a
decimal in word form.

Write the following in word and
expanded form.

1. 12.13

2. 1.09

3. 11.1

4. 88.08

Set G, pages 348–350

Compare 1.35 and 1.26 using place value.

Write the numbers, lining up the decimal
points. Then compare digits by place value.

1.35

1.26

3 tenths > 2 tenths

So, 1.35 > 1.26.

Remember that zeros at the end of the
decimal do not change its value.

Compare. Write >, <, or = for
each ◯.

1. 1.82 ◯ 1.91

2. 1.1 ◯ 1.10

Order the numbers from greatest
to least.

3. 2.2   1.47   2.19

4. 5.6   6.3   6.35

Write 4 dollars, 8 dimes, and 2 pennies with a dollar sign and a decimal point.

Read: four dollars and eighty-two cents

Write: $4.82

Remember that a dime is one tenth of a dollar, and a penny is one hundredth of a dollar.

Write each amount with a dollar sign and a decimal point.

1. 3 dollars + 4 pennies

2. 1 dollar + 5 dimes + 6 pennies

3. 9 dollars + 6 dimes

4. 4 dollars + 9 pennies

5. 7 dollars + 3 dimes + 2 pennies

6. 8 dimes + 1 penny

A biking trail is being planned for a town. Where should the 2-mile marker be placed?

| What do I know? | The biking trail must be at least 2 miles long. The 0.5 mile mark is located on the drawing. |
| What am I asked to find? | Where would the 2-mile mark be located on the drawing? |

Think 1.0 is double 0.5, and 1.0 is half of 2.0.

Measure the distance from 0 to 0.5. Double this distance. Mark 1.0. Now double this distance and mark 2.0.

Remember you can use a ruler to measure the distance between each mark.

1. Look at the walking path below. Will begins at the starting point and walks 0.6 miles. Where on the path would Will end his walk?

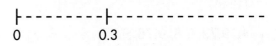

2. An architect has marked a distance of 6 inches or $\frac{1}{2}$ ft on the wall. She wants to make another mark that shows a distance of 3 ft. Where will she make the mark on the wall? How did you determine the location?

Multiple Choice

ASSESSMENT

1. Robert has 5 sports movies. Two out of 5, or $\frac{2}{5}$, of his movies are about baseball. What decimal represents $\frac{2}{5}$? (13-6)

A 0.15

B 0.4

C 0.6

D 6.0

2. What decimal is shown in the grid below? (13-7)

A 6.12

B 2.61

C 1.62

D 1.26

3. Which shows the gymnastic scores in order from least to greatest? (13-8)

A 9.72, 9.8, 9.78, 9.87

B 9.78, 9.72, 9.87, 9.8

C 9.78, 9.8, 9.72, 9.87

D 9.72, 9.78, 9.8, 9.87

4. Which statement is true? (13-8)

0.14   0.09

A 0.14 > 0.09

B 0.14 < 0.09

C 0.09 = 0.14

D 0.09 > 0.14

5. What is 1.47 written as a fraction or mixed number? (13-4)

A $\frac{1}{147}$

B $\frac{47}{100}$

C $1\frac{47}{100}$

D $1\frac{47}{10}$

6. Which number is best represented by point R on the number line? (13-5)

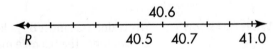

A 40.1

B 40.0

C 39.9

D 39.0

7. What is the missing number? (13-9)

$5.47 = 5 dollars + \blacksquare dimes + 7 pennies

5.47 = 5 ones + \blacksquare tenths + 7 hundredths

A 4   **C** 7

B 5   **D** 9

8. What is 0.63 written as a fraction? (13-4)

9. Find the missing values for the multiplication equation $\frac{7}{8} = \boxed{} \times \frac{\boxed{}}{8}$. (13-1)

10. What fraction is best represented by point D on the number line? (13-5)

11. Louise is creating a 1-foot long comic strip. If she has marked 0.5 ft on her paper, what should she do to find 1 foot? (13-10)

12. Write a multiplication equation with a whole number and a fraction that describes the model shown. (13-2)

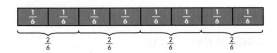

13. Juan is making cookies. He uses $\frac{3}{4}$ cup of flour in each batch of cookies. He is making 6 batches of cookies. How much flour will he use? (13-3)

14. Angie drew a number line and labeled 0 and 1. To show $\frac{5}{12}$, into how many parts should she divide the distance from 0 to 1? (13-10)

15. Quinton's frog leaped $2\frac{3}{4}$ feet on its first leap. Which point on the number line best represents the point where the frog landed? (13-5)

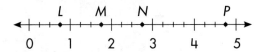

16. What is $\frac{1}{4}$ written as a decimal? (13-4)

17. What fraction and decimal are represented by the shaded area? (13-6)

18. How could you use the least amount of $1 bills, dimes, and pennies to buy a ticket to the movies? (13-9)

Zoe wants to make a clay coaster. First, she makes clay strips from slabs of clay. One slab is green, one slab is blue, and one slab is brown. She cuts each slab into 10 equal strips. Then, Zoe makes her coaster as shown below. The coaster will have 6 horizontal strips and 6 vertical strips woven together.

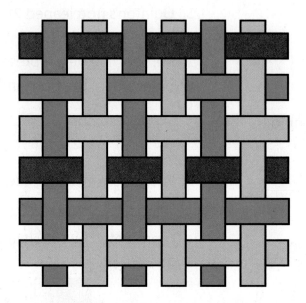

Answer each of the following on a separate piece of paper.

1. How many strips of clay does Zoe use for her coaster?

2. What fraction of the strips used for Zoe's coaster are:
   a green?   **b** blue?   **c** brown?

3. If each slab of clay weighs 1 pound, then how much do each of the clay strips that are used weigh? (Hint: Each slab was cut into 10 equal strips.)

4. Write a multiplication equation to show how much Zoe's coaster will weigh in total. How can you write the total weight as a decimal amount?

5. How many coasters can Zoe make like the one above? How much clay will Zoe have left over?

Topic 14

Measurement Units and Conversions

▼ The Gulf of Mexico is a massive body of water. How much water is deposited into the Gulf of Mexico every second? You will find out in Lesson 14-2.

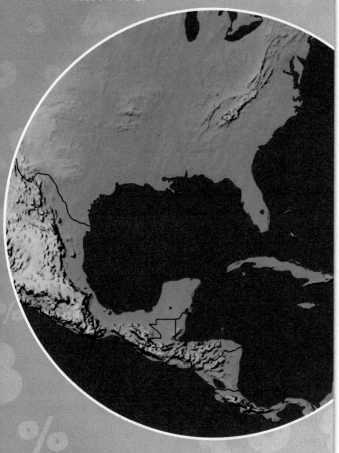

Review What You Know!

Vocabulary

Choose the best term from the box.

- capacity
- length
- foot
- mass

1. A ? is a unit of length equal to 12 inches.

2. ? represents the amount a container can hold in liquid units.

3. ? is the amount of matter that an object contains.

Capacity

Choose the best unit to measure the capacity of each. Write cups or gallons.

4. bathtub

5. fish tank

6. soup bowl

7. mug

8. gasoline tank

9. sugar in a recipe

Weight

Choose the best unit to measure the weight of each. Write ounces or pounds.

10. bicycle

11. slice of bread

12. pencil

13. bag of wood chips

14. bowling ball

15. banana

Perimeter and Area

16. What is the width of a rectangle if its area is 16 square feet, and its length is 8 feet?

© 17. **Writing to Explain** The length of a side of a square is 4 feet. Find the perimeter.

Topic Essential Question

- What are customary and metric units for measuring length, capacity, and weight/mass, and how are they related?

Interactive Learning

Pose the problem. Start each lesson by working together to solve problems. It will help you make sense of math.

Lesson 14-1

© **Be Precise** Which objects in the classroom are about 1 inch long? about 1 foot long? about 1 yard long? Tell how you decided.

Lesson 14-2

© **Reason** Use the objects at the right to complete this task.

Tell whether each of the objects listed at the right holds about a cup, a pint, a quart, or a gallon of the liquid. Tell how you decided.

milk for school lunch   mug of hot chocolate   jug of water   carton of orange juice

Lesson 14-3

© **Communicate** Complete this task. Then explain how you decided.

Name an animal that weighs less than 1 pound (measured in ounces), another animal that weighs slightly more than 1 pound, and an animal that weighs about 1 ton.

Lesson 14-4

© **Use Structure** Solve. Use common measurement relationships you know.

A soccer goal is 24 feet wide and 8 feet high. What are the dimensions of a soccer goal when measured in inches? Show your work.

Lesson 14-5

© **Communicate** Solve any way you choose.

Carson stood next to a tree that is 75 feet taller than she is. Carson is 52 inches tall. Jesse stood next to another tree that is 876 inches taller than he is. Jesse is 5 feet tall. How many inches tall is the first tree? The second tree? Which tree is taller? Explain your solutions.

Lesson 14-6

ⓒ **Use Tools** Use base-ten blocks to find these measurements.

How many centimeters long is 1 decimeter? Use the blocks shown to measure 5 objects in your room. Show how you can write each length using centimeters and decimeters.

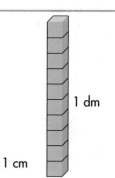

1 dm

1 cm

Lesson 14-7

ⓒ **Reason** Liz has four containers filled with water: a soup can, a bleach bottle, a thimble, and a bucket. What metric unit of capacity should Liz use to measure the amount of water in each container? Explain.

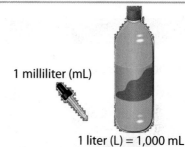

1 milliliter (mL)

1 liter (L) = 1,000 mL

Lesson 14-8

ⓒ **Reason** Decide which unit of mass you would use to measure each of the balls shown at the right. Order the balls from the one with the least mass to one with the greatest mass. Tell how you decided.

Lesson 14-9

ⓒ **Use Structure** Solve. Use common measurement relationships you know.

Maria is 156 centimeters tall. The average 10-year-old girl in the United States is 1 meter, 430 millimeters tall. Is Maria taller than the average 10-year-old girl? Tell how you decided.

Lesson 14-10

ⓒ **Persevere** Solve any way you choose.

Allison skated for 2 hours on Saturday. Kylie skated for 100 minutes. Who skated longer? Tell how you decided.

Lesson 14-11

ⓒ **Persevere** Solve any way you choose.

Between 6:00 A.M. and 7:00 A.M., the temperature outside rose 6°F. Between 7:00 A.M. and 8:00 A.M., the temperature rose 3°F. If the temperature at 8:00 A.M. is 73°F, what was the temperature at 6:00 A.M.? Show all of your work.

Lesson
14-1

© Common Core

4.MD.1 Know relative sizes of measurement units within one system of units including km, m, cm; kg, g; lb, oz.; l, ml; hr, min, sec. Within a single system of measurement, express measurements in a larger unit in terms of a smaller unit. Record measurement equivalents in a two-column table.

Using Customary Units of Length

How do you estimate and measure length?

The United States uses customary units of measure. About how long is Greg's toy car?

About 1 inch (in.)

Other Examples

A notebook is about 1 foot (ft).

Almost 1 foot

1 ft = 12 in.

A baseball bat is about 1 yard (yd).

1 yd = 36 in.   1 yd = 3 ft

1 mile (mi) is about 4 times around the track.

1 mi = 5,280 ft   1 mi = 1,760 yd

Guided Practice*

© **MATHEMATICAL PRACTICES**

Do you know HOW?

For **1** through **4**, choose the most appropriate unit to measure the length of each. Write in., ft, yd, or mi.

1. highway

2. CD case

3. football field

4. room

Do you UNDERSTAND?

© **5. Communicate** How long is your textbook to the nearest inch? Explain how you measured.

© **6. Construct Arguments** Greg wants to measure how tall his 2-year-old sister is. What two units could he use? Explain your answer.

Independent Practice

For **7** through **10**, choose the most appropriate unit to measure the length of each. Write in., ft, yd, or mi.

7. pencil

8. building

9. mountain

10. spool of ribbon

Animated Glossary
www.pearsonsuccessnet.com

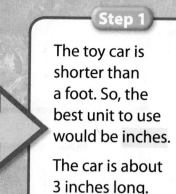

The toy car is shorter than a foot. So, the best unit to use would be inches.

The car is about 3 inches long.

Step 2

Measure to the nearest inch.

Line one end of the toy car up with the zero mark on the ruler. Then, find the inch mark closest to the other end of the toy car.

INCHES

Greg's toy car is about 3 inches long to the nearest inch.

For **11** through **13**, estimate and then measure each length to the nearest inch.

11.

12.

13.

Problem Solving

 MATHEMATICAL PRACTICES

14. If the perimeter of the triangle at the right is 16 yards, what is the length of the third side?

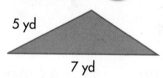

5 yd

7 yd

Ⓒ **15. Writing to Explain** Lionel is building a tree house. The materials list tells the length of the floorboards that are needed. Which would be the best unit of measure to describe the length of the floorboards?

Ⓒ **16. Reason** Trini took some photos. The number of photos she took is a two-digit number. The sum of the digits is 11. The tens digit is 3 more than the ones digit. How many photos did Trini take?

Ⓒ **17. Persevere** In Olivia, Minnesota, there is a giant ear of corn standing over a roadside gazebo. Using the image to the right, which do you think is the actual height of the corn?

   A   25 miles   **C**   25 inches

   B   25 feet   **D**   25 centimeters

Lesson
14-2

Common
Core

4.MD.1 Know relative sizes of measurement units within one system of units including km, m, cm; kg, g; lb, oz.; l, ml; hr, min, sec. Within a single system of measurement, express measurements in a larger unit in terms of a smaller unit. Record measurement equivalents in a two-column table.

Customary Units of Capacity

How do you measure capacity in customary units?

Capacity is the volume of a container measured in liquid units. Here are some customary units for measuring capacity.

How much water can a kitchen sink hold?

1 cup (c)   1 pint (pt)   1 quart (qt)   1 gallon (gal)

Guided Practice*

MATHEMATICAL PRACTICES

Do you know HOW?

Which is the best estimate for the capacity of each item?

1.
3 gallons or 30 gallons?

2.
2 cups or 2 quarts?

3.
1 pint or 4 gallons?

4.
1 cup or 1 quart?

Do you UNDERSTAND?

5. Look at the quart and gallon containers above. Estimate how many quarts are in 1 gallon.

6. **Reason** Estimate how many quarts it would take to fill the kitchen sink.

7. Which is greater, one cup or one quart?

8. Which is greater, one cup or one pint?

Independent Practice

In **9** through **20**, choose the most appropriate unit to measure the capacity of each item. Write c, pt, qt, or gal.

9. juice carton

10. bucket

11. gasoline tank

12. paper cup

13. fish bowl

14. bathtub

15. snow globe

16. cat's water dish

17. spray bottle

18. aquarium

19. soup bowl

20. pond

Animated Glossary
www.pearsonsuccessnet.com

*For another example, see Set B on page 392.

Step 1	Step 2	Step 3

Step 1

Choose the most appropriate unit to measure:

It would take too long to fill the sink with the cup, pint, or quart.

The best unit would be the gallon.

Step 2

Estimate:

Visualize how many gallons of water it would take to fill the sink.

The sink has a capacity of about 4 gallons.

Step 3

Measure:

Fill the gallon jug with water and pour it into the sink. Do this until the sink is full, and count how many gallon jugs were used to fill the sink.

The sink has a capacity of about 5 gallons.

In **21** through **24**, choose the best estimate for the capacity of each item.

21.

1 gallon or
10 gallons?

22.

1 gallon or
1 quart?

23.

20 quarts or
200 quarts?

24.

2 quarts or
2 pints?

Problem Solving

MATHEMATICAL PRACTICES

25. Look for Patterns In one second, 3,300,000 gallons of water from the Mississippi River enters the Gulf of Mexico. In one day, Houston's water system can carry 900,000 gallons. Which is greater, 3,300,000 gallons or 900,000 gallons?

26. Persevere A lemonade recipe calls for 1 cup of sugar and 1 quart of water. This recipe makes 4 servings. If you want to make 12 servings, how many cups of sugar will you need?

27. Be Precise You need 1 teaspoon of bubble bath for every 25 gallons of water. How much bubble bath is needed for a 50-gallon bathtub?

28. The lines on the measuring cup below show fluid ounces (oz) and cups (c). Which is greater, one fluid ounce or one cup?

29. Reason Which would be the better unit to measure the water in a swimming pool, the number of juice glasses or the number of bathtubs?

4.MD.1 Know relative sizes of measurement units within one system of units including km, m, cm; kg, g; lb, oz.; l, ml; hr, min, sec. Within a single system of measurement, express measurements in a larger unit in terms of a smaller unit. Record measurement equivalents in a two-column table.

Units of Weight
How do you measure weight?

Weight is how heavy an object is. Below are some customary units for measuring weight.

How much does a peach weigh?

1 ounce (oz)   1 pound (lb)   1 ton (T)

A key weighs about 1 ounce.

A kitten weighs about 1 pound.

A giraffe weighs about 1 ton.

Guided Practice*

MATHEMATICAL
PRACTICES

Do you know HOW?

For **1** through **4**, give the best unit to measure the weight of each item.

1.

a slice of bread

2.

a sheep

3.

a helicopter

4.

a bicycle

Do you UNDERSTAND?

ⓒ 5. **Writing to Explain** How can you tell that the weight of the peach is **NOT** 8 ounces?

6. If you placed 3 keys on the same pan with the peach, how many ounces would be needed to balance the keys and the peach?

Independent Practice

For **7** through **18**, choose the most appropriate unit to measure the weight of each item.

Tip *Think of a familiar object that weighs one pound, one ounce, or one ton. Use that object to estimate the weight of other objects measured with the same unit.*

7. sea lion   **8.** orange   **9.** nail polish   **10.** greeting card

11. paper clip   **12.** canoe   **13.** ocean liner   **14.** football player

15. telephone   **16.** car   **17.** fork   **18.** bag of potatoes

DIGITAL   Animated Glossary
www.pearsonsuccessnet.com

| Step 1 | Step 2 | Step 3 |

Step 1

Choose the appropriate unit to measure:

A peach weighs less than a pound.

So, the best unit would be the ounce.

Step 2

Estimate:

 A key weighs about one ounce. How many keys would weigh the same as a peach?

About 8 keys would weigh the same.

A peach weighs about 8 ounces.

Step 3

Measure:

Place the peach on one pan of the balance. Place an ounce weight on the other pan. Add ounce weights until the balance is level, and count the ounce weights.

The peach weighs 7 ounces.

Problem Solving

MATHEMATICAL
PRACTICES

19. One of the first computers built weighed 30 tons. What would be an appropriate unit of weight to measure the weight of most desktop computers today?

20. Name 3 things about the box below that you can measure. Give a reasonable estimate for each measure.

© **21. Reason** Which is a greater number, the number of pounds a rooster weighs or the number of ounces the same rooster weighs?

For **22** through **25**, use the chart at the right.

22. About how many ounces do two dozen medium apples weigh?

23. Estimate the weight of one apple.

24. Do five dozen large watermelons weigh more or less than 1,000 pounds?

25. About how many pounds do three dozen bananas weigh?

Fruit	Weight of one dozen
🍎	72 ounces
🍌	3 pounds
🍉	264 pounds

© **26. Persevere** What is a good estimate for the weight of a bicycle?

  A 30 ounces   **C** 30 pounds

  B 3 pounds   **D** 3,000 ounces

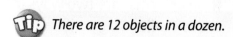 There are 12 objects in a dozen.

4.MD.1 Know relative
sizes of measurement units
within one system of units
including km, m, cm; kg,
g; lb, oz.; l, ml; hr, min, sec.
Within a single system of
measurement, express
measurements in a larger
unit in terms of a smaller
unit. Record measurement
equivalents in a two-
column table.

Changing Customary Units

How do you change customary units?

The table at the right can be used to change one customary unit of measure to another.

Customary Units		
Length	**Capacity**	**Weight**
1 ft = 12 in.	1 tbsp = 3 tsp	1 lb = 16 oz
1 yd = 36 in.	1 fl oz = 2 tbsp	1 T = 2,000 lb
1 yd = 3 ft	1 c = 8 fl oz	
1 mi = 5,280 ft	1 pt = 2 c	
1 mi = 1,760 yd	1 qt = 2 pt	
	1 gal = 4 qt	

Another Example How do you compare customary measures?

Kylie brought 2 gallons of punch to the school picnic. Each person gets 1 cup of punch.

Did Kylie bring enough punch for 24 people?

2 gal ◯ 24 c

Step 1

Change gallons into cups.

Think 1 gal = 4 qt
So, 2 gal × 4 qt = 8 quarts.

Think 1 qt = 2 pt
So, 8 qt × 2 pt = 16 pints.

Think 1 pt = 2 c
So, 16 pt × 2 c = 32 cups.

Kylie brought enough punch for 24 people.

Step 2

Compare.

32 c > 24 c

So, 2 gal > 24 c.

Explain It

1. How do you change quarts to gallons?

2. How do you change pounds to ounces?

© 3. **Reason** What are two ways to find how many inches are in a mile?

How many pints are in five quarts?

To change larger units to smaller units, multiply.

$$5 \text{ qt} = \boxed{} \text{ pt}$$

(Think) 1 qt = 2 pt

$$5 \times 2 = 10$$

$$5 \text{ qt} = 10 \text{ pt}$$

There are 10 pints in five quarts.

How many feet are equal to 84 inches?

To change smaller units to larger units, divide

$$84 \text{ in.} = \boxed{} \text{ ft}$$

(Think) 12 in. = 1 ft

$$84 \div 12 = 7$$

$$84 \text{ in.} = 7 \text{ ft}$$

There are 7 feet in 84 inches.

Guided Practice*

Do you know HOW?

In **1** through **4**, find each missing number.

1. $6 \text{ T} = \boxed{} \text{ lb}$ **2.** $12 \text{ qt} = \boxed{} \text{ gal}$

3. $7 \text{ lb} = \boxed{} \text{ oz}$ **4.** $3 \text{ yd} = \boxed{} \text{ in.}$

In **5** through **8**, compare. Write > or < for each ◯.

5. 5 ft ◯ 57 in. **6.** 16 fl oz ◯ 3 c

7. 2 tbsp ◯ 4 tsp **8.** 3 gal ◯ 8 qt

Do you UNDERSTAND?

9. In the first example, why do you multiply 5 × 2?

10. Do you multiply or divide to change inches to yards?

© **11.** **Writing to Explain** A 4-foot stick is longer than one yard. A 32-inch stick is shorter than one yard. Is a 4-foot stick longer or shorter than a 32-inch stick?

Independent Practice

Leveled Practice For **12** through **19**, find each missing number.

12. $4 \text{ pt} = \boxed{} \text{ qt}$
$4 \div 2 = \boxed{} \text{ qt}$

13. $18 \text{ tsp} = \boxed{} \text{ tbsp}$
$18 \div 3 = \boxed{} \text{ tbsp}$

14. $2 \text{ c} = \boxed{} \text{ fl oz}$
$2 \times 8 = \boxed{} \text{ fl oz}$

15. $4 \text{ tbsp} = \boxed{} \text{ tsp}$
$4 \times 3 = \boxed{} \text{ tsp}$

16. $8 \text{ yd} = \boxed{} \text{ ft}$ **17.** $60 \text{ in.} = \boxed{} \text{ ft}$ **18.** $3 \text{ lb} = \boxed{} \text{ oz}$ **19.** $7 \text{ ft} = \boxed{} \text{ in.}$

For **20** through **27**, compare. Write > or < for each ◯.

20. 1 pt ◯ 1 qt **21.** 16 tbsp ◯ 2 c **22.** 14 in. ◯ 1 yd **23.** 5 c ◯ 2 pt

24. 9 ft ◯ 2 yd **25.** 2 T ◯ 2,500 lb **26.** 2 mi ◯ 2,000 yd **27.** 24 oz ◯ 2 lb

28. The longest tail feathers of any bird are those of the Argus Pheasant. The feathers measure 5 feet 7 inches in length. How many inches long are these feathers?

29. A super-stretch limousine is 240 inches long. A pickup truck is 19 feet long. Which is longer?

30. If one side of a square measures 5 inches, what is the area of the square?

Use the table at the right for **31** through **33**.

The weight of objects on other planets and the Moon is different than it is on Earth.

31. What is the approximate weight in ounces of a fourth grader on Venus?

32. What is the approximate weight in ounces of a fourth grader on the Moon?

Approximate Weight of a 4th-Grader			
Earth	Jupiter	Venus	Moon
85 lb	215 lb	77 lb	14 lb

© **33. Writing to Explain** Would an adult weigh more on Earth or on Venus? Explain your reasoning.

© **34. Critique Reasoning** A magazine reports that a giraffe's height is 180 inches, or 15 yards. What mistake was made?

© **35. Be Precise** Which unit of measure would you use to measure the length of your shoe?

36. Mr. Kunkle uses a bowling ball that weighs 13 pounds. How many ounces does the bowling ball weigh?

A 116 oz   **C** 180 oz

B 140 oz   **D** 208 oz

37. Jeremiah bought 2 pounds of lettuce and 3 pounds of tomatoes for a salad. How many ounces of each did he purchase?

© **38. Persevere** Henry filled a bathtub with 15 gallons of water. How many quarts of water is this?

A 20 qt   **C** 55 qt

B 45 qt   **D** 60 qt

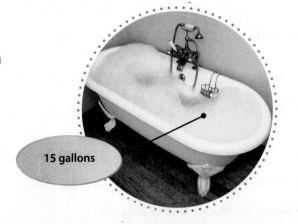

15 gallons

Stop and Practice

Find the difference. Estimate to check if the answer is reasonable.

1. 543 − 28   **2.** 376 − 148   **3.** 1,523 − 317

4. 1,578 − 983   **5.** 345 − 281   **6.** 581 − 127

Find the product. Estimate to check if the answer is reasonable.

7.　　3,418　**8.**　　6,223　**9.**　　3,478　**10.**　　27　**11.**　　40
　　× 　　5　　　× 　　2　　　× 　　5　　× 36　　× 12

Find the sum. Estimate to check if the answer is reasonable.

12.　12,345　**13.**　4,402　**14.**　403　**15.**　5,474　**16.**　13,985
　+ 87,654　　+ 3,912　　+ 737　　+ 　723　　+ 　7,539

© **Critique Reasoning** Find each answer that is not correct. Write it correctly and explain the error.

17.　　3,390　**18.**　　4,890　**19.**　$\frac{\$105}{2)\$210}$　**20.**　$\frac{11}{12}$　**21.**　　57
　+ 2,576　　× 　　8　　　　　　　　　− $\frac{3}{12}$　　× 35
　　5,866　　39,120　　　　　　　　　　　　　　1,965
　　　　　　　　　　　　　　　　　　$\frac{9}{12}$ or $\frac{3}{4}$

Number Sense

© **Construct Arguments** Write whether each statement is true or false. Explain your answer.

22. The product of 3 and $11 is greater than $35.

23. The sum of 59,703 and 24,032 is greater than 70,000, but less than 90,000.

24. The difference of 466 − 103 is 3 less than 366.

25. The product of 21 and 46 is greater than 800.

26. The quotient of 534 ÷ 6 is greater than 90.

27. The sum of 24 and 27 is less than 50.

Common Core

4.MD.1 Know relative sizes of measurement units within one system of units including km, m, cm; kg, g; lb, oz.; l, ml; hr, min, sec. Within a single system of measurement, express measurements in a larger unit in terms of a smaller unit. Record measurement equivalents in a two-column table.

Problem Solving

Writing to Explain

Three students individually measured the width of their classroom. They recorded their data in the chart. Which student made a mistake?

Data	Student	Measurement
	Nancy	44 ft.
	Matt	19 ft 6 in.
	Mike	6 yds 1 ft 6 in.

Guided Practice*

MATHEMATICAL PRACTICES

Do you know HOW?

Solve. Write to explain.

1. A bald eagle can have a wingspan of up to 7 feet 6 inches. A mallard duck can have a wingspan of about 32 inches. How much longer is the bald eagle's wingspan than the mallard duck's wingspan?

Do you UNDERSTAND?

2. How can you explain that one yard is equal to 36 inches?

Ⓒ 3. **Write a Problem** Write a problem in which measurements are compared. Write to explain which measurement is correct.

Independent Practice

MATHEMATICAL PRACTICES

Ⓒ **Be Precise** Solve each problem. Explain your answer.

4. Julia and her brother went deep-sea fishing. They caught a spotted seatrout weighing 5 pounds 10 ounces, a snook weighing 8 pounds 4 ounces, and a redfish weighing 176 ounces. Which was the largest fish they caught?

5. When converting ounces to pounds, you would have to divide the number of ounces by 16 to get the number of pounds. If you get a remainder when converting ounces to pounds, what does the remainder mean?

Applying Math Practices

- What am I asked to find?
- What else can I try?
- How are quantities related?
- How can I explain my work?
- How can I use math to model the problem?
- Can I use tools to help?
- Is my work precise?
- Why does this work?
- How can I generalize?

Convert the students' measurements to inches and compare.

Nancy's measurement:
1 foot = 12 inches
44 × 12 = 528 inches

Matt's measurement:
1 foot = 12 inches
19 × 12 = 228 inches

19 feet = 228 inches
+   6 inches
_____
234 inches

Mike's measurement:
1 yard = 36 inches
6 × 36 = 216 inches

6 yards = 216 inches
1 foot =   12 inches
+   6 inches
_____
234 inches

Mike's and Matt's measurements are both 234 inches.
Nancy's measurement is 528 inches.

Nancy made a mistake. Her calculation is correct, but she may
have measured the length of the classroom not the width.

For **6** and **7**, use the data to the right.

Derek, Kitty, Eva, and Mercedes are measuring
planks of wood to build a tree house.

6. Each plank of wood needs to measure
   5 feet and 10 inches. Derek said his planks
   measure 2 inches less than 2 yards.
   Did Derek measure correctly?

© 7. **Construct Arguments** Whose
   measurement is incorrect? Explain.

Names	Measurements
Derek	2 yds – 2 in.
Kitty	1 yd 34 in.
Eva	70 in.
Mercedes	60 in.

For **8** and **9**, use the drawing to the right.

© 8. **Persevere** What information would
   you need in order to find the length
   of the fourth side of the quadrilateral?

9. If the perimeter of the quadrilateral
   is 25 inches, how long is the final side
   of the quadrilateral?

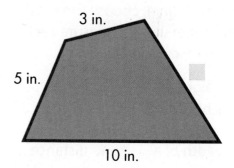

3 in.

5 in.

10 in.

10. Below is a drawing of a race track.
    How many feet would you run if you
    went around the inner track twice?
    Explain.

© 11. **Reason** A millimeter is related to a
    meter in the same way a milligram
    is related to a gram. How many
    millimeters are in one meter?

Tip 1 gram = 1,000 milligrams

One lap around
the inner track is
440 yards

Lesson
14-6

Common
Core

4.MD.1 Know relative sizes of measurement units within one system of units including km, m, cm; kg, g; lb, oz.; l, ml; hr, min, sec. Within a single system of measurement, express measurements in a larger unit in terms of a smaller unit. Record measurement equivalents in a two-column table.

Using Metric Units of Length

How do you estimate and measure length?

The meter is the basic metric unit of length.

How long is the beetle at the right?

About 1 cm

Hands-On
metric ruler
CENTIMETERS

Metric Units of Length

1 centimeter (cm) = 10 millimeters (mm)

1 decimeter (dm) = 10 centimeters (cm)

1 meter (m) = 100 centimeters (cm)

1 kilometer (km) = 1,000 meters (m)

Other Examples

1 millimeter (mm) is about the thickness of a dime.

1 meter (m) is about the length of a snake.

1 kilometer (km) is about the length of 4 city blocks.

Guided Practice*

MATHEMATICAL PRACTICES

Do you know HOW?

For **1** through **4**, choose the most appropriate unit to measure each. Write mm, cm, dm, m, or km.

1. height of a house

2. length of a cat

3. width of a sunflower seed

4. distance traveled by plane

Do you UNDERSTAND?

© **5. Be Precise** How wide is your textbook to the nearest centimeter? Explain how you measured.

6. Joni wants to measure the width of a narrow ribbon she is using to tie around the pinecone. Which metric unit should she use? Explain.

Independent Practice

For **7** through **9**, choose the most appropriate unit to measure each item. Write mm, cm, dm, m, or km.

7. length of a shoe

8. height of a tree

9. width of a strand of yarn

DIGITAL
Animated Glossary
www.pearsonsuccessnet.com

*For another example, see Set F on page 394.

The beetle is shorter than a decimeter, but longer than a millimeter. So the best unit would be centimeters.

The beetle's length is about 4 centimeters long.

Measure to the nearest centimeter.

Line one end of the beetle up with the zero mark on the ruler. Then find the centimeter mark closest to the other end of the beetle.

CENTIMETERS

The beetle is 4 centimeters long to the nearest centimeter.

© **Be Precise** For **10** through **12**, estimate. Then measure each length to the nearest centimeter.

10.

11.

12.

Problem Solving

© **MATHEMATICAL PRACTICES**

13. The fourth-grade teachers are planning a pizza party. Each pizza has 8 slices. The teachers want enough pizza so that each student can have 2 slices. If there are 22 students in each of the 3 fourth-grade classes, how many pizzas must be ordered?

© **14. Writing to Explain** June measured the height from the top of her window to the floor and wrote 3. She forgot to write the unit. Which metric unit of measure did June most likely use?

© **15. Reasonableness** In the year 2000, the world's largest Chinese dancing dragon was part of a celebration at the Great Wall of China. It took 3,200 people working inside the dragon to move it. Which is the best estimate of the length of the dragon?

A 3,048 mm   **C** 3,048 cm

B 3,048 dm   **D** 3,048 m

16. Measure to find the length of the bead below. What is the length of 32 of these beads on a necklace?

A 30 cm   **C** 64 cm

B 32 cm   **D** 100 cm

4.MD.1 Know relative sizes of measurement units within one system of units including km, m, cm; kg, g; lb, oz.; l, ml; hr, min, sec. Within a single system of measurement, express measurements in a larger unit in terms of a smaller unit. Record measurement equivalents in a two-column table. Also **4.MD.2**

Metric Units of Capacity

How do you measure capacity with metric units?

Below are two metric units for measuring capacity. How much liquid can the bottle to the right hold?

1 milliliter (mL)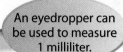

1 liter (L)

An eyedropper can be used to measure 1 milliliter.

Some water bottles hold 1 liter.

Guided Practice*

 MATHEMATICAL PRACTICES

Do you know HOW?

Which is the best estimate for the capacity of each item?

1.

5 liters or 500 liters?

2.

10 liters or 100 liters?

3.

100 milliliters or 10 liters?

4.

10 milliliters or 1 liter?

Do you UNDERSTAND?

5. Which unit of measure is greater, a liter or a milliliter?

6. Reason Which would be the best unit of measure to use to measure the amount of gasoline in a car's gas tank, a milliliter or a liter?

7. Which would be the best unit of measure to use to fill a large milk container, a milliliter or a liter?

Independent Practice

In **8** through **15**, choose the most appropriate unit to measure the capacity of each item. Write L or mL.

8. bucket

9. ink pen

10. juice glass

11. washing machine

12. soup pot

13. coffee mug

14. medicine cup

15. pitcher

Animated Glossary
www.pearsonsuccessnet.com

DIGITAL

*For another example, see Set G on page 394.

Step 1		Step 2		Step 3
Choose the most appropriate unit to measure: The milliliter is a very small amount. A larger unit would be more appropriate to measure with. **The best unit would be the liter.**		**Estimate:** Visualize how many liter bottles it would take to fill the bottle. **The bottle has a capacity of about 2 liters.**		**Measure:** Fill the liter bottle with water and pour it into the bottle. Do this until the bottle is full, and count how many liter bottles were used. **The bottle has a capacity of about 2 liters.**

In **16** through **19**, choose the best estimate for the capacity of each.

16.
200 milliliters or 200 liters?

17.
4 liters or 14 liters?

18.
20 milliliters or 200 milliliters?

19.
3 liters or 300 liters?

Problem Solving **MATHEMATICAL PRACTICES**

20. Reason Which number would be greater, the number of liters of juice in a pitcher or the number of milliliters of juice in the same pitcher?

21. Reasonableness Zack said he poured lemonade from a 300-liter pitcher into a 20-milliliter glass. Are these numbers reasonable? Why or why not?

22. Persevere Which capacities are written in order from greatest to least?

A 5 milliliters, 2 liters, 1 liter

B 2 liters, 5 milliliters, 1 liter

C 1 liter, 2 liters, 5 milliliters

D 2 liters, 1 liter, 5 milliliters

23. Marcus filled a bottle with 1,000 milliliters of water to take with him on his jog. After his jog, he had about 450 milliliters left in his bottle. How much water did he drink while he jogged?

1,000 mL of water	
450	?

24. What is the perimeter of the triangle?

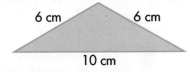
6 cm 6 cm 10 cm

25. How much more water does a 0.75-liter sports bottle hold than a 0.6-liter bottle?

Lesson
14-8

© Common Core

4.MD.1 Know relative sizes of measurement units within one system of units including km, m, cm; kg, g; lb, oz.; l, ml; hr, min, sec. Within a single system of measurement, express measurements in a larger unit in terms of a smaller unit. Record measurement equivalents in a two-column table. Also 4.MD.2

Units of Mass

What are metric units of mass?

Mass is the amount of matter that something contains.

What is the mass of a red brick?

1 gram (g)

1 kilogram (kg)

The mass of a red brick is?

A dollar bill has a mass of about 1 gram (g).

A cantaloupe has a mass of about 1 kilogram (kg).

Other Examples

Weight and Mass are different.

The **weight** of an object changes depending on its location.

The weight of the red brick on the moon is not the same as its weight on Earth.

The **mass** of an object always stays the same.

The mass of the red brick on the moon is the same as its mass on Earth.

Guided Practice*

© MATHEMATICAL PRACTICES

Do you know HOW?

For **1** and **2**, choose the most appropriate unit to measure the mass of each item.

1.

hamster

2.

gorilla

Do you UNDERSTAND?

3. Which number would be less, the mass of a grapefruit in grams or the mass of the same grapefruit in kilograms?

© **4. Reason** How many cantaloupes would be needed to have the same mass as two red bricks?

Independent Practice

For **5** through **12**, choose the most appropriate unit to measure the mass of each item.

5. pencil

6. baseball player

7. baseball

8. honeydew melon

Animated Glossary
www.pearsonsuccessnet.com

Step 1	Step 2	Step 3

Step 1

Choose the appropriate unit to measure:

A brick has a greater mass than a cantaloupe.

So, the best unit would be the kilogram.

Step 2

Estimate:

 Think A cantaloupe has a mass of about one kilogram. How many cantaloupes would have the same mass as a red brick?

About 3 cantaloupes would have the same mass.

The brick has a mass of about 3 kilograms.

Step 3

Measure:

Place the brick on one pan of the balance. Add kilograms to the other pan until the balance is level. Count the kilograms.

The brick has a mass of 3 kilograms.

9. strawberry

10. penguin

11. sailboat

12. dragonfly

Problem Solving

© **MATHEMATICAL PRACTICES**

© **Use Tools** For **13** through **15**, use the table at the right.

13. Order the coins from least mass to greatest mass.

14. A dollar bill has a mass of about 1 gram. About how many dollar bills have the same mass as a nickel?

15. There are 40 nickels in a roll of nickels. What is the total mass of the nickels in one roll?

 Find the mass of 4 nickels and multiply by 10.

Coin	Mass
	2.500 grams
	5.000 grams
	2.268 grams
	5.670 grams

© **16. Writing to Explain** Mandy says that she has a mass of 32 kg on the Earth. What is her mass on the moon?

17. Which number is greater, the mass of a carrot in grams or the mass of the same carrot in kilograms?

18. Use the bar diagram below. José needs $78 for a present. He has already saved $33. How much more does he need to save?

$78 in all

?	$33

© **19. Reasonableness** What is a good estimate for the mass of an American saddlebred horse?

A 5 kg   **C** 500 kg

B 50 kg   **D** 5,000 kg

Common
Core

4.MD.1 Know relative
sizes of measurement units
within one system of units
including km, m, cm; kg,
g; lb, oz.; l, ml; hr, min, sec.
Within a single system of
measurement, express
measurements in a larger
unit in terms of a smaller
unit. Record measurement
equivalents in a two-column
table.

Changing Metric Units

How do you change metric units?

The table at the right can be used to change one metric unit of measure to another.

Metric Units		
Length	**Capacity**	**Mass**
1 m = 1,000 mm	1 L = 1,000 mL	1 g = 1,000 mg
1 cm = 10 mm		1 kg = 1,000 g
1 dm = 10 cm		
1 m = 100 cm		
1 km = 1,000 m		

Another Example How do you compare metric measures?

Sela went to the market to buy some fruit. She bought a bag of oranges that had a mass of 1 kg 125 g and a bag of apples that had a mass of 1,380 g.

Which bag had a greater mass?

1 kg 125 g ◯ 1,380 g

Step 1

Change kilograms into grams.

Think 1 kg = 1,000 g

1,000 + 125 = 1,125

1 kg 125 g = 1,125 g

The bag of apples has a greater mass.

Step 2

Compare.

1,125 kg < 1,380 kg

So, 1 kg 125 g < 1,380 g.

Explain It

1. How do you change centimeters to meters?

2. How do you change liters to milliliters?

© 3. **Reasonableness** Why do you have to change kilograms to grams when comparing these two units of mass?

A large monarch butterfly's wingspan is about 10 centimeters long. How long is this in millimeters?

To change larger units to smaller units, multiply.

10 cm = ▮ **mm**

Think **1 cm = 10 mm**

10 × 10 = 100

10 cm = 100 mm

A large monarch butterfly's wingspan is about 100 mm.

10 cm

A small monarch butterfly's wingspan is about 60 millimeters long. How long is this in centimeters?

To change smaller units to larger units, divide.

60 mm = ▮ **cm**

Think **10 mm = 1 cm**

60 ÷ 10 = 6

60 mm = 6 cm

A small monarch butterfly's wingspan is about 6 cm.

60 mm

Guided Practice*

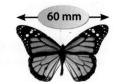

MATHEMATICAL
PRACTICES

Do you know HOW?

In **1** through **4**, find each missing number.

1. 1 kg = ▮ g **2.** 3 cm = ▮ mm

3. 600 cm = ▮ m **4.** 4 dm = ▮ cm

In **5** through **8**, compare. Write > or < for each ◯.

5. 3 m ◯ 200 cm **6.** 4 L ◯ 7,000 mL

7. 1 kg ◯ 100 g **8.** 1 km ◯ 3,000 m

Do you UNDERSTAND?

9. In the second example, why do you divide 60 by 10?

10. Do you multiply or divide to change meters to centimeters?

© **11. Writing to Explain** Explain how to change 600 mm to centimeters.

Independent Practice

Leveled Practice In **12** through **23**, find each missing number.

12. 8 km = ▮ m
8 × 1,000 = ▮ m

13. 6 L = ▮ mL
6 × 1,000 = ▮ mL

14. 32 kg = ▮ g
32 × 1,000 = ▮ g

15. 5 m = ▮ cm

16. 11 kg = ▮ g

17. 57 dm = ▮ cm

18. 8,632 m = ▮ cm

19. 552 km = ▮ m

20. 13,000 g = ▮ kg

21. 680 cm = ▮ dm

22. 61 km = ▮ m

23. 16 L = ▮ mL

Independent Practice

For **24** through **29**, compare. Write > or < for each ◯.

24. 100 mL ◯ 1 L   **25.** 10 cm ◯ 100 dm   **26.** 2 kg ◯ 200 g

27. 30 cm ◯ 30 mm   **28.** 2 km ◯ 200 m   **29.** 600 kg ◯ 6 g

Problem Solving

MATHEMATICAL PRACTICES

Use the data to the right for **30** through **32**.

30. How many meters does a lion travel in 1 minute?

31. List the animals in order from fastest to slowest.

ⓒ **32. Be Precise** Edgar says a giant tortoise is faster than a spider because 450 is greater than 31. Is he correct?

Distances Animals Can Travel in One Minute	
Elephant	670 m
Giant Tortoise	450 cm
Spider	31 m
Lion	1 km 340 m

33. Find the value of $n \div 6$ when n is 4,200.

ⓒ **34. Reason** The mass of 5 tomatoes is about 1 kilogram. Estimate the mass of 1 tomato in grams.

ⓒ **35. Model** Use the diagram below to write a subtraction sentence.

36. Which measure is **NOT** equal to 6 meters?

A   60 kilometers

B   60 decimeters

C   600 centimeters

D   6,000 millimeters

ⓒ **37. Use Structure** Two sides of an equilateral triangle both measure 3 inches. How long is the third side? Explain.

3 inches   3 inches

ⓒ **38. Reason** There are about 5 milliliters in one teaspoon. There are 3 teaspoons in one tablespoon. How many milliliters are there in 10 tablespoons?

Enrichment

Comparing Metric and Customary Measures

The symbol ≈ is read as "is approximately equal to."
The table to the right lists the comparable measures.

Customary and Metric Unit Equivalents

Length:
1 in. = 2.54 cm
1 ft = 30.48 cm
1 m ≈ 3.28 ft
1 m ≈ 1.09 yd
1 km ≈ 0.62 mi
1 mi ≈ 1.61 km

Capacity:
1 L ≈ 1.06 qt
1 gal ≈ 3.79 L

Weight and Mass:
1 oz ≈ 28.35 g
1 kg ≈ 2.2 lb

Examples:

About how many pounds are equal to 5 kilograms?

Think 1 kilogram is approximately equal to 2.2 pounds.

Multiply to convert.

$5 \times 2.2 = 11$

5 kilograms is approximately 11 pounds.

About how many miles are equal to 5 kilometers?

Think 1 kilometer is approximately equal to 0.62 miles.

Multiply to convert.

$5 \times 0.62 = 3.1$

5 kilometers is approximately 3.1 miles.

Practice

For **1** through **8**, copy and complete by writing < or > for each ◯.

1. 1 m ◯ 1 yd
2. 1 mi ◯ 1 km
3. 1 cm ◯ 1 in.
4. 1 gal ◯ 1 L

5. 1 cm ◯ 1 ft
6. 1 L ◯ 1 qt
7. 1 lb ◯ 1 kg
8. 1m ◯ 1 ft

For **9** through **16**, copy and complete.

9. 2 oz ≈ ▢ g
10. 12 in = ▢ cm
11. 5 m ≈ ▢ ft
12. 7 mi ≈ ▢ km

13. 4 gal ≈ ▢ L
14. 3 kg ≈ ▢ lb
15. 10 L ≈ ▢ qt
16. 9 ft = ▢ cm

Lesson
14-10

Common
Core

4.MD.1 Know relative
sizes of measurement units
within one system of units
including km, m, cm; kg,
g; lb, oz.; l, ml; hr, min, sec.
Within a single system of
measurement, express
measurements in a larger
unit in terms of a smaller
unit. Record measurement
equivalents in a two-column
table. Also 4.MD.2

Units of Time

How do you compare units of time?

On her birthday, Kara calculated that she was 108 months old. Her friend Jordan has the same birthday. If Jordan turned 8 years old, who is older, Kara or Jordan?

You can convert different units of time in order to compare them.

Units of Time
1 minute = 60 seconds
1 hour = 60 minutes
1 day = 24 hours
1 week = 7 days
1 month = about 4 weeks
1 year = 52 weeks
1 year = 12 months
1 year = 365 days
1 leap year = 366 days
1 decade = 10 years
1 century = 100 years
1 millennium = 1,000 years

Guided Practice*

MATHEMATICAL PRACTICES

Do you know HOW?

For **1** through **4**, write >, <, or = for each ◯. Use the chart above to help.

1. 9 months ◯ 27 weeks

2. 17 years ◯ 2 decades

3. 5 minutes ◯ 300 seconds

4. 44 months ◯ 3 years

Do you UNDERSTAND?

5. **Writing to Explain** How can you tell which is longer, 63 hours or 3 days?

6. Do you multiply or divide if you want to change months to years?

7. In the example above, how many years old is Kara?

Independent Practice

For **8** through **13**, write >, <, or = for each ◯.

8. 35 weeks ◯ 340 days
9. 7 days ◯ 120 hours
10. 2 years ◯ 730 days

11. 40 hours ◯ 2 days
12. 8 weeks ◯ 56 days
13. 12 months ◯ 40 weeks

For **14** through **22**, complete each number sentence.

14. 6 days = ⬜ hours
15. 2 years = ⬜ months
16. 6 minutes = ⬜ seconds

17. 3 decades = ⬜ years
18. 4 hours = ⬜ minutes
19. 4 centuries = ⬜ years

20. 36 months = ⬜ years
21. 104 weeks = ⬜ years
22. 5,000 years = ⬜ millennia

Change 8 years to months.

1 year = 12 months

To find the number of months in 8 years, multiply.

$8 \times 12 = 96$

So, 8 years = 96 months.

Compare the amounts.

Kara's age   Jordan's age

108 months ◯ 8 years

108 months ⟩ 96 months

So, Kara is older than Jordan.

Problem Solving

MATHEMATICAL
PRACTICES

23. Estimation About how many minutes does it take you to do your homework? How many seconds is this?

24. Reasonableness Trish is going to camp for 2 months. Which is greater than 2 months?

A   35 days   C   6 weeks

B   40 days   D   10 weeks

25. Reason Gina has 3 yards of fabric. She needs to cut 8 pieces, each 1 foot long. Does she have enough fabric? Explain.

26. A girl from England set a world record by sneezing 978 days in a row. About how many weeks did she sneeze in a row?

27. If you brush your teeth 10 minutes a day, about how many hours do you brush in a year?

28. A theater has 358 seats on the main level and 122 seats in the balcony. How many people can see 6 shows in one day?

29. Persevere It is believed that the Mayan pyramid of Kukulkan in Mexico was used as a calendar. It has 4 stairways leading to the top platform. Including the one extra step at the top, it has a total of 365 steps. How many steps are in each stairway?

Tip *Subtract 1 from the total number of steps before you divide.*

Each stairway has the same number of steps.

© Common Core

4.MD.2 Use . . . operations to solve word problems involving distances, intervals of time, . . . and money, including problems involving simple fractions or decimals, and problems that require expressing measurements given in a larger unit in terms of a smaller unit. Represent measurement quantities using diagrams. Also 4.MD.1

Problem Solving

Work Backward

Between 6:00 A.M. and 7:00 A.M., the temperature rose 2 degrees. Every hour after that, the temperature rose 4 degrees. At 1:00 P.M., the temperature was 62°F. What was the temperature at 6:00 A.M.?

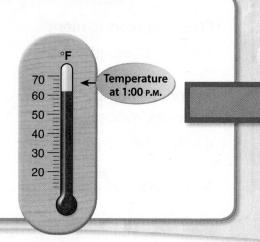
Temperature at 1:00 P.M.

Guided Practice*

MATHEMATICAL PRACTICES

Do you know HOW?

Solve.

1. School starts at 7:45 A.M. It takes Fran 30 minutes to walk to school, 15 minutes to eat, and 20 minutes to get ready. What time should Fran get up?

Do you UNDERSTAND?

© 2. **Reasonableness** Is the answer to the problem above reasonable? Explain.

© 3. **Write a Problem** Write a problem that uses working backward. Then answer your question.

Independent Practice

MATHEMATICAL PRACTICES

Solve. Write the answer in a complete sentence.

4. Wanda walked for 25 minutes from the mall to the train station. She waited 20 minutes for the train, and then had a 20 minute ride. Her train arrived at 12:20 P.M. What time did she leave the mall?

5. Art rode his bike from his house to Jay's house. The boys rode their bikes 3 miles to the park and then 4 miles to the mall. Art rode 9 miles in all. How many miles is Art's house from Jay's house?

Applying Math Practices

- What am I asked to find?
- What else can I try?
- How are quantities related?
- How can I explain my work?
- How can I use math to model the problem?
- Can I use tools to help?
- Is my work precise?
- Why does this work?
- How can I generalize?

What do I know?

The temperature at 1:00 P.M. is 62°F.

The temperature rose 2° between 6:00 A.M. and 7:00 A.M., and 4° every hour after that.

What am I asked to find?

The temperature at 6:00 A.M.

Work backward:

Draw a picture to show each change.
Work backward starting at 1:00 P.M.

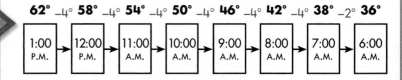

62° _–4°_ **58°** _–4°_ **54°** _–4°_ **50°** _–4°_ **46°** _–4°_ **42°** _–4°_ **38°** _–2°_ **36°**

| 1:00 P.M. | 12:00 P.M. | 11:00 A.M. | 10:00 A.M. | 9:00 A.M. | 8:00 A.M. | 7:00 A.M. | 6:00 A.M. |

The temperature at 6:00 A.M. was 36°F.

6. Communicate Nina walked 1 mile on Monday. She walked twice as far on Tuesday. On Wednesday, she walked three more miles than she did on Monday. On Thursday, she walked a mile less than she had walked on Wednesday. How many miles did Nina walk on Thursday? Explain.

7. Georgette bought some craft items. The silk flowers cost three times as much as the ribbon. The ribbon cost two times what the foam cost. The vase cost $12, which was three times as much as the foam. How much did the silk flowers cost?

8. Sylvia had $43 after she went shopping. She spent $9 on pet food, $6 on salad items, $12 on soup, and $24 on vegetables. How much money did Sylvia start with?

? money Sylvia started with

| $6 | $9 | $12 | $24 | $43 |

9. Persevere Mrs. Harris is planning to drive the twins to a soccer game at 6:00 P.M. They need to arrive 20 minutes early to warm up for the game. It takes 25 minutes to get to the soccer field. What time does Mrs. Harris and the twins need to leave the house?

10. Leslie has 3 boxes of tea in her cupboard. Each box contains 11 tea bags. Each tea bag makes 3 cups of hot tea. How many cups of tea will Leslie make if she uses all the tea bags?

11. The Declaration of Independence was signed in 1776. Three years earlier, the Boston Tea Party took place. Boston was settled 143 years before the Boston Tea Party. What year was Boston settled?

12. Reason Use the digits 7, 1, 5, 9, and 3 to write the largest number possible. Use each digit exactly once.

13. Be Precise Use the digits 6, 2, 5, and 4 to write 2 numbers less than 6,000 but greater than 5,500. Use each digit exactly once.

Set A, pages 366–367

Estimate and measure the length of the piece of ribbon.

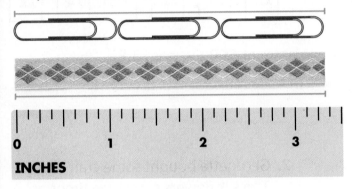

INCHES

The ribbon's length is about 3 small paper clips. It is 3 inches long to the nearest inch.

Remember to add when combining measurements.

Choose the most appropriate unit to measure the length of each.

1. airport runway   **2.** bridge

Estimate and measure the length of the eraser below to the nearest inch.

3.

Set B, pages 368–369

Which is the best estimate for the capacity of the bucket?

2 pints or 2 gallons?

The pint is too small of a unit. The best unit to use is the gallon.

The best estimate is 2 gallons.

Remember that a cup is a smaller measure than a pint.

Which is the best estimate for the capacity of each item?

1.   **2.**

2 cups or
20 cups?

1 gallon or
8 gallons?

Set C, pages 370–371

Which is the best unit to measure the weight of a pear?

Most pears weigh less than a pound.

So, the best unit to use would be the ounce.

Remember to use benchmark weights to compare.

Give the best unit to measure the weight of each item. Write oz, lb, or T.

1. a whale   **2.** an apple

3. a puppy   **4.** a baseball

5. a box of books   **6.** a hippopotamus

Convert 3 gallons to cups.

There are 4 quarts in 1 gallon.
3 gallons × 4 quarts = 12 quarts

There are 2 pints in 1 quart.
12 quarts × 2 pints = 24 pints

There are 2 cups in 1 pint.
24 pints × 2 cups = 48 cups

There are 48 cups in 3 gallons.

Remember when changing from a larger to a smaller unit, you multiply.

1. 5 T = ▨ lb

2. 10 mi = ▨ ft

3. 36 c = ▨ qt

4. 8 fl oz = ▨ tbsp

5. 4 yd = ▨ in.

6. 16 pt = ▨ gal

Jenna, Barbara, and Christina measured the width of their playground. Which measurement is not correct? Why?

Student	Measurement
Jenna	12 yds 1 ft 3 in.
Barbara	400 ft
Christina	37 ft 3 in.

Convert each measurement to feet and compare.

Jenna = 36 ft + 1 ft + 3 in. = 37 ft 3 in.
Barbara = 400 ft
Christina = 37 ft 3 in.

Barbara's measurement is incorrect because the other two measurements are equal.

Remember to explain your answer.

1. One hundred people were surveyed about their favorite flower. Of these, 20 people say their favorite flower is the tulip. What fraction of the people say their favorite flower is **NOT** the tulip? Explain your answer.

2. Mr. Gibson wants to make his driveway longer for more cars to park. It is currently 8 yards long. If the maximum length of a driveway is 30 feet long, how many more yards can he add to his driveway? Explain your answer.

Set F, pages 378–379

Estimate and measure the length of the crayon.

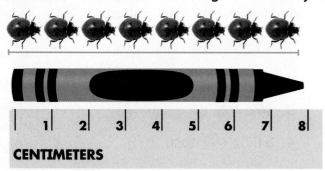

CENTIMETERS

The crayon's length is about 8 ladybugs. It is 8 centimeters long to the nearest centimeter.

Remember you can use objects to help you estimate length.

Give the best unit to measure the length of each. Write cm or m.

1. baseball bat   **2.** penny

Estimate and measure the length of the magnet below to the nearest centimeter.

3.

Set G, pages 380–381

How much liquid will the bucket hold?

8 mL or 8L?

The milliliter is too small of a unit. The best unit to use is the liter.

The best estimate is 8 liters.

Remember that a liter is a greater measure than a milliliter.

Which is the best estimate for the capacity of each item?

1.    **2.**

3 mL or
30 mL?

10 liters or
100 milliliters?

Set H, pages 382–383

What is the mass of a cell phone?

1 kilogram is too large for a cell phone. So, a gram would be a better unit to use.

A dollar bill has a mass of about 1 gram.

Estimate how many one-dollar bills have the same mass as a cell phone. About 20 one-dollar bills would have the same mass. So, the mass of a cell phone is about 20 grams.

Measure the mass of a cell phone on a balance.

Place the cell phone on one pan of the balance. Add 1 gram masses to the other side, and count the number of grams.

The cell phone has a mass of 17 grams.

Remember that weight depends on location. Mass always stays the same.

Choose the most appropriate unit, a gram or kilogram, to measure the mass of each item.

1. crayon   **2.** watermelon

3. carrot   **4.** wallet

5. bicycle   **6.** table

7. penny   **8.** paper clip

Convert 3 kilograms to grams.

1 kg = 1,000 g
3 kg = 3 × 1,000 g
3 kg = 3,000 g

There are 3,000 grams in 3 kilograms.

Remember when going from a smaller unit to a larger unit, you divide.

1. 50 dm = ☐ m

2. 200 mm = ☐ cm

3. 8,000 g = ☐ kg

4. 90 L = ☐ mL

Which is longer, 12 years or 120 months?

Change 12 years to months.

Since 1 year = 12 months, multiply the number of years by 12.

12 years × 12 = 144 months

144 months > 120 months

So, 12 years > 120 months.

Remember to first convert the measurements to the same unit. Then compare the measurements.

1. 36 months ◯ 104 weeks

2. 33 years ◯ 3 decades

3. 90 minutes ◯ 540 seconds

4. 96 months ◯ 8 years

5. 5 centuries ◯ 5,000 years

Solve by working backward.

Jerrold checks the thermometer every hour between 12:00 P.M. and 7:00 P.M. He noticed that the temperature decreased 3° each hour from 12:00 P.M. to 4:00 P.M. Then from 4:00 P.M. to 7:00 P.M., the temperature decreased 4° each hour. At 7:00 P.M., the temperature was 57°F. What was the temperature at 12:00 P.M.?

57°+4°**61°**+4°**65°**+4°**69°**+3°**72°**+3°**75°**+3°**78°**+3°**81°**

| 7:00 P.M. | 6:00 P.M. | 5:00 P.M. | 4:00 P.M. | 3:00 P.M. | 2:00 P.M. | 1:00 P.M. | 12:00 P.M. |

The temperature at 12:00 P.M. was 81°F.

Remember a picture can help you work backward.

1. Brad has trumpet practice at 10:45 A.M. It takes him 15 minutes to get from home to practice and 10 minutes to warm up. What time should he leave home to get to practice on time?

Multiple Choice

1. Which is the best estimate for the length of an earthworm? (14-1)

  A About 3 feet

  B About 3 yards

  C About 3 miles

  D About 3 inches

2. Which is the best estimate of the capacity of a bathroom sink? (14-2)

  A 3 gallons

  B 3 cups

  C 300 cups

  D 300 pints

3. Which is the best estimate of the mass of a football? (14-8)

  A 400 grams

  B 400 kilograms

  C 4,000 grams

  D 4,000 kilograms

4. Rob's backpack weighs 80 ounces. How many pounds does his backpack weigh? (14-4)

  A 3 pounds

  B 4 pounds

  C 5 pounds

  D 1,280 pounds

5. Which of the following holds about 2 liters of water? (14-7)

  A Bathtub

  B Drinking glass

  C Pitcher

  D Eye dropper

6. It takes a guinea pig about 68 days to develop completely before it is born. Which of these is greater than 68 days? (14-10)

  A 1 month

  B 1,200 hours

  C 9 weeks

  D 10 weeks

7. Three friends individually measured the capacity of a goldfish bowl. Which friend do you think measured incorrectly? (14-5)

Student	Measurement
Janell	28 cups
Leah	10 pints
Kathleen	5 quarts

  A Janell, because the other girls' measurements equal 1 gallon 1 quart.

  B Leah, because the other girls' measurements equal 1 gallon 1 quart.

  C Kathleen, because the other girls' measurements equal 1 gallon 1 quart.

  D All 3 girls got the same measurement.

8. What metric unit would best measure the length of a school hallway? (14-6)

9. What unit would best measure the weight of a pair of scissors? (14-3)

10. What symbol makes the comparison true? (14-4)

4 yd ◯ 124 in.

11. The next total solar eclipse that will be able to be seen in the United States will be on August 21, 2017. It will last 160 seconds. What symbol makes the comparison true? (14-10)

160 seconds ◯ 3 minutes

12. Andrea ran 400 meters in gym class. How many centimeters did she run? (14-9)

13. What symbol makes the comparison true? (14-9)

200 mL ◯ 2 L

14. At 4:30 P.M., the thermometer outside of Yasmine's window read 40°C. It had risen 8° between noon and 4:30 P.M. and 5° between 7:00 A.M. and noon. What was the temperature at 7:00 A.M.? (14-11)

15. In 2009, Hawaii celebrated 50 years as a state. How many months are in 50 years? (14-10)

16. Devon counted the number of Kennedy half dollar coins he had. He placed the half dollars in one long line. He counted 32 coins. About how many centimeters long was Devon's line of coins? (14-6)

3 cm

17. Matt hiked the two trails shown below on Monday. He told his friend that he had hiked 7,250 meters in one day. Is that the number of meters Matt hiked? Explain. (14-9)

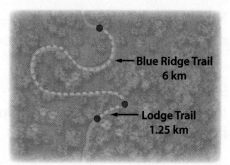

Blue Ridge Trail
6 km

Lodge Trail
1.25 km

Sarah is helping her parents clean up at home. First, she helps her father in his workshop.

1. Sarah helps to organize the car care items. Would a container of windshield washer fluid be measured in cups or gallons? Would a container of car wax be measured in milliliters or liters?

2. Sarah's father says his car can go as fast as 2,682 meters per minute. How many kilometers can the car go in 1 minute? How many centimeters can the car go in 1 minute?

3. After a break, Sarah helps her mother clean up the kitchen. She empties bags of flour into canisters. Which is a reasonable weight for a bag of flour, 5 pounds or 5 tons?

4. Next Sarah organizes the spice rack. If Sarah were to measure the mass of each spice container, would she use grams or kilograms?

5. Sarah's mother puts away bottles of oil and vinegar. What unit of measurement would she use to measure their capacity? Explain how you know.

6. Sarah helped her father in the workshop for 20 minutes and she helped her mother in the kitchen for 40 minutes. She took a half hour break in between. If she finished in the kitchen at 11:15 a.m., what time did she start helping her father in the garage? Explain.

 DOMAIN Measurement and Data

Topic 15
Solving Measurement Problems

▼ Central Park is one of the most visited city parks in the world. What is the total distance around the park? You will find out in Lesson 15-1.

Topic Essential Questions
- What do area and perimeter mean and how can each be found?
- How can line plots and other tools help to solve measurement problems?

Review What You Know!

Vocabulary

Choose the best term from the box.

- addition
- multiplication
- area
- perimeter

1. The ? is the distance around a figure.

2. The number of square units needed to cover a region is the ?.

3. ? is the operation you use to find the area of a region.

Multiplication Facts

Find each product.

4. 6×5 5. 7×9 6. 8×8

7. 7×4 8. 3×6 9. 5×4

10. 4×9 11. 8×5 12. 9×6

13. 8×4 14. 3×9 15. 8×7

Money

Count the bills and coins and write the amount.

16.

17.

18.

© 19. **Writing to Explain** Can you make $1.53 with quarters, dimes, and nickels?

Interactive Learning

Pose the problem. Start each lesson by working together to solve problems. It will help you make sense of math.

Applying Math Practices

- What am I asked to find?
- What else can I try?
- How are quantities related?
- How can I explain my work?
- How can I use math to model the problem?
- Can I use tools to help?
- Is my work precise?
- Why does this work?
- How can I generalize?

Lesson 15-1

Ⓒ **Reason** Solve any way you choose.

What is the maximum length an 8-foot high wall can be so it can be covered with one can of the paint shown at the right? If tape was placed around all sides of this wall before painting, how much tape was used? Show how you found your answers.

Latex
Interior Paint

Covers 225
square ft

Lesson 15-2

Ⓒ **Reason** Solve any way you choose. Pay attention to the measurement units.

A wild bird feeder holds 8 cups of bird seed. The container at the right holds 3 gallons of bird seed. How many times can the feeder be filled with the bird seed from the container? Show how you solved this problem.

Bird Seed
SUPREME

Lesson 15-3

© **Reason** Solve this problem any way you choose. Show how you found the answer.

A certain flash drive costs $24.35 including tax. If you are the sales person and you were given two $20 bills, how much change would you give?

Lesson 15-4

© **Use Tools** Solve using data from the chart. Most people can throw a ball farther with one arm than the other. Make separate line plots for the data given and use the line plots to answer these questions. Use the same scale for each line plot.

1. Were most students better at throwing the ball with their left arm or right arm? Tell how you decided by looking at the line plots.

2. What length throw was most common for each arm?

3. What is the difference between the longest throw and the shortest throw for each arm?

Ball-Throwing Distance, in Yards		
Student	Right Arm	Left Arm
Anita	$3\frac{1}{2}$	$1\frac{3}{4}$
Graciela	$3\frac{3}{4}$	4
Rich	$5\frac{1}{2}$	$2\frac{1}{2}$
Seija	6	8
Cheryl	$4\frac{3}{4}$	$3\frac{1}{4}$
Dan	$4\frac{1}{4}$	$2\frac{1}{2}$
Carrie	$5\frac{1}{2}$	2
Matt	$3\frac{3}{4}$	$3\frac{1}{4}$
Kim	$5\frac{1}{2}$	$1\frac{1}{2}$
Linda	$4\frac{1}{4}$	$3\frac{1}{4}$

Lesson 15-5

© **Model** Solve. Show all of your work.

Lyle has a square fenced-in garden with sides of 10 ft. For every 5 ft, one fence post was placed. He and some friends are going to make the garden bigger, but Lyle still wants to have a fence post every 5 ft. The new garden will have sides of 40 ft. How many fence posts will the friends need for a new fence?

Lesson
15-1
© Common Core

4.MD.3 Apply the area and perimeter formulas for rectangles in real world and mathematical problems.

Solving Perimeter and Area Problems

How can you use perimeter and area to solve problems?

Perimeter is the distance around a figure. Area is the amount of surface a figure covers. What is the area of the new state park shown at the right?

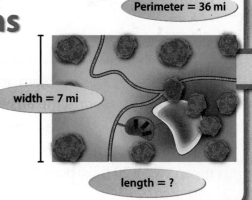

Perimeter = 36 mi

width = 7 mi

length = ?

Guided Practice*

Do you know HOW?

Find the missing dimension or dimensions.

1.

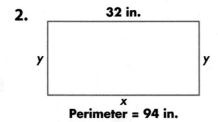

Area = 216 sq in.   8 in.

x

2.

32 in.

y ⬚ y

x

Perimeter = 94 in.

Do you UNDERSTAND?

3. A sandbox is shaped like a rectangle. Its area is 48 square feet. The side lengths are whole numbers. What are possible dimensions of this sandbox? Do all possible dimensions make sense? Explain.

4. The length of a garden is 25 feet. What must the width of the garden be, in a whole number of feet, so the area is greater than 200 square feet but less than 300 square feet?

Independent Practice

© **MATHEMATICAL PRACTICES**

© **Model** Find the missing dimension or dimensions.

5.

Area = 60 sq ft   6 ft

x

6.

x

y ⬚ 5 in.

Perimeter = 30 in.

7.

22 yd

⬚ y

x

Perimeter = 84 yd

8.

x

Area = 81 sq mi   9 mi

Animated Glossary
www.pearsonsuccessnet.com
DIGITAL

For another example, see Set A on page 414.

Answer the hidden question.

Area = length × width

Think I know only the width. The hidden question is, "What is the length of the park?" I can use what I know to find the length.

7 + 7 = 14   Add the two known sides, since opposite sides of a rectangle are equal.

36 − 14 = 22   Subtract the total of the two known sides from the perimeter to find the total of the two unknown sides.

22 ÷ 2 = 11   Divide to find the length of one side.

The length of the park is 11 miles.

Use the answer to the hidden question to answer the original question.

$\ell = 11$ miles
$w = 7$ miles
$A = \ell \times w$
   $= 11 \times 7$
   $= 77$

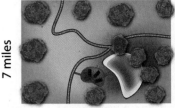

7 miles

11 miles

The area of the park is 77 square miles.

Problem Solving

MATHEMATICAL PRACTICES

9. Mr. Chen is putting tile down in his kitchen. The kitchen is 16 feet long and 8 feet wide. The tile costs $5 per square foot. How much will it cost Mr. Chen to tile his kitchen?

10. Greg built a picture frame with a perimeter of 50 inches. It is 14 inches long. How wide is it?

© 11. Model Julie planted a rectangular garden that is 20 feet long. She placed 56 feet of fencing around her garden. Draw and label a sketch of her garden. What is the width of her garden? What is the area?

12. Central Park in New York City has a length of $2\frac{1}{2}$ miles and a width of $\frac{1}{2}$ mile. What is the perimeter of the park?

A $6\frac{1}{2}$ miles   **C** $5\frac{1}{2}$ miles

B 6 miles   **D** $4\frac{1}{2}$ miles

© 13. Reason Nancy wove a pot holder with an area of 80 square inches. The lengths and widths of the sides are whole numbers. Which dimensions make the most sense for a potholder? Explain.

14. The Green Darner is one of the largest dragonflies. It weighs about four hundredths of an ounce. Write four hundredths in standard form.

© 15. Persevere An art class is planning to paint a rectangular mural with an area of 60 square feet. It has to be at least 4 feet high but no more than 6 feet high. How long could it be if the length and width have to be whole numbers?

Common
Core

4.MD.2 Use the four operations to solve word problems involving distances, intervals of time, liquid volumes, masses of objects, and money, including problems involving simple fractions or decimals, and problems that require expressing measurements given in a larger unit in terms of a smaller unit. Represent measurement quantities using diagrams such as number line diagrams that feature a measurement scale.

Solving Measurement Problems

How can you use diagrams to solve measurement problems?

Andy is using a roll of fabric to make a sofa cushion like the one at the right. What is the total length of fabric Andy needs to make the cushion?

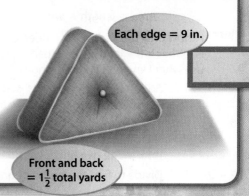

Each edge = 9 in.

Front and back = $1\frac{1}{2}$ total yards

Another Example

A runner finished a race in 2 hours 32 minutes. A walker finished the same race in 5 hours 8 minutes. How much faster was the runner's time than the walker's time? Use a bar diagram to compare the quantities and choose the operation.

x = 5 h 8 min − 2 h 32 min

   = 4 h 68 min − 2 h 32 min

   = 2 h 36 min

The runner finished 2 hours 36 minutes faster than the walker.

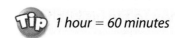

Tip *1 hour = 60 minutes*

Walk	5 h 8 min	
Run	2 h 32 min	x

Guided Practice*

MATHEMATICAL PRACTICES

Do you know HOW?

Draw a bar diagram to help solve the problem.

1. A recipe for fruit punch is shown below. How much punch does the recipe make?

   FRUIT PUNCH

   $2\frac{1}{2}$ gallons orange juice
   3 quarts cranberry juice
   2 quarts apple juice

Do you UNDERSTAND?

2. **Reason** In the example above, what fraction of a yard is 9 inches? How can fractions be used to find the total number of yards needed to make one of the sofa cushions?

3. A small sofa has a mass of 30 kilograms. A pillow on the sofa has a mass of 300 grams. How many pillows would it take to equal the mass of the sofa?

For another example, see Set B on page 414.

Draw a diagram to show the data.
Change to common units.

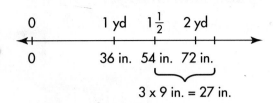

0   1 yd   1½   2 yd

0   36 in.   54 in.   72 in.

3 × 9 in. = 27 in.

 Tip *1 yard = 36 inches*

Use the given data to solve the problem.

$1\frac{1}{2}$ yards = 54 inches

3 sides × 9 inches = 27 inches

54 in. + 27 in. = 81 in.

1 yd = 36 in.   2 yd = 72 in.

81 in. − 72 in. = 9 in.

So, 81 inches = 2 yards 9 inches

81 inches or 2 yards 9 inches of material are needed for the cushion.

Independent Practice

Use the diagram to help solve each problem.

4. A water jug has a capacity of $3\frac{1}{2}$ gallons. How many times will the coach have to fill a 2-cup measuring cup to fill the water jug?

			1 gal			
	1 qt					
1 pt						
1 c						

5. Geneva cut $1\frac{1}{4}$ yards from a spool of ribbon. Then she cut two 27-inch pieces of ribbon from the spool. How many inches of ribbon in all did Geneva cut from the spool? How many yards of ribbon did she cut?

0   1 yd   2 yd   3 yd

0   9 in.   18 in.   27 in.   36 in.

Problem Solving

 **MATHEMATICAL PRACTICES**

© 6. **Reason** The trail to a waterfall is $2\frac{1}{3}$ miles long. Signs are placed at the beginning and the end of the trail. There are also signs placed at each $\frac{1}{3}$ mile mark along the trail. How many signs are there on the trail?

© 7. **Model** Mrs. Reed collects rocks. Each rock in her collection weighs about 4 ounces. Her collection weighs about 12 pounds in all. About how many rocks are in her collection?

    A 3 rocks   **C** 36 rocks

    B 4 rocks   **D** 48 rocks

Common Core

4.MD.2 Use the four operations to solve word problems involving distances, intervals of time, liquid volumes, masses of objects, and money, including problems involving simple fractions or decimals, and problems that require expressing measurements given in a larger unit in terms of a smaller unit. Represent measurement quantities using diagrams such as number line diagrams that feature a measurement scale.

Solving Problems Involving Money

How can you use counting up to make change?

How can you count to make change from a $20 bill used to buy the toy airplane?

penny
1¢

nickel
5¢

dime
10¢

quarter
25¢

half dollar
50¢

$8.36

Guided Practice*

 **MATHEMATICAL PRACTICES**

Do you know HOW?

For **1** and **2**, tell the amount of change for each situation.

1. You give the salesperson a $10 bill and three $5 bills to buy two movie tickets. How much change should you get?

MOVIE TICKET **$11.25**

2. A new jacket costs $65.89. How much change should you get if you give the salesperson four $20 bills?

Do you UNDERSTAND?

© **3. Reason** In the example above, how could mental math be used to find the amount of change, rather than counting up with coins?

© **4. Reason** If an item costs $19.54, why might someone give the sales clerk a $20 bill and 4 pennies?

Independent Practice

For **5–8**, tell the amount of change for each situation.

5. Andie buys a sandwich from the deli for $4.45. She pays for the sandwich with a $5 bill. How much change should she receive?

6. A new drawing pad costs $6.89. How much change should you get if you give the salesperson a $20 bill?

7. Carlos buys some knee pads and elbow pads. The total cost of the pads is $14.38. How much change should Carlos receive if he pays for the pads with two $10 bills?

8. Dana buys a poster that costs $8.15. She pays for the poster with a $10 dollar bill and one quarter. How much change should she receive?

For another example, see Set C on page 415.

One Way

Start with $8.36. Count up using the fewest coins.

Give this		Get this
4 pennies	→	$8.40
1 dime	→	$8.50
1 half dollar	→	$9
1 $1 bill	→	$10
1 $10 bill	→	$20

Another Way

Start with $8.36. Count up a different way.

Give this		Get this
4 pennies	→	$8.40
2 nickels	→	$8.50
2 quarters	→	$9
1 $1 bill	→	$10
2 $5 bills	→	$20

The change is the total amount given, $11.64.

Problem Solving

MATHEMATICAL PRACTICES

9. Reason Lucy buys a magazine for $4.19. She gives the sales clerk a $5 bill and two dimes. What is her change?

10. Marco used a $10 bill to pay for a jump rope. He received $3.08 in change. How much did the jump rope cost?

11. Reason Leo went to lunch with his parents. The bill was $17.85. What are two different combinations of coins and bills that can be used to make this amount?

12. Reason Leo's family used a $20 bill to pay the $17.85 lunch bill. What are three different combinations of coins and bills that can be used to make the change?

13. Blake bought two concert tickets for a total of $38.75. She gave the salesperson three $10 bills and two $5 bills. How much change should the salesperson give Blake?

14. Model Rajeev bought a skateboard that cost $37.74. How much change will he get back if he paid with two $20 bills?

A $2.26   C $2.74

B $3.26   D $3.74

15. Ana Maria wants to buy a sweater and a scarf that cost a total of $31.24. She has three $10 bills. How much more money does she need to buy both items?

16. Critique Reasoning Matthew buys a video game for $34.28. He pays for the game using two $20 bills. Matthew thinks he should receive $6.72 in change. Is he correct? Explain.

17. Communicate Jenna bought a hand pump for $12.19. She gave the sales clerk one $20 bill and one quarter. How can you find Jenna's change?

18. Greg buys three tickets. Each ticket costs $4.25. He pays for the tickets with three $5 bills. How much change should Greg get back?

Lesson
15-4

Common
Core

4.MD.4 Make a line plot to display a data set of measurements in fractions of a unit ($\frac{1}{2}$, $\frac{1}{4}$, $\frac{1}{8}$). Solve problems involving addition and subtraction of fractions by using information presented in line plots.

Solving Problems Involving Line Plots

How can you use line plots to solve problems?

The results of a catch-and-release salmon fishing contest are shown in the chart at the right. What length of fish was caught most often? What is the difference between the longest and shortest lengths?

Fish Lengths, in inches

$24\frac{1}{2}$, $25\frac{3}{4}$, $26\frac{1}{4}$, $25\frac{1}{4}$, 23, $22\frac{3}{4}$,

$22\frac{3}{4}$, $21\frac{1}{4}$, $25\frac{1}{4}$, $25\frac{1}{4}$, $24\frac{1}{2}$, $22\frac{3}{4}$,

$22\frac{1}{4}$, $27\frac{1}{2}$, $25\frac{1}{4}$, $24\frac{1}{2}$, $22\frac{1}{4}$,

$22\frac{3}{4}$, $25\frac{1}{4}$, $27\frac{1}{2}$

Guided Practice*

MATHEMATICAL
PRACTICES

Do you know HOW?

For **1** and **2**, use the line plot showing results to a survey question.

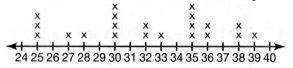

Number of Cell Phone Calls Made Today

1. What was the greatest number of cell phone calls made?

2. What is the difference between the greatest and least number of calls?

Do you UNDERSTAND?

For **3–4**, use the data set below.

Shoe Sizes from a Survey

4, $7\frac{1}{2}$, 9, $9\frac{1}{2}$, 6, $5\frac{1}{2}$, 7, 8, $8\frac{1}{2}$, $8\frac{1}{2}$, $9\frac{1}{2}$,

$6\frac{1}{2}$, 8, $6\frac{1}{2}$, 6, $5\frac{1}{2}$, $6\frac{1}{2}$, 6, $8\frac{1}{2}$, $6\frac{1}{2}$

3. Make a line plot of the data.

© 4. **Use Tools** What is the most common shoe size?

Independent Practice

MATHEMATICAL
PRACTICES

For **5** and **6**, use the line plot below.

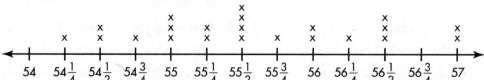

Heights in inches of Dr. Chen's Patients

5. What is the difference between the tallest height and the shortest height?

© 6. **Critique Reasoning** Oscar says that 55 inches is the most common height Dr. Chen measured. Do you agree? Explain.

Animated Glossary
www.pearsonsuccessnet.com

DIGITAL

Make line plots to show the data.

Remember a line plot <u>shows data along a</u> <u>number line.</u>

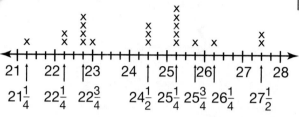

Fish Length—Catch-and-Release Salmon Contest

Use the line plot to solve the problems.

The most Xs are for $25\frac{1}{4}$ in. This is the length of fish caught most often.

Longest fish: $27\frac{1}{2}$ in.

Shortest fish: $21\frac{1}{4}$ in.

$27\frac{1}{2} - 21\frac{1}{4} = 27\frac{2}{4} - 21\frac{1}{4} = 6\frac{1}{4}$

The difference between the longest fish and the shortest fish was $6\frac{1}{4}$ in.

Problem Solving

MATHEMATICAL PRACTICES

For **7** through **9**, use the line plot on the right.

© 7. Reason How many students are in Mrs. Harper's class? Explain how you found your answer.

Number of Pets Each Student Has

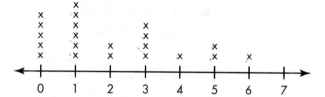

8. How many students have 3 pets? How many pets in all is that?

9. What is the total number of pets the students in Mrs. Harper's class have?

  A 25   **C** 42

  B 34   **D** 52

For **10** through **12**, use the results of the men's and women's races, shown on the right.

© 10. Use Tools Make a line plot of each set of times.

11. Which race had the smallest difference between the fastest and slowest times? Show how you found your answer.

12. Using the line plots you made, what can you tell about how the runners in each race were grouped when they crossed the finish line?

Data		
Men's Times (seconds)	10.38, 10.32, 10.31, 10.41, 10.41, 10.25, 10.41, 10.38, 10.38, 10.32, 10.38, 10.41, 10.32, 10.38, 10.38
Women's Times (seconds)	10.45, 10.31, 10.32, 10.37, 10.32, 10.32, 10.36, 10.32, 10.37, 10.41, 10.31, 10.31, 10.45, 10.31, 10.32

Common
Core

4.MD.2 Use the four operations to solve world problems involving distances, intervals of time, liquid volumes, masses of objects, and money, including problems involving simple fractions or decimals, and problems that require expressing measurements given in a larger unit in terms of a smaller unit. Represent measurement quantities using diagrams such as number line diagrams that feature a measurement scale.

Problem Solving

Solve a Simpler Problem and Make a Table

Each side of a triangle cracker below is one inch long. If there are 12 triangle crackers in a row, what is the perimeter of the figure?

1 inch

Guided Practice*

MATHEMATICAL
PRACTICES

Do you know HOW?

1. Cora is cutting a piece of paper to get equal sized pieces. After the first cut, she stacks the two pieces and makes another cut. After she makes the second cut, she stacks the pieces again. If this pattern continues, how many pieces will she have after the fourth cut?

Do you UNDERSTAND?

2. **Reason** How was the problem above broken into simpler problems?

3. **Write a Problem** Write a problem that you can solve by making a table.

Independent Practice

MATHEMATICAL
PRACTICES

Solve.

4. **Model** Troy is helping his father build a fence. Each section of the fence has a post at each end. Make a table showing how many posts will be needed if there are 1, 3, 5, 10, 15, or 20 sections of the fence. Look for a pattern.

5. How many posts will be needed if the fence has 47 sections?

Applying Math Practices

- What am I asked to find?
- What else can I try?
- How are quantities related?
- How can I explain my work?
- How can I use math to model the problem?
- Can I use tools to help?
- Is my work precise?
- Why does this work?
- How can I generalize?

Change the problem into problems that are simpler to solve.

Look at 1 triangle, then 2 triangles, then 3 triangles.

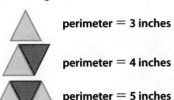

perimeter = 3 inches

perimeter = 4 inches

perimeter = 5 inches

The perimeter is 2 more than the number of triangles.

Number of triangles	1	2	3
Perimeter (inches)	3	4	5

So, for 12 triangles the perimeter is 14 inches.

6. Helen is part of a 32-player one-on-one basketball tournament. As soon as a player loses, she is out of the tournament. The winners will continue to play until there is one champion. How many games are there in all in this tournament?

© 7. Persevere The figure below is a square. If sides A and B are doubled, will this figure still be a square?

For **8** through **10**, use the table at the right.

8. The missing classes in the schedule to the right are Math, Science, Reading, Spelling, and Social Studies. Math is after morning break. Spelling is at 9:40. Reading and Science are the two afternoon classes. At what time is Math class?

9. What class is at 8:45?

10. Science class is before Reading. What time is Science class?

Class Schedule

Morning	Afternoon
8:30: Opening	12:15:
8:45:	1:00: Break
9:30: Break	1:30:
9:40:	1:55: Recess
10:25: Recess	2:05: Art, Music or P.E.
10:55:	2:40: Pack Up
11:30: Lunch	2:45: School's Out

11. Six friends are playing checkers. If each friend plays against every other friend once, how many games of checkers will they play all together?

12. Mr. McNulty's classroom library has 286 books. If he buys 12 books each month for five months, how many books will he have in all?

13. Jolene, Timmy, Nicholas, Paul, and Kathryn are all planting in a community garden. If each of their plots holds 7 rows and 13 columns, how many plants will they be able to grow all together?

14. Thomas is training for a marathon. He runs for 2 miles and then he walks for a half a mile. If he trains by running 22 miles every day, how many miles will he walk?

15. Every day, James spends $\frac{5}{10}$ of an hour on the phone, $\frac{6}{12}$ of an hour reading, and $\frac{3}{6}$ of an hour on the computer. Use the fraction strips to the right to tell which activity James spends the most time doing.

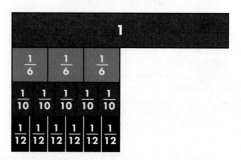

16. Maya is putting 3 ice cubes in each red cup and 4 ice cubes in each blue cup. The cups alternate colors starting with red. How many ice cubes will she use if she has 15 cups?

17. Shaina has a necklace she wants to have cut to give to her friends. The jeweler chargers $3 for each cut. How much does Shaina need to pay for 5 cuts?

18. Reasonableness Danielle can type 15 words per minute. How many words can she type in 7 minutes?

Minutes	1	2	3
Words Typed	15	30	45

© Think About the Structure

19. It takes a plumber 4 minutes to cut a pipe. Which expression would you use to find how long it would take the plumber to cut 7 pipes?

A $4 + 7$

B 4×4

C 7×4

D 7×7

20. On every train car there are two connectors, one at the front and one at the back. These connectors are there so each car can be linked with another car. If a train has 30 cars, how would you find out the number of connections made?

A The number of cars minus 1

B The number of connectors on all the cars minus 1

C Same as the number of cars

D The number of cars plus 1

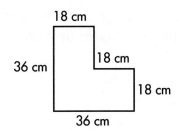

Going Digital

Finding Area with a Calculator

One Way Find the area of the figure shown at the right:

Divide the figure into two rectangles.
Rectangle A is 18 cm by 18 cm.
Rectangle B is 18 cm by 36 cm.

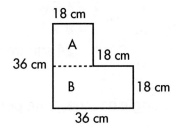

Find the area of each rectangle and add.

Press: 18 × 18 **ENTER =**   18 × 36 **ENTER =**   324 + 648 **ENTER =**

Display: *324*   *648*   *972*

Another Way Find the area of the figure in one step.

Press: 18 × 18 + 18 × 36 **ENTER =**

Display: *972*

The area of the figure is 972 square centimeters.

Practice

Use a calculator to find the area of each figure.

1.

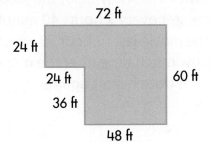

72 ft
24 ft
24 ft
36 ft
60 ft
48 ft

2.

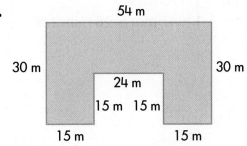

54 m
30 m
30 m
24 m
15 m 15 m
15 m
15 m

Set A, pages 402–403

Draw a different rectangle with the same perimeter as the one shown, and find its area.

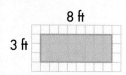

8 ft
3 ft

$P = (2 \times \ell) + (2 \times w) \qquad A = \ell \times w$
$\quad = (2 \times 8) + (2 \times 3) \qquad \quad = 8 \times 3$
$\quad = 16 + 6 \qquad\qquad\qquad = 24$ square feet
$\quad = 22$ ft

A 4 ft by 7 ft rectangle has the same perimeter.

$P = (2 \times 7) + (2 \times 4) = 22$ ft
$A = 7 \times 4$
$A = 28$ square feet

7 ft
4 ft

Remember that two rectangles can have the same area but different perimeters.

Draw two different rectangles with the perimeter listed. Find the area of each rectangle.

1. $P = 24$ feet

2. $P = 40$ centimeters

Draw two different rectangles with the area listed. Find the perimeter of each rectangle.

3. $A = 64$ square feet

4. $A = 80$ square yards

Set B, pages 404–405

You can use diagrams to solve measurement problems.

Daria went to the beach with her family. The ride to the beach took 2 hours 13 minutes. The ride home from the beach took 1 hour 47 minutes. How much longer was the ride to the beach than the ride from the beach?

2 h 13 min	

1 h 47 min	?

2 h 13 min = 1 h 73 min
1 h 73 min − 1 h 47 min = 26 minutes

Remember you can use number lines to solve many measurement problems.

1. Utility poles are spaced 200 feet along one part of Main Street. That part of Main Street is 3,600 feet long. There are poles at both ends of that length. How many poles are there along this part of Main Street?

2. A movie is showing at the local theater every 2 hours 40 minutes. The movie lasts 1 hour 50 minutes. How much time after the movie ends does it start again?

You can find the amount of change by counting up from the cost to the amount of money given.

You buy lunch for yourself and a friend that costs $12.46. How much change should you get if you give the cashier a $20 bill?

Count up to $20 using coins and bills.

$12.46 + 4 pennies = $12.50

$12.50 + 2 quarters = $13.00

$13.00 + 2 $1 bills = $15.00

$15.00 + 1 $5 bill = $20.00

4 pennies + 2 quarters + 2 $1 bills + 1 $5 bill = $7.54

Remember you can use different combinations of money to make change.

1. Gary buys three tickets to a movie for a total of $26.25. He pays with a $20 bill and a $10 bill. How much change should he get back?

2. A carpenter buys a tool box and hand tools for a total of $32.56. How much change will the carpenter receive if he pays with two $20 bills?

The line plot shows the grades on a quiz. How many students took the quiz in all?

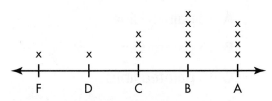

Add the total number shown in the plot.
1 F, 1 D, 3 Cs, 5 Bs, 4 As
1 + 1 + 3 + 5 + 4 = 14 students

Remember a line plot shows data along a number line.

1. The line plot shows how many siblings each student has. How many more students have only one sibling than have at least 3 siblings?

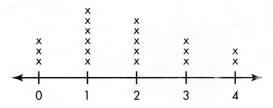

Each side of each triangle is two inches. What is the perimeter of the figure with 5 triangles?

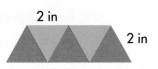

The perimeter increases by 2.

Number of Triangles	1	2	3	4	5
Perimeter	6 in.	8 in.	10 in.	12 in.	14 in.

The perimeter of 5 triangles is 14 inches.

Remember you can break the problem apart and solve.

1. Each side of a square in the figure is one inch. If there are 14 squares in a row, what is the perimeter of the figure?

Multiple Choice

ⓒ **ASSESSMENT**

1. Each cube has 6 faces. If Tandra connects 2 cubes, she can see 10 faces. If Tandra connects 7 cubes, how many faces of the cubes will she be able to see? (15-5)

Cubes	2	3	4	5	6	7
Faces	10	14	18			

A 42

B 32

C 30

D 28

2. Howie used 20 feet of edging to design four different gardens. He wants the garden with the greatest area. Which should Howie use? (15-1)

A

6 ft
4 ft

B
8 ft
2 ft
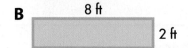

C
7 ft
3 ft
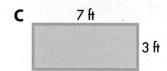

D
5 ft
5 ft
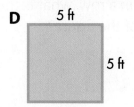

3. Maggie buys three sandwiches to share with her friends for a total of $20.25. She pays with a $20 bill and a $5 bill. How much change should she get back? (15-3)

A $4.25

B $4.65

C $4.75

D $5.25

4. Painted lines separate parking spaces in one row of a parking lot. The lines are spaced 9 feet apart. One row of the lot is 153 feet long. There are painted lines at both ends of the row. How many painted lines are there in the row? (15-2)

A 18 painted lines

B 17 painted lines

C 16 painted lines

D 15 painted lines

5. A picnic table is 9 feet long and 3 feet wide. What is the area of the rectangular surface of the table? (15-1)

A 27 square feet

B 36 square feet

C 45 square feet

D 54 square feet

6. Clarence worked in the garden for 1 hour 52 minutes. Later he worked inside the house. He worked 3 hours 26 minutes in all that day. How long did he work inside the house? (15-2)

7. Aden buys a ticket to the museum. His ticket costs $7.75. He pays with two $5 bills. How much change should he get back? (15-3)

8. Pepper's dog pen measures 4 meters wide and 5 meters long. What is the perimeter of the pen? (15-1)

For problems **9** and **10,** use the line plot that shows students' grades for the year in math class.

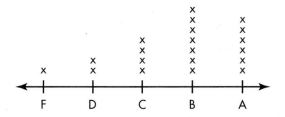

9. How many more students got an A than a D? (15-4)

10. How many more students got a grade better than a C than got a grade worse than a B? (15-4)

11. What is the perimeter of the flag? (15-1)

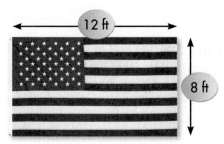

12. Cindy is making a pattern with triangle tiles like below. Each side of a triangle is 2 inches long. What is the perimeter when the pattern has 7 rows of triangles? (15-5)

Number of rows of triangles	1	2	3	4
Perimeter (inches)	6	12	18	24

13. Meghan is building a fence around her garden. The garden is a rectangle 12 feet long and 24 feet wide. She wants to put a post up at each corner and every 3 feet along the sides. How many posts will Meghan need for her garden? (15-5)

14. Justin has a cat that eats 3 cups of dry cat food every week. He bought a large bag of food that has 21 quarts of food. How many weeks of cat food does Justin have in the bag? (15-2)

Suppose you are going to design a small quilt using squares and rectangles. You want to use three different colors of fabric for the quilt. You need to find out how much of each fabric you need.

1. Use grid paper to design your quilt. Each square in the grid will represent a one-inch square of the quilt. The quilt should be no larger than 20 inches long and 10 inches wide.

2. What is the perimeter of your quilt?

3. What is the total area of your quilt?

4. Make a table listing the pieces of each color fabric you will need for your quilt, the dimensions of each piece, and the total area for all of the pieces of each shape. Use the headings below to make your table.

Shape	Color	Number of Pieces	Dimensions	Total Area

5. What is the total amount of fabric that you need for each color?

6. How do you know that the design you have drawn and the dimensions of the pieces in the design will fit the overall size of the quilt?

Topic 16

Lines, Angles, and Shapes

▼ How could you use geometric terms to describe items on a map of Nevada? You will find out in Lesson 16-2.

Review What You Know!

Vocabulary

Choose the best term from the box.

- triangle
- quadrilateral
- plane figure
- line

1. A polygon with four sides is a __?__ .

2. A polygon with three sides is a __?__ .

3. A __?__ is a straight path of points that goes on forever in two directions.

4. A figure with only two dimensions is a __?__ .

Solids

Name what each object looks like.

5.

6.

7.

8.

Addition

Solve.

9. 35 + 39   10. 72 + 109   11. 44 + 12

12. 145 + 238   13. 642 + 8   14. 99 + 41

15. 984 + 984   16. 22 + 888   17. 72 + 391

© 18. **Writing to Explain** To find the sum of 438 + 385, how many times will you need to regroup? Explain.

Topic Essential Questions

- How can lines, angles, and shapes be described, analyzed, and classified?
- How are angles measured, added and subtracted?

Pose the problem. Start each lesson by working together to solve problems. It will help you make sense of math.

Lesson 16-1

ⓒ **Use Tools** Use grid paper to complete these tasks.

a. Draw a pair of straight lines on grid paper, and label these lines Pair A. Write a description of how the lines in Pair A are related to each other.

b. Make a second pair of straight lines, labeled Pair B, that are related to each other in a different way. Write a description of how the lines in Pair B are related to each other.

Lesson 16-2

ⓒ **Use Tools** Draw the figures described below. Remember, a ray is part of a line that has one endpoint and goes on forever in one direction.

Make a square corner with two rays sharing one endpoint. Then make two more pairs of rays sharing one endpoint but not making a square corner. Make these as different as possible. Tell how your drawings are alike and how they are different.

Lesson 16-3

ⓒ **Use Tools** The hands of the clock shown form an angle. Where is the vertex of the angle? Describe the angle made by the two hands in different ways.

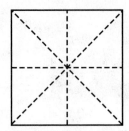

Lesson 16-4

ⓒ **Use Tools** Use a measuring tool like the one at the right to measure an angle.

Imagine that we are walking along a street and then turn at an angle down another street. Draw an angle to represent this situation. What is the measure of the angle we turned?

Lesson 16-5

ⓒ **Use Tools** The tool at the right can be used to measure angles.

Where would 0° be on this tool? Where would 90° be? Label as many other points as you can on your angle-measuring tool. Explain how you decided.

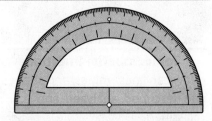

Lesson 16-6

© **Use Structure** Use a protractor to complete this task.

Draw an angle on your paper and label it ABC. Draw CBD so that the two angles share a ray but do not overlap. How many angles do you have? Measure each angle. Describe ways in which the measures are related.

Lesson 16-7

© **Reason** How can you sort the shapes at the right into two or more groups? Can you find more than one way? Explain how you sorted the shapes.

Lesson 16-8

© **Reason** Work with a partner and use the triangles in your set of polygons to complete this task.

Sort the triangles into two or more groups. Can you find more than one way? Explain how you sorted them.

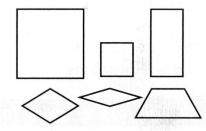

Lesson 16-9

© **Reason** Use the quadrilaterals in your set of polygons.

Find a quadrilateral to match each description. Name it in any way you can.

1. Opposite sides parallel; all sides the same length
2. Only 1 pair of parallel sides
3. 2 pairs of parallel sides
4. 4 right angles
5. 4 right angles; all sides the same length

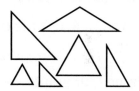

Lesson 16-10

© **Reason** Solve using a paper square. There is more than one answer.

How many ways can you fold a square so that one half fits exactly on top of the other half? You may cut and fold a square to help you.

Lesson 16-11

© **Generalize** Use the triangles at the right to complete this task.

Test each generalization below, and explain if it works.

All right triangles have 2 acute angles.

All right triangles have two equal sides.

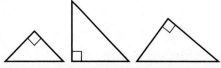

Lesson
16-1

© Common Core

4.G.1. Draw points, lines, line segments, rays, angles (right, acute, obtuse), and perpendicular and parallel lines. Identify these in two-dimensional figures.

Points, Lines, and Planes

What are some important geometric terms?

A point <u>is an exact location in space</u>.

A line <u>is a straight path of points that goes on and on in two directions.</u>

A plane <u>is an endless flat surface.</u>

Guided Practice*

 MATHEMATICAL PRACTICES

Do you know HOW?

For **1** through **4**, use the diagram at the right.

1. Name four points.

2. Name four lines.

3. Name two pairs of parallel lines.

4. Name two pairs of perpendicular lines.

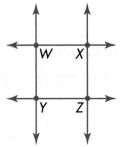

Do you UNDERSTAND?

© 5. **Writing to Explain** What geometric term could you use to describe the top and bottom sides of a chalkboard? Why?

6. What geometric term could you use to describe a chalkboard?

7. What geometric term could you use to describe the tip of your pencil?

Independent Practice

In **8** through **14**, use geometric terms to describe what is shown.

8.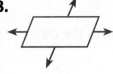

9.
L M I H

10.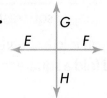

11. • A

12.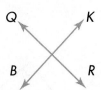

13.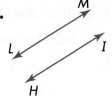

14.

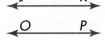
Animated Glossary
www.pearsonsuccessnet.com

*For another example, see Set A on page 444.

Pairs of lines are given special names depending on their relationship.

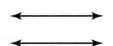

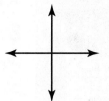

Parallel lines
never intersect.

Intersecting lines
pass through the
same point.

Perpendicular lines
are lines that form
square corners.

For **15** through **17**, describe each image shown using a geometric term.

15.

16.

17.

Problem Solving

© **MATHEMATICAL PRACTICES**

18. Georgia purchased items to make dinner. She bought chicken for $5.29, salad items for $8.73, and rice for $1.99. Estimate how much Georgia spent in all.

© **19. Persevere** I have 6 square faces and 8 vertices. What am I?

   A Cube   **C** Pyramid

   B Square   **D** Circle

For **20**, use the diagram at the right.

© **20. Reason** Line *AB* is parallel to line *CD*, and line *CD* is perpendicular to line *EF*. What can you conclude about *AB* and *EF*?

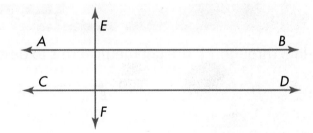

21. The web site of a company that sells sports equipment averages 850 visitors a day. How many visitors would the web site average in 7 days?

22. Which geometric term below best describes the surface of a desk?

   A Point   **C** Line

   B Plane   **D** Parallel

© **23. Writing to Explain** If all perpendicular lines are also intersecting lines, are all intersecting lines also perpendicular? Explain.

24. If $40 \times 8 = 320$, how many zeros will there be in the product $4{,}000 \times 8$?

4.G.1 Draw points, lines, line segments, rays, angles (right, acute, obtuse), and perpendicular and parallel lines. Identify these in two-dimensional figures.

Line Segments, Rays, and Angles

What geometric terms are used to describe parts of lines and types of angles?

A line segment <u>is a part of a line with two endpoints.</u>

A ray <u>is a part of a line that has one endpoint and continues on forever in one direction.</u>

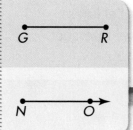

Guided Practice*

© **MATHEMATICAL PRACTICES**

Do you know HOW?

In **1** through **4**, use geometric terms to describe what is shown.

1. P ————— X

2.

3. B ————→ Y

4.

Do you UNDERSTAND?

5. What geometric term describes a line that has only one endpoint?

6. What geometric term describes a line that has two endpoints?

© **7. Reason** Which geometric term describes what two edges of a book make when a corner is formed?

Independent Practice

In **8** through **11**, use geometric terms to describe what is shown.

8.

9. B ————— D

10. X ————→ Y

11.

For **12** through **14**, use the figure shown to the right.

12. Name four line segments.

13. Name four rays.

14. Name 2 right angles.

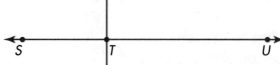

*For another example, see Set B on page 444.

An angle <u>is a figure formed by two rays that have the same endpoint</u>.
Angles are given special names depending upon their size.

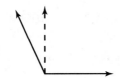

A right angle is a square corner.

An acute angle is open less than a right angle.

An obtuse angle is open more than a right angle but less than a straight angle.

A straight angle forms a straight line.

Problem Solving

MATHEMATICAL PRACTICES

© **15. Writing to Explain** Is the figure shown below formed by two rays with a common endpoint? If so, is it an angle? Explain.

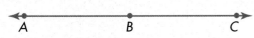

16. Which choice names the figure shown below?

G   H

A Ray *GH*   **C** Ray *HG*

B Line *GH*   **D** Angle *GH*

17. What three capital letters can be written by drawing two parallel line segments and then one line segment that is perpendicular to the line segments you already drew?

© **18. Model** Lexi said that two lines can both intersect a line and form perpendicular lines. Draw a picture to explain what she means.

For **19** through **21**, use the map of Nevada to the right. Which geometric term best fits each description?

19. The route between 2 cities

20. The cities

21. The north and west borders

© **22. Model** Randy used 92 sticks to build a model project. Bryan used 3 times as many. Draw a diagram showing how many sticks Bryan used.

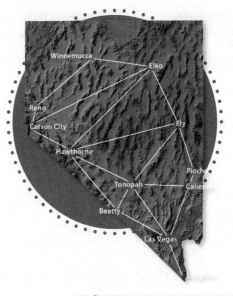

DIGITAL
Animated Glossary
www.pearsonsuccessnet.com

Common
Core

4.MD.5a An angle is measured with reference to a circle with its center at the common endpoint of the rays, by considering the fraction of the circular arc between the points where the two rays intersect the circle. An angle that turns through 1/360 of a circle is called a "one-degree angle," and can be used to measure angles. Also **4.MD.5, 4.G.1**

Understanding Angles and Unit Angles

What is the unit used to measure angles?

Jill drew a right angle and wants to find its measurement. Angles can be measured in units called degrees (°). A unit angle is an angle that cuts off $\frac{1}{360}$ of a circle and measures 1°. When you find the degrees of an angle, you find its angle measure.

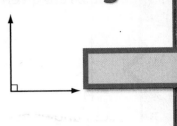

$1° = \frac{1}{360}$ of a circle

Guided Practice*

MATHEMATICAL
PRACTICES

Do you know HOW?

Find the measure of each angle.

1. A circle is divided into 9 equal parts. What is the angle measure of one of those parts?

2. The angle cuts off $\frac{1}{8}$ of the circle.

Do you UNDERSTAND?

3. Critique Reasoning Susan thinks Angle B is greater than Angle A. Do you agree? Explain.

4. Mike cuts a pie into 6 equal pieces. What is the angle measure of each piece? Explain.

Independent Practice

MATHEMATICAL
PRACTICES

Use Structure For **5** through **12**, find the measure of each angle.

5. The angle cuts off $\frac{1}{5}$ of the circle.

6. The angle cuts off $\frac{3}{8}$ of the circle.

7.

8.

9.

10.

11. A circle is divided into 20 equal parts. Find the angle measure of one of the parts.

12. Find the measure of an angle that cuts off $\frac{3}{10}$ of a circle.

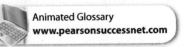
Animated Glossary
www.pearsonsuccessnet.com

Divide to find the angle measure of a right angle.

Right angles divide a circle into 4 equal parts.

$$360° \div 4 = 90°$$

The angle measure of a right angle is 90°.

What is the angle measure of a straight angle?

A straight angle divides a circle into 2 equal parts.

$$360° \div 2 = 180°$$

The angle measure of a straight angle is 180°.

Find the measure of an angle that cuts off $\frac{1}{6}$ of a circle.

Remember, $\frac{1}{6}$ means 1 of 6 equal parts, so divide by 6 to find the angle measure.
$$360° \div 6 = 60°$$
The angle measure is 60°.

Problem Solving

MATHEMATICAL PRACTICES

For **13** through **21**, solve each problem.

13. Lanie cut a large circular rice cake into 3 pieces with equal angles. What is the angle measure of each piece?

14. What is the measure of the smaller angle when it is 8:00?

15. Megan has a very large round table. In order for her to seat her guests, she divided it into 15 equal sections. What is the angle measure of each section of the table?

© **16. Reason** Joanne cut a round pizza into equal wedges with angles measuring 36°. How many pieces of pizza does she have?

© **17. Construct Arguments** Jacey wrote an equation to find an angle measure. What do *a* and *b* stand for in Jacey's equation?

$$360 \div a = b$$

© **18. Writing to Explain** Why is 360 used as the dividend when dividing to find the measure of an angle?

19. Four pieces of pie were eaten from a pie cut in equal parts. The 5 pieces that remained measured 200°. What was the angle measure of one piece of pie?

© **20. Persevere** Jake cut a round gelatin dessert into 8 equal pieces. Five of the pieces were eaten. What angle measure of the dessert was left?

21. Estimation Paul drew a clock face that showed the time 5:00. What is the measure of the smaller angle shown by that time?

A 50°   **B** 120°   **C** 135°   **D** 150°

Lesson
16-4

©
Common
Core

4.MD.5b An angle that turns through *n* one-degree angles is said to have an angle measure of *n* degrees. Also 4.MD.5, 4.MD.5.a, 4.G.1

Measuring with Unit Angles

Hands-On
pattern blocks

How are angles measured?

Holly traced around a trapezoid pattern block. She wants to find the measure of the angle formed at the vertex shown at the right. What can Holly use to measure the angle?

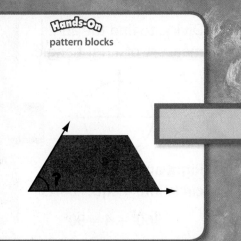

Guided Practice*

© MATHEMATICAL PRACTICES

Do you know HOW?

Use angles you know to find the measure of each angle. Explain how to use the measures of the angles in the squares to help.

1.   **Tip** *The corners of a square form 90° angles.*

2.

Do you UNDERSTAND?

© 3. **Communicate** Explain how you could draw a 210° angle.

4. How many 30° angles are there in a 180° angle? How do know?

5. How many 45° angles are there in a 180° angle? How do you know?

Independent Practice

© MATHEMATICAL PRACTICES

© **Use Tools** For **6** through **14**, find the measure of each angle. Use pattern blocks to help.

6.

7.

8.

9.

10.

11.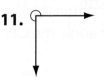

12.

13.

14.

DIGITAL eTools
www.pearsonsuccessnet.com

For another example, see Set D on page 445.

Use an angle you know to find the measure of another angle.

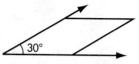

The smaller angle of this pattern block measures 30°.

It turns through 30 unit angles of 1°.

The smaller angle of the trapezoid pattern block matches two of the smaller angles on the long rhombus pattern block. Each smaller angle is 30°.

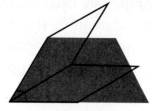

$2 \times 30° = 60°$

The measure of the angle is 60°.

Problem Solving

For **15** through **22**, solve each problem. Use pattern blocks to help.

15. What is the measure of each angle of the yellow hexagon pattern block?

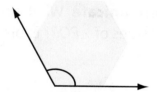

16. What is the measure of the smaller angle formed at 5:00?

17. Cory cut a pizza into 45° slices. Five of the slices were eaten. What is the angle measure of the pizza that is left?

18. What is the measure of the two different-sized angles of the blue rhombus pattern block?

© **19. Be Precise** A classroom table top is shaped like a trapezoid but with different pairs of angles than the red pattern block. What are the angle measures formed on the inside of the classroom table?

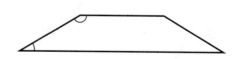

20. Using pattern blocks, what is the measure of the larger angle formed at 8:00?

   A 60°   **C** 175°

   B 120°   **D** 240°

© **21. Writing to Explain** How can you use pattern blocks to measure or draw an angle of 150°?

22. Critique Reasoning Jared said that the angle formed to show the time 10:00 is a 45° angle. Is he correct? Explain.

Lesson
16-5

©
Common Core

4.MD.6 Measure angles in whole-number degrees using a protractor. Sketch angles of specified measure. Also 4.MD.5.a, 4.MD.5.b, 4.G.1

Measuring Angles

Hands-On protractor

How do you measure and draw angles?

Angles are usually measured in units called degrees. The symbol ° indicates degrees. A protractor is <u>a tool that is used to measure and draw angles</u>.

A partially folded crane is shown at the right. Measure ∠PQR.

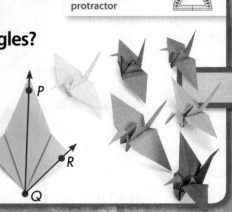

Guided Practice*

MATHEMATICAL **PRACTICES**

Do you know HOW?

For **1** and **2**, measure each angle.

1.   **2.**

For **3** and **4**, draw an angle with each measure.

3. 110°   **4.** 50°

Do you UNDERSTAND?

5. What is the angle measure of a straight line?

© **6. Communicate** What are the vertex and sides of ∠PQR? Explain your answers.

Independent Practice

For **7** through **14**, measure each angle. Tell if each angle is acute, right, or obtuse.

Tip To measure an angle, you may need to trace it and extend its sides.

7. 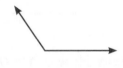   **8.**   **9.**   **10.**

11.   **12.**   **13.**   **14.**

DIGITAL   Animated Glossary
www.pearsonsuccessnet.com

Measure ∠PQR.

Place the protractor's center on the angle's vertex, Q. Place one side of the bottom edge on one side of the angle. Read the measure where the other side of the angle crosses the protractor. If the angle is acute, use the smaller number. If the angle is obtuse, use the larger number.

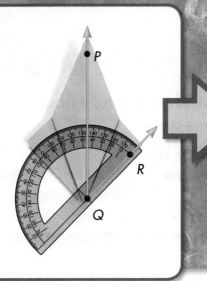

The measure of ∠PQR is 45°.

Draw an angle that measures 130°.

Draw a ray. Label the endpoint T. Place the protractor so that the middle of the bottom edge is over the endpoint of the ray. Place a point at 130°. Label it W. Draw ray TW.

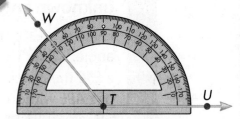

The measure of ∠WTU is 130°.

For **15** through **22**, draw an angle with each measure.

15. 140°   **16.** 180°   **17.** 20°   **18.** 65°

19. 45°   **20.** 115°   **21.** 90°   **22.** 155°

Problem Solving

MATHEMATICAL
PRACTICES

23. Jorge is reading a book containing 3 chapters. The first chapter is 20 pages long. The second chapter is 36 pages long. There are 83 pages in the book. How many pages are in the third chapter?

24. Mariah made 5 three-point shots in her first game and 3 in her second game. She also made 4 two-point shots in each game and no one-point free throws in either game. How many total points did she score?

Use the diagram at the right for **25**.

ⓒ **25. Use Tools** Measure all of the angles created by the intersections of Main Street and Pleasant Street.

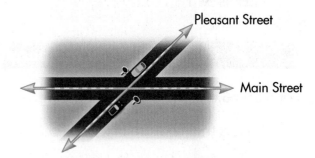

ⓒ **26. Reason** If ∠ABC is an obtuse angle, which of the following could **NOT** be its measure?

    A 140°   **C** 105°

    B 95°   **D** 90°

27. A newspaper stand orders 325 newspapers every day. How many newspapers will be ordered in the month of May?

Tip *There are 31 days in May.*

Lesson
16-6
ⓒ
Common
Core

4.MD.7 Recognize angle
measure as additive. When
an angle is decomposed
into non-overlapping
parts, the angle measure
of the whole is the sum of
the angle measures of the
parts. Solve addition and
subtraction problems to
find unknown angles … by
using an equation … . Also
4.MD.5.a, 4.MD.5.b, 4.MD.6

Adding and Subtracting Angle Measures

Hands-On
protractors

How can you add and subtract to find unknown angle measures?

Elinor is creating a design. First she draws a right angle, ∠ABC. Then she draws a ray BE. She finds that ∠EBC measures 60°. How can she find the measure of ∠ABE without using a protractor?

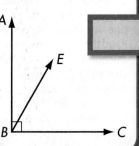

Guided Practice*

MATHEMATICAL
PRACTICES

Do you know HOW?

For **1 and 2**, use the diagram next to each exercise. Add or subtract to find the angle measure.

1. What is the measure of ∠EBC if ∠ABE measures 25°?

2. What is the measure of ∠AEB if measures ∠CEB is 68°?

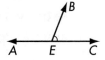

Do you UNDERSTAND?

ⓒ 3. **Use Structure** Write the equation you used to find the answer to Exercise **2**. What is another way to write it using a different operation?

ⓒ 4. **Model** Use the information below to draw a diagram.
　　∠PQR measures 42°.
　　∠RQS measures 39°.
　　∠PQR and ∠RQS do not overlap.
What is the measure of ∠PQS?

Independent Practice

For **5** and **6**, use the diagram at the right.

5. What is the measure of ∠FGJ if ∠JGH measures 22°?

6. What is the measure of ∠KGF if ∠EGK measures 68°?

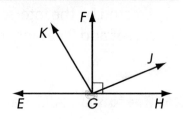

For **7** and **8**, use the diagram at the right.

7. Joe makes a design by turning quadrilateral ABCD 72° about point A. He rotates it 72° about point A again. What is the measure of ∠DAZ?

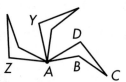

8. The measure of ∠YAD is 72°. The measure of ∠YAB is 95°. What is the measure of ∠DAB?

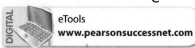
eTools
www.pearsonsuccessnet.com
DIGITAL

∠EBC and ∠ABE do not overlap, so the measure of right angle ABC is equal to the sum of the measures of its parts.

The measure of ∠ABC equals the measure of ∠ABE plus the measure of ∠EBC.

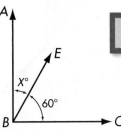

Tip All right angles measure 90°.

Write an equation to find the missing angle measure:

$$x + 60 = 90$$

Solve the equation.

$$x = 90 - 60 = 30$$

$$x = 30$$

The measure of ∠ABE is 30°.

So, Elinor uses subtraction instead of a protractor to find the measure of ∠ABE.

Problem Solving

Ⓒ MATHEMATICAL PRACTICES

Ⓒ **9. Mental Math** Alex draws an angle that measures 110°. He then draws a ray that divides the angle into 2 equal parts. What is the measure of each smaller angle?

10. Talia receives a total of 85¢ for cans she recycles. If she gets a nickel for each can, how many cans does she recycle?

Ⓒ **11. Use Tools** Li uses pattern blocks to make a design. He puts 5 parallelogram blocks together, as shown in the diagram. The measure of ∠LJK is 30°. Use this information and the diagram to answer the following questions.

a What is the measure of ∠MJK?

b What is the measure of ∠NJK?

c What is the measure of ∠OJK?

d What is the measure of ∠PJK?

Tip Remember the parallelograms have the same angle measures.

12. Write 5 hundredths as a decimal and as a fraction.

13. Twenty equal angles share a vertex. The sum of the measures of the angles is 360°. What is the measure of one angle?

Ⓒ **14. Reason** ∠EFG is divided into 2 parts by a ray. One of the smaller angles formed is an obtuse angle and the other is an acute angle. Which of these cannot be the measure of ∠EFG?

    A 89°   **B** 98°   **C** 109°   **D** 118°

©
Common
Core

4.G.2 Classify two-dimensional figures based on the presence or absence of parallel or perpendicular lines, or the presence or absence of angles of a specified size. Recognize right triangles as a category, and identify right triangles.

Polygons

How do you identify polygons?

A polygon is a closed plane figure made up of line segments. Each line segment is a side. The point where two sides meet is called a vertex.

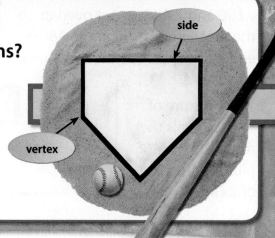

side

vertex

Guided Practice*

© MATHEMATICAL PRACTICES

Do you know HOW?

Draw an example of each polygon. Write the number of sides and vertices it has.

1. pentagon

2. triangle

3. octagon

4. quadrilateral

Do you UNDERSTAND?

5. Is a circle a polygon? Why or why not?

© **6. Writing to Explain** Does every hexagon have the same shape?

Independent Practice

In **7** through **18**, name each polygon if possible. Write the number of sides and vertices it has.

7.

8.

9.

10.

11.

12.

13.

14.

15.

16.

17.

18.

DIGITAL

Animated Glossary
www.pearsonsuccessnet.com

For another example, see Set G on page 446.

Here are some examples of polygons.

Triangle
3 sides

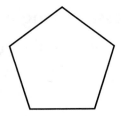
Quadrilateral
4 sides

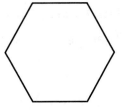
Pentagon
5 sides

Hexagon
6 sides

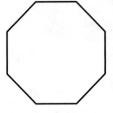
Octagon
8 sides

Problem Solving

MATHEMATICAL
PRACTICES

19. The building to the right is named for the polygon it looks like. What is the name of the polygon?

A Quadrilateral   **C** Hexagon

B Pentagon   **D** Octagon

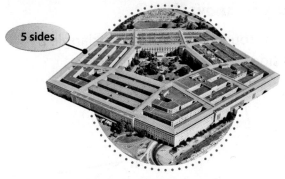

5 sides

20. What rule could be used to sort these polygons?

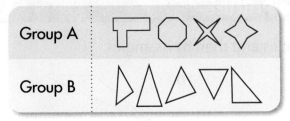

Group A

Group B

© **21. Model** Tim and Peter both are on a swimming team. In one week, Tim swam 244 laps and Peter swam 196 laps. Draw a bar diagram to show how many more laps Tim swam than Peter.

22. Carla gathered a total of 124 seashells. How many seashells would she have if she gathered 4 times that amount?

23. Tasha is hosting a party for 216 people. If 6 people can sit at each table, how many tables will Tasha need to set up?

© **24. Writing to Explain** What do you notice about the number of sides and the number of vertices a polygon has? How many vertices would a 20-sided polygon have?

25. Which polygon does **NOT** have at least 4 sides?

A Octagon   **C** Quadrilateral

B Hexagon   **D** Triangle

Lesson
16-8

© Common Core

4.G.2 Classify two-dimensional figures based on the presence or absence of parallel or perpendicular lines, or the presence or absence of angles of a specified size. Recognize right triangles as a category, and identify right triangles.

Triangles

How can you classify triangles?

Triangles can be classified by their sides.

Equilateral Triangle
3 equal sides

Isosceles Triangle
2 equal sides

Scalene Triangle
0 equal sides

Guided Practice*

 MATHEMATICAL PRACTICES

Do you know HOW?

In **1** through **4**, classify each triangle by its sides and then by its angles.

1.

2.

3.

4.

Do you UNDERSTAND?

© 5. **Reason** Can a triangle have more than one obtuse angle? Explain.

6. Is it possible to draw a right isosceles triangle? If so, draw an example.

7. Can a triangle have more than one right angle? If so, draw an example.

Independent Practice

In **8** through **16**, classify each triangle by its sides and then by its angles.

8.

9.

10.

11.

12.

13.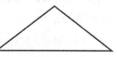

14.

15.

16.

Animated Glossary
www.pearsonsuccessnet.com

For another example, see Set H on page 447.

Triangles also can be classified by their angles.

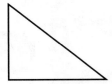

A right triangle <u>has one right angle</u>.

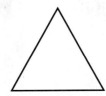

An acute triangle <u>has three acute angles</u>. All of its angles measure less than a right angle.

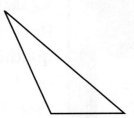

An obtuse triangle <u>has one obtuse angle</u>. One angle has a measure greater than a right angle.

In **17** through **19**, classify each triangle by its sides and then by its angles.

17.

18.

19.

Problem Solving

Ⓒ **MATHEMATICAL PRACTICES**

Ⓒ **20. Reason** Use the diagram below. If the backyard is an equilateral triangle, what do you know about the lengths of the other two sides?

45 feet

21. If Chris uses a third line to make a triangle, what kind of triangle will it be?

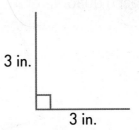

3 in.

3 in.

Ⓒ **22. Writing to Explain** Is an equilateral triangle always an isosceles triangle?

23. When you multiply any number by 1, what is the product?

Use the diagram at the right for **24**.

24. Which is the best name for this muscle group shown at the right?

  A Right muscle group

  B Scalene muscle group

  C Isosceles muscle group

  D Equilateral muscle group

no equal sides

Lesson
16-9

© Common Core

4.G.2 Classify two-dimensional figures based on the presence or absence of parallel or perpendicular lines, or the presence or absence of angles of a specified size. Recognize right triangles as a category, and identify right triangles.

Quadrilaterals

How can you classify quadrilaterals?

Quadrilaterals can be classified by their angles or pairs of sides.

Square

Rectangle

Other Examples

A rhombus is a quadrilateral that has opposite sides that are parallel and all of its sides are the same length.

A trapezoid is a quadrilateral with only one pair of parallel sides.

Guided Practice*

MATHEMATICAL PRACTICES

Do you know HOW?

In **1** through **4**, write all the names you can use for each quadrilateral.

1.

2.

3.

4.

Do you UNDERSTAND?

5. What is true about all quadrilaterals?

© **6. Communicate** Why is a trapezoid not a parallelogram?

7. What is the difference between a square and a rhombus?

Independent Practice

In **8** through **15**, write all the names you can use for each quadrilateral.

8.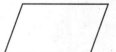

9.

10.

11.

DIGITAL

Animated Glossary
www.pearsonsuccessnet.com

A parallelogram <u>has</u> <u>2 pairs of parallel sides</u>.

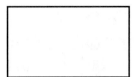

A rectangle <u>has</u> <u>4 right angles</u>. It is also a parallelogram.

A square <u>has 4 right angles and</u> <u>all sides are the same length</u>. It is a parallelogram, rectangle, and rhombus.

12.

13.

14.

15.

Problem Solving

 MATHEMATICAL PRACTICES

16. A quadrilateral has two pairs of parallel sides and exactly 4 right angles. What quadrilateral is being described?

17. Reason Is it possible for a quadrilateral to be both a rhombus and a parallelogram?

18. What number comes next in the pattern?

4, 16, 64, 256,

19. Writing to Explain All the sides of an equilateral triangle are congruent. Is an equilateral triangle also a rhombus? Explain.

20. Valley Ridge Elementary has 108 fourth-grade students and 4 fourth-grade teachers. If split equally, how many students should be in each class?

21. If a theater can hold 235 people for one showing of a movie and they show the movie 5 times a day, how many people could view the movie in one day?

22. In math class, Mr. Meyer drew a quadrilateral on the board. It had just one set of parallel sides and no right angles. What shape was it?

  A Square   **C** Rectangle

  B Rhombus   **D** Trapezoid

23. Jamie went to exercise at a swimming pool. The length of the pool was 25 yards. If she swam the length of the pool 6 times, how many yards did Jamie swim?

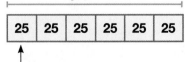

? yards in all

| 25 | 25 | 25 | 25 | 25 | 25 |

Length of pool

Lesson
16-10

© Common Core

4.G.3 Recognize a line of symmetry for a two-dimensional figure as a line across the figure such that the figure can be folded along the line into matching parts. Identify line-symmetric figures and draw lines of symmetry.

Line Symmetry

Hands-On
grid paper

What is a line of symmetry?

A figure is symmetric if it can be folded on a line to form two equal halves that fit on top of each other.

The fold line is called a line of symmetry. This truck has one line of symmetry.

Guided Practice*

© MATHEMATICAL PRACTICES

Do you know HOW?

For **1** and **2**, tell if each line is a line of symmetry.

1.   **2.**

For **3** and **4**, tell how many lines of symmetry each figure has.

3. 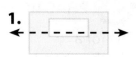   **4.**

Do you UNDERSTAND?

5. Do some figures have no lines of symmetry?

6. How many lines of symmetry does the figure below have?

© **7. Writing to Explain** How many lines of symmetry does a bicycle tire have?

Independent Practice

For **8** through **11**, tell if each line is a line of symmetry.

8. 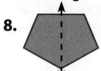   **9.** 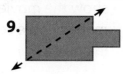   **10.**   **11.**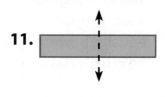

For **12** through **15**, tell how many lines of symmetry each figure has.

12.    **13.**   **14.**    **15.**

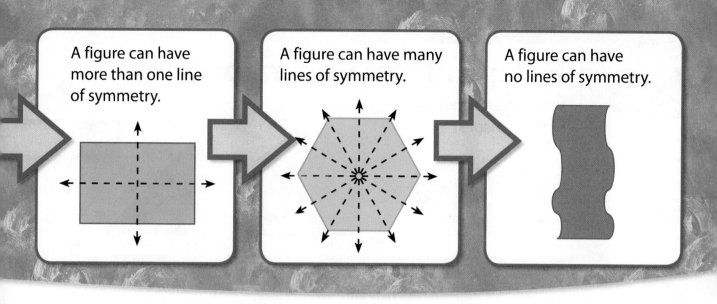

A figure can have more than one line of symmetry.

A figure can have many lines of symmetry.

A figure can have no lines of symmetry.

For **16** through **23**, trace each figure on grid paper, and draw lines of symmetry if you can.

16.

17.

18.

19.

20.

21.

22.

23.

Problem Solving

MATHEMATICAL PRACTICES

24. How many lines of symmetry does a scalene triangle have?

25. How many lines of symmetry does an isosceles triangle have?

© **26. Use Structure** Vanessa drew a figure and said that it had an infinite number of lines of symmetry. What figure did she draw?

27. Draw a quadrilateral that does not have a line of symmetry.

28. The Thomas Jefferson Memorial in Washington, D.C. has one line of symmetry. Use the picture at the right to describe where the line of symmetry is.

© **29. Reason** Write 5 capital letters that have at least one line of symmetry.

30. How many lines of symmetry does a square have?

   A None   **C** 4 lines

   B 2 lines   **D** 6 lines

Animated Glossary
www.pearsonsuccessnet.com
DIGITAL

Lesson
16-11

@
Common Core

4.G.2. Classify two-dimensional figures based on the presence or absence of parallel or perpendicular lines, or the presence or absence of angles of a specified size. Recognize right triangles as a category, and identify right triangles. Also **4.OA.5.**

Problem Solving

Make and Test Generalizations

What is true about all of these shapes?

Guided Practice*

 MATHEMATICAL PRACTICES

Do you know HOW?

1. Look at each group of three letters below. Give a generalization for each group of letters that does not apply to the other group of three letters.

| E F T | C O S |

Do you UNDERSTAND?

© **2. Writing to Explain** Is the generalization that every four sided polygon has at least one right angle correct? If not, draw a picture to show why not.

© **3. Write a Problem** Select 3 items and make two correct generalizations about them.

Independent Practice

 **MATHEMATICAL PRACTICES**

Solve.

4. Look at each group of numbers below. Compare the size of the factors to each product. What generalization can you make about factors and products for whole numbers?

$6 \times 8 = 48$ $46 \times 5 = 230$ $1 \times 243 = 243$

5. Write the factors for 8, 16, and 20. What generalization can you make about all multiples of 4?

Applying Math Practices
- What am I asked to find?
- What else can I try?
- How are quantities related?
- How can I explain my work?
- How can I use math to model the problem?
- Can I use tools to help?
- Is my work precise?
- Why does this work?
- How can I generalize?

For another example, see Set J on page 447.

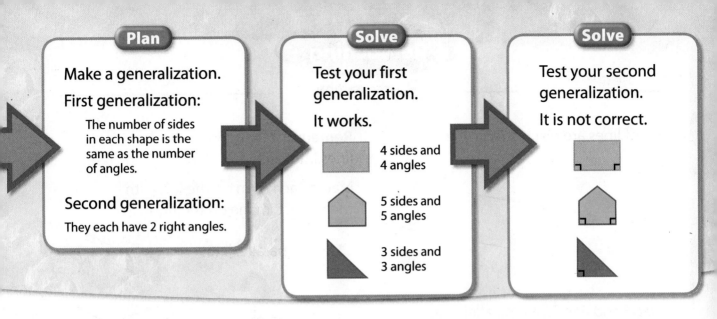

Plan

Make a generalization.

First generalization:

The number of sides in each shape is the same as the number of angles.

Second generalization:

They each have 2 right angles.

Solve

Test your first generalization.

It works.

4 sides and 4 angles

5 sides and 5 angles

3 sides and 3 angles

Solve

Test your second generalization.

It is not correct.

6. What generalization can you make about each of the polygons at the right?

A All sides of each polygon are the same length.

B All polygons have 5 sides.

C All polygons have 4 angles.

D All polygons have 3 angles.

7. The factors for 3 and 6 are shown in the table to the right. Jan concluded if you double a number, then you double the number of factors. Is Jan correct? Why or why not?

Number	3	6
Factors	1, 3	1, 2, 3, 6

8. How many sides does an octagon have? vertices?

9. How many acute angles can an isosceles triangle have?

© 10. **Look for Patterns** Look at the pattern below. Draw the shape that would come next.

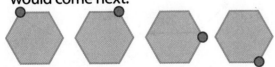

© 11. **Generalize** What generalization could be made about the triangles below?

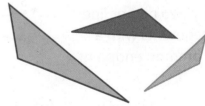

© 12. **Critique Reasoning** Susan said that all squares are rectangles and therefore all rectangles are squares. Is Susan correct? Why or why not?

13. Michael lives on the 22nd floor of a 25 story building. If each floor is 12 feet in height, how many feet above ground level is Michael's apartment?

Set A, pages 422–423

Pairs of lines are given special names.

Line *DE* and line *FG* are parallel lines.

Remember that perpendicular lines intersect.

Match each term on the left with the correct image on the right.

1. _____ parallel lines   **a**

2. _____ point   **b**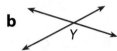

3. _____ perpendicular lines   **c** *B*

4. _____ intersecting lines   **d**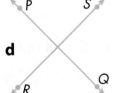

Set B, pages 424–425

Geometric terms are used to describe figures.

A ray has one endpoint and continues on forever in one direction.

An angle is formed by two rays or line segments with a common endpoint.

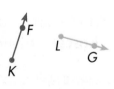

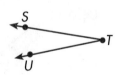

Remember that a line segment does not continue beyond its endpoints.

Use geometric terms to describe what is shown.

1. 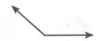   **2.**

3.   **4.**

5.   **6.**

You can find the measure of an angle using fractions of a circle. The angle below is $\frac{1}{3}$ of the circle. How can you measure this angle?

$\frac{1}{3}$ means 1 of 3 equal parts.

$360 \div 3 = 120$

The measure of this angle is 120°.

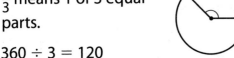

Remember there are always 360° in a complete circle.

1. A circular pizza is cut into 8 pieces of the same size. What is the angle measure of each piece?

You can use an angle you know to find the measure of other angles. Use the smaller angle of the pattern block.

It has a measure of 30°.
Find the measure of the angle below.

Three of the 30° angles will fit into the angle.
Add: 30° + 30° + 30° = 90°.
The measure of this angle is 90°.

Remember you can use any angle that you know the measure of to find the measure of other angles.

Find the measure of each angle. Use pattern blocks.

1. 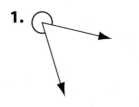   2.

3.    4.

Angles are measured by placing the center of the protractor on the vertex and the 0° mark on one side.

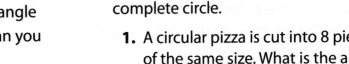

The measurement of the angle is 57°.

Remember that a straight line forms an angle of 180°.

Measure the angles.

1.   2.

3. 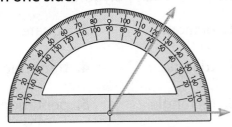   4.

Set F, pages 432–433

If two angles share a ray, then the sum of the measures of the angles is equal to the measure of the larger angle that is made up by the two angles.

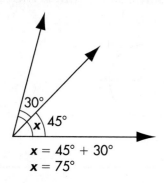

$x = 45° + 30°$
$x = 75°$

You can use subtraction to find the measure of the missing angle in the figure shown below.

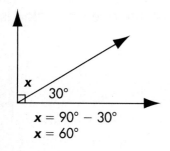

$x = 90° - 30°$
$x = 60°$

Remember you can subtract to find angle measures.

1. $\angle ABC$ and $\angle CBD$ together make the larger $\angle ABD$. Copy and complete the table with the missing angle measures.

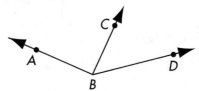

Angle Measure (degrees)		
$\angle ABC$	$\angle CBD$	$\angle ABD$
100°	45°	
95°		155°
105°		170°
	25°	140°
122°	36°	

2. A ray is drawn that splits a right angle into two smaller angles. One angle measures 27 degrees. What is the measure of the other angle?

Set G, pages 434–435

A polygon is a closed figure made up of line segments called sides. Each side meets at a point called a vertex.

Count the number of sides and vertices to identify the polygon.

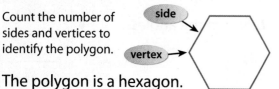

The polygon is a hexagon.

Remember that polygons have the same number of sides and vertices.

Write the number of sides and vertices of each polygon.

1. octagon

2. square

3. triangle

4. trapezoid

5. rectangle

6. pentagon

Triangles can be classified by their sides and angles.

Two sides are the same length and all angles are acute. It is an isoceles, acute triangle.

Name the quadrilateral.

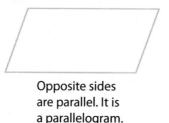

Opposite sides are parallel. It is a parallelogram.

Remember that a quadrilateral can be a rectangle, square, trapezoid, parallelogram, or rhombus.

Classify each shape by its sides and angles.

1.   **2.**

3.   **4.**

How many lines of symmetry does the figure have?

Fold the figure along the dashed line. The two halves are equal and fit one on top of the other.

It has 1 line of symmetry.

Remember that figures can have many lines of symmetry.

Draw the lines of symmetry for each figure.

1. **2.** **3.**

What is true about all of these shapes?

The number of sides in each is the same as the number of angles. Test your generalization.

4 sides, 4 angles   3 sides, 3 angles   4 sides, 4 angles

Remember to test your generalizations.

1. Look at each group of numbers below. Give a generalization for each group of numbers that does not apply to the other group of three numbers.

1 **4**   **3**
  7   **6** **9**

Multiple Choice

1. Which triangle has no equal sides? (16-8)

   A Isosceles

   B Scalene

   C Equilateral

   D Right isosceles

2. Which polygon has more than 5 vertices? (16-7)

   A Pentagon

   B Quadrilateral

   C Triangle

   D Hexagon

3. Laney used drinking straws in art to form a figure that had perpendicular sides. Which could be her figure? (16-1)

   A

   B

   C

   D

4. Which geometric term best describes the light that shines from a flashlight? (16-2)

   A Point

   B Ray

   C Line segment

   D Plane

5. Which quadrilateral has less than 2 pairs of parallel sides? (16-9)

   A Square

   B Parallelogram

   C Trapezoid

   D Rhombus

6. Thomas chose these shapes.

He said the following shapes did not belong with the ones he chose.

Which is the best description of the shapes Thomas chose? (16-11)

   A Polygons with more than 4 sides

   B Polygons with parallel sides

   C Polygons with all sides equal

   D Polygons with a right angle

7. Which stick is parallel to stick *S*? (16-1)

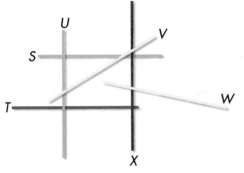

8. What type of angle is angle *A*? (16-2)

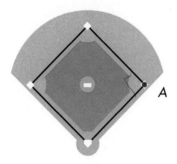

9. What polygon has 5 sides? (16-7)

10. Four of Mrs. Li's students decorated a bulletin board with the shapes shown below. Who made a shape with 8 lines of symmetry? (16-10)

Ralph   Liza

Patricia   Dan

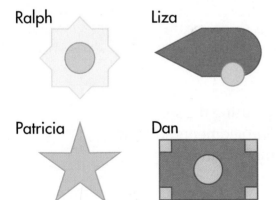

11. What is the measure of the angle shown below? (16-5)

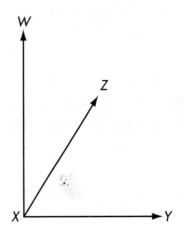

12. Gisela cuts an apple pie into 8 pieces of the same size. What is the angle measure of each piece? (16-3)

13. Terry is measuring an angle using pattern blocks. The smaller angle of each of the pattern blocks shown below measures 30°. What is the measure of the angle shown? (16-4)

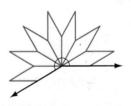

14. If the measure of ∠*WXY* is 90° and the measure of ∠*WXZ* is 33°, what is the measure of ∠*ZXY*? (16-6)

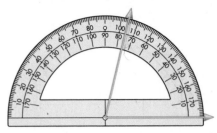

Mrs. Sweeney made some shape patterns for the students to use in art class. Write your answers on a separate page.

1. List the letters of the shapes that match each description. Some shapes will be listed more than once.

   a equilateral triangle   **e** hexagon

   b square   **f** parallelogram

   c pentagon   **g** rectangle

   d isosceles triangle

2. Answer each of the following questions about the shapes shown above. Some shapes will be listed more than once.

   a How many triangles are there?

   b How many quadrilaterals are there?

   c Which shapes have parallel lines?

   d Which are acute triangles?

   e Which are obtuse triangles?

3. On a separate sheet of paper, create a design using the shape pattern pieces shown above. Also include line segments and rays in the design. Color your design, using no more than three different colors.

4. Write a paragraph that describes your design. Don't forget to tell about the shapes!

Step Up to Grade 5

The following lessons provide a step up to, or preview of, Grade 5 Common Core.

Lessons

Scott Foresman-Addison Wesley

enVisionMATH®
Common Core

Step-UP
Lesson

1

Common
Core

5.OA.1 Use parentheses,
brackets, or braces in
numerical expressions, and
evaluate expressions with
these symbols.

The Distributive Property

How can you use the Distributive Property to evaluate expressions?

The Distributive Property states that multiplying a sum (or difference) by a number gives the same result as multiplying each number in the sum (or difference) by the number and adding (or subtracting) the products.

Distributive Property

$a(b + c) = a(b) + a(c)$ $a(b - c) = a(b) - a(c)$

Guided Practice

© MATHEMATICAL PRACTICES

Do you know HOW?

In **1** through **4**, find each missing number.

1. $8(7 + 23) = 8(7) + 8(\ )$

2. $4(28) = 4(20) + 4 (\ )$

3. $8(57) - 8(7) = 8(\ )$

4. $5(26 - 3) = 5 (\ ) - 5(3)$

Do you UNDERSTAND?

5. Why is it easier to evaluate 7×60 than to evaluate $7 \times 55 + 7 \times 5$?

© **6. Communicate** Tony read 22 pages in the morning and 28 pages in the afternoon for 5 days. Lois read 47 pages each day for 5 days. Explain how to use the Distributive Property to find how many pages each of them read.

Independent Practice

Leveled Practice In **7** through **16**, use the Distributive Property to find each missing number.

7. $6(32) = 6(\ ) + 6(2)$

8. $20(5) - 20(2) = 20(\ )$

9. $3(28) + 3(2) = \ (30)$

10. $9(23) = 9(\ ) + 9(3)$

11. $6(46) - 6(6) = 6(\ )$

12. $4(33) = 4(30) + 4(\ )$

13. $30(22 - 10) = 30(22) - 30(\ )$

14. $8(99) = 8(100) - 8(\ )$

15. $20(33 - 5) = 20(\ )$
$= 20(\ ) + 20(8)$

16. $5(42) + 5(5) = 5(\ )$
$= 5(\ ) + 5(7)$

Animated Glossary
www.pearsonsuccessnet.com

DIGITAL

Use the Distributive Property to break apart a number to find the product for 5 × 27.

5×27 ← Break 27 apart.

$5(20 + 7)$ ← $27 = $ 20 7

$5(20) + 5(7)$ ← Multiply each addend.

$100 + 35$ ← Add.

135

$5 \times 27 = 135$

Use the Distributive Property to join numbers together to find 8(32) − 8(2).

$8(32) - 8(2)$

$8(32 - 2)$ ← Join factors.

$8(30)$ ← Subtract.

240 ← Multiply.

$8(32) - 8(2) = 240$

Independent Practice

© **MATHEMATICAL PRACTICES**

© **Persevere** Use the Distributive Property and mental math to evaluate.

 Tip When doing mental math, choose to join or break apart based on which is easier.

17. 7(29) **18.** 6(21) + 6(31) **19.** 5(22) + 5(8) **20.** 8(47)

21. 6(41) + 6(9) **22.** 30(3) + 30(5) **23.** 3(21) − 3(11) **24.** 5(25 − 3)

Problem Solving

© **MATHEMATICAL PRACTICES**

© **25. Writing to Explain** The sixth graders ordered lunch from the Big Group Menu. They ordered 22 organic chilis and 8 veggie plates. Their order can be expressed as 6(22) + 6(8). Explain what mental math steps you would use to find the total cost of the order.

Big Group Menu	
Organic Chili	$6.00
Chicken Tacos	$4.00
Fruit Salad	$5.00
Organic Salad	$5.00
Veggie Plate	$6.00

26. Using the Big Group Menu, write and solve a problem where you can use the Distributive Property.

© **27. Writing to Explain** Jamal said that 9.45 is greater than 9.8 because 45 is greater than 8. Is he correct? Explain.

28. Hiroko put money in a savings account each week. After 9 weeks, there was $49.50 in the account. If Hiroko put the same amount in each week, how much did she save each week?

49.50

?

↑
Amount saved each week

© **29. Think About the Structure** Which choice shows a problem with common factors that could be used for mental math?

A 3(45) + 3(5) **B** 4(18) − 7(8) **C** 2(22) + 3(33) **D** 8(39) + 4(40)

Step-UP
Lesson
2
ⓒ
**Common
Core**

5.OA.2 Write simple expressions that record calculations with numbers, and interpret numerical expressions without evaluating them.

Using Variables to Write Expressions

How can you write an algebraic expression?

Donnie bought CDs for $10 each. How can you represent the total cost of the CDs?

A variable is <u>a quantity that can change or vary and is often represented with a letter</u>. Variables help you translate word phrases into algebraic expressions.

$10 each

Other Examples

The table shows algebraic expressions for given situations.

Word Phrase	Operation	Algebraic Expression
5 dollars more than cost c	addition	$c + 5$
eleven pencils decreased by a number n	subtraction	$11 - n$
six times a distance d	multiplication	$6 \times d$ or $6d$
b bananas divided by seven	division	$b \div 7$ or $\frac{b}{7}$
four less than two times an amount x	multiplication and subtraction	$2x - 4$

Guided Practice

 MATHEMATICAL PRACTICES

Do you know HOW?

Write an algebraic expression for each situation.

1. the difference of a number s and 33

2. m muffins added to 14 muffins

3. 9 times a number n

4. 3 less than 4 times a number f

Do you UNDERSTAND?

5. In the example at the top of the page, what does the variable n represent?

6. Identify the variable and the operation in the algebraic expression $7h$.

ⓒ 7. **Model** Write an algebraic expression for this situation: n more students than the 9 students sitting in each of 4 rows.

DIGITAL Animated Glossary
www.pearsonsuccessnet.com

CDs cost $10 each. The operation is multiplication.

Number of CDs	Total Cost
1	$10 × 1
2	$10 × 2
3	$10 × 3
4	$10 × 4

Use the variable *n* to represent the number of CDs and write an algebraic expression.

$$\$10 \times n$$

An algebraic expression is <u>a mathematical phrase that has at least one variable and one operation</u>. The total cost of the CDs is represented by

$$10 \times n$$
or 10*n*.

The operation is multiplication. The variable is *n*.

Independent Practice

For **8** through **13**, write algebraic expressions.

8. A number *h* increased by 13

9. 10 divided by a number *q*

10. 10 more points than a number *k* times 6

11. 3 less than 8 times a number *e*

12. 7 more than the product of *y* and 5

13. 9 times the difference of *b* and 2

Problem Solving

MATHEMATICAL PRACTICES

14. The distance around a closed shape can be expressed as 3 times side *s*, or 3*s*. Draw an example of this geometric shape.

15. Travis sold *g* cartons of grapes and *s* cartons of strawberries. Write an algebraic expression to represent how many cartons were sold.

16. One float for the Tournament of Roses parade uses as many flowers as a florist usually uses in 5 years. If *x* is the number of flowers a florist uses in 1 year, write an algebraic expression for the number of flowers used to make a float.

17. Writing to Explain Manuel's DVD case has 4 rows of slots, but 6 slots are broken. If *x* equals the number of slots in a row, explain how the expression 4*x* − 6 relates to Manuel's DVD case.

18. A group of hens laid the same number of eggs each day for a week. Meagan collected the eggs for four days. Write an expression to show the number of eggs Meagan did not collect.

19. Think About the Structure Which expression shows a quantity of footballs, *f*, added to 10 basketballs?

A 10 − *f*

C 10 + *f*

B 10*f*

D *f* ÷ 10

Step-UP
Lesson
3

**Common
Core**

5.NBT.2 Explain patterns in the number of zeros of the product when multiplying a number by powers of 10, and explain patterns in the placement of the decimal point when a decimal is multiplied or divided by a power of 10. Use whole-number exponents to denote powers of 10.

Using Patterns to Divide

How can patterns help you divide large multiples of 10?

A jet carries 18,000 passengers in 90 trips. The plane is full for each trip. How many passengers does the plane hold?

Choose an Operation Divide to find how many people were on each trip.

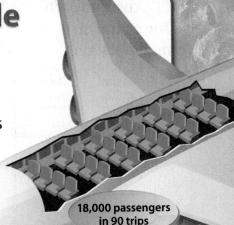

18,000 passengers in 90 trips

Guided Practice

MATHEMATICAL PRACTICES

Do you know HOW?

In **1** through **4**, find each quotient. Use mental math.

1. 180 ÷ 90 = 18 tens ÷ 9 tens = ▩

2. 400 ÷ 50 = 40 tens ÷ 5 tens = ▩

3. 5,400 ÷ 60 = ▩

4. 2,400 ÷ 40 = ▩

Do you UNDERSTAND?

5. In Exercise 1, why is 180 ÷ 90 the same as 18 tens ÷ 9 tens?

Ⓒ **6. Use Structure** In the example at the top, if the jet carried 12,000 people in 30 trips, how many people did it carry for each trip?

Independent Practice

In **7** through **22**, use mental math to find the missing number.

7. 450 ÷ 90 = 45 tens ÷ 9 tens = ▩

8. 500 ÷ 50 = 50 tens ÷ 5 tens = ▩

9. 3,200 ÷ 40 = 320 tens ÷ 4 tens = ▩

10. 24,000 ÷ 60 = 2,400 tens ÷ 6 tens = ▩

11. 2,000 ÷ 20 = ▩

12. 6,300 ÷ 90 = ▩

13. 430 ÷ 10 = ▩

14. 36,000 ÷ ▩ = 90

15. 270 ÷ 30 = ▩

16. 36,000 ÷ ▩ = 300

17. 30,000 ÷ ▩ = 600

18. 1,600 ÷ ▩ = 40

19. 72,000 ÷ ▩ = 800

20. 1,000 ÷ 10 = ▩

21. 3,500 ÷ 50 = ▩

22. 20,000 ÷ 40 = ▩

Think of a basic fact to help you solve.

$18 \div 9 = 2$

Think about multiples of 10:

$180 \div 90 = 18 \text{ tens} \div 9 \text{ tens} = 2$

$1,800 \div 90 = 180 \text{ tens} \div 9 \text{ tens} = 20$

$18,000 \div 90 = 1,800 \text{ tens} \div 9 \text{ tens} = 200$

The pattern shows us that
$18,000 \div 90 = 200$.

So, the jet can hold 200 people during each trip.

You can multiply to check your answer.

$200 \times 90 = 18,000$

Problem Solving

MATHEMATICAL PRACTICES

For **23** and **24**, use the information at the right.

23. If each flight was stocked with the same number of bags of pretzels how many bags of pretzels were on each flight?

Data		
Total passengers	:	4,000
Flights per day	:	20
Bags of pretzels	:	2,000

24. If all the flights were full and all planes carried the same number of passengers, how many people were on each flight?

25. There are 7 schools in the district. Each school receives a $400 donation. What is the total amount of the donation?

26. Caty bowled 4 games. Her scores were 102, 97, 126, and 118. What was the total of her scores?

Ⓒ **27. Think About the Structure** Dividing 420 by 60 is the same as

   A dividing 42 ones by 6 tens.

   B dividing 42 tens by 6 ones.

   C dividing 42 tens by 6 tens.

   D dividing 42 hundreds by 6 tens.

28. Suppose there are 2,750 rubber bands in 25 bins. You want to put the same number of rubber bands in each bin. Which expression shows how to find the number of rubber bands in each bin?

   A $2,750 - 25$ **C** $2,750 \div 25$

   B $2,750 + 25$ **D** $2,750 \times 25$

29. One dozen bagels is 12 bagels. Pat baked 2,472 bagels. Which expression shows how to find how many dozen bagels Pat baked?

   A $2,472 + 12$ **C** $2,472 \times 12$

   B $2,472 - 12$ **D** $2,472 \div 12$

30. It takes 2,500 kg of sand to fill 25 school sandboxes. How much sand will a construction company need to put in each of the 25 sandboxes to get ready for the new school year?

Step-UP
Lesson

4

Common
Core

5.NBT.3 Read, write, and
compare decimals to
thousandths.

Connecting Decimal and Whole Number Numeration

5,342.435 feet

How are whole number place values related to decimal place values?

A telephone company has large spools of cable that they use to install phone lines. Suppose each spool is 5,342.435 feet long.

Show this number in a place-value chart.

Guided Practice

 MATHEMATICAL PRACTICES

Do you know HOW?

In **1** through **4**, write the place value for the red digit.

1. 54.67   **2.** 856.583

3. 372.359   **4.** 5,069.375

For **5** through **8**, write the number that is ten times as many.

5. 0.01   **6.** 0.001

7. 1   **8.** 100

Do you UNDERSTAND?

9. A telephone worker used 340.75 feet of cable. What is the place value of the 5 in 340.75?

10. Reason The grid below shows one hundred equal parts. Each part is equal to one hundredth. How many hundredths are in one tenth?

1 whole

Independent Practice

 MATHEMATICAL PRACTICES

Persevere In **11** through **22**, write the place value for the red digit.

11. 547.76   **12.** 2,368.795   **13.** 1,435.312   **14.** 9,456.782

15. 207.65   **16.** 9,213.709   **17.** 2,468.624   **18.** 5,221.470

19. 2,867.217   **20.** 6,754.392   **21.** 1,843.2   **22.** 5,642.437

For **23** through **26**, write the number that is ten times as many.

23. 0.04   **24.** 20   **25.** 0.006   **26.** 0.5

Each place-value position is ten times as much as the place value to its right.

thousands	hundreds	tens	ones		tenths	hundredths	thousandths
1,000	100	10	1		$0.1 = \frac{1}{10}$	$0.01 = \frac{1}{100}$	$0.001 = \frac{1}{1,000}$
5	3	4	2	•	4	3	5

Problem Solving

MATHEMATICAL
PRACTICES

Ⓒ **27. Look for Patterns** There are 200 fiction books in Mr. Kent's classroom library. The school library has ten times as many fiction books. What is the number of fiction books in the school library?

Ⓒ **28. Look for Patterns** Jaques found two shells. One weighs 0.01 pound. The other weighs ten times as much. How much does the heavier shell weigh?

29. Jennifer and Linda collected aluminum cans for one month. Look at the table at the right to see how many aluminum cans each student collected.

Data	Jennifer	1,353 cans
	Linda	1,328 cans

a Who collected more cans?

b Find the difference between the number of cans collected.

30. Angela baked 3 times as many muffins as Jasmine for the bake sale. If Jasmine baked 36 muffins, how many did Angela bake?

? muffins

Angela	36	36	36	3 times as many
Jasmine	36			

31. Name the place-value position that is ten times as great as the hundredths position.

A Ones

B Tenths

C Hundredths

D Thousands

Ⓒ **32. Reason** Mr. Rodgers has 7 gallons of gas in his car. His tank can hold 15 gallons of gas. Will Mr. Rodgers need more or less than 10 gallons to fill his tank?

Ⓒ **33. Critique Reasoning** Bob says the value of the first 1 is greater than the value of the second 1 in 4.115. Is he correct? Explain.

Step-UP
Lesson
5
ⓒ
**Common
Core**

5.NBT.4 Use place value
understanding to round
decimals to any place.

Rounding Decimals

How can you round decimals?

Rounding replaces one number
with another number that tells
about how many or how much.
Round 2.36 to the nearest tenth.

halfway
↓ 2.36

2.3   2.35   2.4

Think Is 2.36 closer to 2.3 or 2.4?

Another Example **How do you round to the nearest whole number?**

Round 3.2 to the nearest whole number.

Think Is 3.2 closer to 3 or 4?

halfway
3.2   ↓

3   3.5   4

Step 1

Find the rounding place.
Look at the digit to the
right of the rounding
place.

3.2

Step 2

If the digit is 5 or greater, add
1 to the rounding digit. If
the digit is less than 5, leave
the rounding digit alone.

Since 2 < 5,
leave 3 the same.

Step 3

Drop the digits to the
right of the decimal point.
Drop the decimal point.

3.2 rounds to 3.

Guided Practice

 MATHEMATICAL
PRACTICES

Do you know HOW?

In **1** through **6**, round each number to
the place of the underlined digit.

1. 23.7

2. 32.4

3. 5.41

4. 16.89

5. 1.128

6. 457.02

Do you UNDERSTAND?

ⓒ **7. Use Structure** To round 63.82 to
the nearest tenth, which digit do
you look at? What is 63.82 rounded
to the nearest tenth?

ⓒ **8. Communicate** A car-rental service
charges customers for the number of
miles they travel, rounded to the
nearest whole mile. Victor travels 32.6
miles. For how many miles will he be
charged? Explain.

Animated Glossary
www.pearsonsuccessnet.com

DIGITAL

460

Step 1

Find the rounding place. Look at the digit to the right of the rounding place.

2.3̲6

Step 2

If the digit is 5 or greater, add 1 to the rounding digit. If the digit is less than 5, leave the rounding digit alone.

Since 6 > 5, add 1 to the 3.

Step 3

Drop the digits to the right of the rounding digit.

2.36 rounds to 2.4.

Independent Practice

In **9** through **16**, round each decimal to the nearest whole number.

9. 4.2   **10.** 9.7   **11.** 1.0523   **12.** 17.3

13. 51.8   **14.** 77.7   **15.** 154.1   **16.** 362.5

In **17** through **24**, round each number to the place of the underlined digit.

17. 8.2̲64   **18.** 0.47̲3   **19.** 5.3̲291   **20.** 0.981̲3

21. 67.5̲28   **22.** 3.148̲4   **23.** 5.03̲9   **24.** 36.007̲4

Problem Solving

MATHEMATICAL PRACTICES

25. One of the largest dinosaurs ever found, the *Puertasaurus,* measured 39.92 meters long. Round 39.92 to the nearest whole number and to the nearest tenths place.

Ⓒ **26. Writing to Explain** In the first 3 quarters of a basketball game, a team scored 19, 23, and 13 points. The final score was 75. Explain how to find how many points the team scored in the last quarter.

27. The typical wingspan for a red-tailed hawk is 4.17 feet. What is 4.17 when rounded to the nearest tenth? What is 4.17 when rounded to the nearest whole number?

28. **Science** The picture at the right shows the length of an average American alligator. What is the length of the alligator rounded to the nearest whole number?

4.39 meters

A 4 meters   **B** 4.3 meters   **C** 3 meters   **D** 4.4 meters

Step-UP
Lesson

6

ⓒ

Common Core

5.NBT.6 Find whole-number quotients of whole numbers with up to four-digit dividends and two-digit divisors, using strategies based on place value, the properties of operations, and/or the relationship between multiplication and division. Illustrate and explain the calculation by using equations, rectangular arrays, and/or area models.

Estimating Quotients with 2-Digit Divisors

How can you use compatible numbers to estimate quotients?

$159 for 75 bracelets

Betty made $159 by selling 75 bracelets. Each bracelet cost the same. About how much did each bracelet cost?

Choose an Operation We know the total amount made and the number of bracelets. Divide to find the price.

Guided Practice

ⓒ MATHEMATICAL PRACTICES

Do you know HOW?

In **1** through **6**, estimate using compatible numbers.

1. 167 ÷ 21

2. 298 ÷ 21

3. 355 ÷ 49

4. 473 ÷ 83

5. 2,400 ÷ 61

6. 2,019 ÷ 38

Do you UNDERSTAND?

7. In the example above, find another way to estimate the cost of each bracelet.

ⓒ **8. Reason** Betty has 375 more bracelets to sell. She wants to store these in plastic bags that hold 20 bracelets each. She estimates she will need about 20 bags. Is she right? Why or why not?

Independent Practice

In **9** through **26**, estimate using compatible numbers.

9. 308 ÷ 11

10. 322 ÷ 37

11. 3,022 ÷ 61

12. 195 ÷ 19

13. 1,784 ÷ 24

14. 3,620 ÷ 53

15. 1,179 ÷ 30

16. 455 ÷ 85

17. 542 ÷ 56

18. $32\overline{)2,100}$

19. $67\overline{)5,591}$

20. $11\overline{)232}$

21. $48\overline{)4,900}$

22. $44\overline{)8,090}$

23. $94\overline{)6,431}$

24. $84\overline{)7,238}$

25. $29\overline{)2,045}$

26. $63\overline{)5,384}$

The question asks, "About how much?" So, an estimate is enough.

Use compatible numbers to estimate 159 ÷ 75.

Find compatible numbers for 159 and 75.

Think 16 can be divided evenly by 8.

160 and 80 are close to 159 and 75.

So, 160 and 80 are compatible numbers.

Divide.

160 ÷ 80 = 2.

So, Betty charged *about* $2 for each bracelet.

Check for reasonableness:

2 × 80 = 160

Problem Solving

MATHEMATICAL PRACTICES

27. A high school hockey team has made it to the state tournament. There are 315 students who want to go, and 38 students can fit on each bus. How many buses are needed?

28. Each hockey player contributed $8 for a gift for the head coach. The two assistant coaches each donated $15. If there were 18 players on the team, how much money did the team raise in all?

29. A comet orbits the Sun 39 times in 129 years. About how long does it take the comet to complete one orbit?

30. Anthony bought 5 CDs on sale for $60. The regular price for 5 CDs is $75. How much did Anthony save per CD by buying them on sale?

31. Which is the best estimate of the product for the following expression?

395×52

A 2,000

B 20,000

C 24,000

D 200,000

32. Which property does the following equation illustrate?

$42 + 54 = 54 + 42$

A Commutative Property of Addition

B Associative Property of Addition

C Identity Property of Addition

D Commutative Property of Multiplication

33. Ayira bought a skate board. She paid $10 less than the regular price. If the regular price was $62, how much did Ayira spend on the skate board?

© **34. Writing to Explain** Ryley needs to estimate the quotient of 565 ÷ 82. Explain how he can use compatible numbers to make a reasonable estimate.

Step-UP
Lesson
7

ⓒ
**Common
Core**

5.NBT.7 Add, subtract,
multiply, and divide
decimals to hundredths,
using concrete models or
drawings and strategies
based on place value,
properties of operations,
and/or the relationship
between addition and
subtraction; relate the
strategy to a written
method and explain the
reasoning used.

Modeling Addition and ~Hands-On~
grid paper

Subtraction of Decimals

How do you add decimals using grids?

Use the table at the right to find the total monthly cost of using the dishwasher and the DVD player.

Data

Device	Cost/month
DVD player	$0.40
Microwave oven	$3.57
Ceiling light	$0.89
Dishwasher	$0.85

Another Example **How do you subtract decimals with grids?**

Find the difference between the cost per month to run the microwave oven and the ceiling light.

Use hundredths grids to subtract 3.57 − 0.89.

Step 1 Shade three grids and 57 squares to show 3.57.

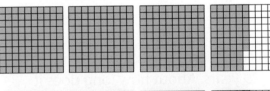

Step 2 Cross out 8 columns and 9 squares of the shaded grid to show 0.89 being subtracted from 3.57.

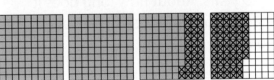

Count the squares that are shaded but not crossed out to find the difference.
3.57 − 0.89 = 2.68

Explain It

ⓒ 1. **Reasonableness** How could you use the grids to check your answer above?

2. How would the grids above be different if the cost per month to run the microwave were $2.57?

Step 1

Use hundredths grids to add $0.85 + $0.40.

It costs $0.85 to use the dishwasher per month.

 Shade 85 squares to show $0.85.

Step 2

It costs $0.40 to use the DVD player per month.

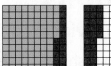 Use a different color and shade 40 more squares to show $0.40. Count all of the shaded squares to find the sum.

$0.85 + $0.40 = $1.25

The monthly cost of using the dishwasher and DVD player is $1.25.

Guided Practice

© **MATHEMATICAL PRACTICES**

Do you know HOW?

In **1** through **4**, use hundredths grids to add or subtract.

1. $4.45 + 0.34$

2. $0.72 + 0.86$

3. $5.32 - 0.54$

4. $2.57 - 0.42

Do you UNDERSTAND?

© **5. Model** Show the difference between the monthly cost of using the dishwasher and the ceiling light.

Independent Practice

© **MATHEMATICAL PRACTICES**

© **Model** In **6** through **9**, add or subtract. Use hundredths grids to help.

6. $0.26 + 0.58$

7. $0.30 + 0.53

8. $2.0 - 1.27$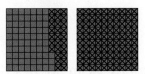

9. $1.42 - 0.29

© **10. Writing to Explain** How is adding $5.17 + 6.40$ similar to adding $5.17 + $6.40?

11. Do you think the difference of $1.6 - 0.99$ is less than one or greater than one? Explain.

Step-UP
Lesson

8

Common
Core

5.NF.3 Interpret a fraction
as division of the numerator
by the denominator ($a/b =$
$a \div b$). Solve word
problems involving division
of whole numbers leading
to answers in the form of
fractions or mixed numbers,
e.g., by using visual fraction
models or equations to
represent the problem.

Relating Division to Multiplication of Fractions

How can you divide by a fraction?

Joyce is making sushi rolls. She needs $\frac{1}{4}$ cup of rice for each sushi roll. How many sushi rolls can she make if she has 3 cups of rice?

MATHEMATICAL
PRACTICES

Guided Practice

Do you know HOW?

In **1** and **2**, use the picture below to find each quotient. Simplify, if necessary.

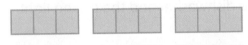

1. How many $\frac{1}{3}$s are in 3? $3 \div \frac{1}{3} = $ ▢

2. How many $\frac{2}{3}$s are in 6? $6 \div \frac{2}{3} = $ ▢

Do you UNDERSTAND?

© 3. **Model** In the example above, if Joyce had 4 cups of rice, how many rolls could she make?

© 4. **Writing to Explain** In the example above, how does the diagram help to show that $3 \div \frac{1}{4}$ is equal to 3×4?

Independent Practice

In **5** and **6**, use the picture to find each quotient.

5. How many $\frac{1}{6}$s are in 1? $1 \div \frac{1}{6} = $ ▢   6. How many $\frac{1}{6}$s are in 5? $5 \div \frac{1}{6} = $ ▢

In **7** through **11**, draw a picture to find each quotient.

7. $4 \div \frac{1}{2}$ 8. $8 \div \frac{1}{4}$ 9. $2 \div \frac{1}{8}$ 10. $4 \div \frac{2}{3}$ 11. $6 \div \frac{3}{4}$

In **12** through **16**, use multiplication to find each quotient.

12. $3 \div \frac{1}{5}$ 13. $8 \div \frac{1}{3}$ 14. $3 \div \frac{1}{10}$ 15. $9 \div \frac{3}{8}$ 16. $15 \div \frac{3}{5}$

Animated Glossary
www.pearsonsuccessnet.com

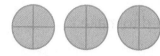

One Way

Draw a diagram.

How many $\frac{1}{4}$s are in 3?

Think $3 \div \frac{1}{4}$.

There are twelve $\frac{1}{4}$s in three whole cups.

So, Joyce can make 12 sushi rolls.

Another Way

The diagram shows $3 \div \frac{1}{4} = 12$.
You also know that $3 \times 4 = 12$.
This suggests that you can also use multiplication to divide by a fraction.

Two fractions whose product is 1 are reciprocals. For example, $\frac{1}{4} \times \frac{4}{1} = 1$, so $\frac{1}{4}$ and $\frac{4}{1}$ are reciprocals. Dividing by a fraction is the same as multiplying by its reciprocal.

$$3 \div \frac{1}{4} = 3 \times \frac{4}{1} = 12$$

So, Joyce can make 12 sushi rolls.

Problem Solving

 MATHEMATICAL PRACTICES

For **17** and **18**, use the following information.

Bijan is making a banner for his school. Along the bottom edge of the banner is a row of small squares. Each square is 6 inches by 6 inches.

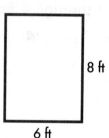

8 ft

6 ft

17. How many small squares can Bijan put along the bottom of the banner?

18. If every fourth square is colored blue, how many blue squares are along the bottom?

© **19. Reason** When you divide a whole number by a fraction with a numerator of 1, explain how you can find the quotient.

© **20. Write a Problem** Write a word problem that can be solved by dividing 10 by $\frac{2}{3}$. Include the answer to the problem.

21. As of 2006, the world's largest leather work boot is 16 feet tall. A typical men's work boot is $\frac{1}{2}$ foot tall. How many times as tall is the largest boot as the height of a typical work boot?

© **22. Estimation** The Nile River is 4,160 miles long. You want to spend three weeks traveling the entire length of the river. Estimate the number of miles you should travel each day.

23. Maria used one bag of flour. She baked two loaves of bread. Each loaf required $2\frac{1}{4}$ cups of flour. Then she used the remaining $6\frac{1}{2}$ cups of flour to make muffins. How much flour was in the bag to begin with?

24. Rudy has 8 yards of twine. If he cuts the twine into $\frac{3}{4}$-foot pieces, how many pieces can he cut?

A $10\frac{1}{2}$ C 32

B 24   D $96\frac{1}{2}$

Step-Up Lesson 8   467

Step-UP
Lesson

9

Common
Core

5.NF.4 Apply and extend
previous understandings of
multiplication to multiply a
fraction or whole number
by a fraction.

Multiplying Fractions and Whole Numbers

What are some ways to think about multiplying fractions and whole numbers?

How many cups of orange juice are needed to make 8 batches of fruit drink?

One way to find $8 \times \frac{3}{4}$ is to use repeated addition.

$$8 \times \frac{3}{4} = \frac{3}{4} + \frac{3}{4} + \frac{3}{4} + \frac{3}{4} + \frac{3}{4} + \frac{3}{4} + \frac{3}{4} + \frac{3}{4} = \frac{8 \times 3}{4} = \frac{24}{4} = 6$$

$\frac{3}{4}$ cup of orange juice for each batch

Guided Practice

MATHEMATICAL PRACTICES

Do you know HOW?

In **1** through **4**, find each product.

1. $\frac{1}{7}$ of 21

2. $\frac{3}{7}$ of 21

3. $35 \times \frac{1}{5}$

4. $\left(\frac{5}{6} - \frac{2}{6}\right) \times 20$

Do you UNDERSTAND?

© **5. Use Structure** How is finding $8 \times \frac{3}{4}$ similar to finding $\frac{3}{4}$ of 8?

6. If you wanted to make 8 batches using the recipe above, how many cups of orange juice would you need?

Independent Practice

In **7** through **38**, find each product.

7. $\frac{1}{3}$ of 30

8. $\frac{1}{3}$ of 18

9. $\frac{1}{5}$ of 20

10. $\frac{1}{7}$ of 35

11. $\frac{2}{9}$ of 90

12. $\frac{2}{5}$ of 50

13. $\frac{1}{2}$ of 60

14. $\frac{5}{8}$ of 24

15. $\frac{2}{3}$ of 12

16. $\frac{6}{7}$ of 49

17. $\frac{3}{5}$ of 25

18. $\frac{2}{5}$ of 35

19. $\frac{5}{8}$ of 48

20. $\frac{3}{7}$ of 21

21. $\frac{8}{9}$ of 72

22. $\frac{7}{8}$ of 56

23. $\frac{2}{3} \times 27$

24. $\frac{3}{8} \times 32$

25. $\frac{2}{3} \times 27$

26. $30 \times \frac{7}{10}$

27. $35 \times \frac{4}{5}$

28. $12 \times \frac{2}{3}$

29. $28 \times \frac{1}{4}$

30. $18 \times \frac{2}{9}$

31. $\frac{2}{5} \times 45$

32. $\frac{8}{9} \times 27$

33. $\frac{4}{7} \times 35$

34. $\frac{5}{8} \times 8$

35. $\frac{3}{8} \times 24$

36. $\frac{7}{9} \times 36$

37. $\left(\frac{3}{4} - \frac{1}{4}\right) \times 50$

38. $\left(\frac{3}{5} - \frac{3}{10}\right) \times 40$

To find $8 \times \frac{3}{4}$, you can multiply first and then divide.

$8 \times \frac{3}{4} = \frac{24}{4} = 6$

Another way to think about multiplication of a whole number and a fraction is to find a part of a whole group.

Martin has 8 oranges to make juice. If he uses $\frac{3}{4}$ of the oranges, how many will he use? To find $\frac{3}{4}$ of 8, you can draw a picture.

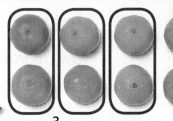

To find $\frac{3}{4}$ of 8, you can divide first and then multiply.

Think $\frac{1}{4}$ of 8 = 2.
So, $\frac{3}{4}$ of 8 = 3×2 or 6.
Remember that $\frac{3}{4}$ of 8 means $\frac{3}{4} \times 8$.
So, $\frac{3}{4} \times 8 = 6$.

Problem Solving

MATHEMATICAL PRACTICES

© **39. Reason Quantitatively** Explain how you would find $32 \times \frac{3}{4}$ mentally.

40. Lions spend about $\frac{5}{6}$ of their days sleeping. How many hours a day does a lion sleep?

© **41. Writing to Explain** Diego said that when you multiply a nonzero whole number by a fraction less than 1, the product is always less than the whole number. Do you agree?

43. On Mars, your weight is about $\frac{1}{3}$ of your weight on Earth. If a fourth grader weighs 69 pounds on Earth, about how much would be his or her weight on Mars?

42. Who ran the most miles by the end of the week? Use the table below.

	Tuesday	Thursday	Saturday
Lorne	3.75 mi	3 mi	2.5 mi
Dave	3 mi	2.25 mi	3.5 mi

44. How much change will Kaleena get if she buys three CDs and six books and gives the clerk three $20 bills?

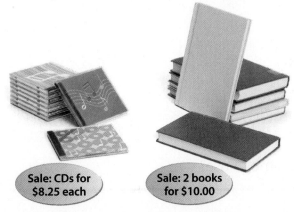

Sale: CDs for $8.25 each

Sale: 2 books for $10.00

45. A recipe calls for $\frac{1}{2}$ cup of raisins and $\frac{3}{16}$ cup of chocolate chips. Which of the following shows the correct relationship?

A $\frac{1}{2} > \frac{3}{16}$ **C** $\frac{3}{8} < \frac{1}{4}$

B $\frac{1}{2} = \frac{3}{16}$ **D** $\frac{1}{2} < \frac{3}{16}$

46. A 1965 U.S. half dollar contains $\frac{2}{5}$ ounce of silver. How many ounces of silver do 50 of those coins contain?

Step-UP
Lesson

10

Common
Core

5.MD. 4 Measure volumes
by counting unit cubes,
using cubic cm, cubic in,
cubic ft, and improvised
units.

Volume

How do you find the volume of a prism?

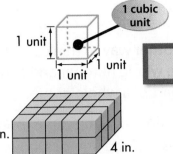

1 cubic unit

Volume is the number of cubic units needed to fill a solid figure.

A cubic unit is the volume of a cube 1 unit on each edge. Each cube = 1 cubic unit. Find the volume of the rectangular prism.

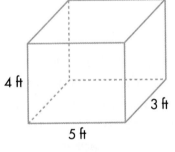

2 in.

4 in.

5 in.

Another Example **How do you use a formula to find volume?**

If the measurements of a prism are given in length ℓ, width w, and height h, then use this formula to find volume V:

Volume = (length × width) × height
$V = (\ell \times w) \times h$

Use a formula to find the volume of the prism.

$V = (\ell \times w) \times h$
$V = (5 \times 3) \times 4$
$V = 60$ cubic feet

4 ft

3 ft

5 ft

The volume of the prism is 60 cubic feet.

Sometimes the area of the base will be given.

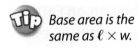
Tip *Base area is the same as $\ell \times w$.*

If a rectangular prism has a base area B and a height h, use this formula:

Volume = base × height
$V = B \times h$

Find the volume of a rectangular prism with a base area of 49 square centimeters and a height of 6 cm.

$V = B \times h$
$V = 49 \times 6$
$V = 294$ cubic centimeters

Explain It

1. How is counting cubes related to the formulas for finding volume?

2. How do you know which formula for volume to use?

Count cubes to find volume.

If the cubic units are shown, you can count the cubes inside the rectangular prism. Begin with the base layer of the prism. It has 5 cubes each in 4 rows.

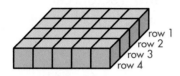

There are 20 cubic units in the base layer of the prism.

There are two layers.

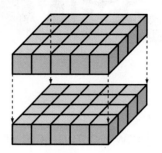

20 cubes × 2 layers = 40 cubic units.

The measures are in inches, so the volume of the rectangular prism is 40 cubic inches.

Guided Practice

© MATHEMATICAL PRACTICES

Do you know HOW?

In **1** and **2**, find the volume of each rectangular prism.

1.

2.

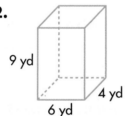

9 yd
4 yd
6 yd

Do you UNDERSTAND?

© **3. Construct Arguments** In the example above, how do you know both of the layers are the same?

4. A cereal box measures 6 in. by 2 in. by 10 in. Draw a rectangular prism and label it. What is the volume of the figure you drew?

Independent Practice

© MATHEMATICAL PRACTICES

© **Be Precise** In **5** through **10**, find the volume of each rectangular prism.

5.

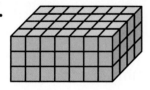

6.

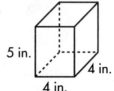

5 in.
4 in.
4 in.

7.

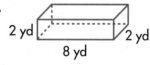

2 yd
8 yd
2 yd

8. Base area: 40 square inches height: 9 in

9. Base area: 100 square feet height: 21 ft

10. Base area: 64 square yards height: 8 yds

11. What is the perimeter of this figure?

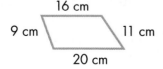

16 cm
9 cm
11 cm
20 cm

12. A refrigerator measures about 6 feet tall, 4 feet wide, and 3 feet deep. Estimate the volume of the refrigerator.

DIGITAL
Animated Glossary
www.pearsonsuccessnet.com

Glossary

A.M. Time between midnight and noon.

acute angle An angle that is less than a right angle.

acute triangle A triangle with three acute angles.

addends The numbers that are added together to find a sum.
Example: 2 + 7 = 9

Addends

algebraic expression An expression with variables.

analog clock Shows time by pointing to numbers on a face.

angle A figure formed by two rays that have the same endpoint.

angle measure The degrees of an angle.

area The number of square units needed to cover a region.

array A way of displaying objects in rows and columns.

Associative Property of Addition Addends can be regrouped and the sum remains the same.

Associative Property of Multiplication Factors can be regrouped and the product remains the same.

average The mean, found by adding all numbers in a set and dividing by the number of values.

bar graph A graph using bars to show data.

benchmark fractions Fractions that are commonly used for estimation: $\frac{1}{4}$, $\frac{1}{3}$, $\frac{1}{2}$, $\frac{2}{3}$, and $\frac{3}{4}$.

breaking apart Mental math method used to rewrite a number as the sum of numbers to form an easier problem.

capacity The volume of a container measured in liquid units.

center A point within a circle that is the same distance from all points on a circle.

centimeter (cm) A metric unit of length. 100 centimeters = 1 meter

century A unit of time equal to 100 years.

chord Any line segment that connects any two points on the circle.

circle A closed plane figure in which all the points are the same distance from a point called the center.

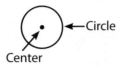
←Circle
Center

circle graph A graph in the shape of a circle that shows how the whole is broken into parts.

circumference The distance around a circle.

common factor A factor that two or more numbers have in common.

Commutative Property of Addition Numbers can be added in any order and the sum remains the same.

Commutative Property of Multiplication Factors can be multiplied in any order and the product remains the same.

compare To decide if one number is greater than or less than another number.

compatible numbers Numbers that are easy to compute mentally.

compensation Choosing numbers close to the numbers in a problem to make the computation easier, and then adjusting the answer for the numbers chosen.

composite number A whole number greater than 1 that has more than two factors.

coordinate grid A grid used to show ordered pairs.

counting on Counting up from the smaller number to find the difference of two numbers.

cube A solid figure with six congruent squares as its faces.

cup (c) A customary unit of capacity. 1 cup = 8 fluid ounces

customary units of measure Units of measure that are used in the United States.

cylinder A solid figure with two congruent circular bases.

D

data Pieces of collected information.

day A unit of time equal to 24 hours.

decade A unit of time equal to 10 years.

decimal point A dot used to separate dollars from cents or ones from tenths in a number.

decimeter (dm) A metric unit of length equal to 10 centimeters.

degree (°) A unit of measure for angles.

degrees Celsius (°C) A metric unit of temperature.

degrees Fahrenheit (°F) A standard unit of temperature.

denominator The number below the fraction bar in a fraction. The total number of equal parts in all.

diameter A line segment that connects two points on a circle and passes through the center.

difference The answer when subtracting two numbers.

digital clock Shows time with numbers. Hours are separated from minutes with a colon.

digits The symbols used to write a number: 0, 1, 2, 3, 4, 5, 6, 7, 8, and 9.

Distributive Property Breaking apart problems into two simpler problems. *Example*: (3 × 21) = (3 × 20) + (3 × 1)

divide An operation to find the number in each group or the number of equal groups.

dividend The number to be divided.

divisibility rules The rules that state when a number is divisible by another number.

divisible Can be divided by another number without leaving a remainder. *Example*: 10 is divisible by 2

divisor The number by which another number is divided. *Example*: 32 ÷ 4 = 8

Divisor

elapsed time The amount of time between the beginning of an event and the end of the event.

equally likely (event) Just as likely to happen as not to happen.

equation A number sentence that uses the equal sign (=) to show that two expressions have the same value.

equilateral triangle A triangle in which all sides are the same length.

equivalent Numbers that name the same amount.

equivalent fractions Fractions that name the same region, part of a set, or part of a segment.

expanded form A number written as the sum of the values of its digits. *Example*: 2,000 + 400 + 70 + 6

F

fact family A group of related facts using the same set of numbers.

factors The numbers multiplied together to find a product.
Example: 3 × 6 = 18

Factor

fluid ounce (fl oz) A customary unit of capacity.
1 fluid ounce = 2 tablespoons

foot (ft) A customary unit of length.
1 foot = 12 inches

fraction A fraction is a symbol, such as $\frac{2}{3}$, $\frac{5}{1}$, or $\frac{8}{5}$, used to name a part of a whole, a part of a set, a location on a number line, or a division of whole numbers.

front-end estimation A way to estimate a sum by adding the first digit of each addend and adjusting the result based on the remaining digits.

G

gallon (gal) A customary unit of capacity. 1 gallon = 4 quarts

gram (g) A metric unit of mass.
1,000 grams = 1 kilogram

H

hexagon A polygon with 6 sides.

hour A unit of time equal to 60 minutes.

hundredth One part of 100 equal parts of a whole.

I

Identity Property of Addition The sum of any number and zero is that number.

Identity Property of Multiplication The product of any number and one is that number.

impossible (event) An event that cannot occur.

improper fraction A fraction in which the numerator is greater than or equal to the denominator.

inch (in.) A customary unit of length.
12 inches = 1 foot

inequality A number sentence that uses the greater than sign (>) or the less than sign (<) to show that two expressions do not have the same value.

intersecting lines Lines that cross at one point.

interval A number which is the difference between two consecutive numbers on the scale of a graph.

inverse operations Operations that undo each other.
Examples: Adding 6 and subtracting 6 are inverse operations. Multiplying by 4 and dividing by 4 are inverse operations.

isosceles triangle A triangle that has at least two equal sides.

key Part of a pictograph that tells what each symbol stands for.

kilogram (kg) A metric unit of mass.
1 kilogram = 1,000 grams

kilometer (km) A metric unit of length.
1 kilometer = 1,000 meters

leap year A unit of time equal to 366 days.

likely (event) An event that probably will happen.

line A straight path of points that goes on and on in two directions.

line graph A graph that connects points to show how data changes over time.

line of symmetry A line on which a figure can be folded so that both halves are the same.

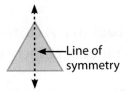

line plot A display of data along a number line.

line segment A part of a line that has two endpoints.

liter (L) A metric unit of capacity.
1 liter = 1,000 milliliters

mass The amount of matter that something contains.

meter (m) A metric unit of length.
1 meter = 100 centimeters

mile (mi) A customary unit of length.
1 mile = 5,280 feet

millennium A unit for measuring time equal to 1,000 years.

milliliter (mL) A metric unit of capacity.
1,000 milliliters = 1 liter

millimeter (mm) A metric unit of length.
1,000 millimeters = 1 meter

minute A unit of time equal to 60 seconds.

mixed number A number that has a whole number and a fraction.

month One of the 12 parts into which a year is divided.

multiple The product of a given factor and any whole number.

number expression An expression that contains numbers and at least one operation. A number expression is also called a numerical expression.

numerator The number above the fraction bar in a fraction.

obtuse angle An angle whose measure is between 90° and 180°.

obtuse triangle A triangle in which there is one obtuse angle.

octagon A polygon with 8 sides.

ounce (oz) A customary unit of weight.
16 ounces = 1 pound

outcome A possible result of a game or experiment.

overestimate An estimate that is greater than the exact answer.

P.M. Time between noon and midnight.

parallel lines In a plane, lines that never intersect.
Example:

parallelogram
A quadrilateral in which opposite sides are parallel.

partial products Products found by breaking one factor in a multiplication problem into ones, tens, hundreds, and so on and then multiplying each of these by the other factor.

pentagon A plane figure with 5 sides.

perimeter The distance around a figure.

period In a number, a group of three digits, separated by commas, starting from the right.

perpendicular lines Two intersecting lines that form right angles. *Example:*

pictograph A graph using pictures or symbols to show data.

pi (π) The ratio of the circumference of a circle to its diameter. Pi is approximately 3.14.

pint (pt) A customary unit of capacity. 1 pint = 2 cups

place value The value given to the place a digit has in a number. *Example*: In 3,946, the place value of the digit 9 is in the hundreds. So, the 9 has a value of 900.

plane An endless flat surface.

point An exact location in space.

polygon A closed plane figure made up of line segments.

pound (lb) A customary unit of weight. 1 pound = 16 ounces

prediction An informed guess about what will happen.

prime number A whole number greater than 1 that has exactly two factors, 1 and itself.

prism A solid object that has two identical ends and all flat sides.

product The answer to a multiplication problem.

protractor A tool used to measure and draw angles.

quadrilateral A polygon with 4 sides.

quart (qt) A customary unit of capacity. 1 quart = 2 pints

quotient The answer to a division problem.

radius Any line segment that connects the center to a point on the circle.

ray A part of a line that has one endpoint and continues endlessly in one direction.

rectangle A quadrilateral with 4 right angles.

remainder The number that remains after the division is complete.

repeating pattern A pattern that is made up of shapes or numbers that form a part that repeats.

rhombus A quadrilateral in which opposite sides are parallel and all sides are the same length.

right angle An angle that forms a square corner.

right triangle A triangle in which there is one right angle.

rounding Replacing a number with a number that tells about how many or how much.

scale Numbers that show the units used on a graph.

scalene triangle A triangle in which no sides are the same length.

second A unit of time. 60 seconds = 1 minute

side Each of the line segments of a polygon.

simplest form A fraction in which the numerator and denominator have no common factors other than 1.

solid figure A figure that has length, width, and height.

solution The value of the variable that makes an equation true.

solve Find a solution to an equation.

sphere A solid figure that includes all points the same distance from a center point.

square A quadrilateral with 4 right angles and all sides the same length.

standard form A way to write a number showing only its digits. *Example*: 2,613

stem-and-leaf plot A display that shows data in order of place value.

straight angle An angle that forms a straight line.

sum The result of adding numbers together.

survey Collecting information by asking a number of people the same question and recording their answers.

symmetric A figure is symmetric if it can be folded into two congruent halves that fit on top of each other.

tablespoon (tbsp) A customary unit of capacity. 1 tablespoon = 3 teaspoons

teaspoon (tsp) A customary unit of capacity. 3 teaspoons = 1 tablespoon

tenth One of ten equal parts of a whole.

ton (T) A customary unit of weight. 1 ton = 2,000 pounds

trapezoid A quadrilateral with only one pair of parallel sides.

tree diagram A display to show all possible outcomes.

trend A pattern in the data on a line graph, shown by an increase or decrease.

triangle A polygon with 3 sides.

underestimate An estimate that is less than the exact answer.

unit angle An angle that cuts off $\frac{1}{360}$ of a circle and measures 1°.

unit fraction A fraction with a numerator of 1.
Example: $\frac{1}{2}$

variable A symbol or letter that stands for a number.

Venn diagram A diagram that uses circles to show the relationships between groups of data.
Example:

vertex (plural, vertices) The point where two rays meet to form an angle. The points where the sides of a polygon meet.

volume The number of cubic units needed to fill a solid figure.

week A unit of time equal to 7 days.

weight How heavy an object is.

word form A number written in words.
Example: Four thousand, six hundred, thirty-two.

yard (yd) A customary unit of length.
1 yard = 3 feet

year A unit of time equal to 365 days or
52 weeks or 12 months.

Zero Property of Multiplication The
product of any number and zero is zero.

Illustrations

68, 89, 121, 137, 210, 227, 229, 230, 244, 254, 289, 314, 315, 316, 326, 332, 333, 364, 365, 398, 400, 406 Rob Schuster; **115** Nathan Jarvis.

Photographs

Every effort has been made to secure permission and provide appropriate credit for photographic material. The publisher deeply regrets any omission and pledges to correct errors called to its attention in subsequent editions.

Unless otherwise acknowledged, all photographs are the property of Pearson Education, Inc.

Photo locators denoted as follows: Top (T), Center (C), Bottom (B), Left (L), Right (R), Background (Bkgd)

Cover

Luciana Navarro Powell

3 (CL) zingiber/Fotolia; **11** (C) Henrik Larsson/Shutterstock, (CL) Ioanis Pantziaras/Shutterstock; **37** (L) ©Directphoto/Alamy; **43** (CR) ©Directphoto/Alamy; **48** (CR) Eric Isselée/Fotolia; **60** Photos to Go/Photolibrary; **66** 2010/Photos to Go/Photolibrary; **70** (TR) Elwynn/Fotolia, (TR) Getty Images/Jupiterimages/Thinkstock; **72** (C, BC) 2010/Photos to Go/Photolibrary, (CR) Getty Images/Jupiterimages/Thinkstock; **77** (TL) Getty Images/Jupiterimages/Thinkstock; **87** (CL) NASA; **92** (BR) Digital Vision/Thinkstock; **96** (TR) Alexey Usachev/Fotolia, (TL) Andy Thorington/Fotolia; **101** (BR) Digital Vision/Thinkstock; **104** (TC) ©Mark Sykes/Alamy; **113** (L) Thinkstock; **116** (TR) Photos to Go/Photolibrary; **117** (BR) tsach/Fotolia; **123** (BR) SuperStock; **135** (CL) GIS/Fotolia; **140** (BR) percent/Fotolia; **143** (BR) ©tbkmedia.de/Alamy; **149** (CR, CL, BR, BL) ©Royalty-Free/Corbis; **155** (BR) 2010/Photos to Go/Photolibrary, (BR) Eric Isselée/Fotolia; **163** (CL) Rubberball/Getty Images; **183** (TL) Photos to Go/Photolibrary, (L) Rikke/Fotolia; **191** (BR) 2011/Photos to Go/Photolibrary; **195** (CR) Rikke/Fotolia, (BR) s/Fotolia; **203** (L) ©JSC/NASA; **205** (BL) Goodshoot/Thinkstock; **225** (BL) Cristian Ciobanu/Fotolia; **234** (BR) Joe Gough/Fotolia; **255** (L) Courtesy of New Bremen Giant Pumpkin Growers; **259** (BR) ©Comstock Images/Jupiter Images; **287** (BL) selfnouvau/Shutterstock; **312** (TR) Image Source/Jupiter Images, (TR) Jupiter Images; **327** (L) Getty Images; **334** (T) JLV Image Works/Fotolia; **337** (BR) piotrwzk@go2.pl/Fotolia; **346** (T) ©VStock/Index Open; **363** (L) Cartographer/Fotolia; **366** (C) Jupiter Images;

369 jenoe/Fotolia; **370** (CL) ©photolibrary/Index Open, (TC, C) Getty Images, (CL) Hemera Technologies, (TR) Jupiter Images; **378** (TC) Alekss/Fotolia, (C) fivespots/Fotolia, (T) Hemera Technologies; **382** (BL) ©face to face Bildagentur GMBH/Alamy; **383** (C) Goodshoot/Jupiter Images, (C) Ingram Publishing, (TR) vnlit/Fotolia; **385** (TR, TL) Getty Images; **389** (BR) Jcella/Fotolia; **399** (L) ablestock/Thinkstock; **419** (CL) Getty Images; **425** (BR) Getty Images; **434** (TR) Getty Images; **435** (TR) Getty Images; **437** (BR) Goodshoot/Thinkstock; **441** (BR) Gary Blakeley/Fotolia.

Index